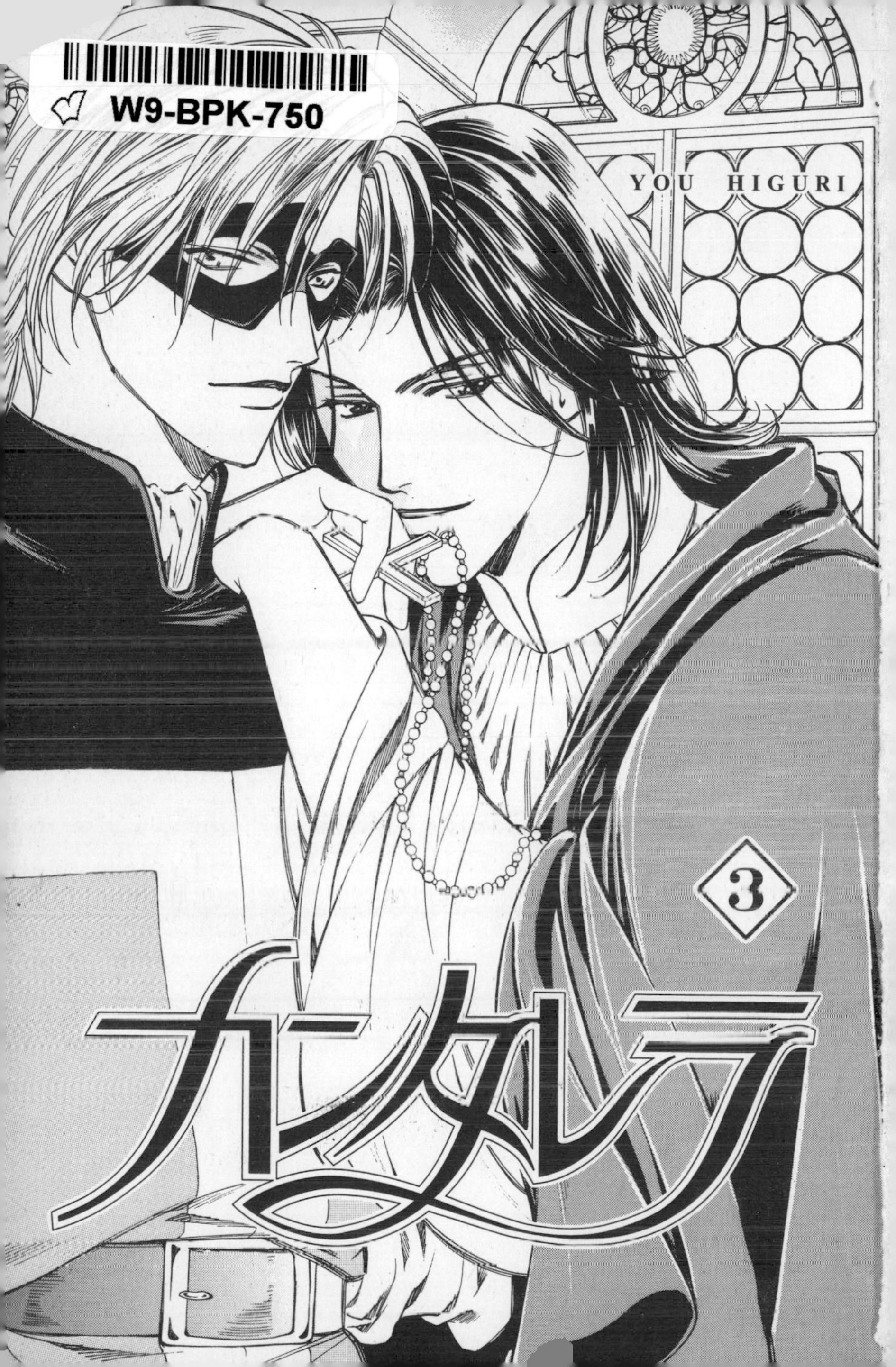
YOU HIGURI
3

Translation – Chrissy Schilling
Adaptation – Audry Taylor
Production Assistant – Mallory Reaves
Lettering & Design– Fawn Lau
Production Manager – James Dashiell
Editor – Jake Forbes

A Go! Comi manga

Published by Go! Media Entertainment, LLC

Cantarella Volume 3

Originally published in Japan in 2002 by Akita Publishing Co., Ltd., Tokyo.
English translation rights arranged with Akita Publishing Co., Ltd.
through TOHAN CORPORATION, Tokyo.

This edition is struck from the original Japanese film for the best possible reproduction. Absolutely no artwork has been censored.

This book is a work of fiction. Names, places and incidents are either a product of the author's imagination or are used fictitiously.

Visit us online at www.gocomi.com
e-mail: info@gocomi.com

ISBN 0-9768957-8-1

First printed in April 2006

1 2 3 4 5 6 7 8 9

Manufactured in the United States of America

Cantarella

STORY AND ART BY
YOU HIGURI

VOLUME 3

go!comi

Cantarella ◆ 3

TABLE OF CONTENTS

First appeared in:
GOLD September issue (2001)
GOLD October Special issue (2001)
GOLD November & December issues (2001)
GOLD January issue (2002)

OUR STORY SO FAR AND INTRODUCTION OF CHARACTERS

Enter the forsaken Cesare Borgia, whose soul was sold to the devil by his father, Cardinal Rodrigo, in exchange for the Papal throne. In the throes of hopelessness, he tried to kill himself rather than face the inner darkness of his soul. Even this relief was not granted him, as he was saved by his own enemy, the assassin Michelotto, whose pity eased Cesare's pain. Rodrigo took on the robes of the papacy and named himself Pope Alexander VI. Granting his son the position of Cardinal, Alexander hoped to quietly quell Cesare's greater ambitions. But Cesare now lives only for his ambitions, and with the assassin at his side, he plots a future both magnificent and terrifying in its scope, even as the threat of invasion gathers around Italy...

CESARE BORGIA

The hero of our story. His father sold the boy's soul to the devil in exchange for religious power. Now a Cardinal, Cesare will wear the sacred scarlet robe even when his eyes glow golden with wicked intent.

JUAN BORGIA

Unlike his older brother, Juan is favored by his father. A position has been secured for him in the Spanish court, though lately he's spent all his time in Rome with the mysterious foreigner, Prince Djem.

LUCREZIA BORGIA

A sweet girl who adores her older brother Cesare. She was forced to wed the Lord of Pasaro in an arranged marriage.

POPE ALEXANDER VI

An ambitious man who sold his own son's soul in exchange for the title of Pope. His birth name was Rodrigo Borgia.

MICHELOTTO (CHIARO)

A legendary assassin. After saving Cesare's life, he now serves him, and goes in public by the false name of Michele da Corella. His real name is Chiaro.

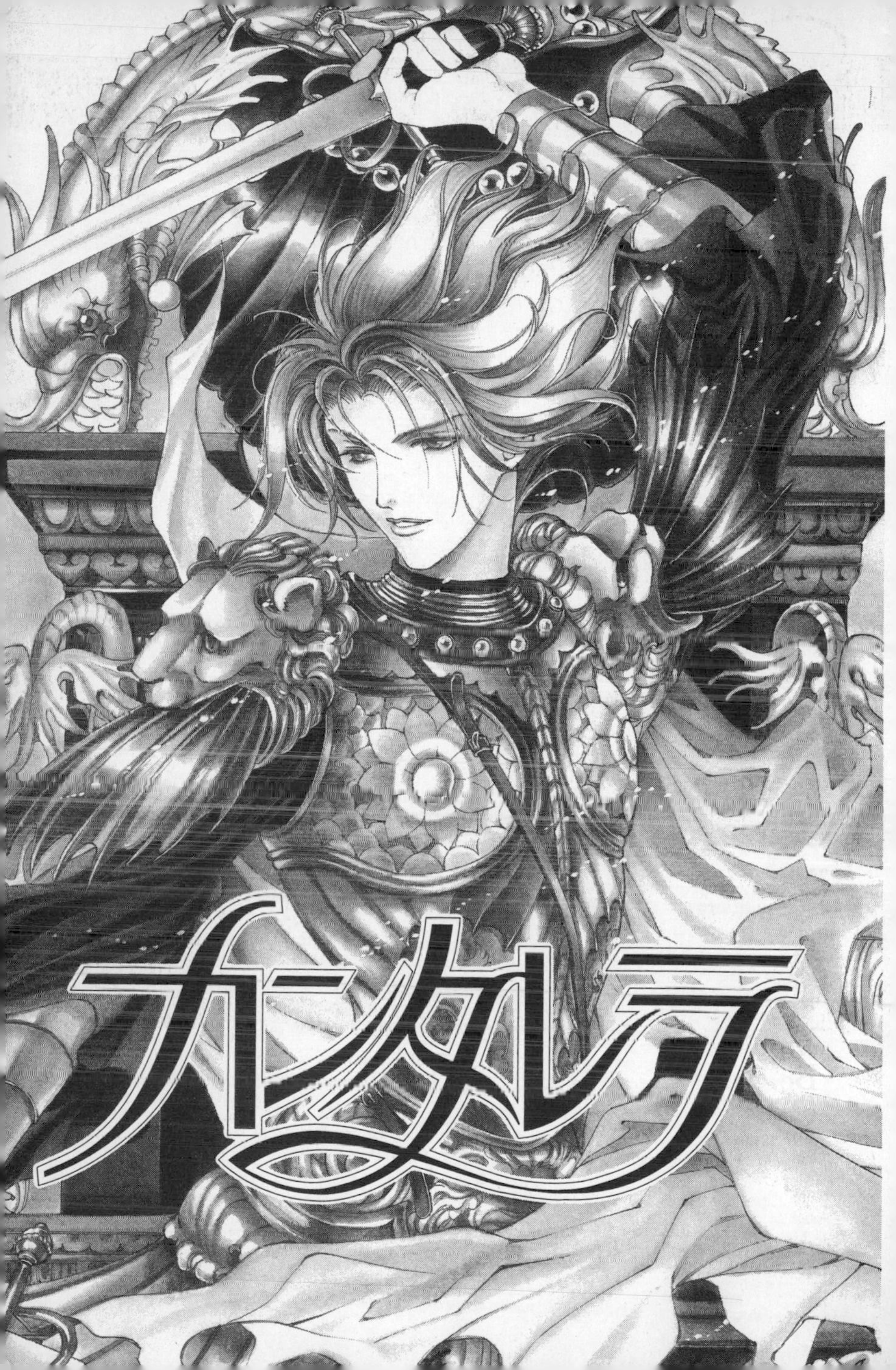
カンタレラ

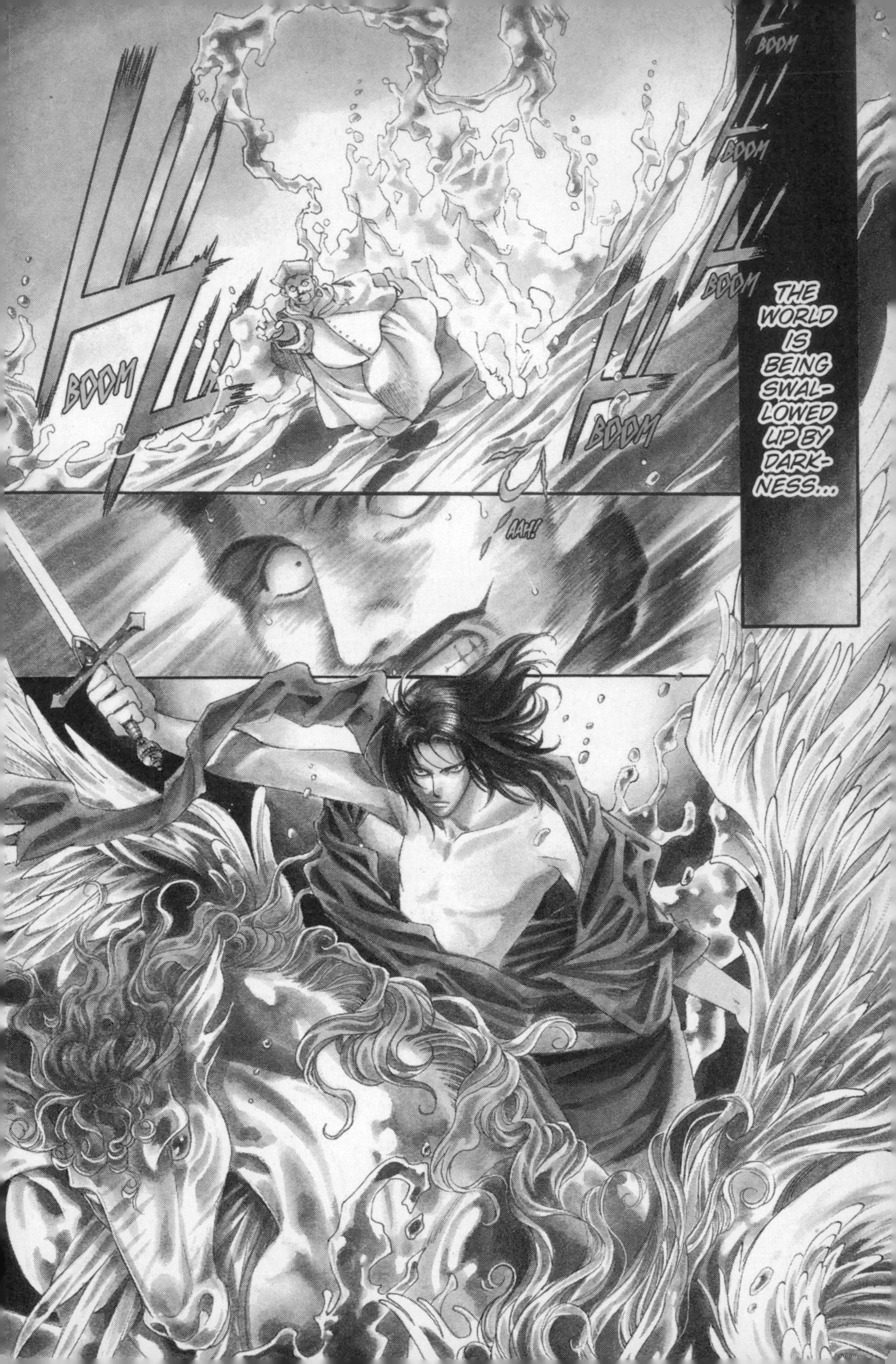
BOOM
BOOM
BOOM
BOOM
BOOM
THE WORLD IS BEING SWAL-LOWED UP BY DARK-NESS...
AAH!

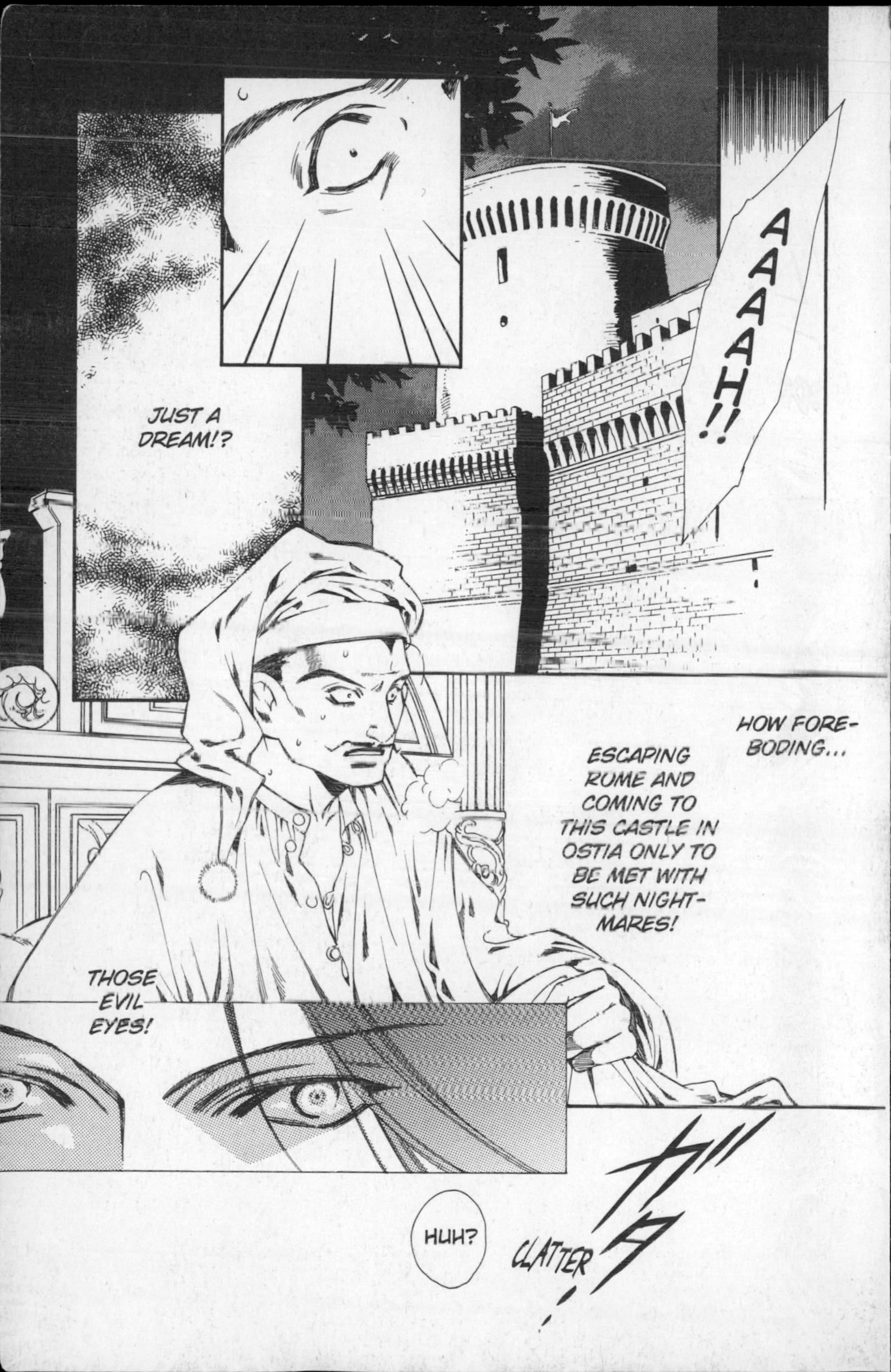
AAAAAH!!
JUST A DREAM!?
HOW FORE-BODING...
ESCAPING ROME AND COMING TO THIS CASTLE IN OSTIA ONLY TO BE MET WITH SUCH NIGHT-MARES!
THOSE EVIL EYES!
CLATTER
HUH?

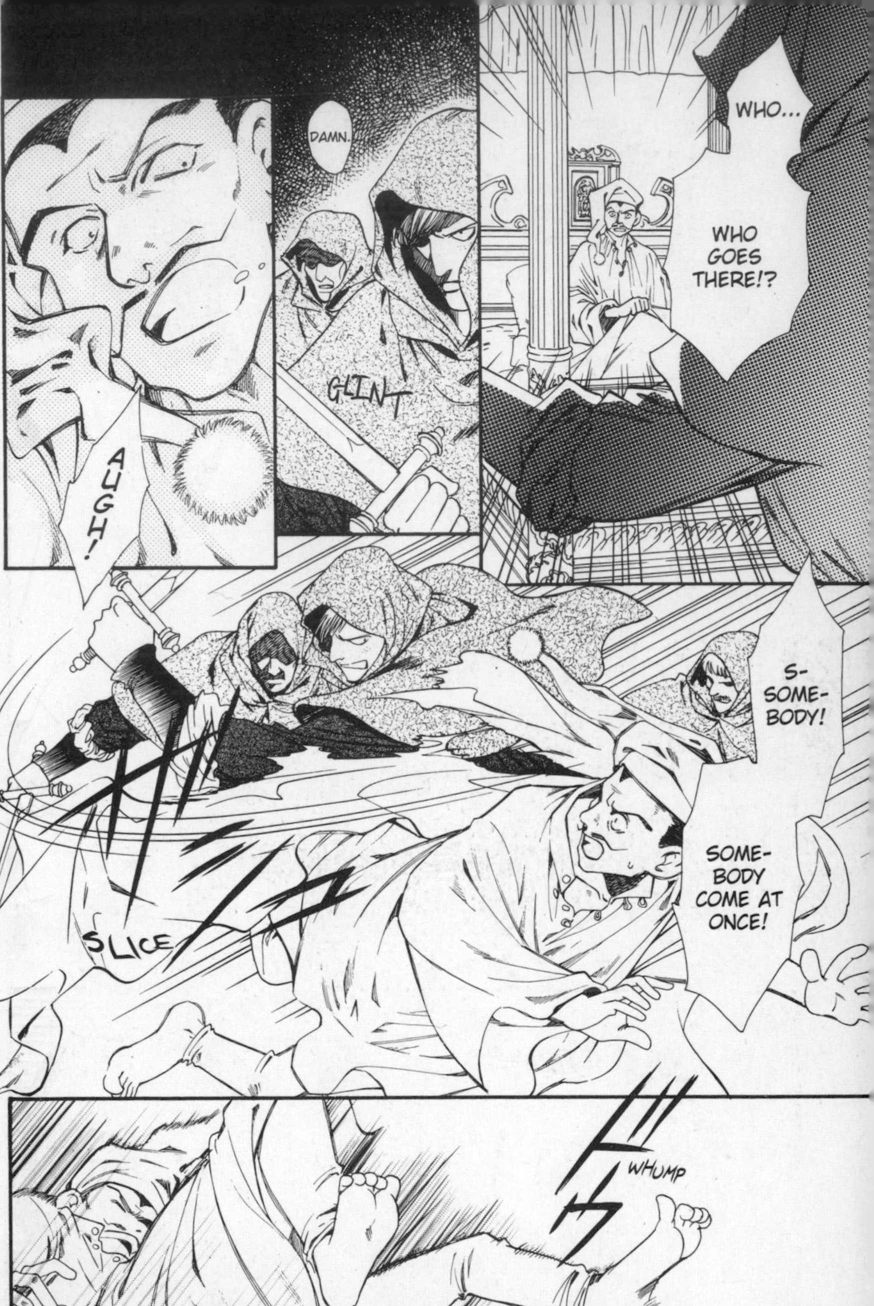
WHO...
WHO GOES THERE!?
DAMN.
GLINT
AUGH!
S- SOMEBODY!
SOMEBODY COME AT ONCE!
SLICE
WHUMP

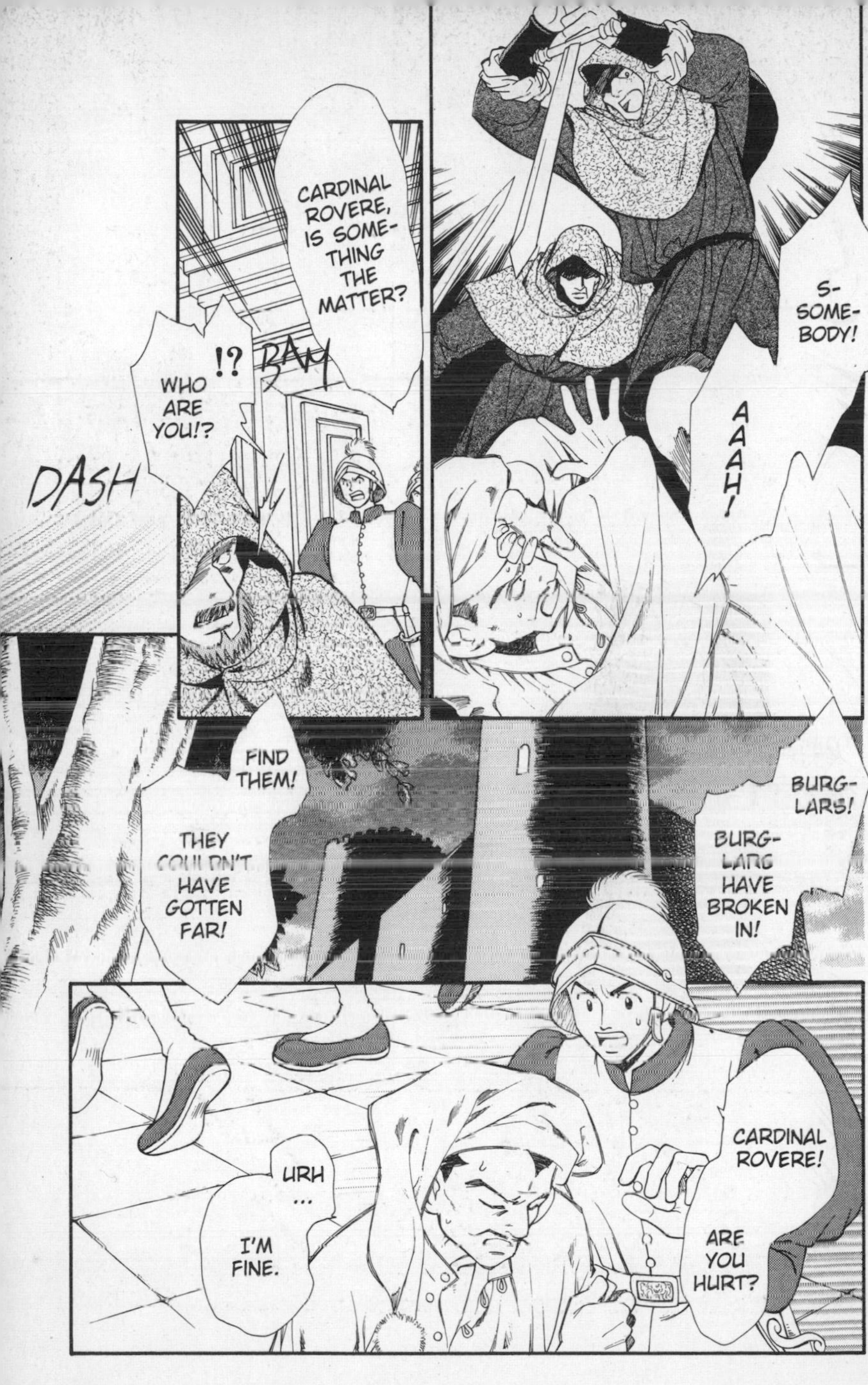
S-SOMEBODY!
AAAAH!
CARDINAL ROVERE, IS SOMETHING THE MATTER?
BAM
!?
WHO ARE YOU!?
DASH
BURGLARS!
BURGLARS HAVE BROKEN IN!
FIND THEM!
THEY COULDN'T HAVE GOTTEN FAR!
CARDINAL ROVERE!
ARE YOU HURT?
URH ...
I'M FINE.

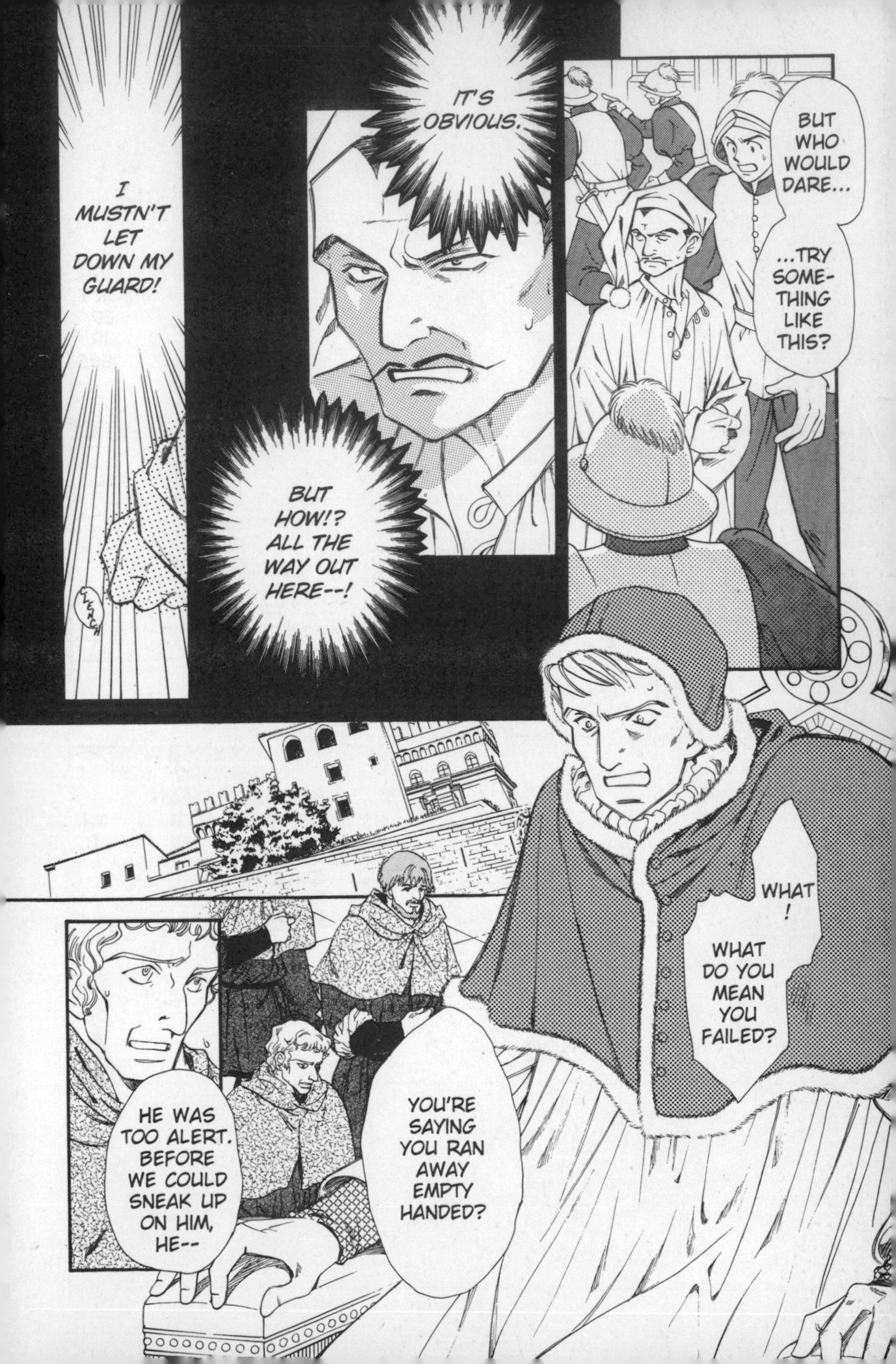
BUT WHO WOULD DARE...
...TRY SOME-THING LIKE THIS?
IT'S OBVIOUS.
BUT HOW!? ALL THE WAY OUT HERE--!
I MUSTN'T LET DOWN MY GUARD!
CLENCH
WHAT!
WHAT DO YOU MEAN YOU FAILED?
YOU'RE SAYING YOU RAN AWAY EMPTY HANDED?
HE WAS TOO ALERT. BEFORE WE COULD SNEAK UP ON HIM, HE--

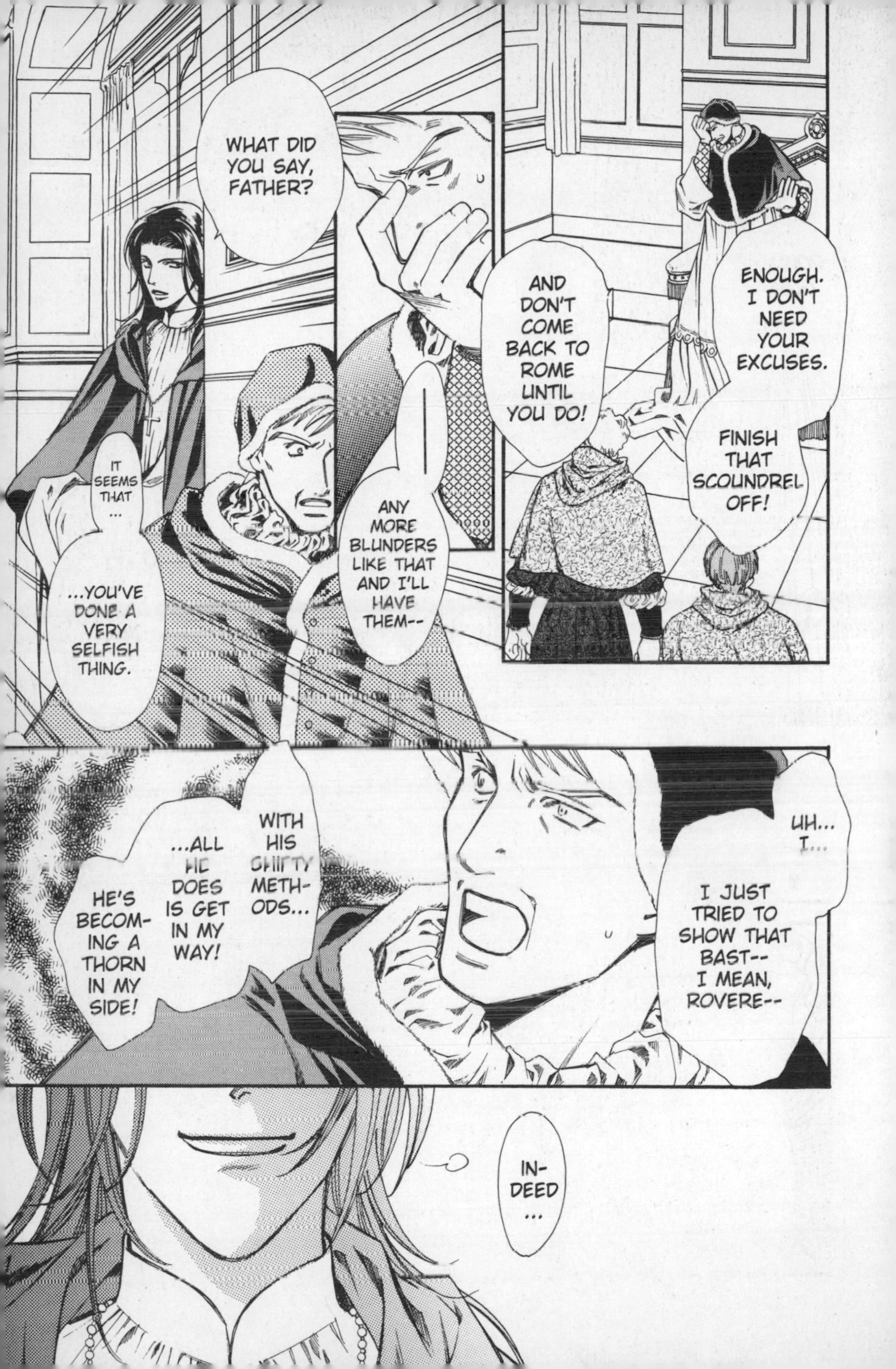
ENOUGH. I DON'T NEED YOUR EXCUSES.
FINISH THAT SCOUNDREL OFF!
AND DON'T COME BACK TO ROME UNTIL YOU DO!
ANY MORE BLUNDERS LIKE THAT AND I'LL HAVE THEM--
WHAT DID YOU SAY, FATHER?
IT SEEMS THAT...
...YOU'VE DONE A VERY SELFISH THING.
UH... I...
I JUST TRIED TO SHOW THAT BAST-- I MEAN, ROVERE--
WITH HIS SHIFTY METH-ODS...
...ALL HE DOES IS GET IN MY WAY!
HE'S BECOM-ING A THORN IN MY SIDE!
IN-DEED...

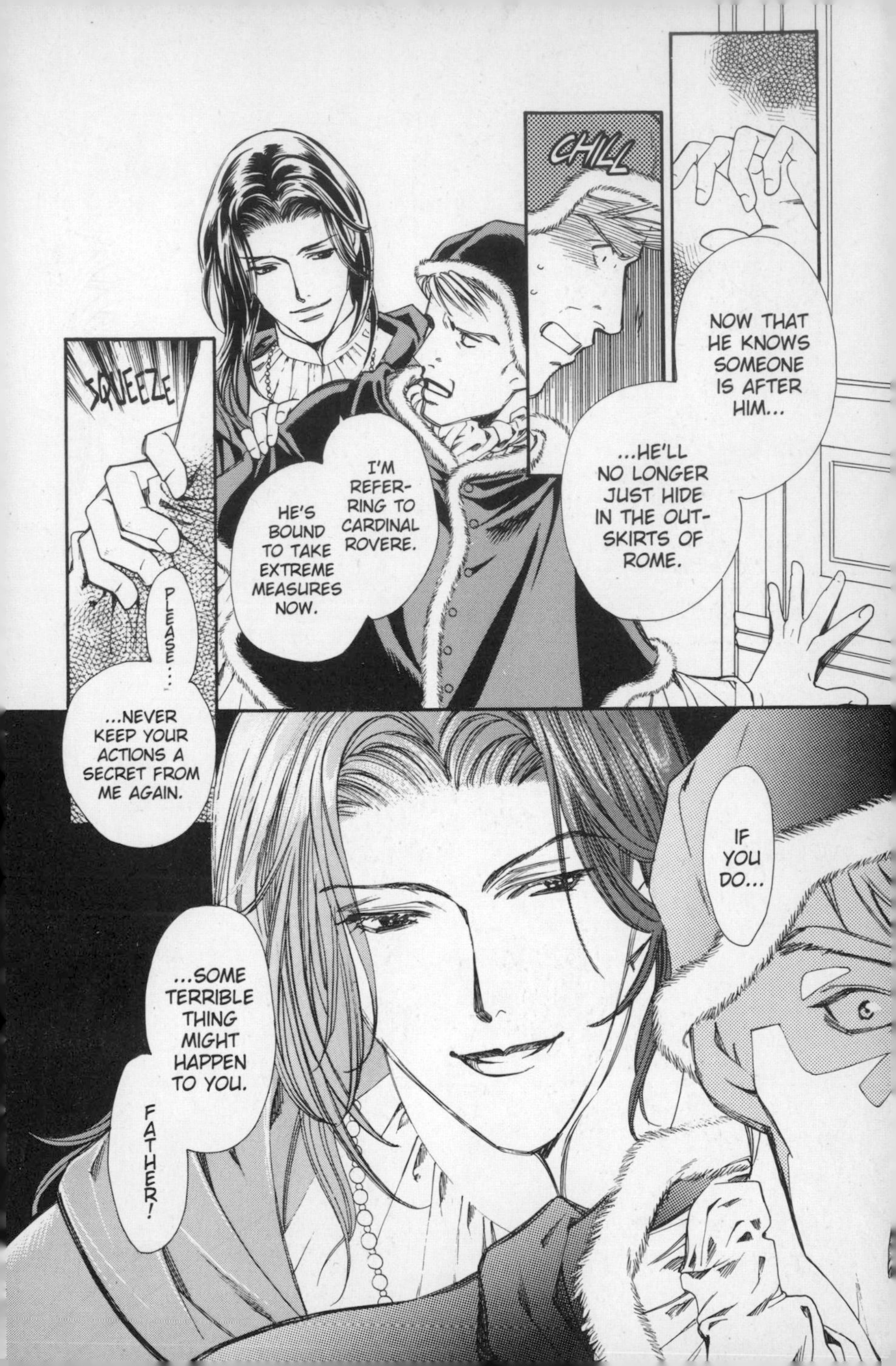
NOW THAT HE KNOWS SOMEONE IS AFTER HIM...
...HE'LL NO LONGER JUST HIDE IN THE OUT-SKIRTS OF ROME.
CHILL
I'M REFER-RING TO CARDINAL ROVERE.
HE'S BOUND TO TAKE EXTREME MEASURES NOW.
SQUEEZE
PLEASE...
...NEVER KEEP YOUR ACTIONS A SECRET FROM ME AGAIN.
IF YOU DO...
...SOME TERRIBLE THING MIGHT HAPPEN TO YOU.
FATHER!

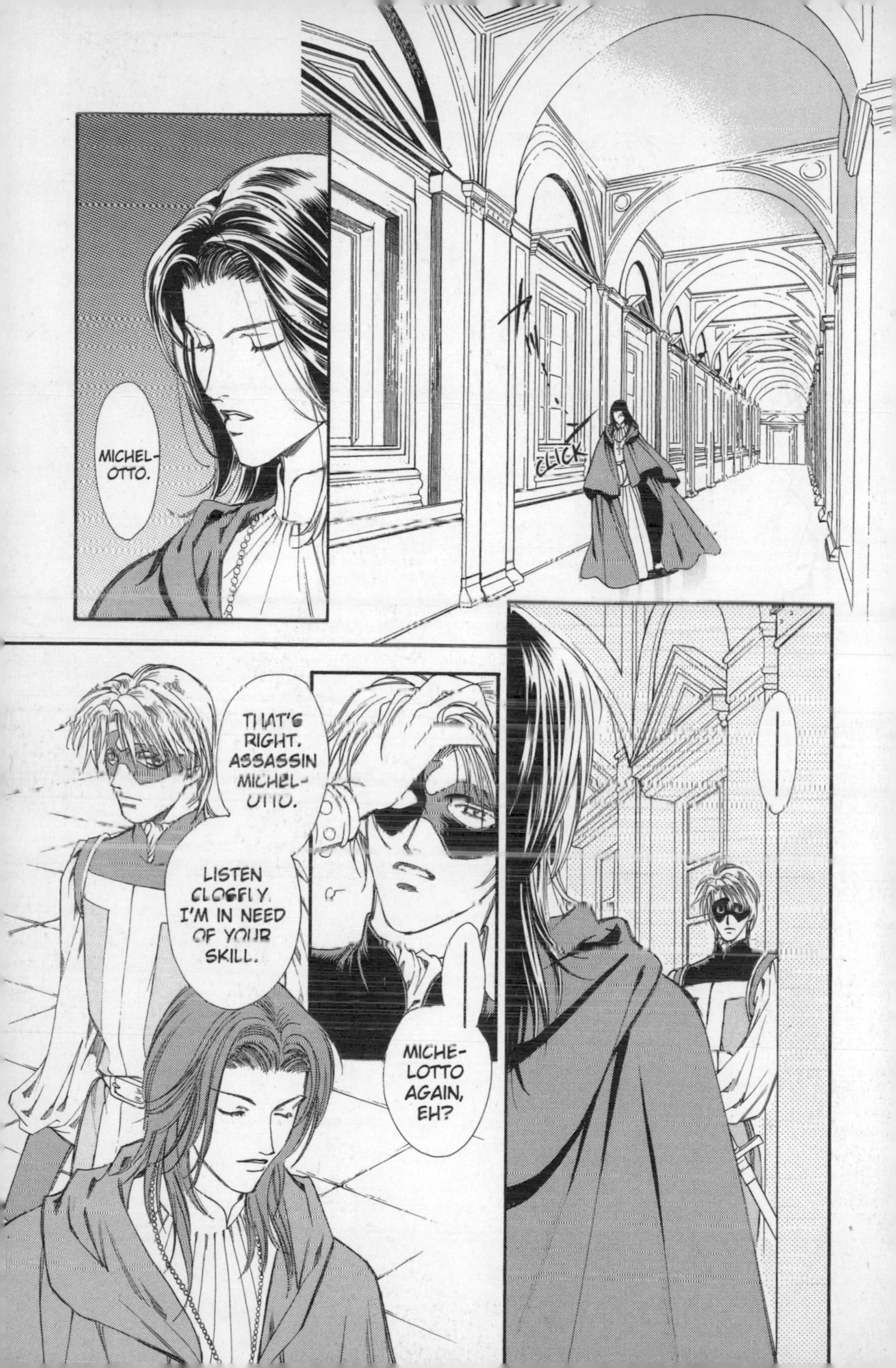
CLICK
MICHEL-OTTO.
MICHE-LOTTO AGAIN, EH?
THAT'S RIGHT. ASSASSIN MICHEL-OTTO.
LISTEN CLOSELY. I'M IN NEED OF YOUR SKILL.

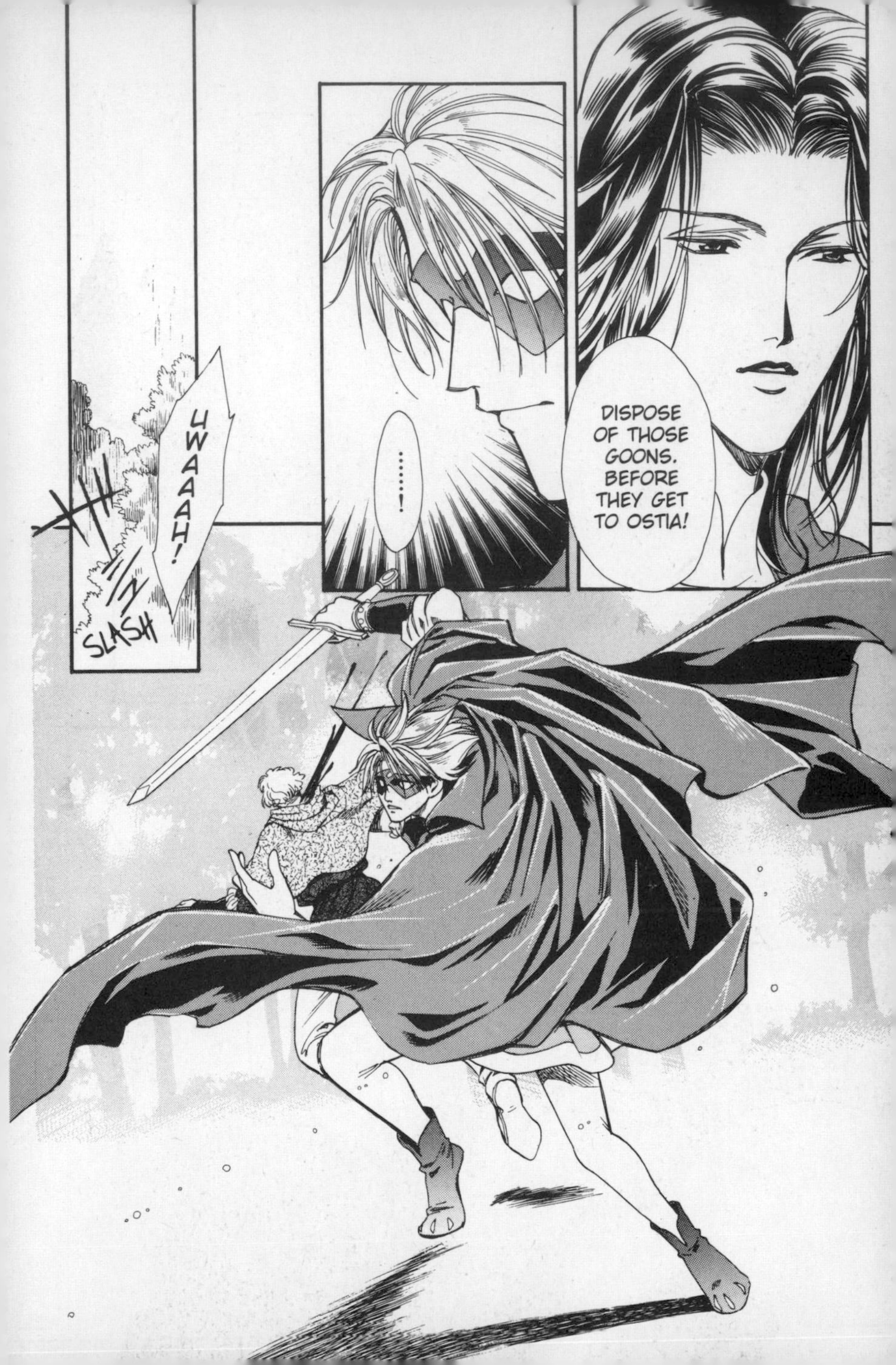

DISPOSE OF THOSE GOONS. BEFORE THEY GET TO OSTIA!
......!
UWAAAAH!
SLASH

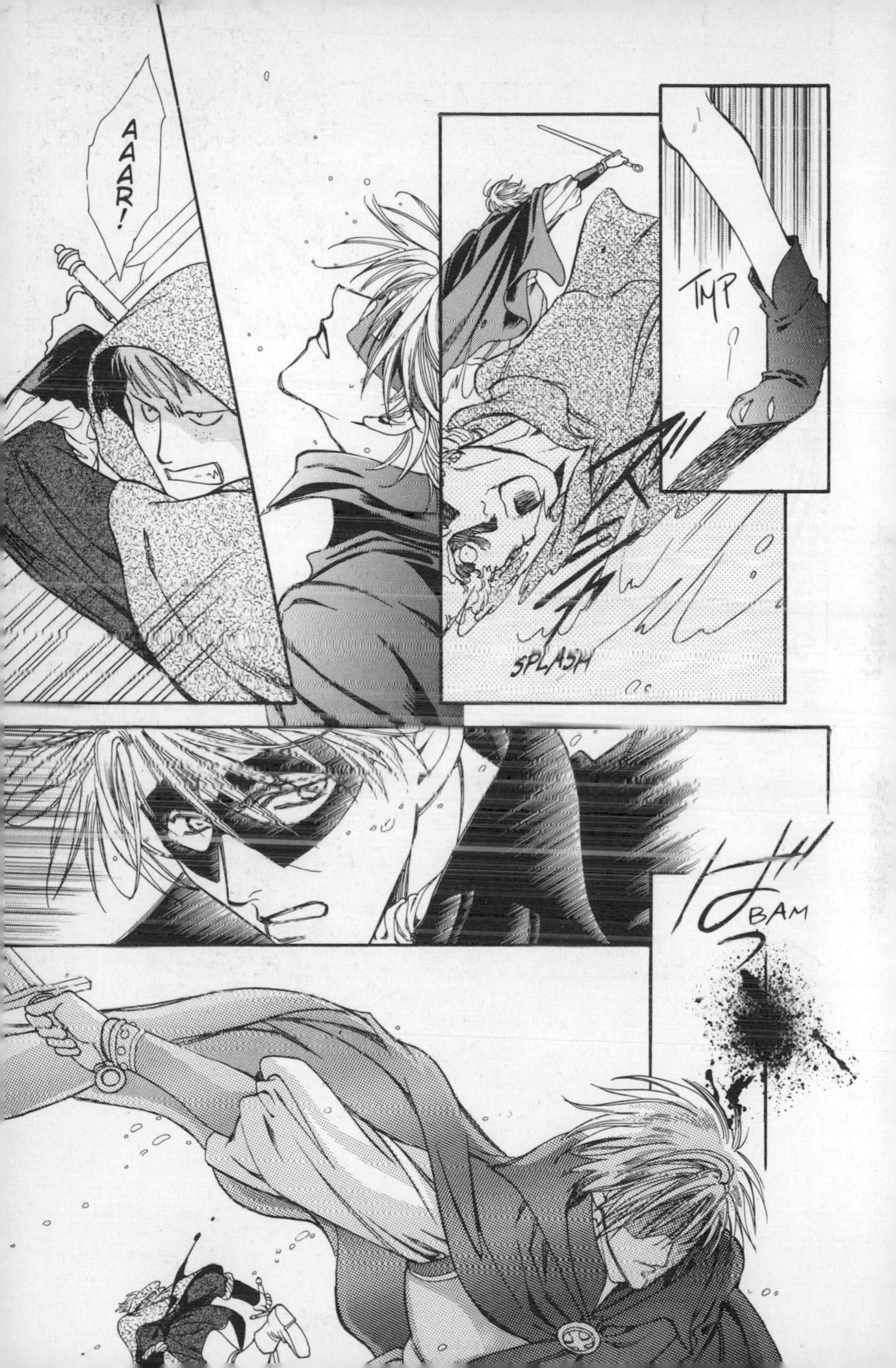
TMP
SPLASH
AAAR!
BAM

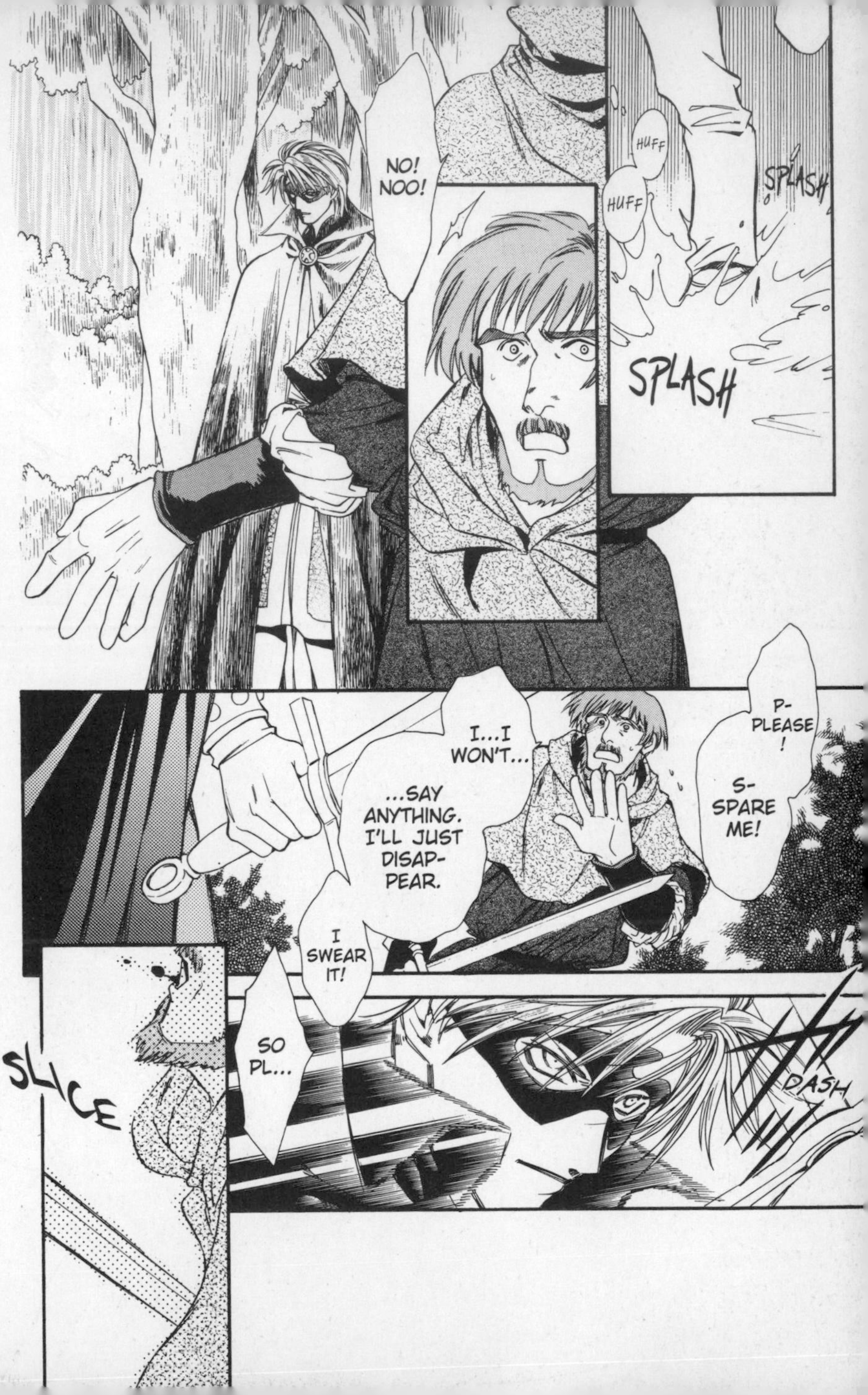
HUFF
HUFF
SPLASH
SPLASH
NO! NOO!
P-PLEASE!
S-SPARE ME!
I...I WON'T...
...SAY ANYTHING. I'LL JUST DISAP-PEAR.
I SWEAR IT!
DASH
SO PL...
SLICE

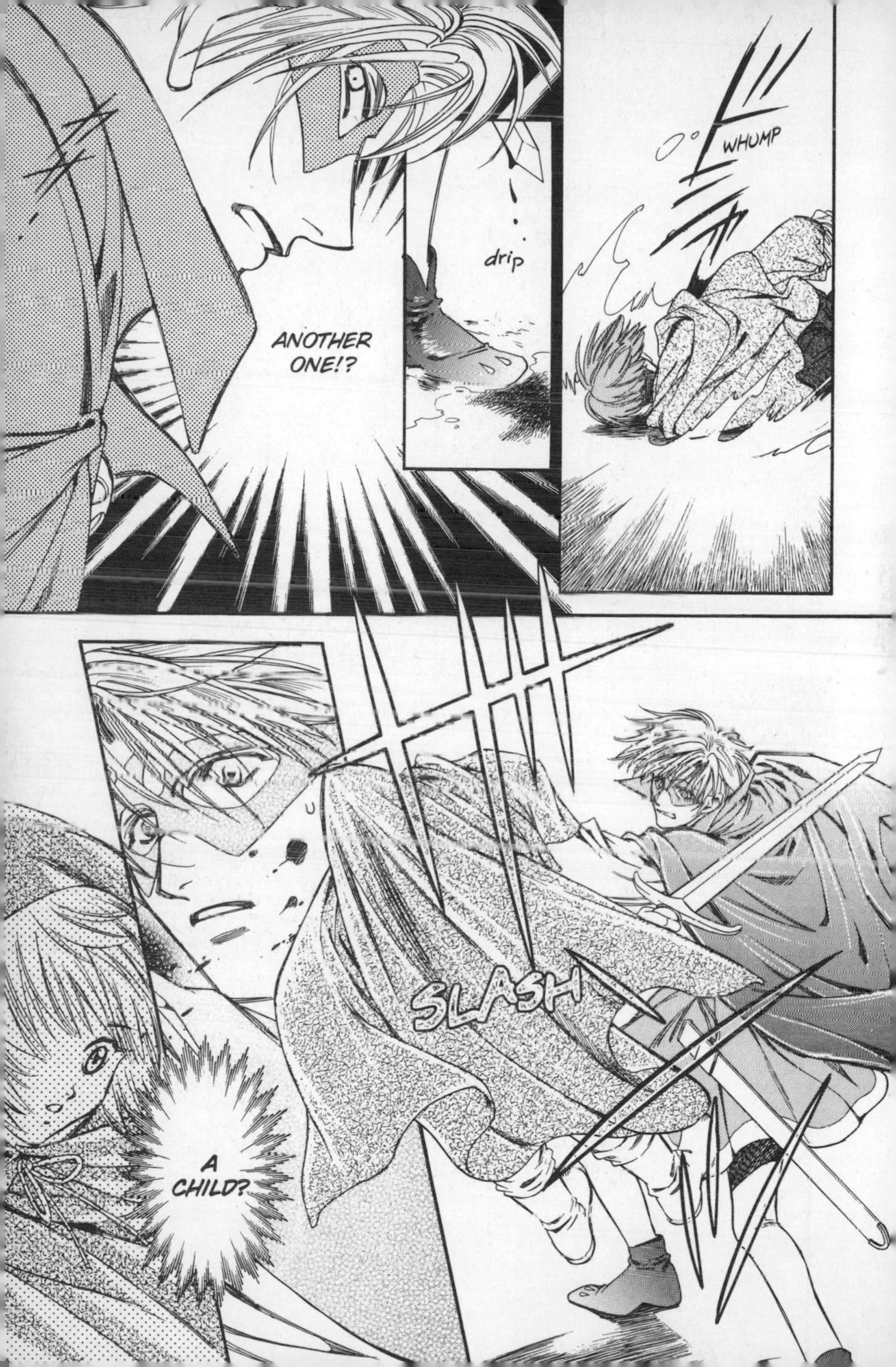
WHUMP
drip
ANOTHER ONE!?
SLASH
A CHILD?

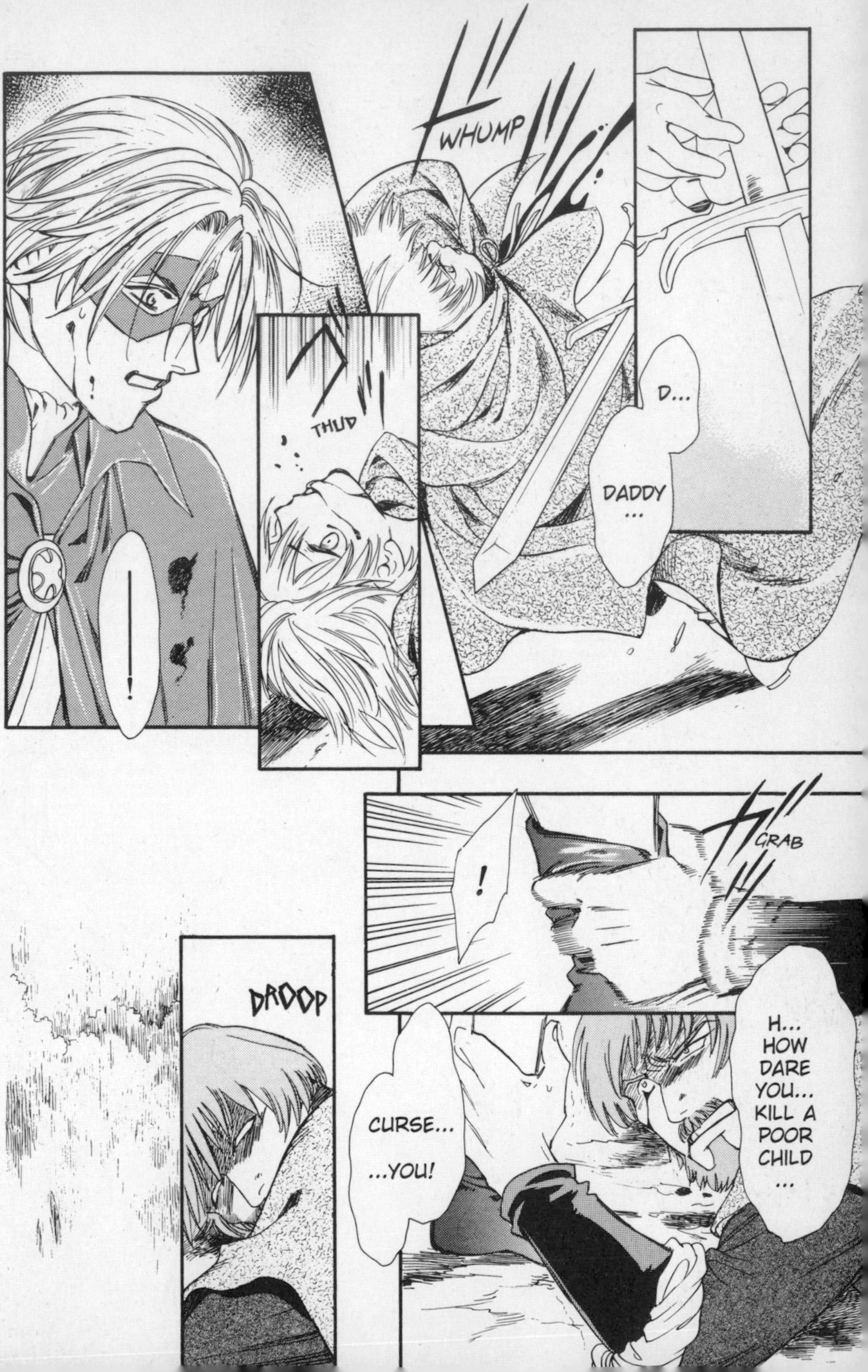
WHUMP
D...
DADDY ...
THUD
!
GRAB
!
H... HOW DARE YOU... KILL A POOR CHILD ...
CURSE...
...YOU!
DROOP

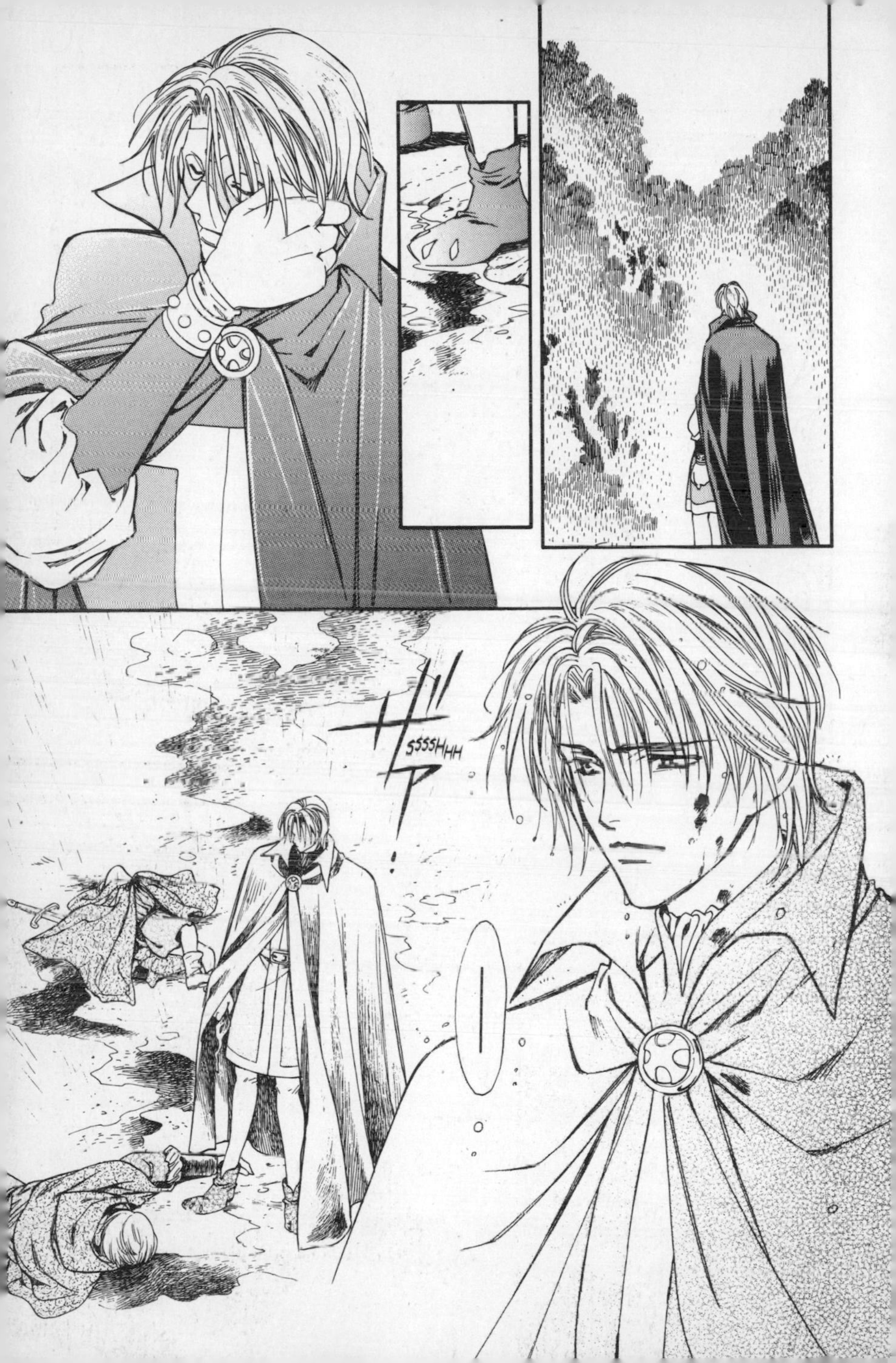
SSSSHHH
!
!

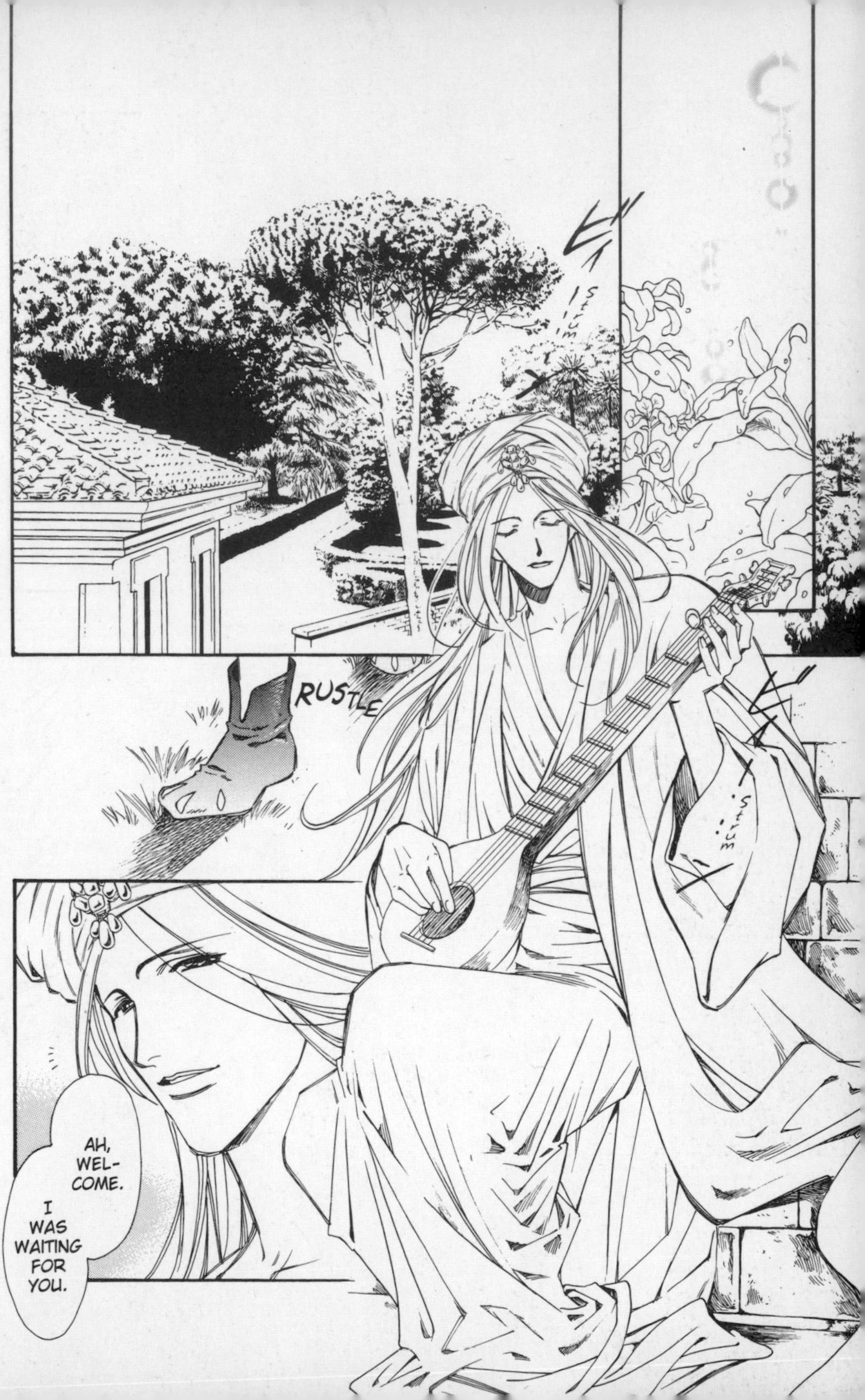
strum
strum
RUSTLE
AH, WEL-COME. I WAS WAITING FOR YOU.

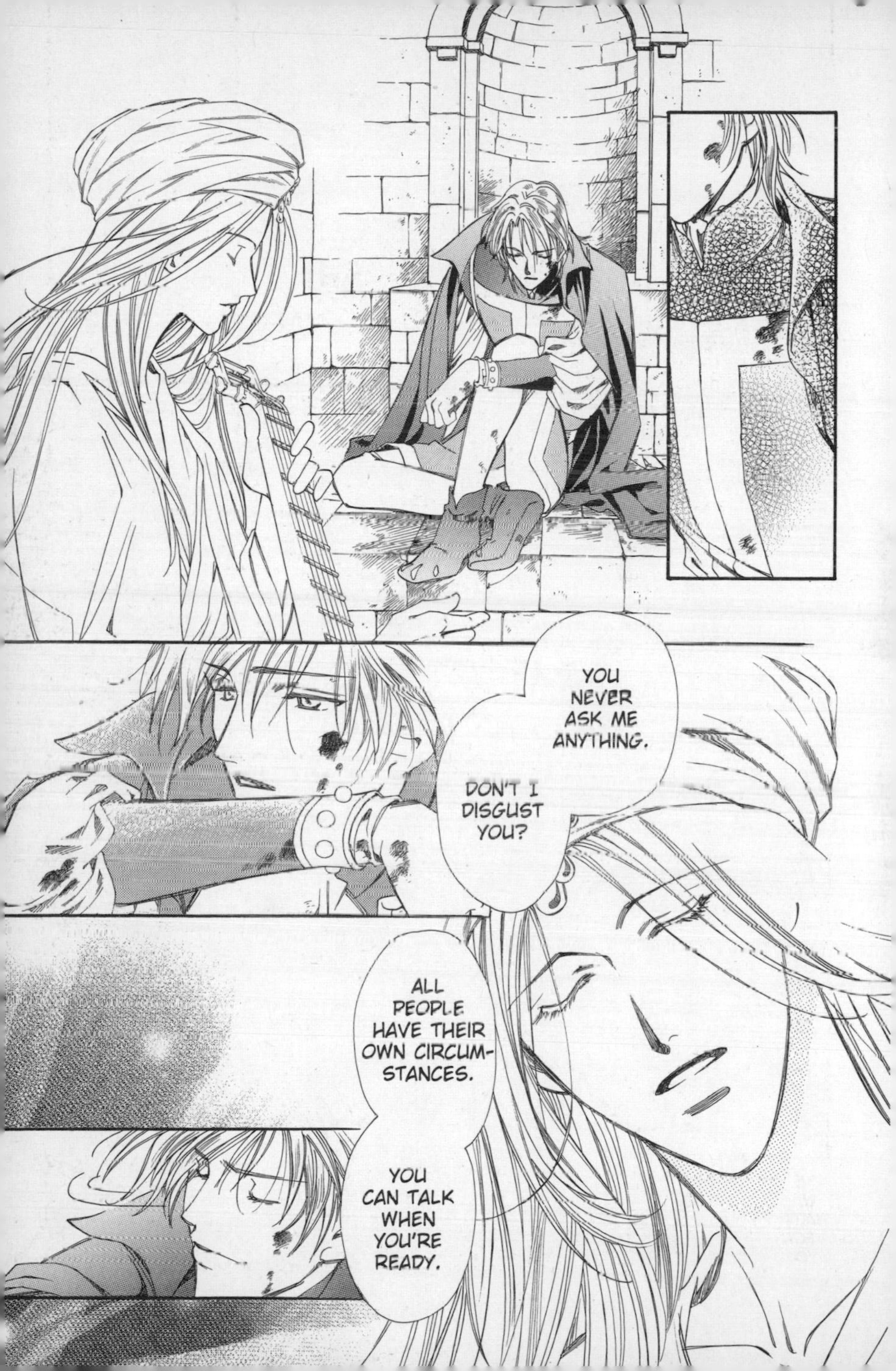
YOU NEVER ASK ME ANYTHING.
DON'T I DISGUST YOU?
ALL PEOPLE HAVE THEIR OWN CIRCUM-STANCES.
YOU CAN TALK WHEN YOU'RE READY.

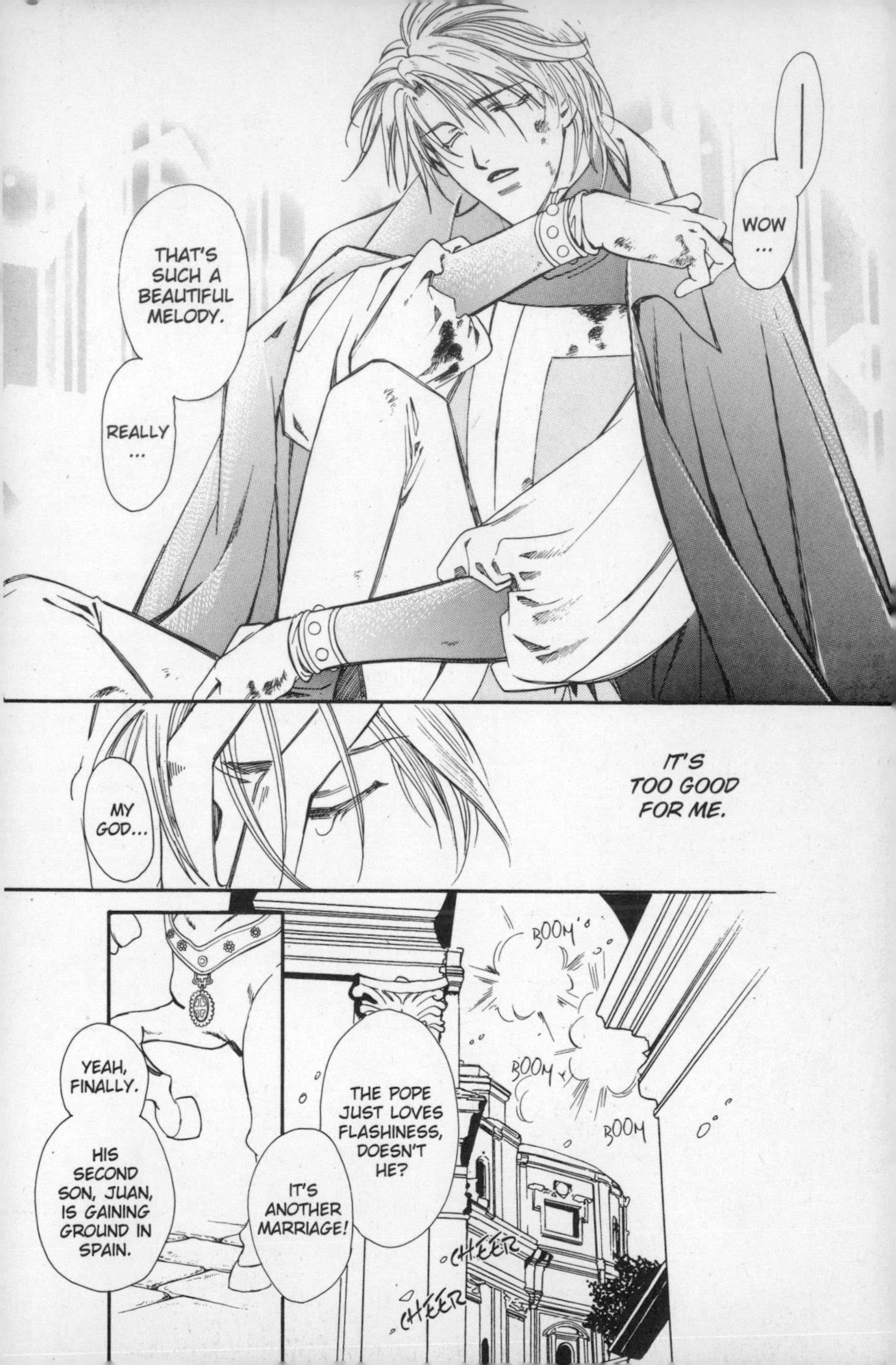
!
WOW ...
THAT'S SUCH A BEAUTIFUL MELODY.
REALLY ...
IT'S TOO GOOD FOR ME.
MY GOD...
BOOM
BOOM
BOOM
CHEER
CHEER
THE POPE JUST LOVES FLASHINESS, DOESN'T HE?
IT'S ANOTHER MARRIAGE!
YEAH, FINALLY.
HIS SECOND SON, JUAN, IS GAINING GROUND IN SPAIN.

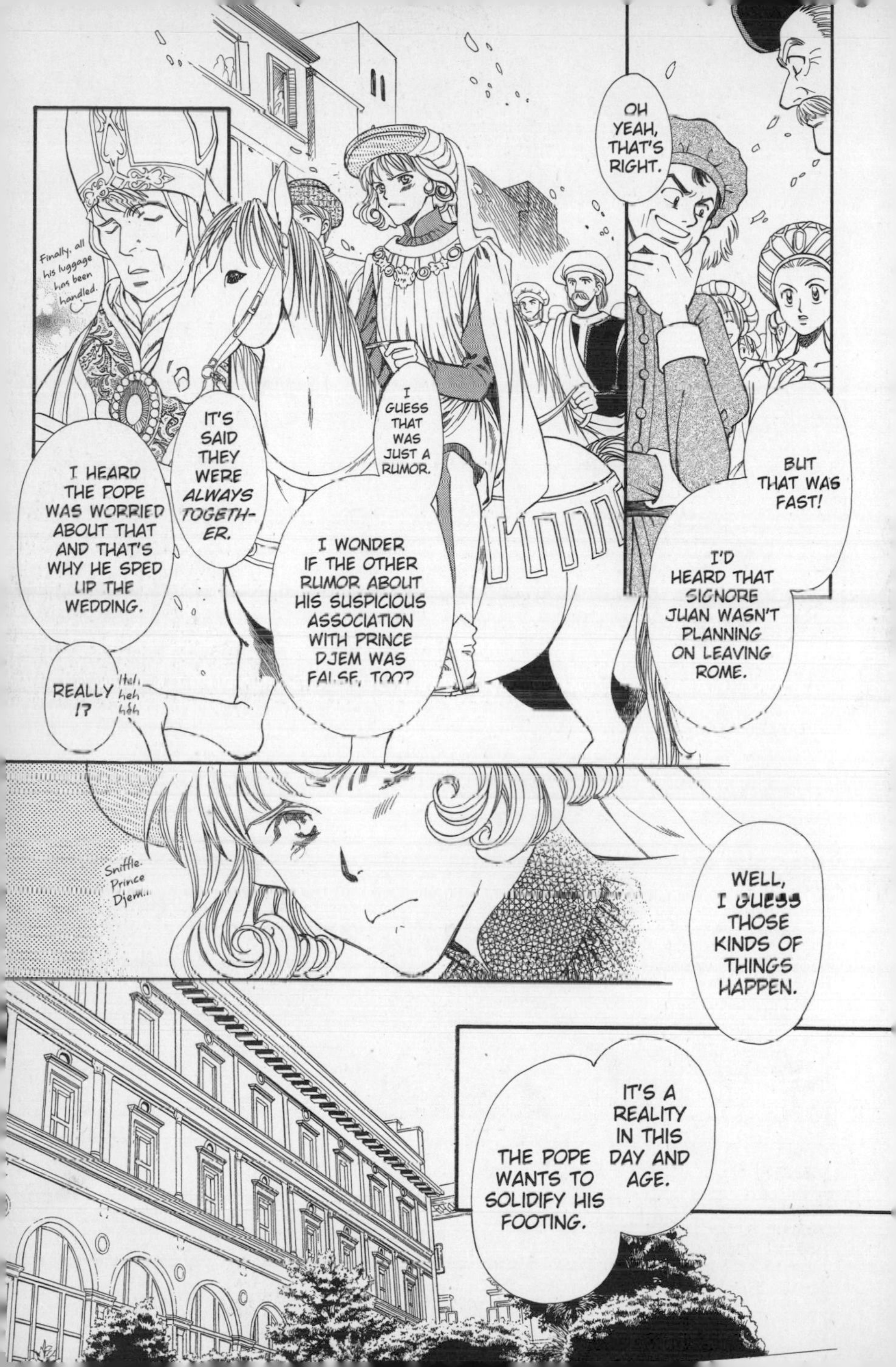
OH YEAH, THAT'S RIGHT.
BUT THAT WAS FAST!
I'D HEARD THAT SIGNORE JUAN WASN'T PLANNING ON LEAVING ROME.
I GUESS THAT WAS JUST A RUMOR.
IT'S SAID THEY WERE *ALWAYS TOGETHER.*
I HEARD THE POPE WAS WORRIED ABOUT THAT AND THAT'S WHY HE SPED UP THE WEDDING.
I WONDER IF THE OTHER RUMOR ABOUT HIS SUSPICIOUS ASSOCIATION WITH PRINCE DJEM WAS FALSE, TOO?
REALLY!?
Heh heh heh
Finally, all his luggage has been handled.
WELL, I GUESS THOSE KINDS OF THINGS HAPPEN.
Sniffle. Prince Djem...
IT'S A REALITY IN THIS DAY AND AGE.
THE POPE WANTS TO SOLIDIFY HIS FOOTING.

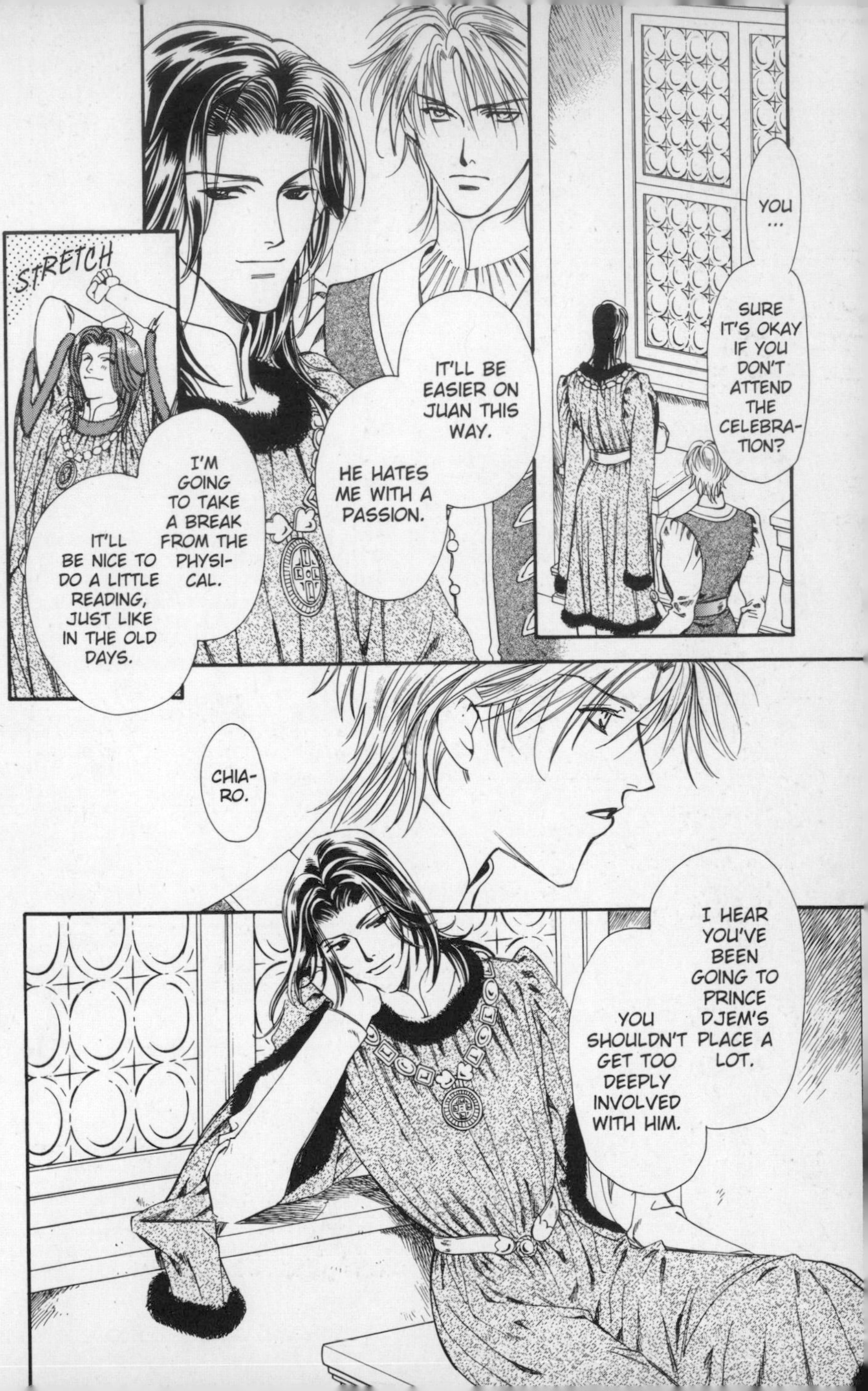
YOU...
SURE IT'S OKAY IF YOU DON'T ATTEND THE CELEBRATION?
IT'LL BE EASIER ON JUAN THIS WAY.
HE HATES ME WITH A PASSION.
STRETCH
I'M GOING TO TAKE A BREAK FROM THE PHYSICAL.
IT'LL BE NICE TO DO A LITTLE READING, JUST LIKE IN THE OLD DAYS.
CHIARO.
I HEAR YOU'VE BEEN GOING TO PRINCE DJEM'S PLACE A LOT.
YOU SHOULDN'T GET TOO DEEPLY INVOLVED WITH HIM.

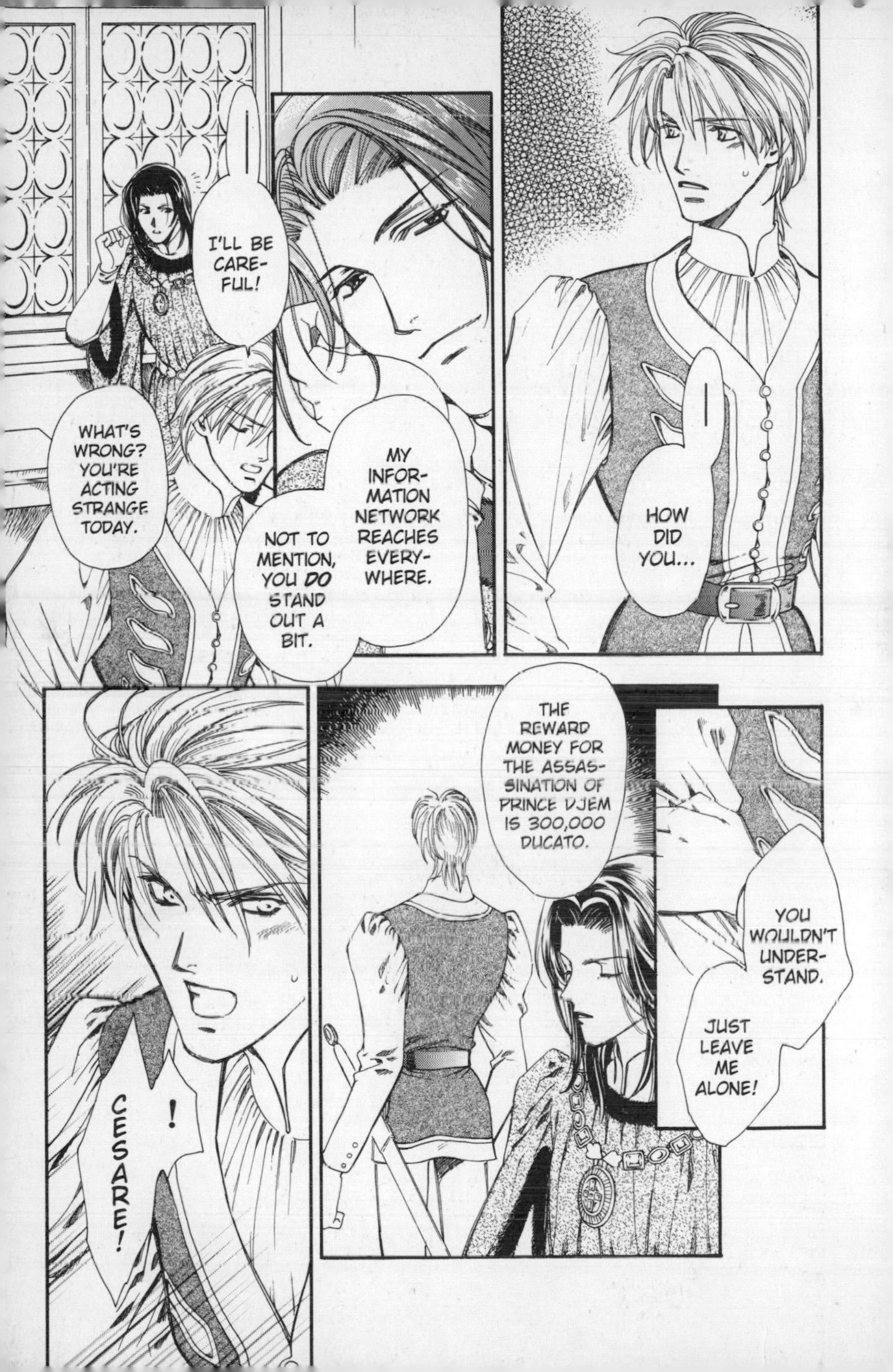
HOW DID YOU...
MY INFORMATION NETWORK REACHES EVERYWHERE.
NOT TO MENTION, YOU *DO* STAND OUT A BIT.
I'LL BE CAREFUL!
WHAT'S WRONG? YOU'RE ACTING STRANGE TODAY.
YOU WOULDN'T UNDERSTAND.
JUST LEAVE ME ALONE!
THE REWARD MONEY FOR THE ASSASSINATION OF PRINCE DJEM IS 300,000 DUCATO.
!
CESARE!

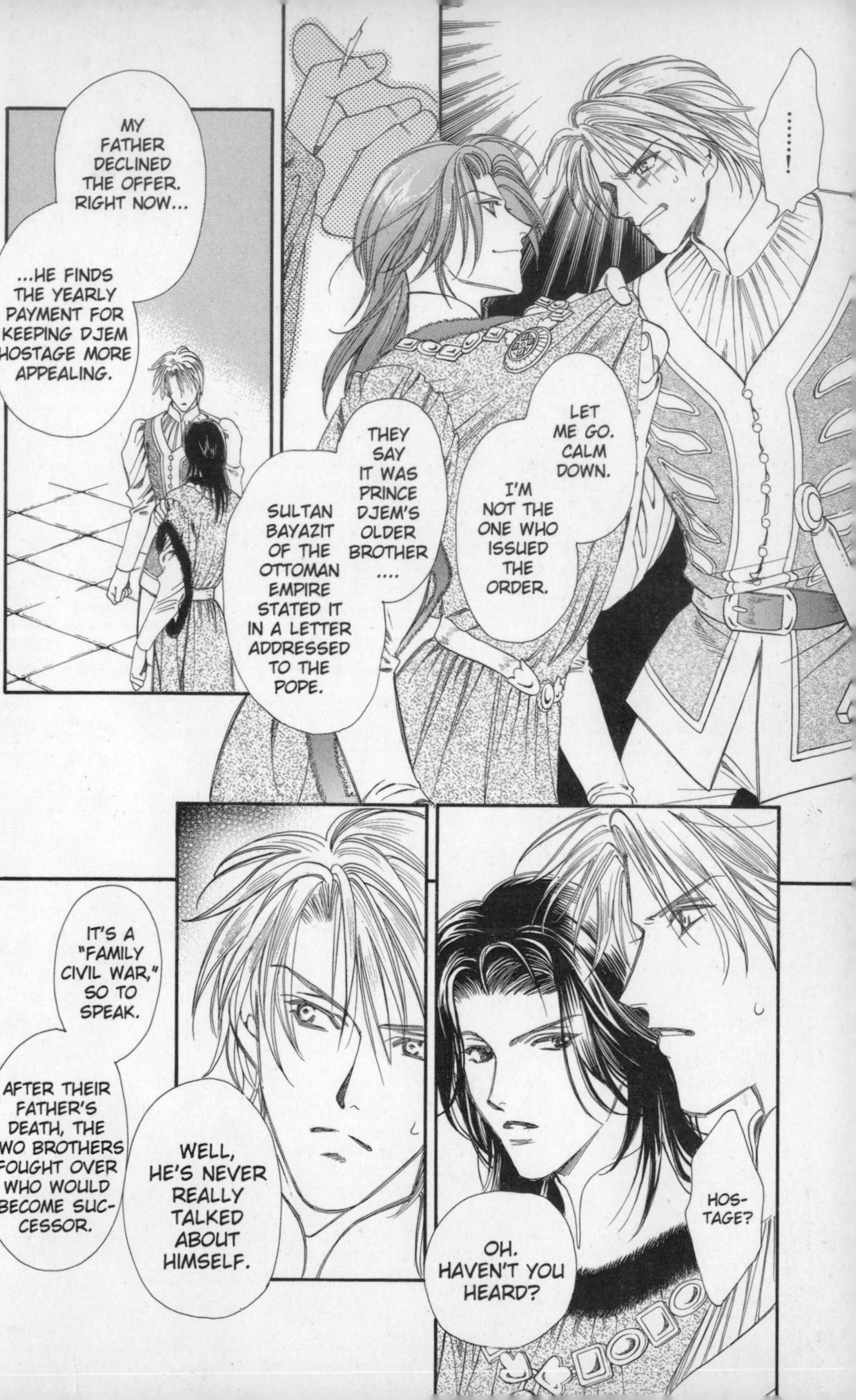

......!
LET ME GO. CALM DOWN.
I'M NOT THE ONE WHO ISSUED THE ORDER.
THEY SAY IT WAS PRINCE DJEM'S OLDER BROTHER ....
SULTAN BAYAZIT OF THE OTTOMAN EMPIRE STATED IT IN A LETTER ADDRESSED TO THE POPE.
MY FATHER DECLINED THE OFFER. RIGHT NOW...
...HE FINDS THE YEARLY PAYMENT FOR KEEPING DJEM HOSTAGE MORE APPEALING.
HOS-TAGE?
OH. HAVEN'T YOU HEARD?
WELL, HE'S NEVER REALLY TALKED ABOUT HIMSELF.
IT'S A "FAMILY CIVIL WAR," SO TO SPEAK.
AFTER THEIR FATHER'S DEATH, THE TWO BROTHERS FOUGHT OVER WHO WOULD BECOME SUC-CESSOR.

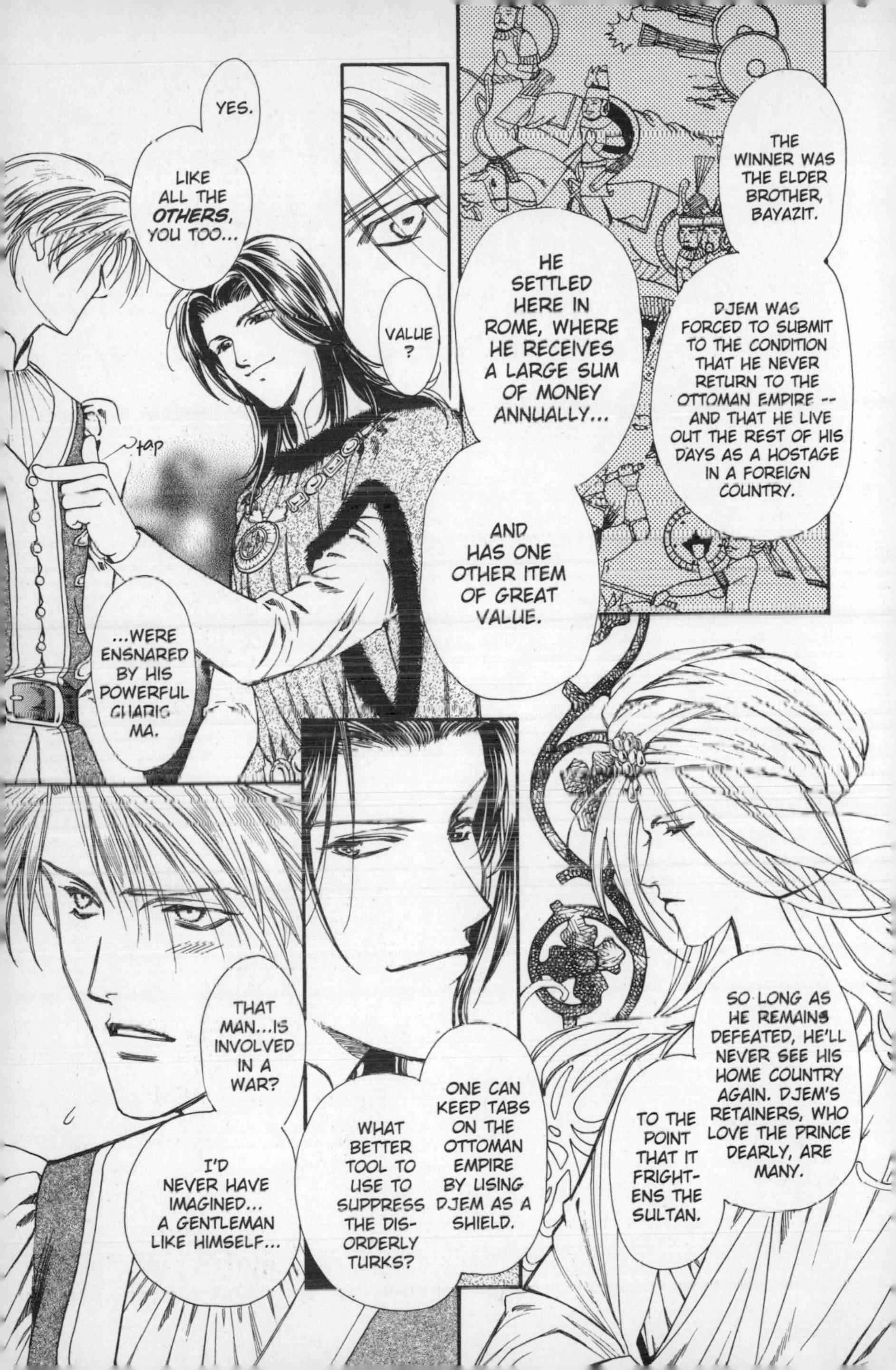
THE WINNER WAS THE ELDER BROTHER, BAYAZIT.
DJEM WAS FORCED TO SUBMIT TO THE CONDITION THAT HE NEVER RETURN TO THE OTTOMAN EMPIRE -- AND THAT HE LIVE OUT THE REST OF HIS DAYS AS A HOSTAGE IN A FOREIGN COUNTRY.
HE SETTLED HERE IN ROME, WHERE HE RECEIVES A LARGE SUM OF MONEY ANNUALLY...
AND HAS ONE OTHER ITEM OF GREAT VALUE.
VALUE?
YES.
LIKE ALL THE *OTHERS*, YOU TOO...
tap
...WERE ENSNARED BY HIS POWERFUL CHARISMA.
SO LONG AS HE REMAINS DEFEATED, HE'LL NEVER SEE HIS HOME COUNTRY AGAIN. DJEM'S RETAINERS, WHO LOVE THE PRINCE DEARLY, ARE MANY.
TO THE POINT THAT IT FRIGHTENS THE SULTAN.
ONE CAN KEEP TABS ON THE OTTOMAN EMPIRE BY USING DJEM AS A SHIELD.
WHAT BETTER TOOL TO USE TO SUPPRESS THE DISORDERLY TURKS?
THAT MAN...IS INVOLVED IN A WAR?
I'D NEVER HAVE IMAGINED... A GENTLEMAN LIKE HIMSELF...

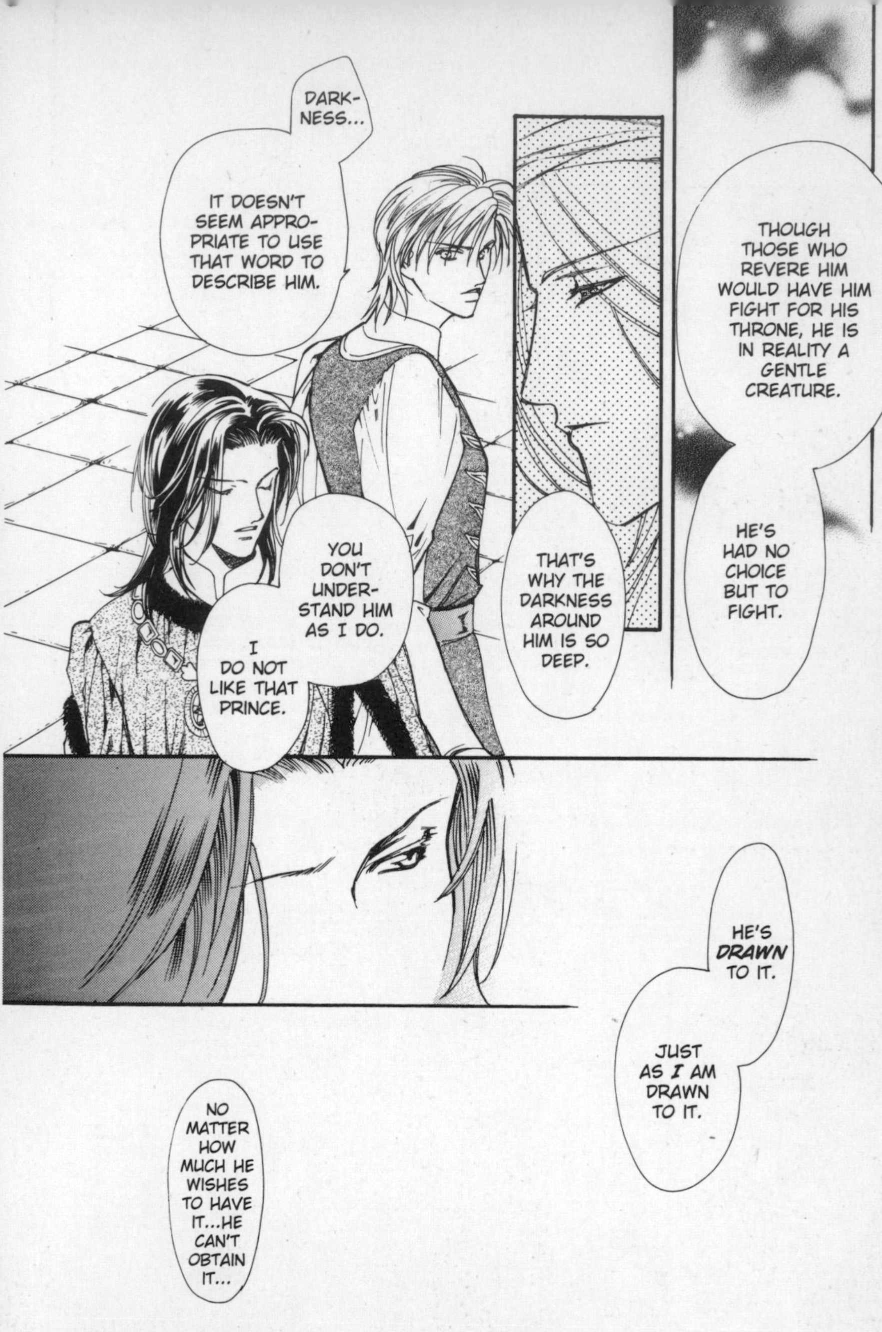

THOUGH THOSE WHO REVERE HIM WOULD HAVE HIM FIGHT FOR HIS THRONE, HE IS IN REALITY A GENTLE CREATURE.
HE'S HAD NO CHOICE BUT TO FIGHT.
THAT'S WHY THE DARKNESS AROUND HIM IS SO DEEP.
DARKNESS...
IT DOESN'T SEEM APPROPRIATE TO USE THAT WORD TO DESCRIBE HIM.
YOU DON'T UNDERSTAND HIM AS I DO.
I DO NOT LIKE THAT PRINCE.
HE'S *DRAWN* TO IT.
JUST AS *I* AM DRAWN TO IT.
NO MATTER HOW MUCH HE WISHES TO HAVE IT...HE CAN'T OBTAIN IT...

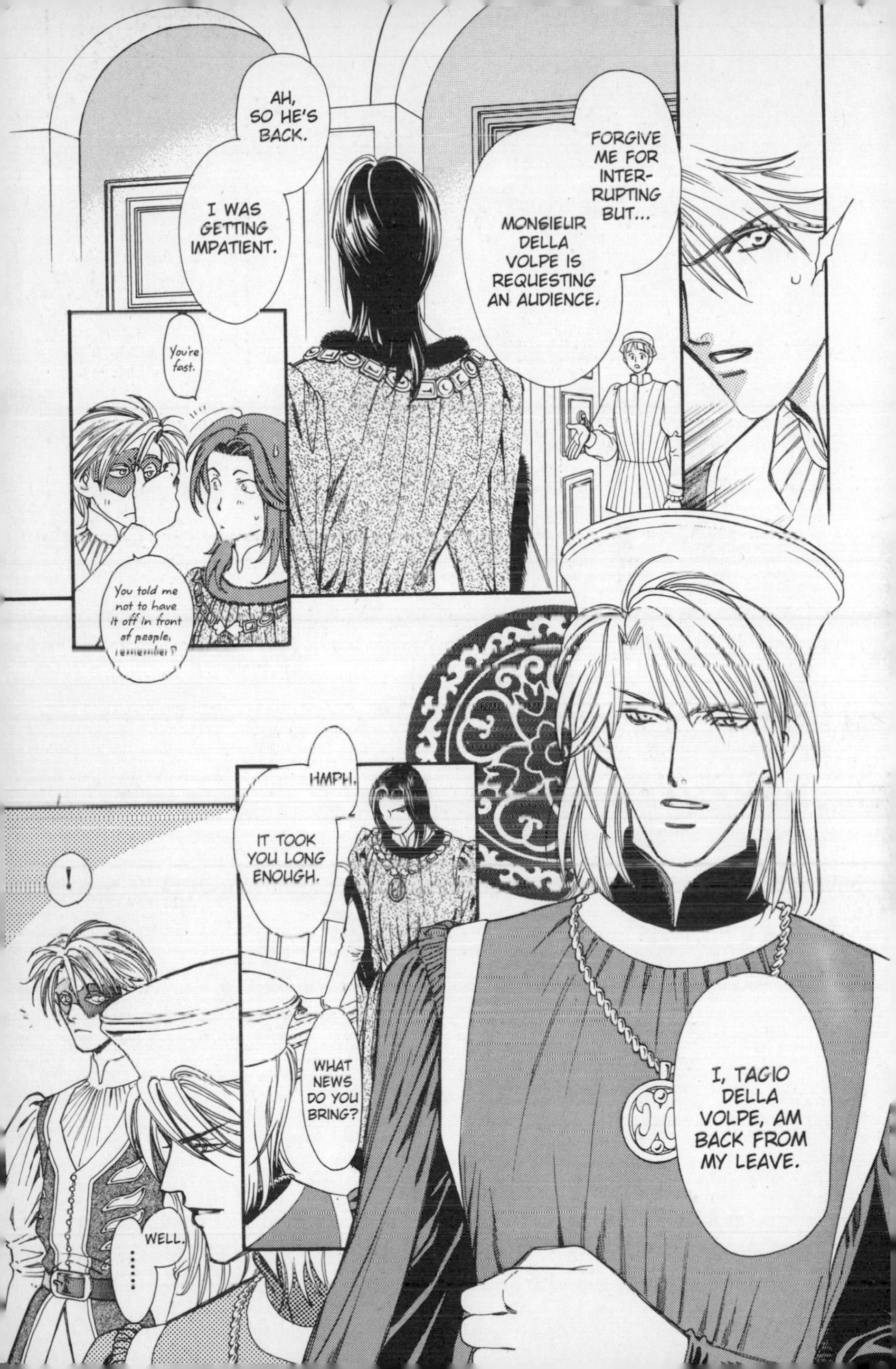
FORGIVE ME FOR INTER-RUPTING BUT...
MONSIEUR DELLA VOLPE IS REQUESTING AN AUDIENCE.
AH, SO HE'S BACK.
I WAS GETTING IMPATIENT.
You're fast.
You told me not to have it off in front of people, remember?
I, TAGIO DELLA VOLPE, AM BACK FROM MY LEAVE.
HMPH.
IT TOOK YOU LONG ENOUGH.
WHAT NEWS DO YOU BRING?
!
WELL.
......

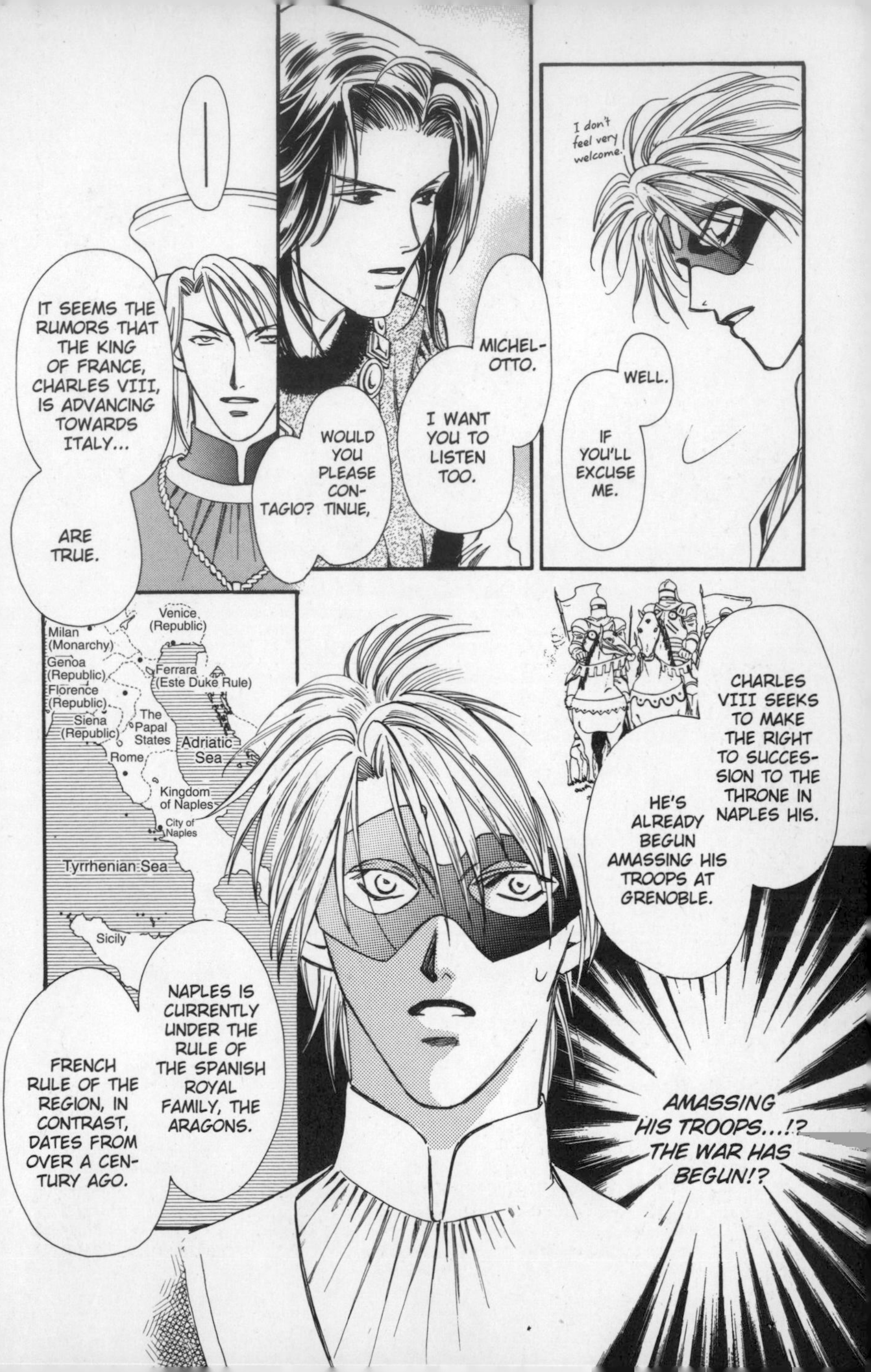
I don't feel very welcome.
WELL.
IF YOU'LL EXCUSE ME.
MICHEL-OTTO.
I WANT YOU TO LISTEN TOO.
WOULD YOU PLEASE CON-TINUE, TAGIO?
IT SEEMS THE RUMORS THAT THE KING OF FRANCE, CHARLES VIII, IS ADVANCING TOWARDS ITALY...
ARE TRUE.
CHARLES VIII SEEKS TO MAKE THE RIGHT TO SUCCES-SION TO THE THRONE IN NAPLES HIS.
HE'S ALREADY BEGUN AMASSING HIS TROOPS AT GRENOBLE.
AMASSING HIS TROOPS...!? THE WAR HAS BEGUN!?
Venice (Republic)
Milan (Monarchy)
Genoa (Republic)
Ferrara (Este Duke Rule)
Florence (Republic)
The Papal States
Siena (Republic)
Adriatic Sea
Rome
Kingdom of Naples
City of Naples
Tyrrhenian Sea
Sicily
NAPLES IS CURRENTLY UNDER THE RULE OF THE SPANISH ROYAL FAMILY, THE ARAGONS.
FRENCH RULE OF THE REGION, IN CONTRAST, DATES FROM OVER A CEN-TURY AGO.

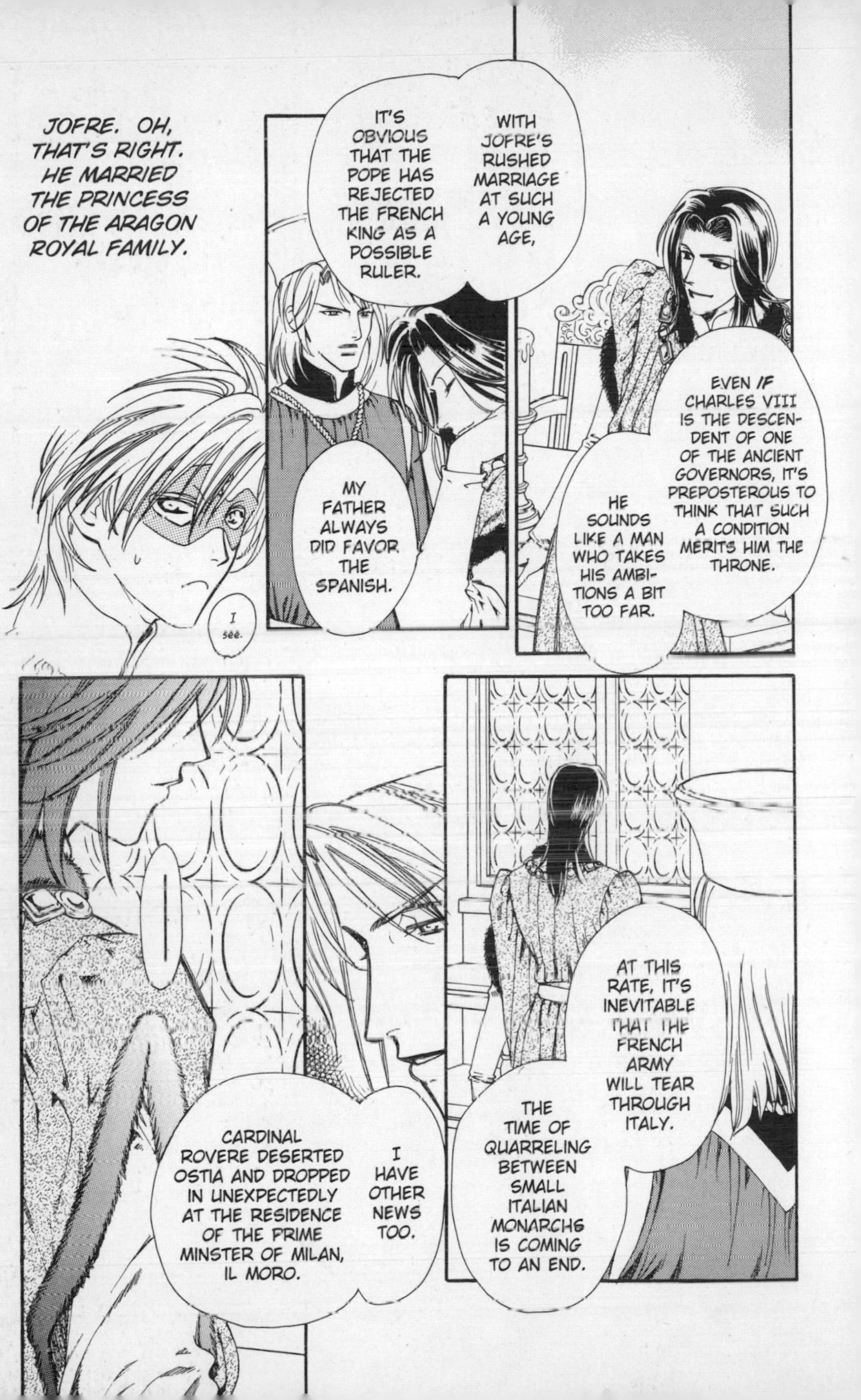
WITH JOFRE'S RUSHED MARRIAGE AT SUCH A YOUNG AGE,
IT'S OBVIOUS THAT THE POPE HAS REJECTED THE FRENCH KING AS A POSSIBLE RULER.
EVEN IF CHARLES VIII IS THE DESCENDENT OF ONE OF THE ANCIENT GOVERNORS, IT'S PREPOSTEROUS TO THINK THAT SUCH A CONDITION MERITS HIM THE THRONE.
HE SOUNDS LIKE A MAN WHO TAKES HIS AMBITIONS A BIT TOO FAR.
MY FATHER ALWAYS DID FAVOR THE SPANISH.
JOFRE. OH, THAT'S RIGHT. HE MARRIED THE PRINCESS OF THE ARAGON ROYAL FAMILY.
I see.
AT THIS RATE, IT'S INEVITABLE THAT THE FRENCH ARMY WILL TEAR THROUGH ITALY.
THE TIME OF QUARRELING BETWEEN SMALL ITALIAN MONARCHS IS COMING TO AN END.
I HAVE OTHER NEWS TOO.
CARDINAL ROVERE DESERTED OSTIA AND DROPPED IN UNEXPECTEDLY AT THE RESIDENCE OF THE PRIME MINSTER OF MILAN, IL MORO.

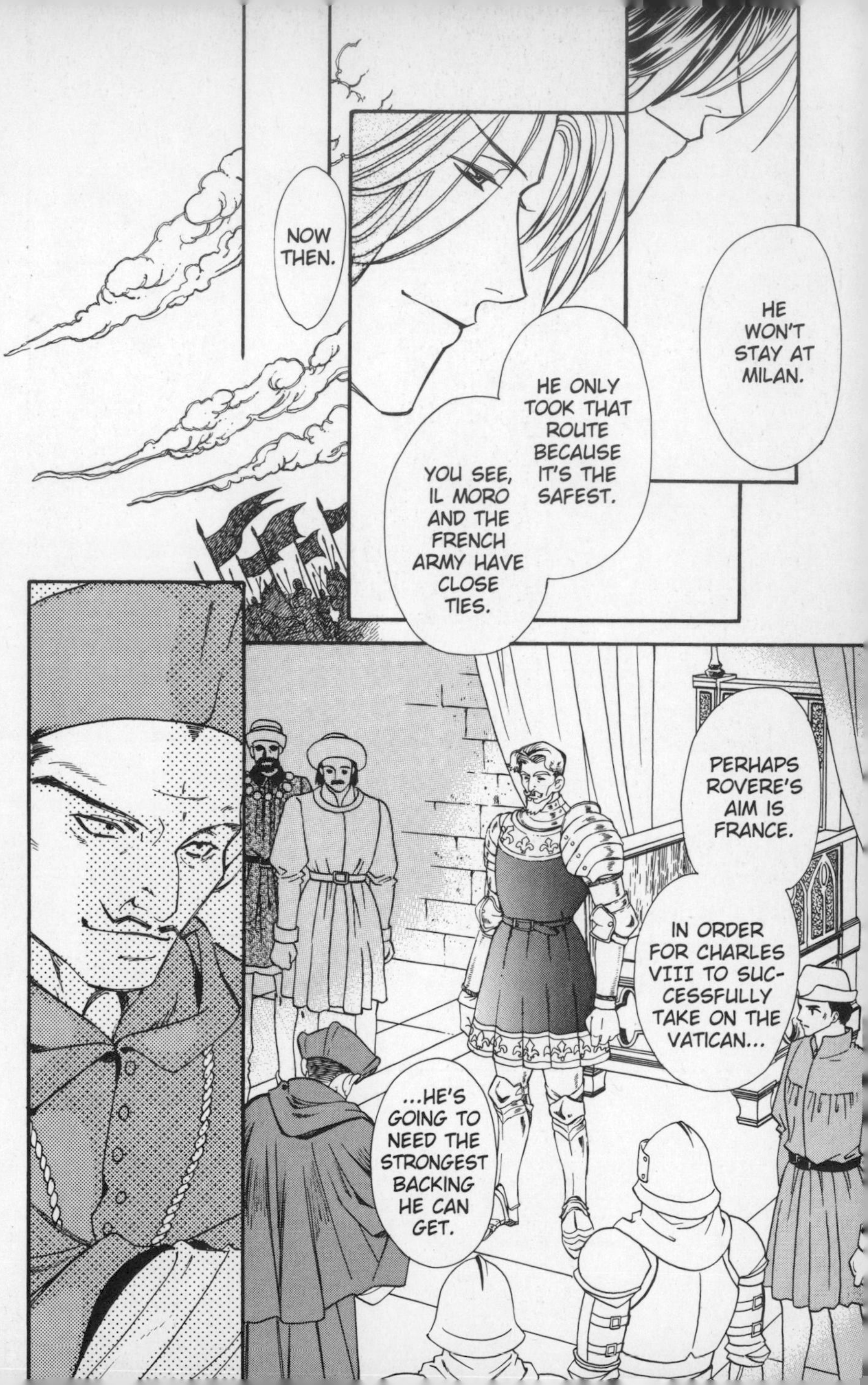
HE WON'T STAY AT MILAN.
HE ONLY TOOK THAT ROUTE BECAUSE IT'S THE SAFEST.
YOU SEE, IL MORO AND THE FRENCH ARMY HAVE CLOSE TIES.
NOW THEN.
PERHAPS ROVERE'S AIM IS FRANCE.
IN ORDER FOR CHARLES VIII TO SUC-CESSFULLY TAKE ON THE VATICAN...
...HE'S GOING TO NEED THE STRONGEST BACKING HE CAN GET.

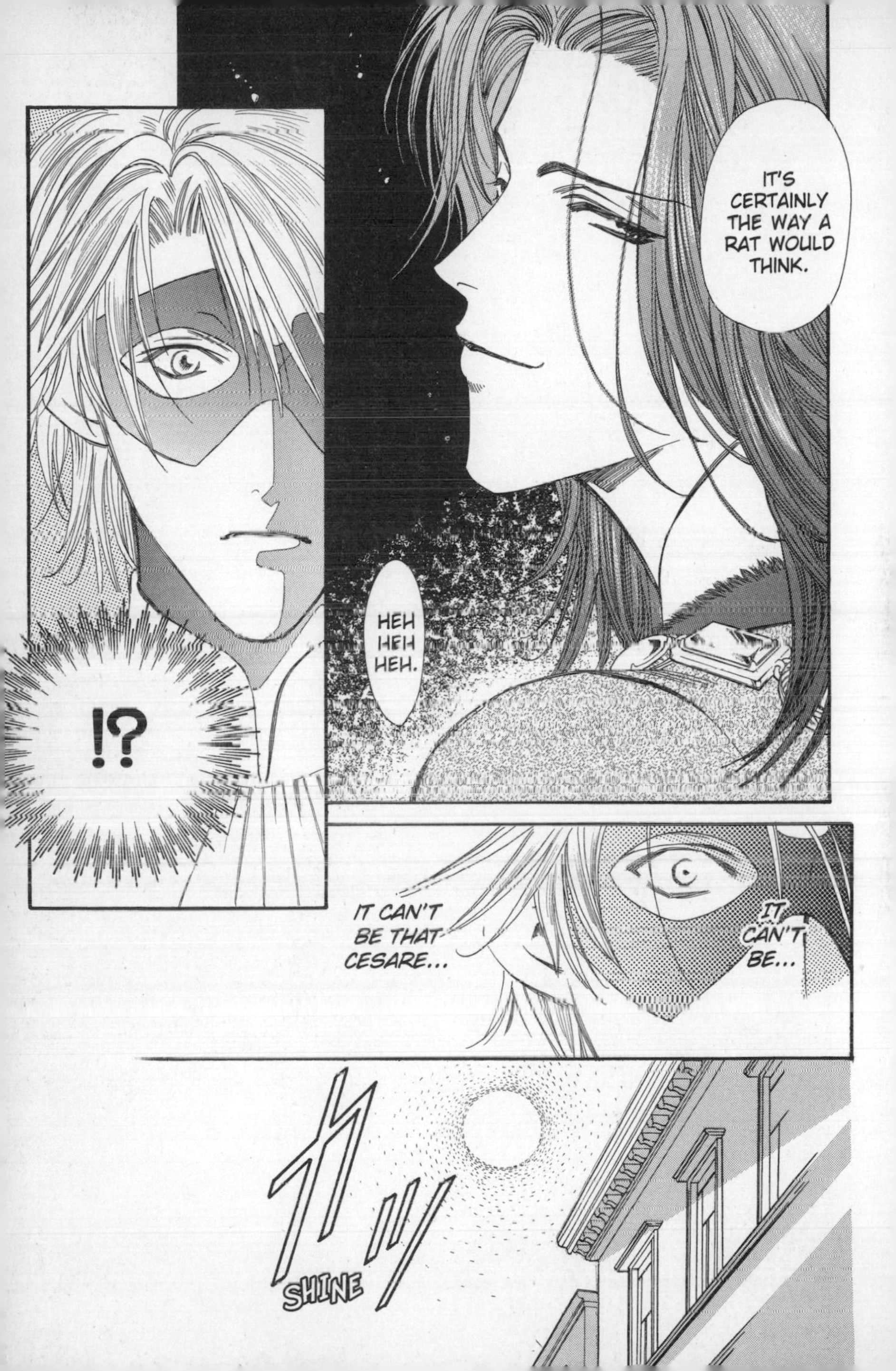
IT'S CERTAINLY THE WAY A RAT WOULD THINK.
HEH HEH HEH.
!?
IT CAN'T BE...
IT CAN'T BE THAT CESARE...
SHINE

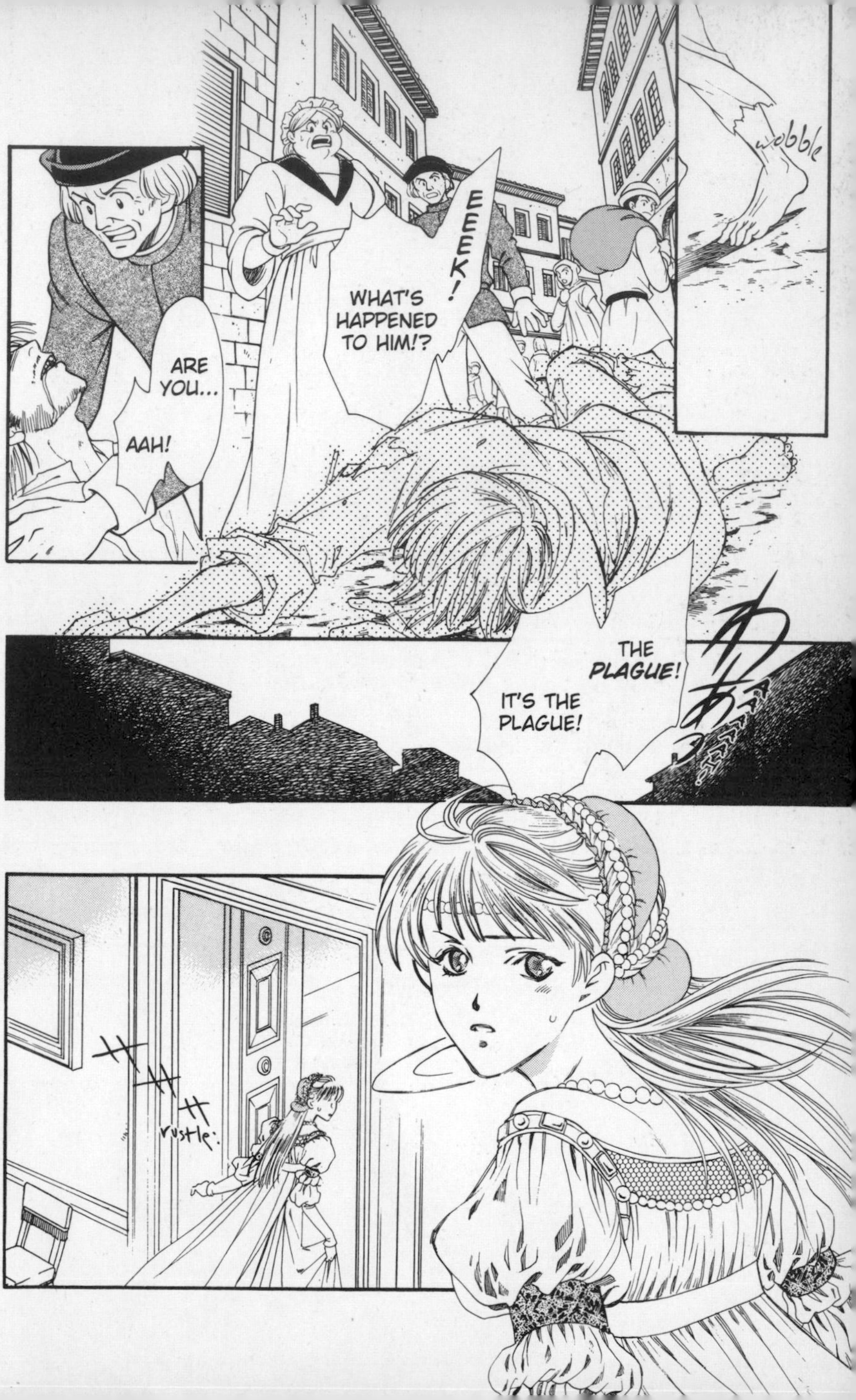
wobble
EEEK!
WHAT'S HAPPENED TO HIM!?
ARE YOU...
AAH!
THE PLAGUE!
IT'S THE PLAGUE!
rustle

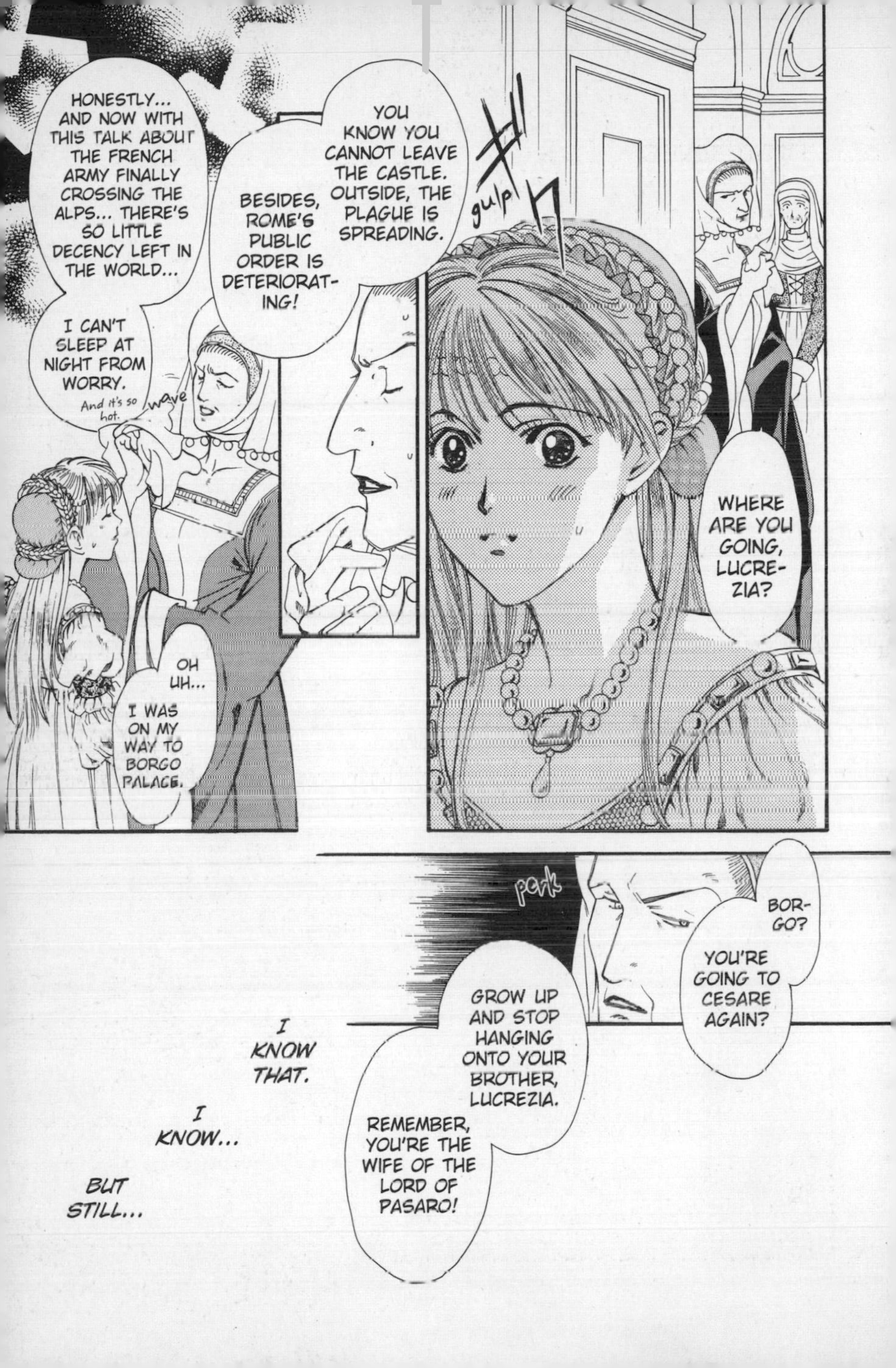
gulp
WHERE ARE YOU GOING, LUCREZIA?
YOU KNOW YOU CANNOT LEAVE THE CASTLE. OUTSIDE, THE PLAGUE IS SPREADING.
BESIDES, ROME'S PUBLIC ORDER IS DETERIORATING!
HONESTLY... AND NOW WITH THIS TALK ABOUT THE FRENCH ARMY FINALLY CROSSING THE ALPS... THERE'S SO LITTLE DECENCY LEFT IN THE WORLD...
I CAN'T SLEEP AT NIGHT FROM WORRY.
wave
And it's so hot.
OH UH... I WAS ON MY WAY TO BORGO PALACE.
perk
BORGO?
YOU'RE GOING TO CESARE AGAIN?
GROW UP AND STOP HANGING ONTO YOUR BROTHER, LUCREZIA.
REMEMBER, YOU'RE THE WIFE OF THE LORD OF PASARO!
I KNOW THAT.
I KNOW...
BUT STILL...

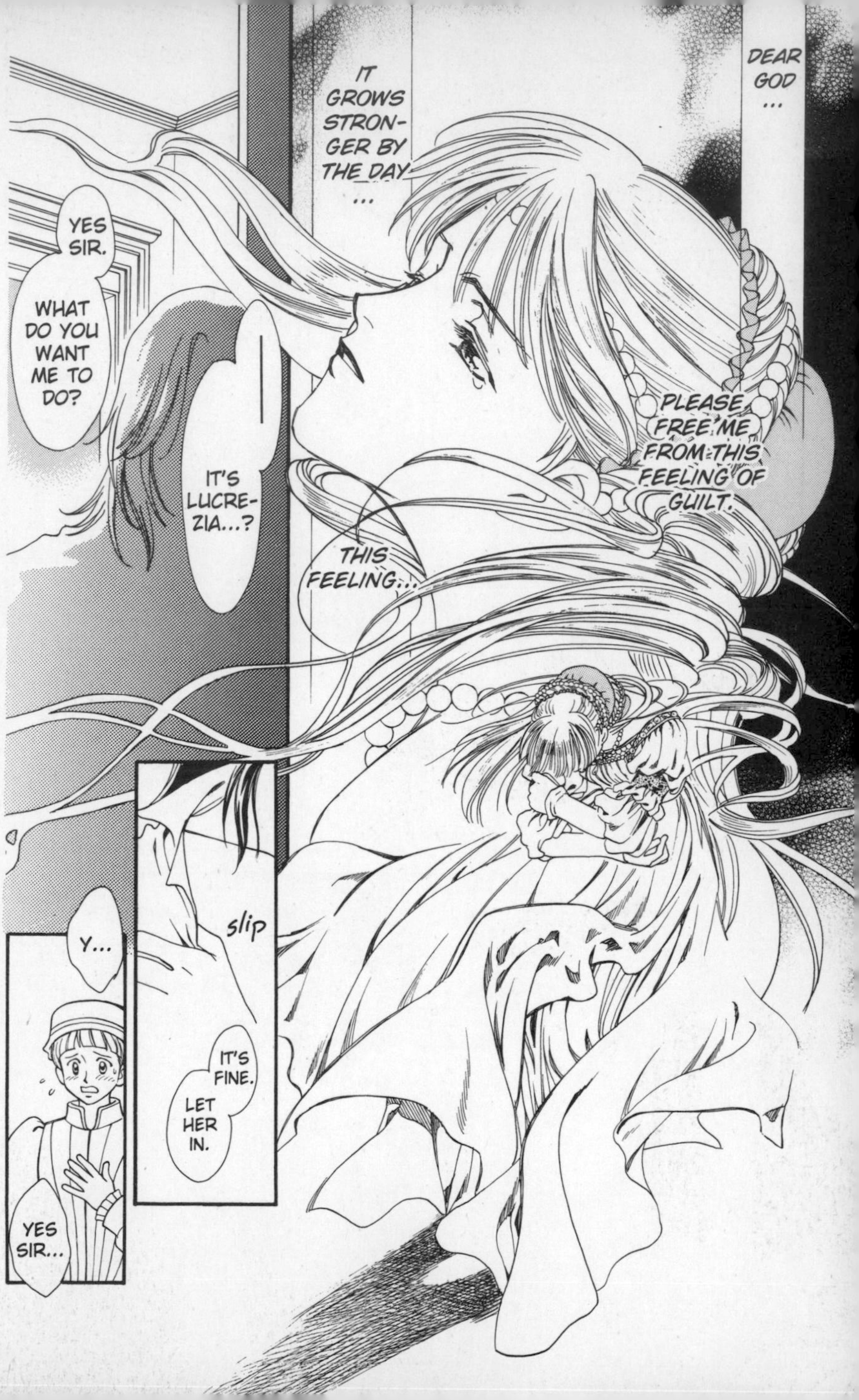
DEAR GOD ...
IT GROWS STRONGER BY THE DAY ...
PLEASE FREE ME FROM THIS FEELING OF GUILT.
THIS FEELING...
IT'S LUCREZIA...?
YES SIR.
WHAT DO YOU WANT ME TO DO?
slip
IT'S FINE. LET HER IN.
Y...
YES SIR...

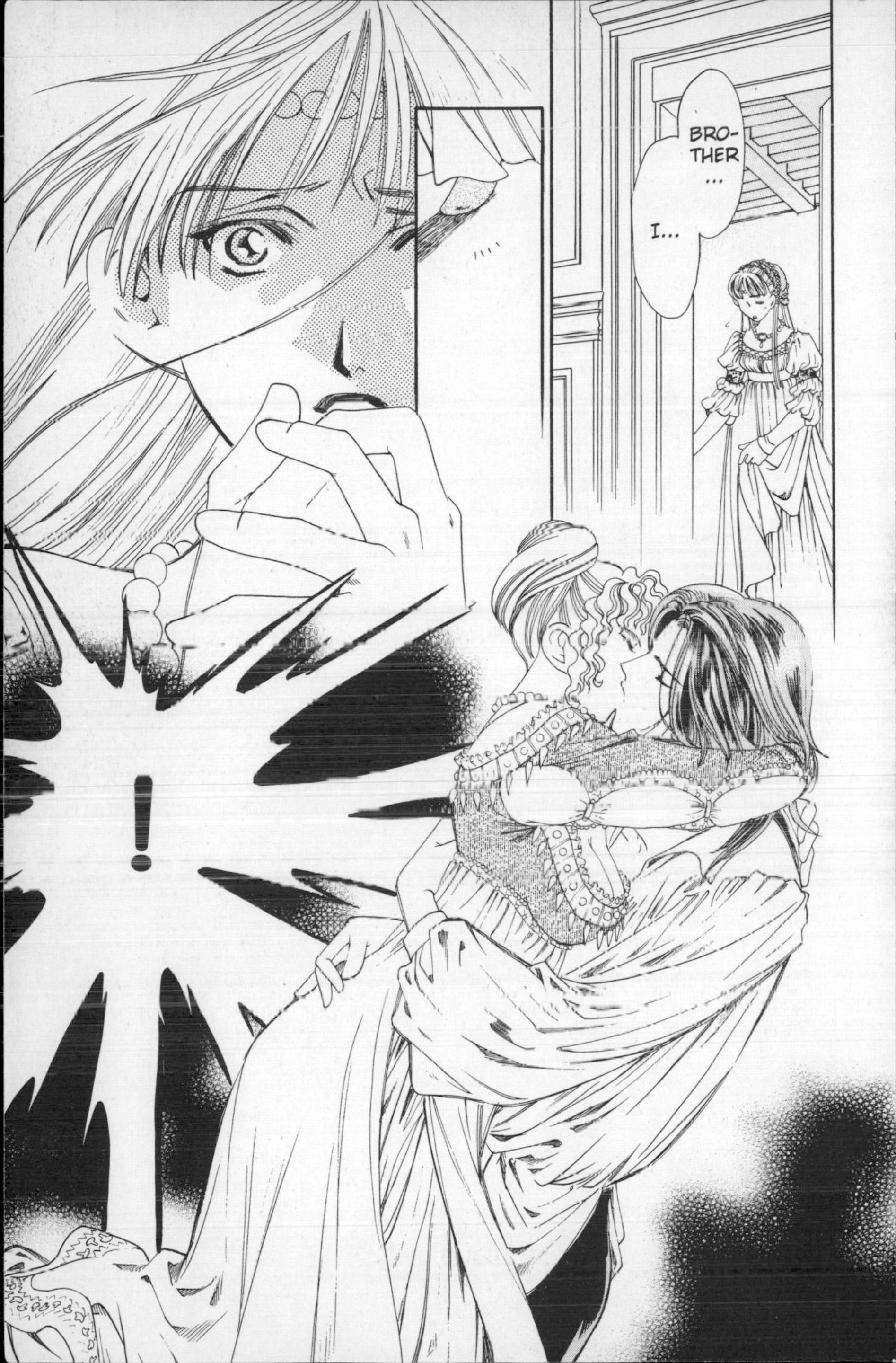
BRO-THER ... I...
!

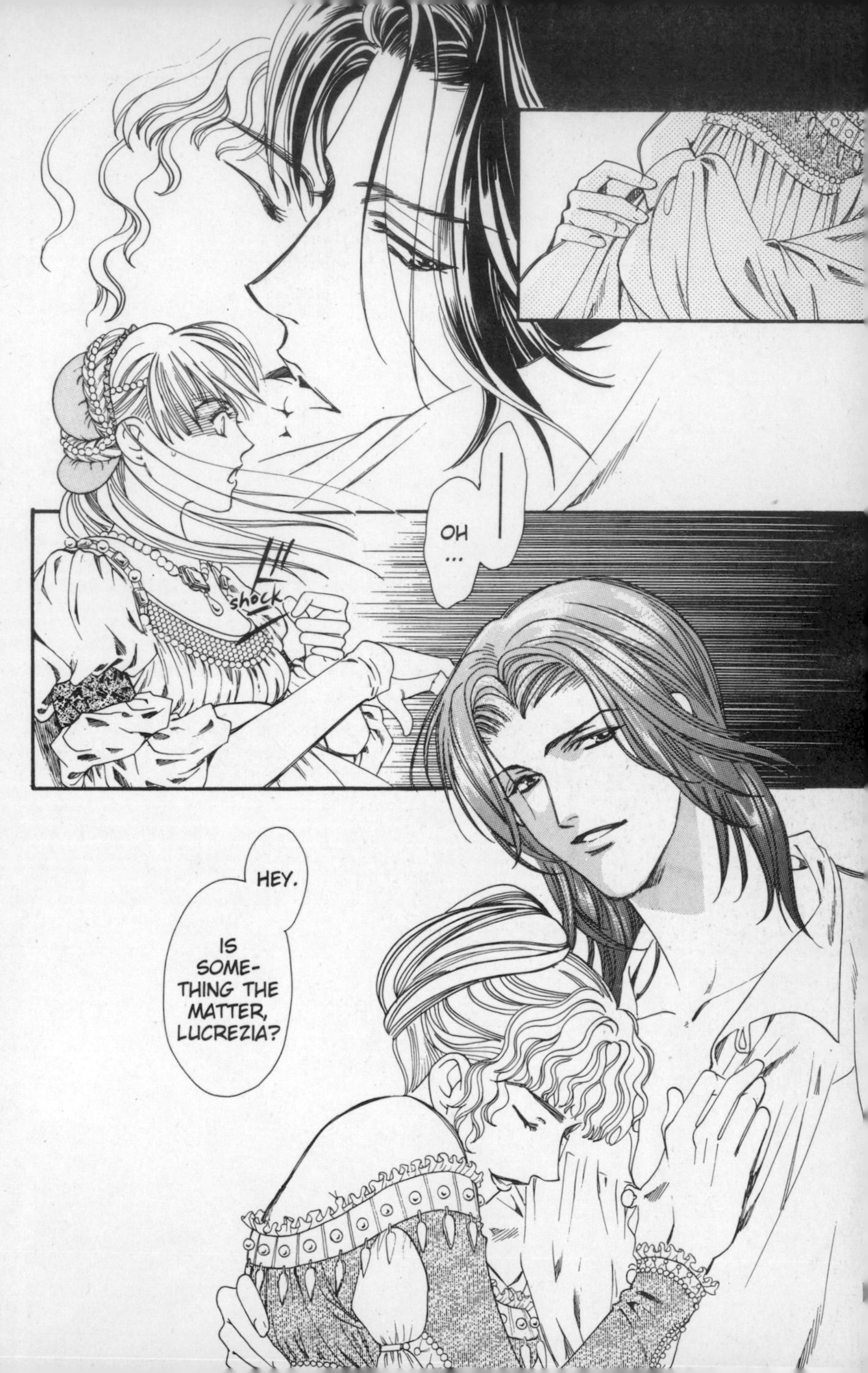

OH ...
shock
HEY.
IS SOME-THING THE MATTER, LUCREZIA?

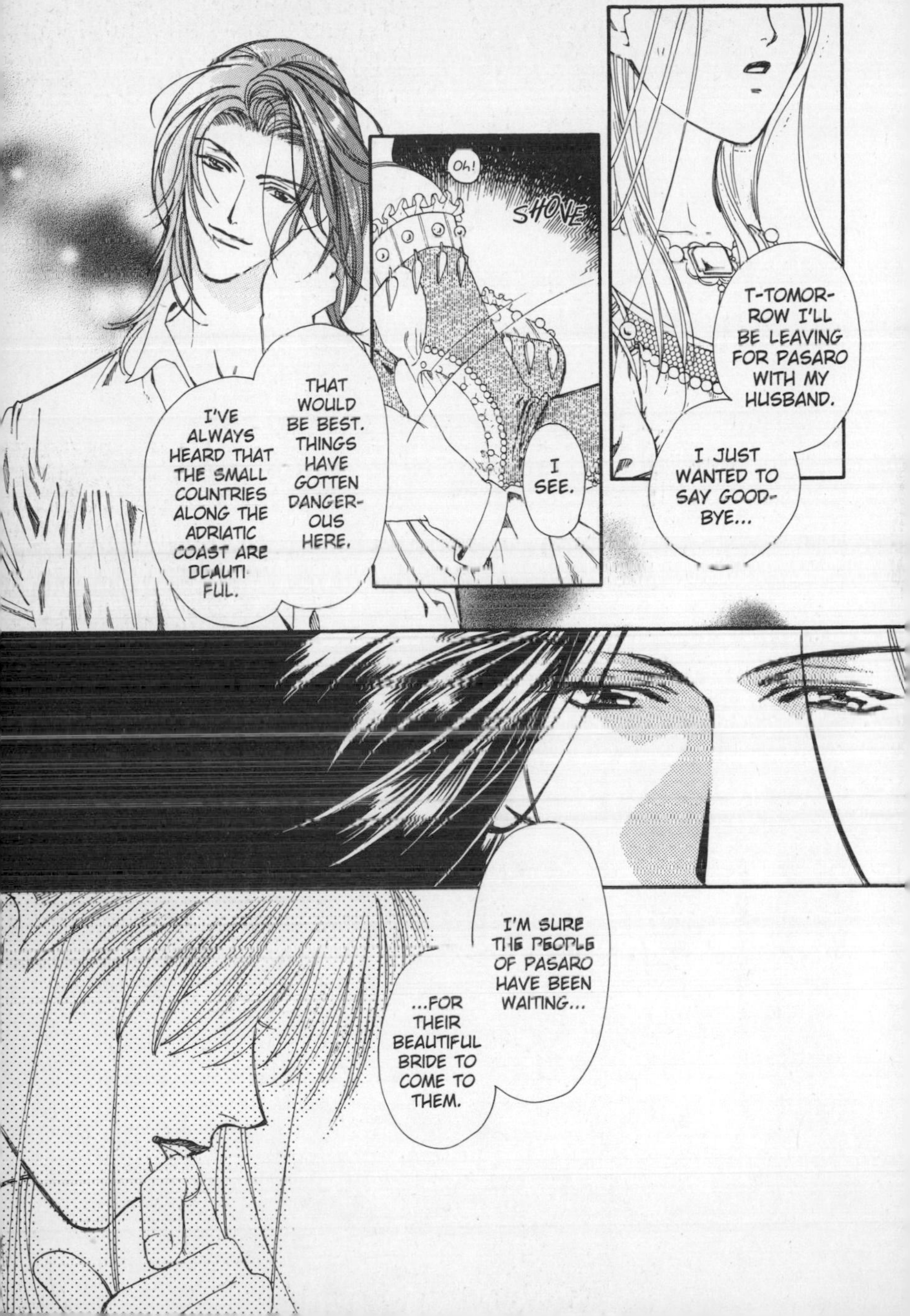
T-TOMORROW I'LL BE LEAVING FOR PASARO WITH MY HUSBAND.
I JUST WANTED TO SAY GOOD-BYE...
Oh!
SHOVE
I SEE.
THAT WOULD BE BEST. THINGS HAVE GOTTEN DANGEROUS HERE.
I'VE ALWAYS HEARD THAT THE SMALL COUNTRIES ALONG THE ADRIATIC COAST ARE BEAUTIFUL.
I'M SURE THE PEOPLE OF PASARO HAVE BEEN WAITING...
...FOR THEIR BEAUTIFUL BRIDE TO COME TO THEM.

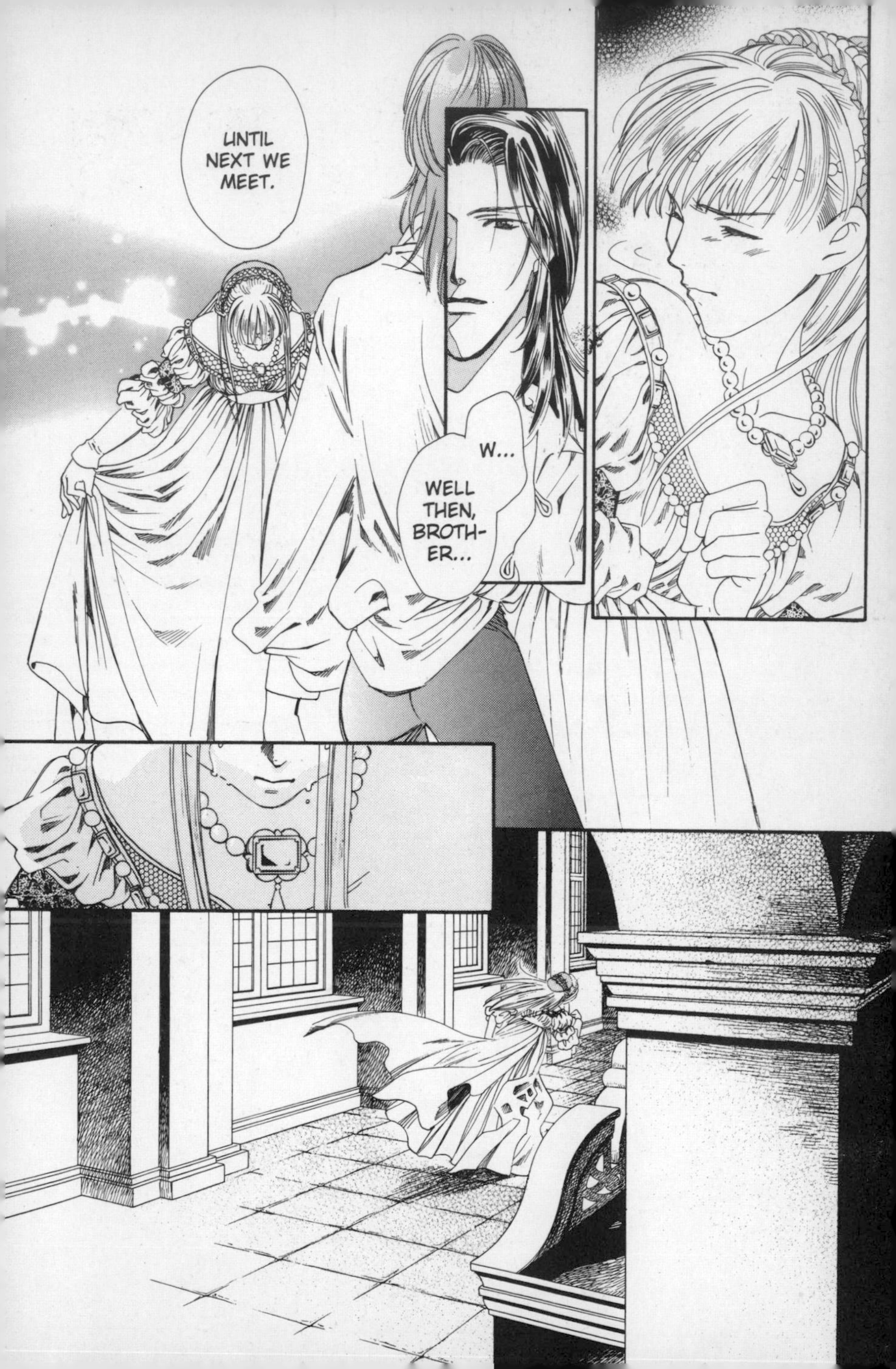
W... WELL THEN, BROTHER...
UNTIL NEXT WE MEET.

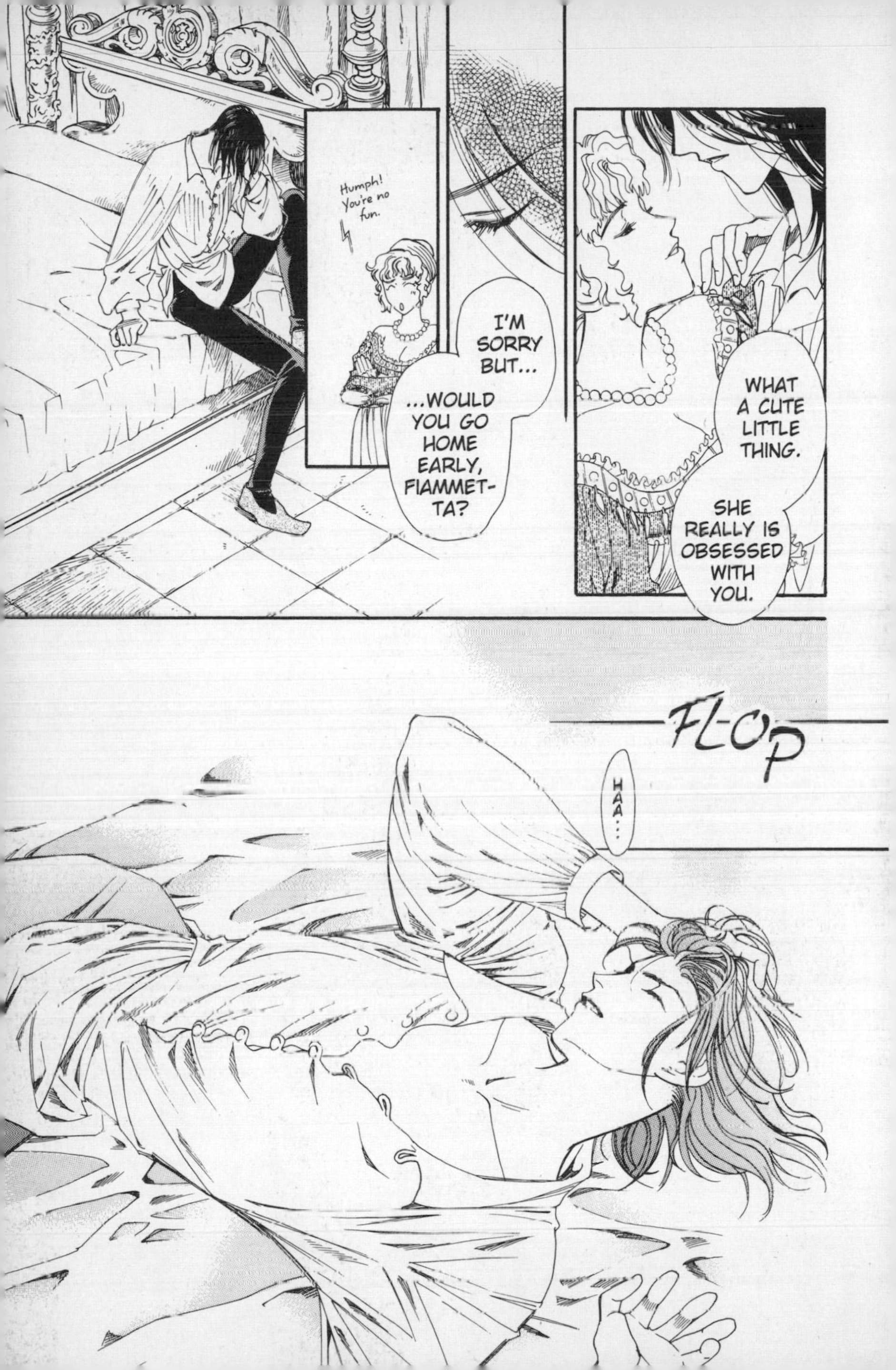
WHAT A CUTE LITTLE THING.
SHE REALLY IS OBSESSED WITH YOU.
I'M SORRY BUT...
...WOULD YOU GO HOME EARLY, FIAMMETTA?
Humph! You're no fun.
FLOP
HAA...

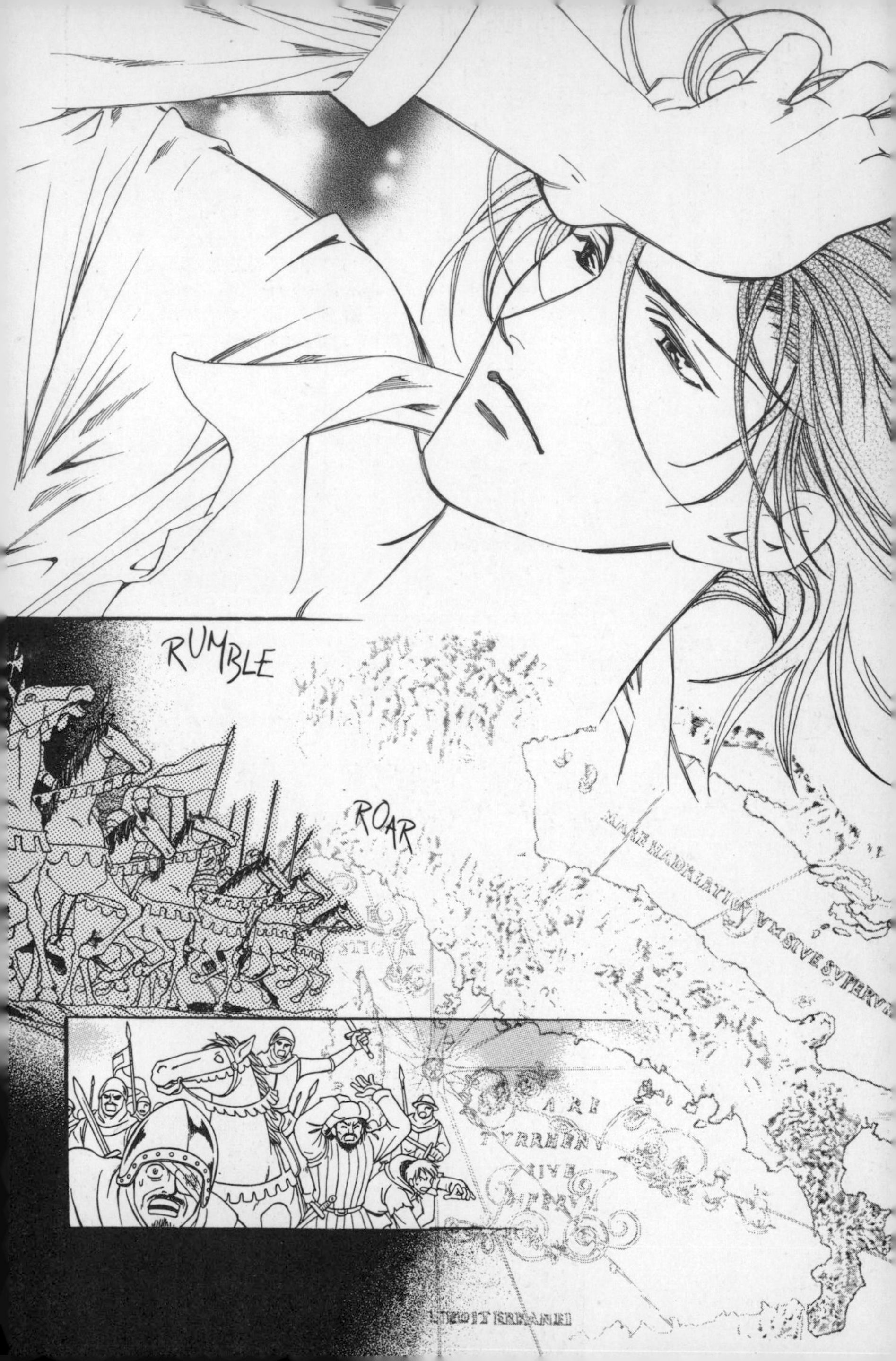
RUMBLE
ROAR

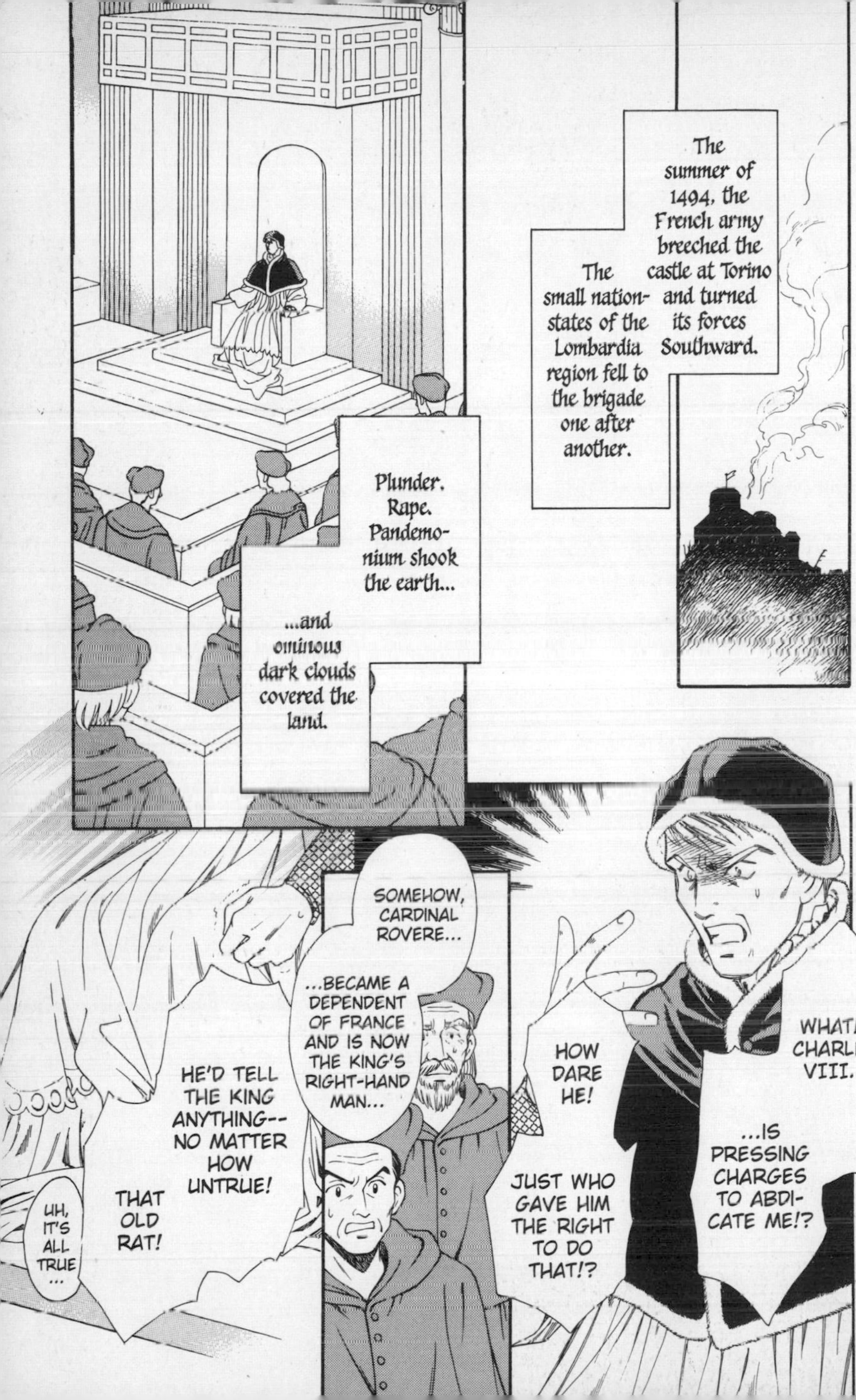
The summer of 1494, the French army breeched the castle at Torino and turned its forces Southward.
The small nation-states of the Lombardia region fell to the brigade one after another.
Plunder. Rape. Pandemonium shook the earth...
...and ominous dark clouds covered the land.
WHAT!? CHARLES VIII...
...IS PRESSING CHARGES TO ABDICATE ME!?
HOW DARE HE!
JUST WHO GAVE HIM THE RIGHT TO DO THAT!?
SOMEHOW, CARDINAL ROVERE...
...BECAME A DEPENDENT OF FRANCE AND IS NOW THE KING'S RIGHT-HAND MAN...
HE'D TELL THE KING ANYTHING-- NO MATTER HOW UNTRUE!
THAT OLD RAT!
UH, IT'S ALL TRUE...

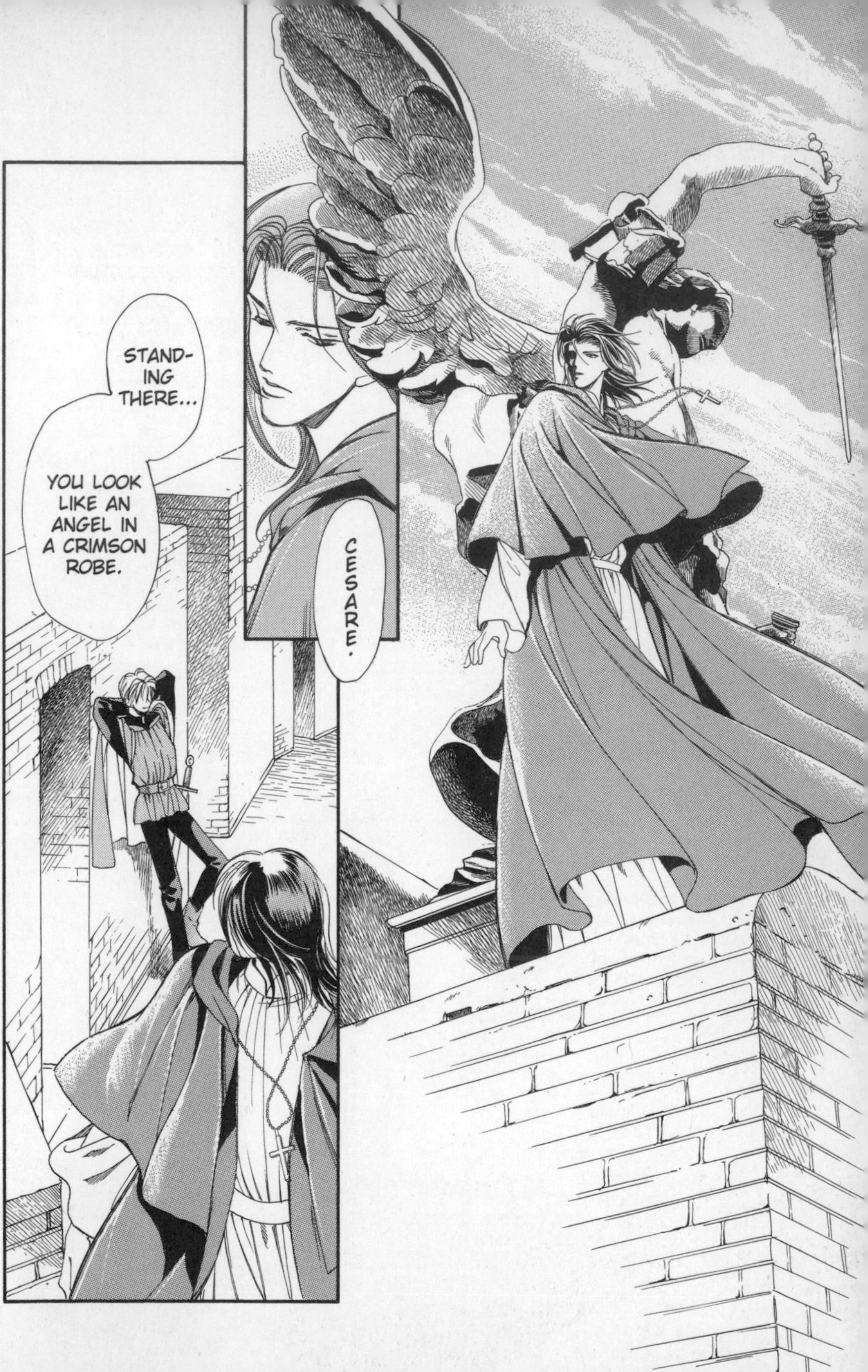
CESARE.
STANDING-ING THERE...
YOU LOOK LIKE AN ANGEL IN A CRIMSON ROBE.

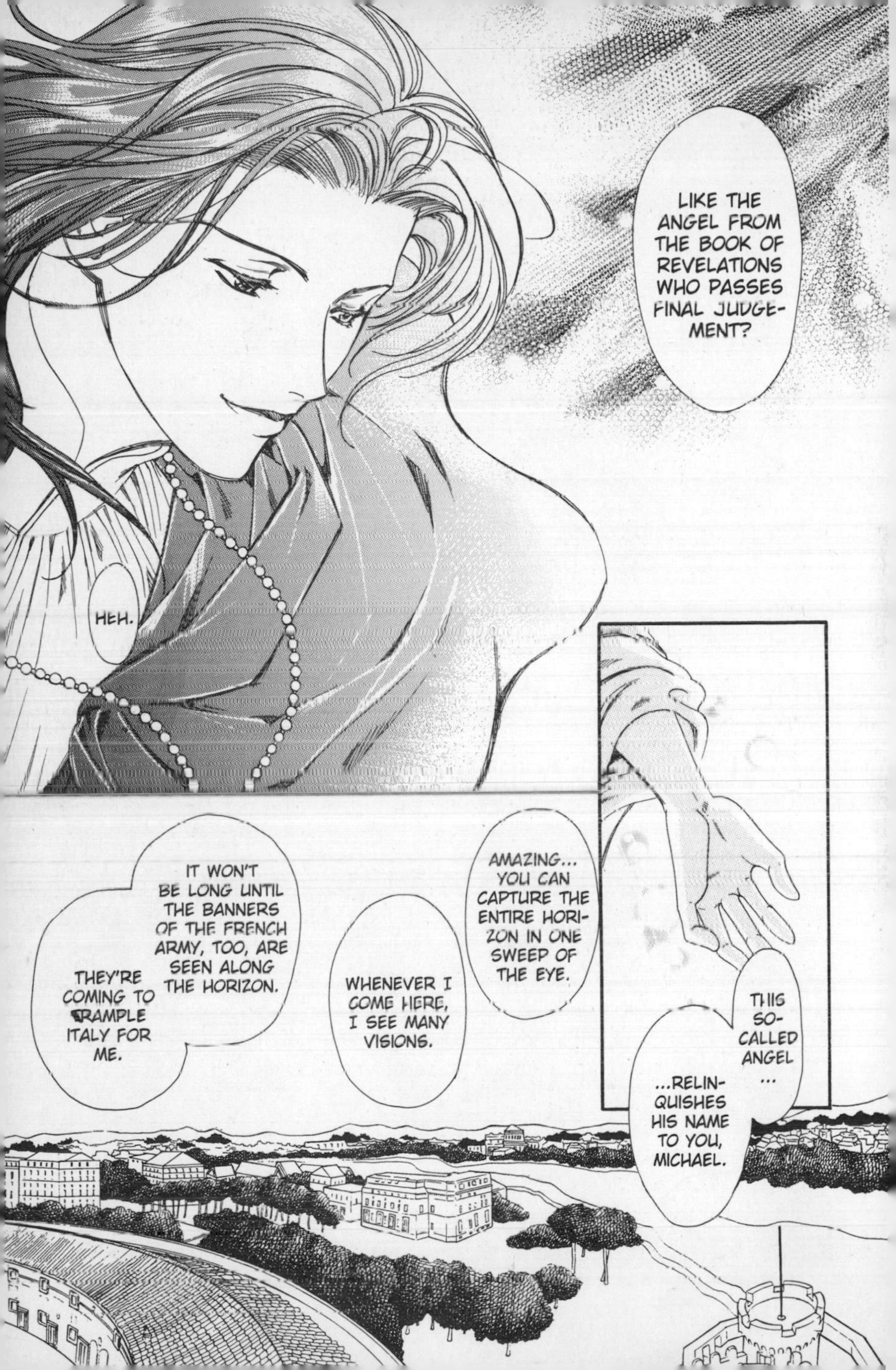
LIKE THE ANGEL FROM THE BOOK OF REVELATIONS WHO PASSES FINAL JUDGE-MENT?
HEH.
THIS SO-CALLED ANGEL ...
...RELIN-QUISHES HIS NAME TO YOU, MICHAEL.
AMAZING... YOU CAN CAPTURE THE ENTIRE HORI-ZON IN ONE SWEEP OF THE EYE.
WHENEVER I COME HERE, I SEE MANY VISIONS.
IT WON'T BE LONG UNTIL THE BANNERS OF THE FRENCH ARMY, TOO, ARE SEEN ALONG THE HORIZON.
THEY'RE COMING TO TRAMPLE ITALY FOR ME.

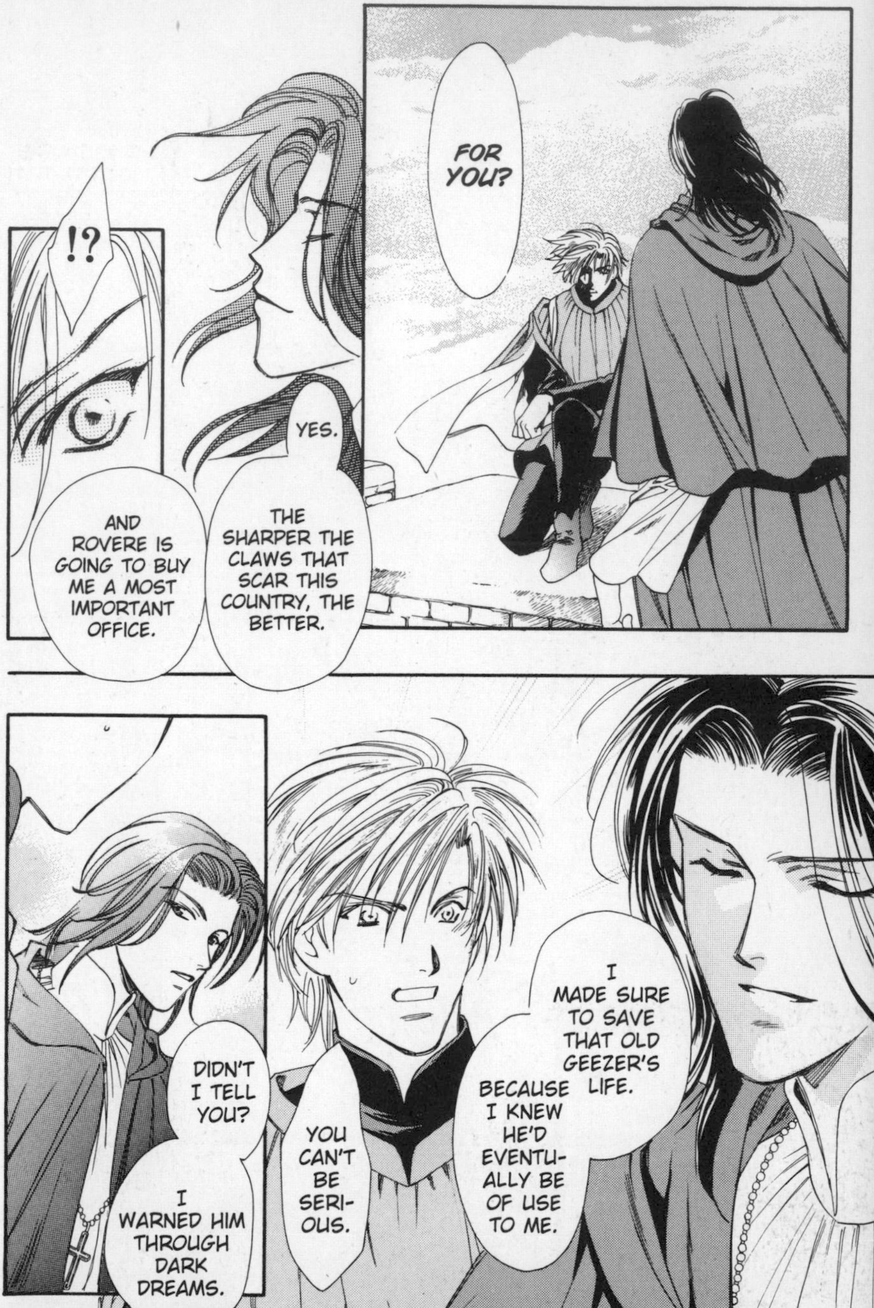
FOR YOU?
YES.
THE SHARPER THE CLAWS THAT SCAR THIS COUNTRY, THE BETTER.
AND ROVERE IS GOING TO BUY ME A MOST IMPORTANT OFFICE.
!?
I MADE SURE TO SAVE THAT OLD GEEZER'S LIFE.
BECAUSE I KNEW HE'D EVENTU-ALLY BE OF USE TO ME.
YOU CAN'T BE SERI-OUS.
DIDN'T I TELL YOU?
I WARNED HIM THROUGH DARK DREAMS.

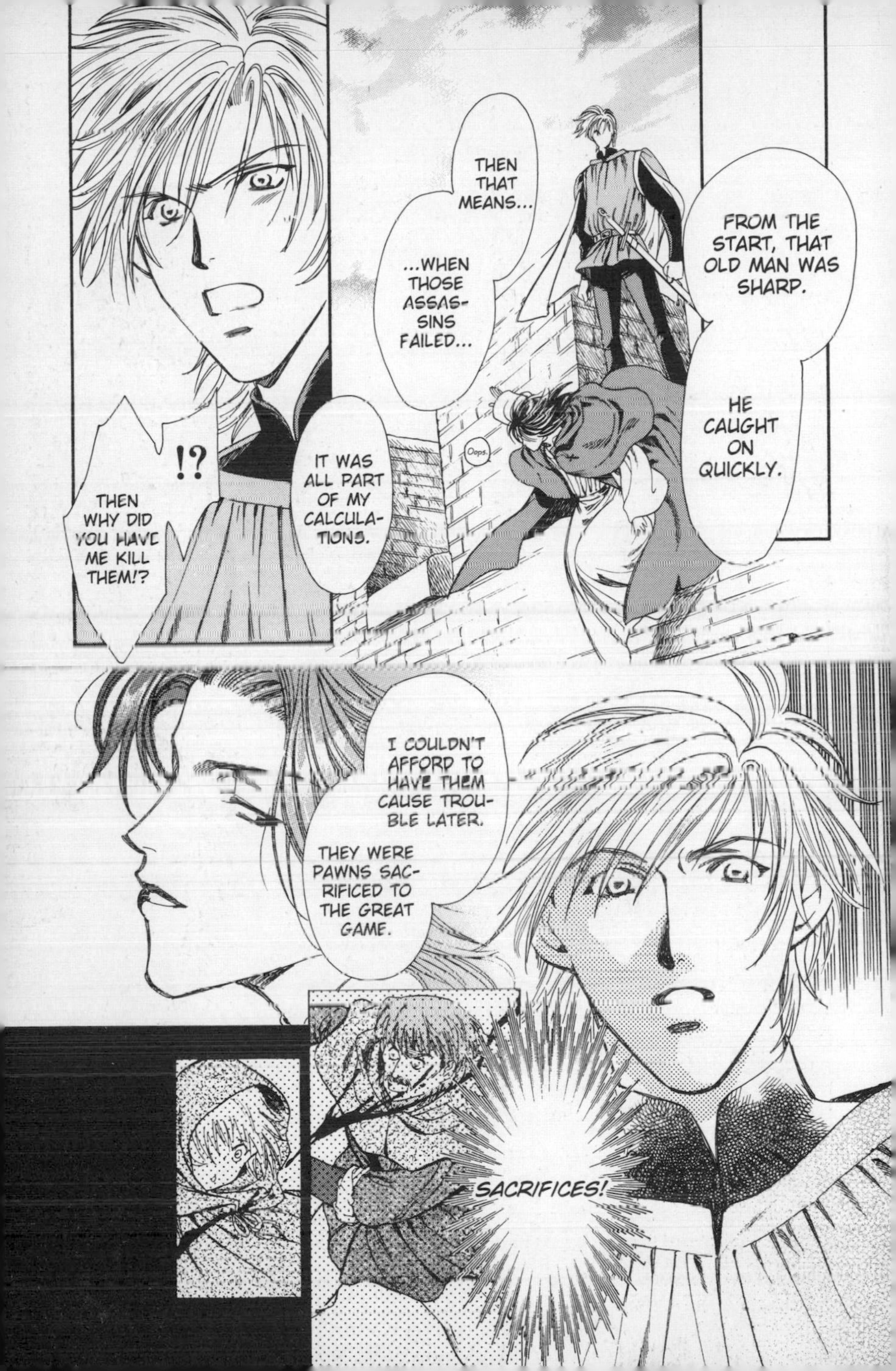

FROM THE START, THAT OLD MAN WAS SHARP.
HE CAUGHT ON QUICKLY.
THEN THAT MEANS...
...WHEN THOSE ASSASSINS FAILED...
Oops.
IT WAS ALL PART OF MY CALCULATIONS.
!?
THEN WHY DID YOU HAVE ME KILL THEM!?
I COULDN'T AFFORD TO HAVE THEM CAUSE TROUBLE LATER.
THEY WERE PAWNS SACRIFICED TO THE GREAT GAME.
SACRIFICES!

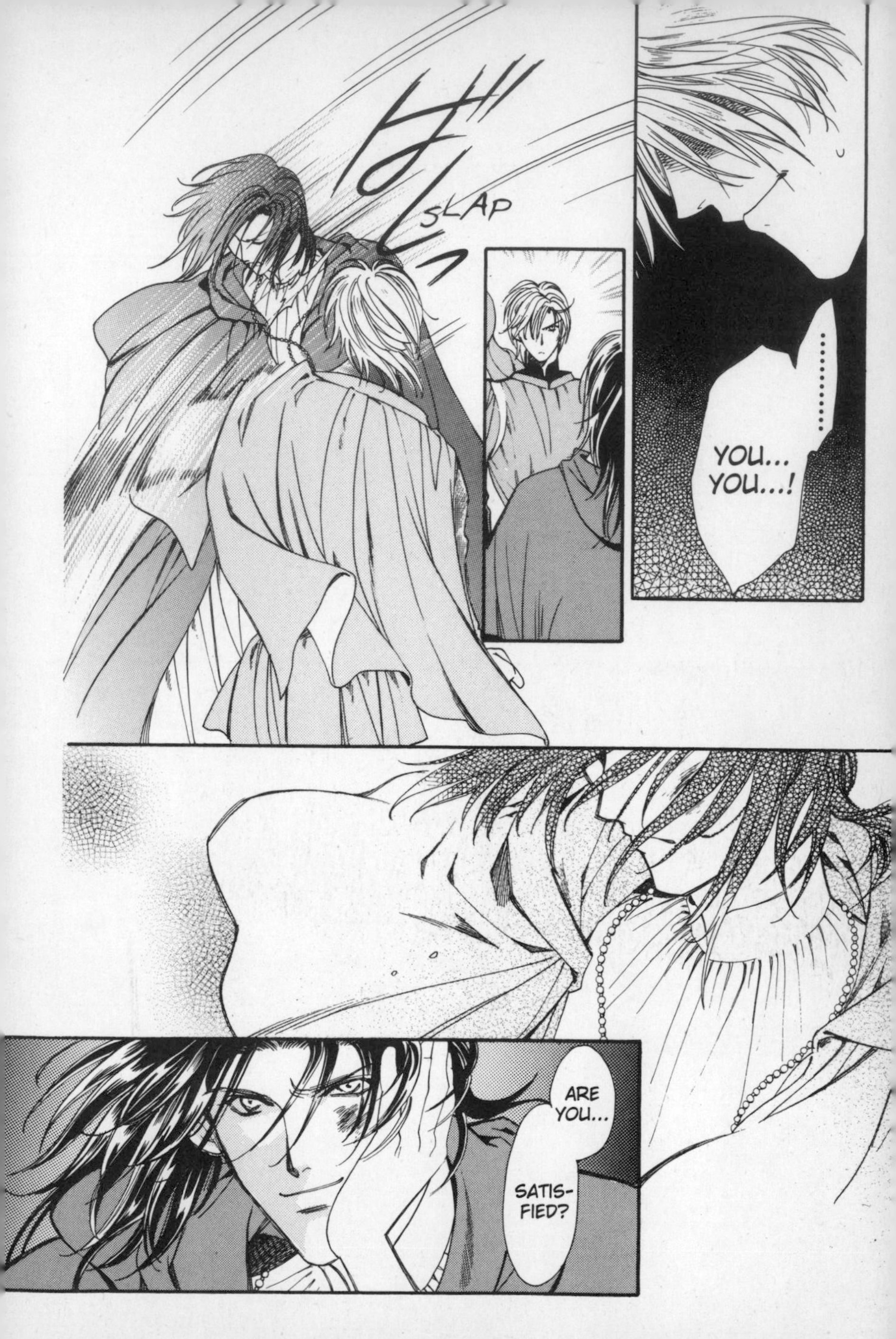
......
YOU... YOU...!
SLAP
ARE YOU...
SATIS-FIED?

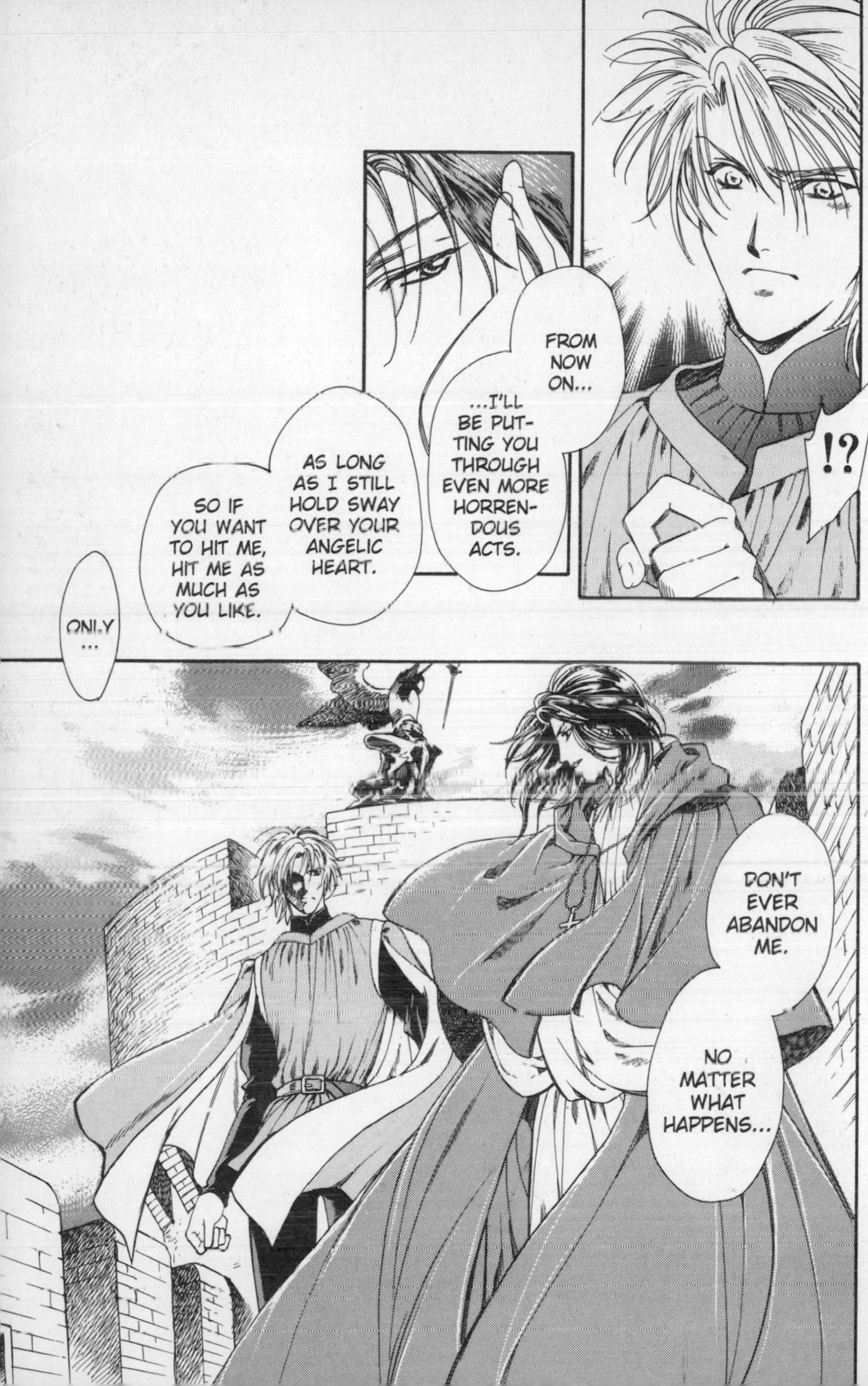
!?
FROM NOW ON...
...I'LL BE PUTTING YOU THROUGH EVEN MORE HORRENDOUS ACTS.
AS LONG AS I STILL HOLD SWAY OVER YOUR ANGELIC HEART.
SO IF YOU WANT TO HIT ME, HIT ME AS MUCH AS YOU LIKE.
ONLY ...
DON'T EVER ABANDON ME.
NO MATTER WHAT HAPPENS...

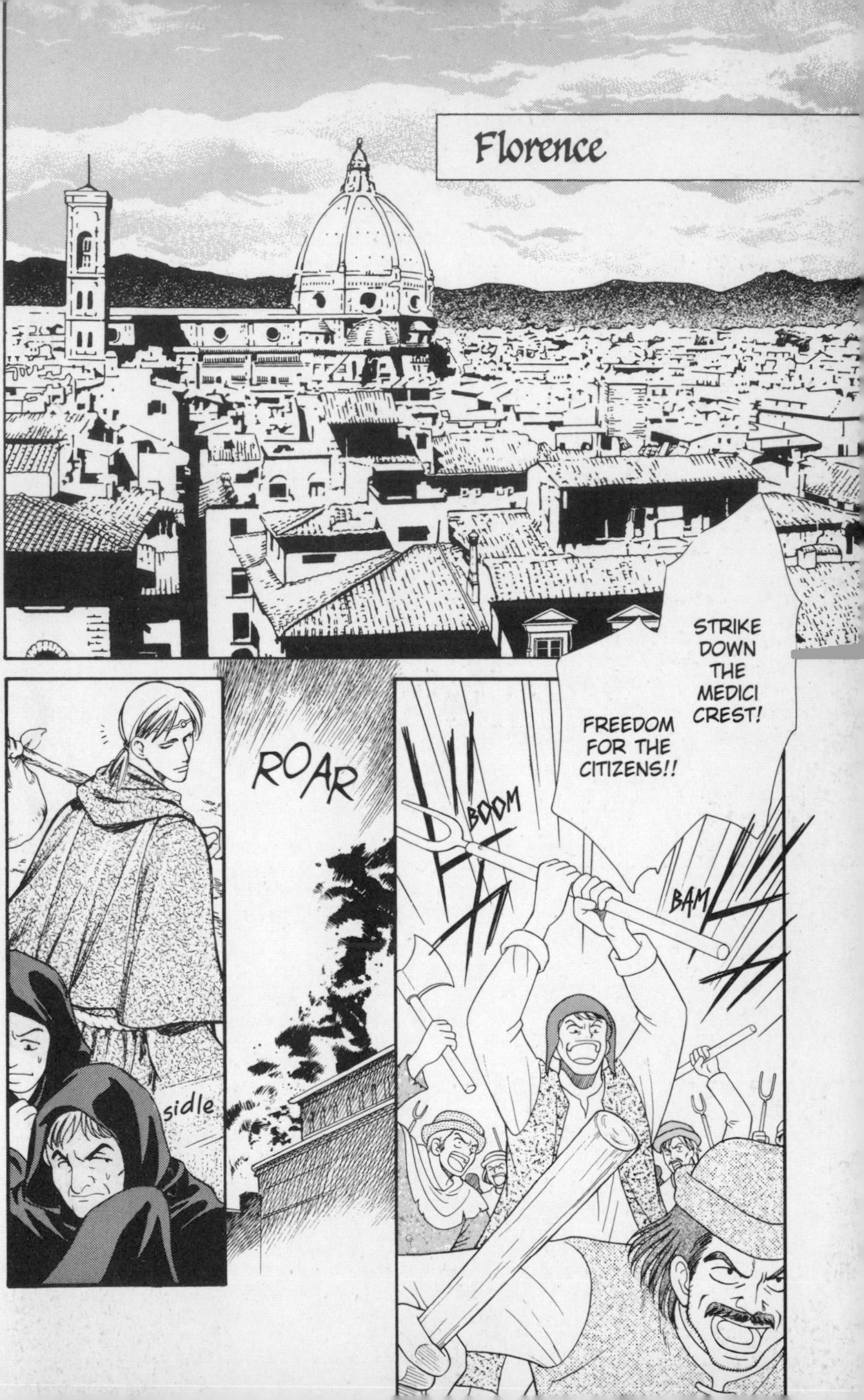
Florence
STRIKE DOWN THE MEDICI CREST!
FREEDOM FOR THE CITIZENS!!
BOOM
BAM
ROAR
sidle

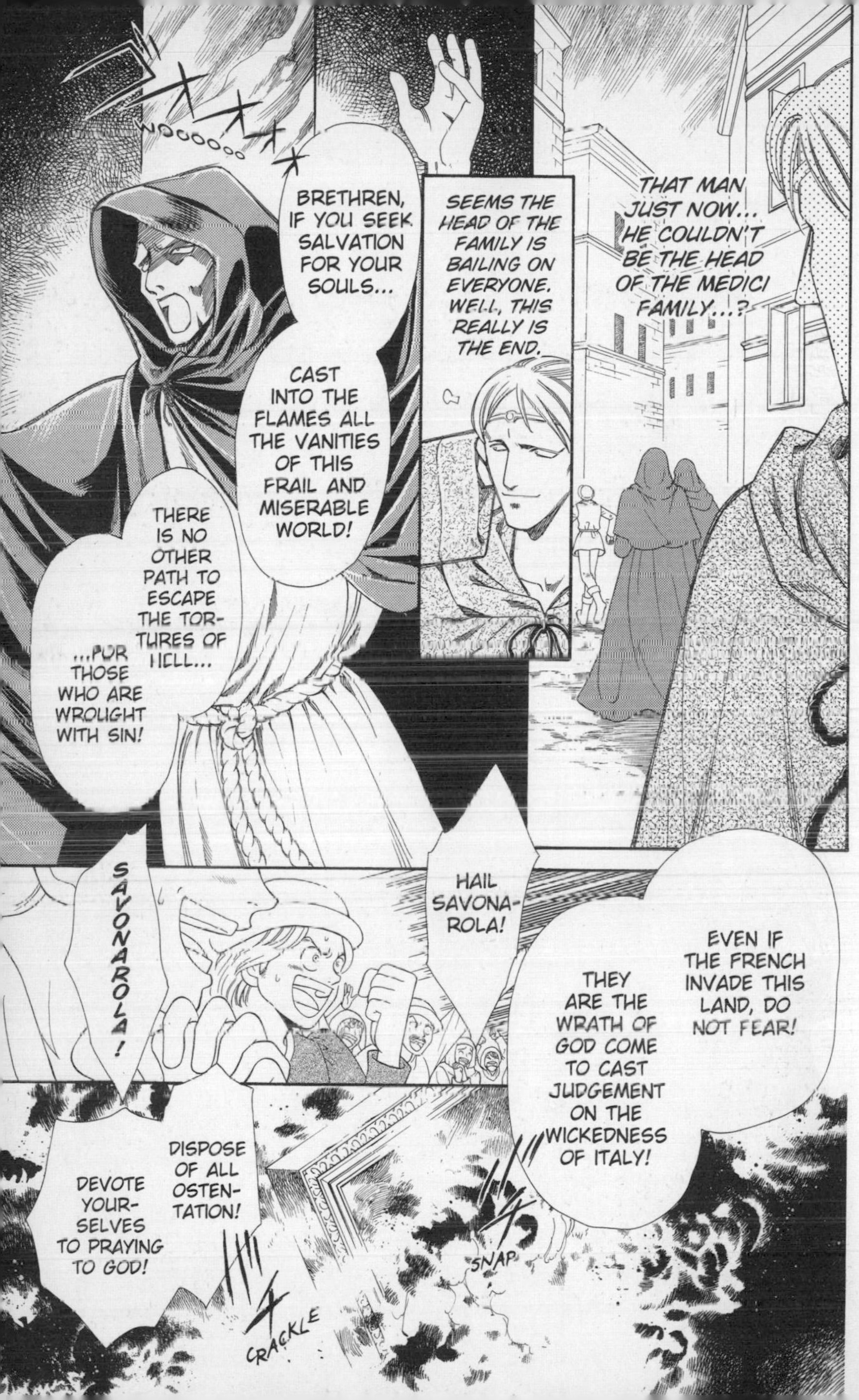
THAT MAN JUST NOW... HE COULDN'T BE THE HEAD OF THE MEDICI FAMILY...?
SEEMS THE HEAD OF THE FAMILY IS BAILING ON EVERYONE. WELL, THIS REALLY IS THE END.
WOOOOOO
BRETHREN, IF YOU SEEK SALVATION FOR YOUR SOULS...
CAST INTO THE FLAMES ALL THE VANITIES OF THIS FRAIL AND MISERABLE WORLD!
THERE IS NO OTHER PATH TO ESCAPE THE TORTURES OF HELL...
...FOR THOSE WHO ARE WROUGHT WITH SIN!
EVEN IF THE FRENCH INVADE THIS LAND, DO NOT FEAR!
THEY ARE THE WRATH OF GOD COME TO CAST JUDGEMENT ON THE WICKEDNESS OF ITALY!
HAIL SAVONAROLA!
SAVONAROLA!
SNAP
DISPOSE OF ALL OSTENTATION!
DEVOTE YOURSELVES TO PRAYING TO GOD!
CRACKLE

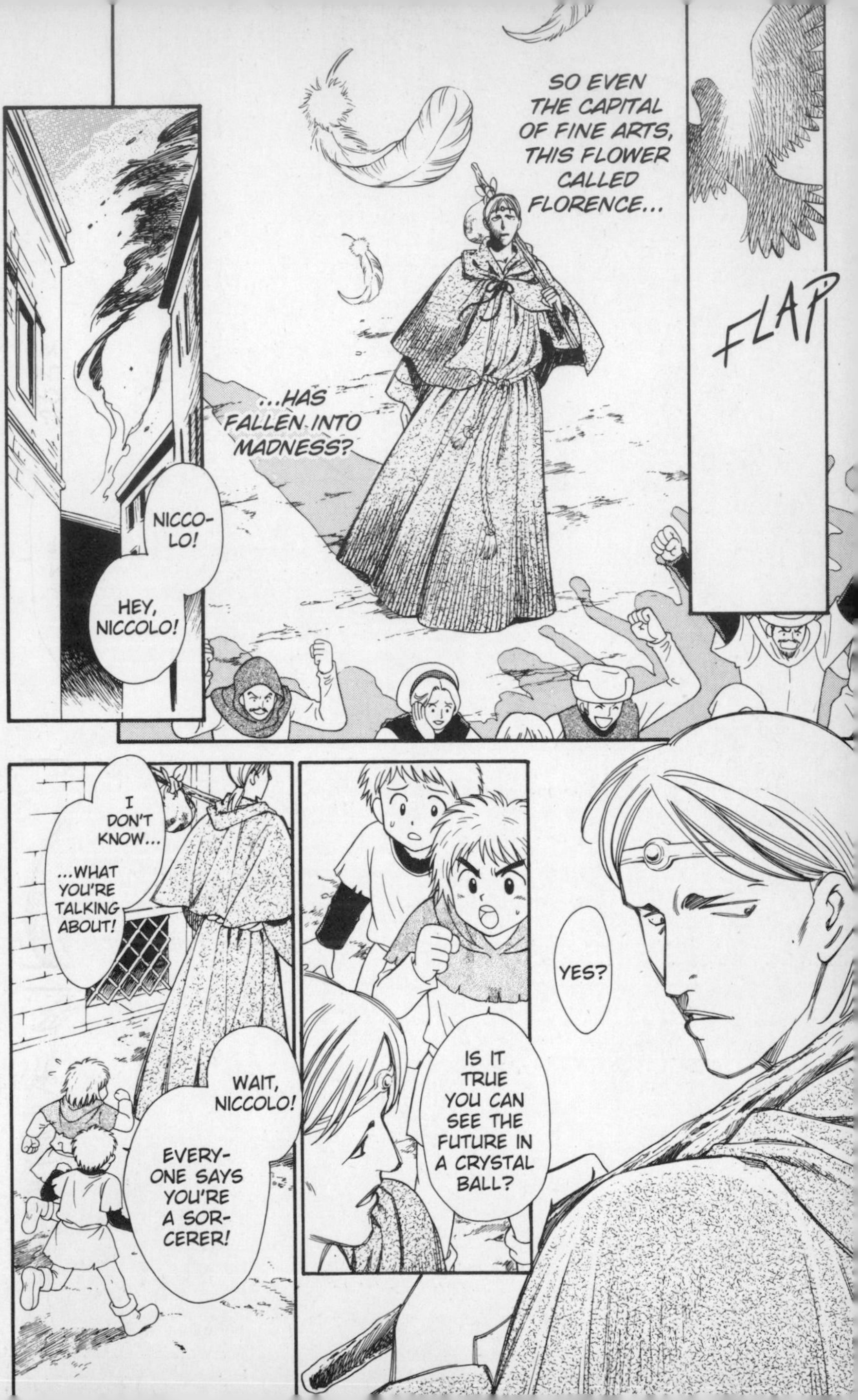
FLAP
SO EVEN THE CAPITAL OF FINE ARTS, THIS FLOWER CALLED FLORENCE...
...HAS FALLEN INTO MADNESS?
NICCOLO!
HEY, NICCOLO!
YES?
IS IT TRUE YOU CAN SEE THE FUTURE IN A CRYSTAL BALL?
I DON'T KNOW...
...WHAT YOU'RE TALKING ABOUT!
WAIT, NICCOLO!
EVERYONE SAYS YOU'RE A SORCERER!

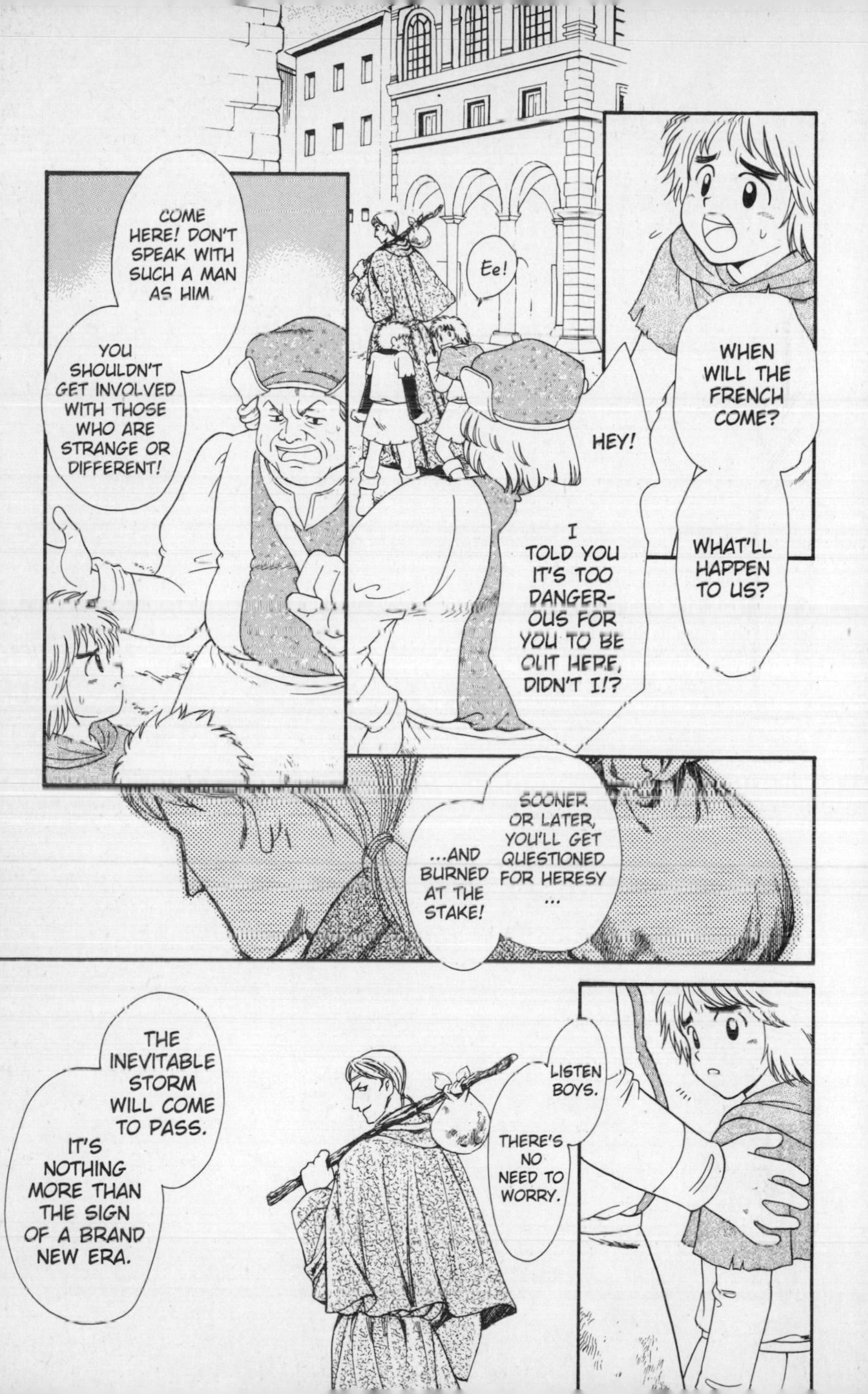
WHEN WILL THE FRENCH COME?
WHAT'LL HAPPEN TO US?
Ee!
HEY!
I TOLD YOU IT'S TOO DANGER-OUS FOR YOU TO BE OUT HERE, DIDN'T I!?
COME HERE! DON'T SPEAK WITH SUCH A MAN AS HIM.
YOU SHOULDN'T GET INVOLVED WITH THOSE WHO ARE STRANGE OR DIFFERENT!
SOONER OR LATER, YOU'LL GET QUESTIONED FOR HERESY ...
...AND BURNED AT THE STAKE!
LISTEN BOYS.
THERE'S NO NEED TO WORRY.
THE INEVITABLE STORM WILL COME TO PASS.
IT'S NOTHING MORE THAN THE SIGN OF A BRAND NEW ERA.

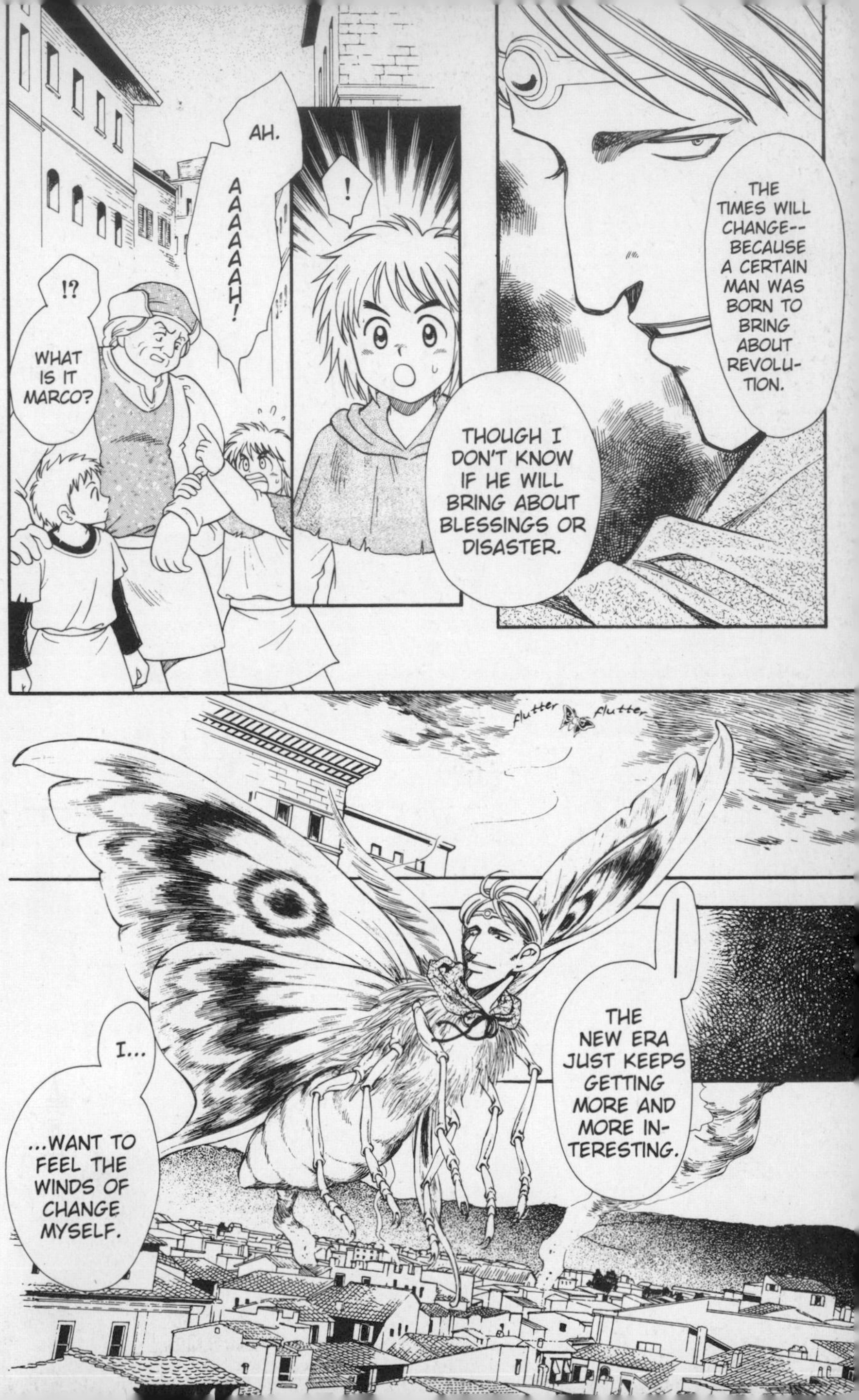
THE TIMES WILL CHANGE-- BECAUSE A CERTAIN MAN WAS BORN TO BRING ABOUT REVOLUTION.
THOUGH I DON'T KNOW IF HE WILL BRING ABOUT BLESSINGS OR DISASTER.
!
AH.
AAAAAAH!
!?
WHAT IS IT MARCO?
flutter flutter
THE NEW ERA JUST KEEPS GETTING MORE AND MORE INTERESTING.
I...
...WANT TO FEEL THE WINDS OF CHANGE MYSELF.

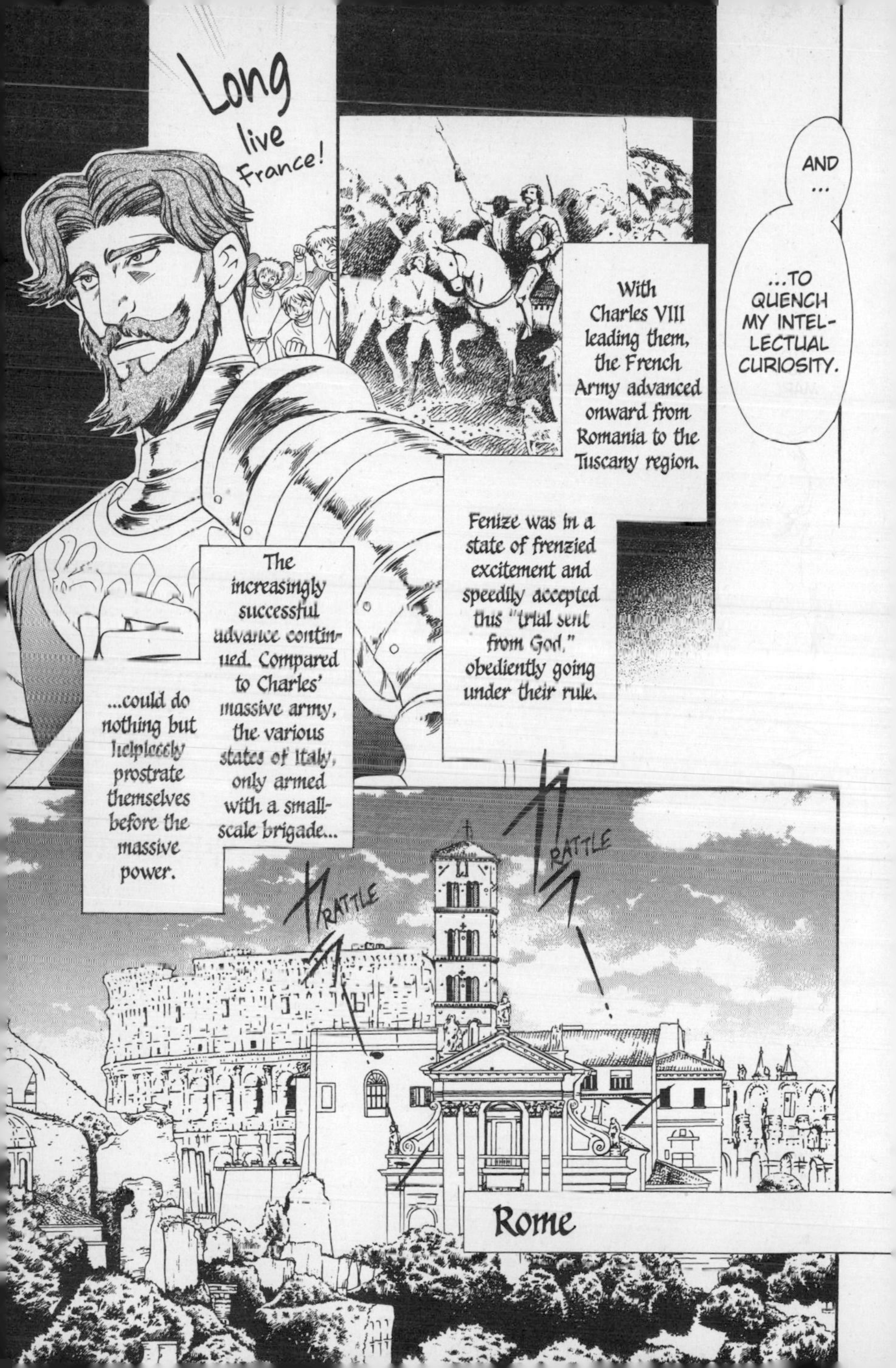

AND ...
...TO QUENCH MY INTEL-LECTUAL CURIOSITY.
With Charles VIII leading them, the French Army advanced onward from Romania to the Tuscany region.
Long live France!
Fenize was in a state of frenzied excitement and speedily accepted this "trial sent from God," obediently going under their rule.
The increasingly successful advance contin-ued. Compared to Charles' massive army, the various states of Italy, only armed with a small-scale brigade...
...could do nothing but helplessly prostrate themselves before the massive power.
RATTLE
RATTLE
Rome

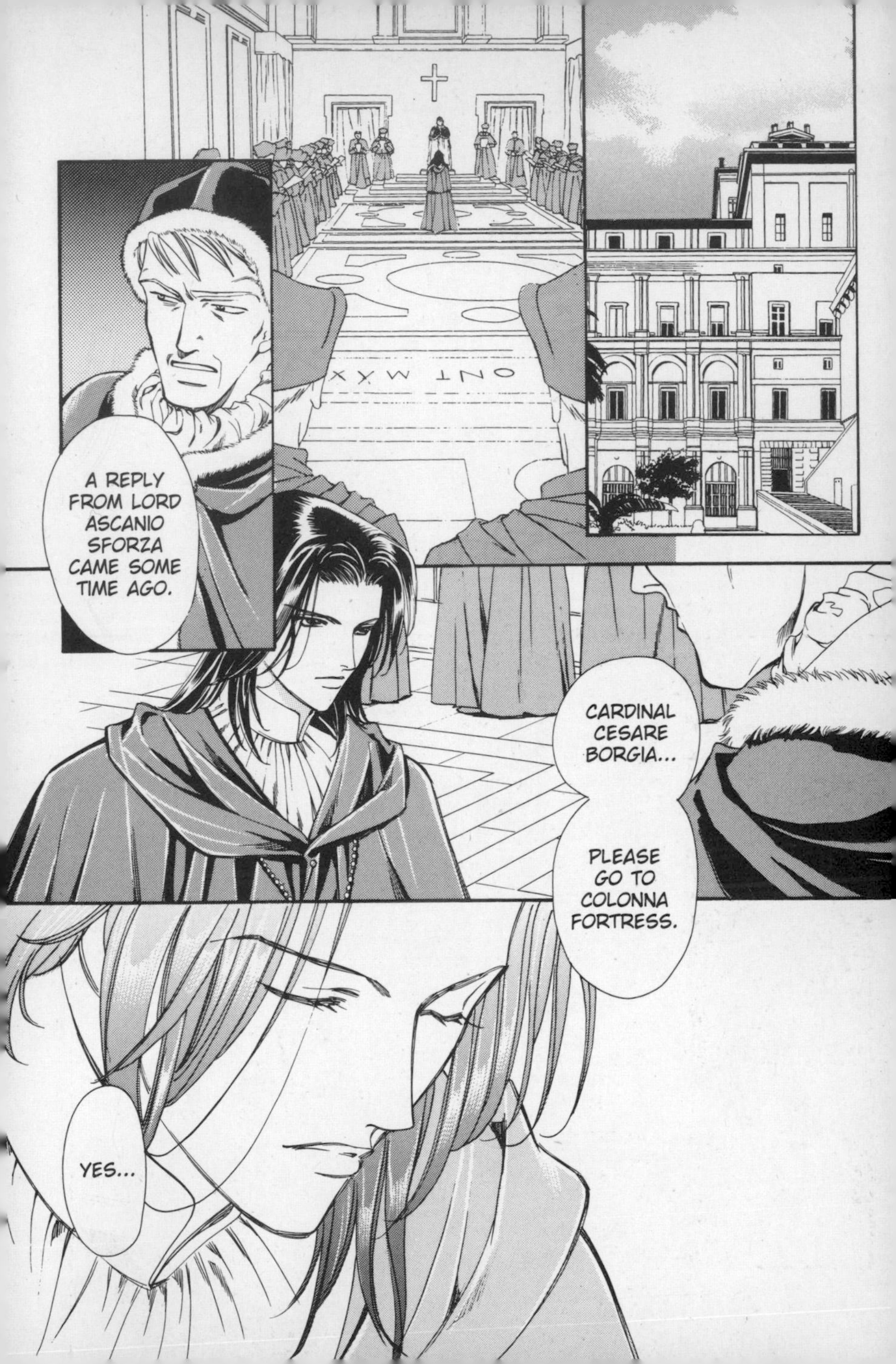
A REPLY FROM LORD ASCANIO SFORZA CAME SOME TIME AGO.
CARDINAL CESARE BORGIA...
PLEASE GO TO COLONNA FORTRESS.
YES...

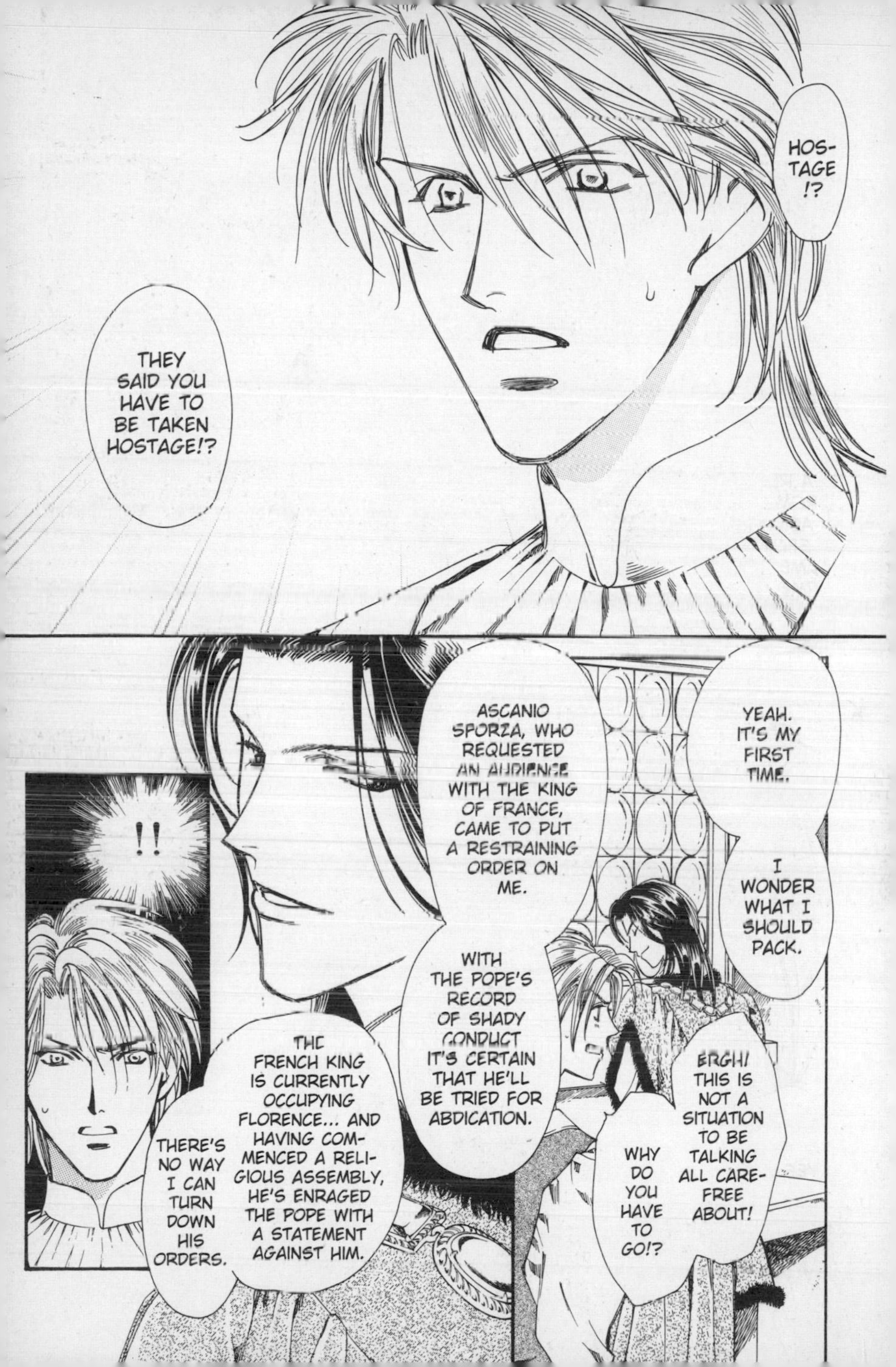
HOS-TAGE!?
THEY SAID YOU HAVE TO BE TAKEN HOSTAGE!?
YEAH. IT'S MY FIRST TIME.
I WONDER WHAT I SHOULD PACK.
ERGH! THIS IS NOT A SITUATION TO BE TALKING ALL CARE-FREE ABOUT!
WHY DO YOU HAVE TO GO!?
ASCANIO SPORZA, WHO REQUESTED AN AUDIENCE WITH THE KING OF FRANCE, CAME TO PUT A RESTRAINING ORDER ON ME.
WITH THE POPE'S RECORD OF SHADY CONDUCT IT'S CERTAIN THAT HE'LL BE TRIED FOR ABDICATION.
THE FRENCH KING IS CURRENTLY OCCUPYING FLORENCE... AND HAVING COM-MENCED A RELI-GIOUS ASSEMBLY, HE'S ENRAGED THE POPE WITH A STATEMENT AGAINST HIM.
THERE'S NO WAY I CAN TURN DOWN HIS ORDERS.
!!

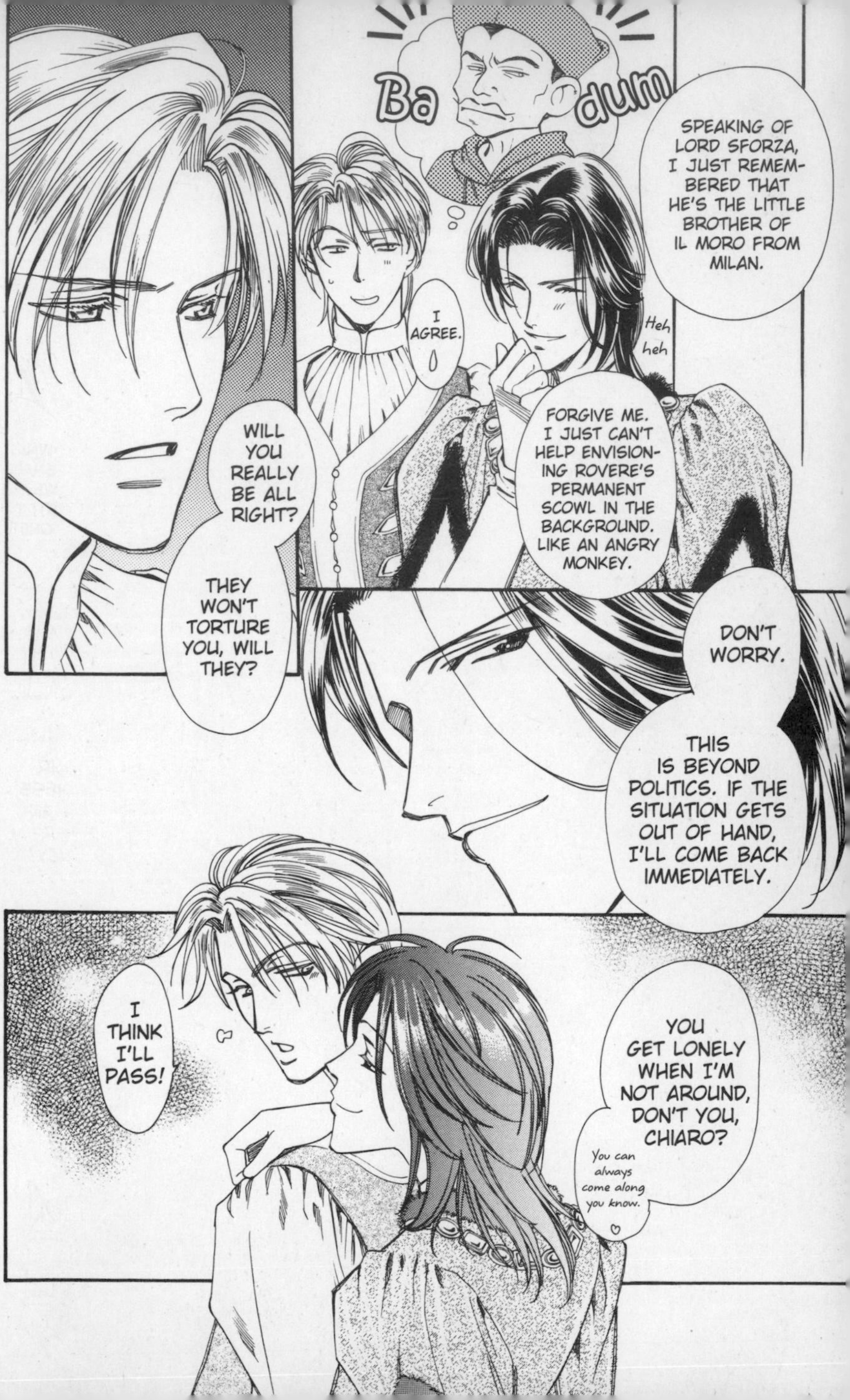
Ba dum
SPEAKING OF LORD SFORZA, I JUST REMEMBERED THAT HE'S THE LITTLE BROTHER OF IL MORO FROM MILAN.
I AGREE.
Heh heh
FORGIVE ME. I JUST CAN'T HELP ENVISIONING ROVERE'S PERMANENT SCOWL IN THE BACKGROUND. LIKE AN ANGRY MONKEY.
WILL YOU REALLY BE ALL RIGHT?
THEY WON'T TORTURE YOU, WILL THEY?
DON'T WORRY.
THIS IS BEYOND POLITICS. IF THE SITUATION GETS OUT OF HAND, I'LL COME BACK IMMEDIATELY.
YOU GET LONELY WHEN I'M NOT AROUND, DON'T YOU, CHIARO?
You can always come along you know.
I THINK I'LL PASS!

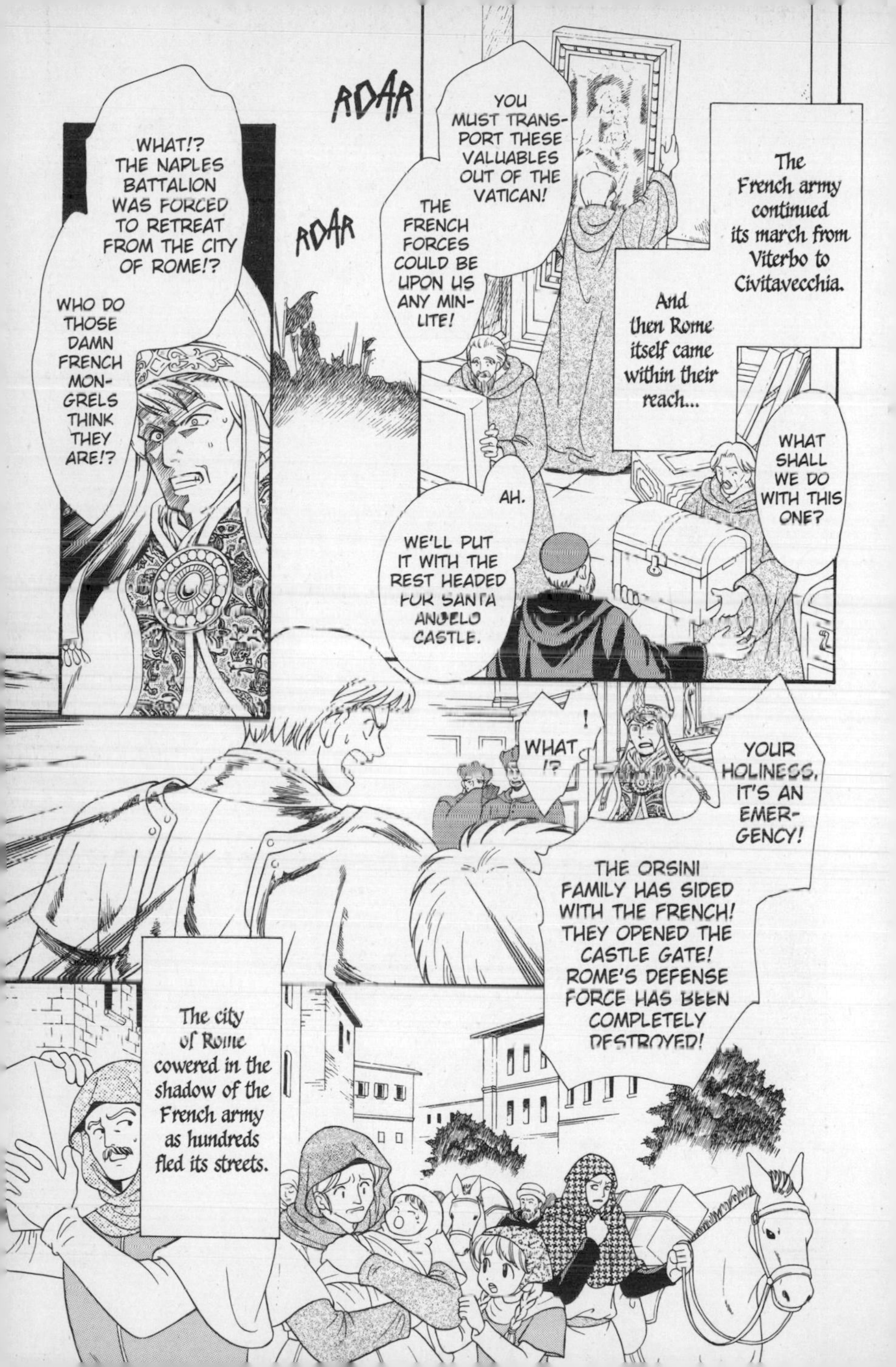
The French army continued its march from Viterbo to Civitavecchia.
RDAR
YOU MUST TRANSPORT THESE VALUABLES OUT OF THE VATICAN!
RDAR
THE FRENCH FORCES COULD BE UPON US ANY MINUTE!
And then Rome itself came within their reach...
WHAT SHALL WE DO WITH THIS ONE?
AH.
WE'LL PUT IT WITH THE REST HEADED FOR SANTA ANGELO CASTLE.
WHAT!? THE NAPLES BATTALION WAS FORCED TO RETREAT FROM THE CITY OF ROME!?
WHO DO THOSE DAMN FRENCH MONGRELS THINK THEY ARE!?
YOUR HOLINESS, IT'S AN EMERGENCY!
!
WHAT !?
THE ORSINI FAMILY HAS SIDED WITH THE FRENCH! THEY OPENED THE CASTLE GATE! ROME'S DEFENSE FORCE HAS BEEN COMPLETELY DESTROYED!
The city of Rome cowered in the shadow of the French army as hundreds fled its streets.

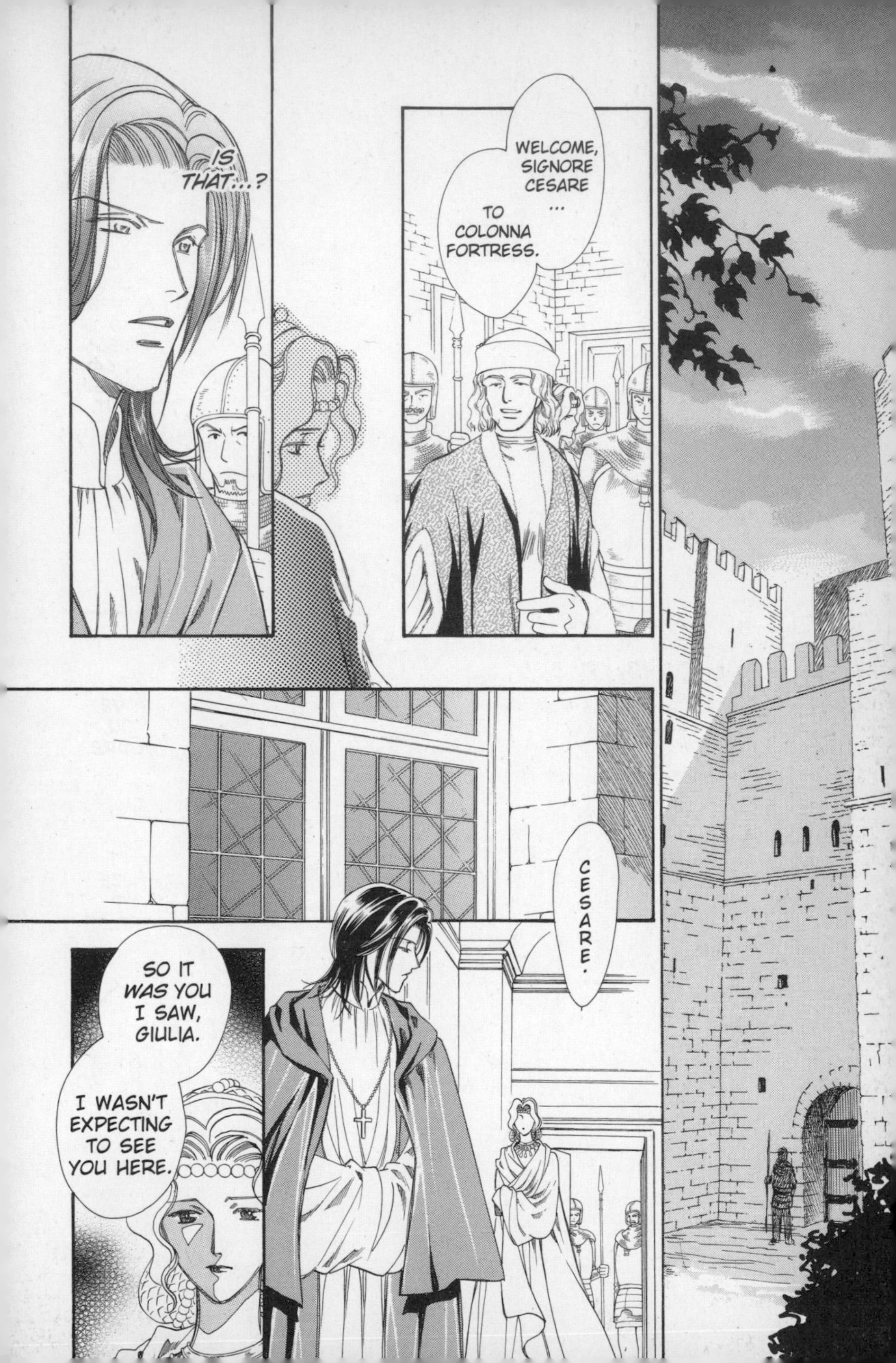
WELCOME, SIGNORE CESARE ... TO COLONNA FORTRESS.
IS THAT...?
CESARE.
SO IT WAS YOU I SAW, GIULIA.
I WASN'T EXPECTING TO SEE YOU HERE.

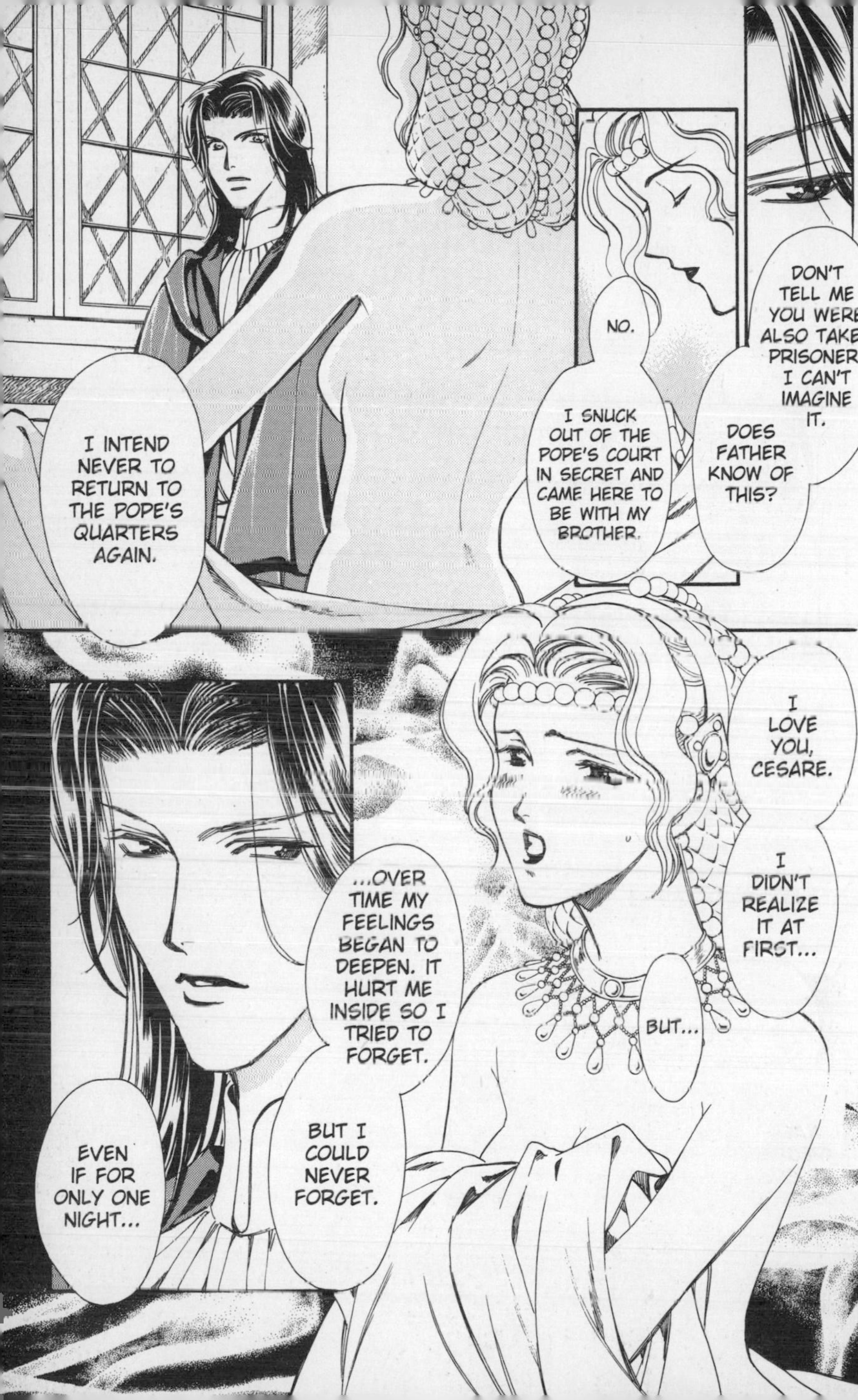
DON'T TELL ME YOU WERE ALSO TAKEN PRISONER. I CAN'T IMAGINE IT.
DOES FATHER KNOW OF THIS?
NO.
I SNUCK OUT OF THE POPE'S COURT IN SECRET AND CAME HERE TO BE WITH MY BROTHER.
I INTEND NEVER TO RETURN TO THE POPE'S QUARTERS AGAIN.
I LOVE YOU, CESARE.
I DIDN'T REALIZE IT AT FIRST...
BUT...
...OVER TIME MY FEELINGS BEGAN TO DEEPEN. IT HURT ME INSIDE SO I TRIED TO FORGET.
BUT I COULD NEVER FORGET.
EVEN IF FOR ONLY ONE NIGHT...

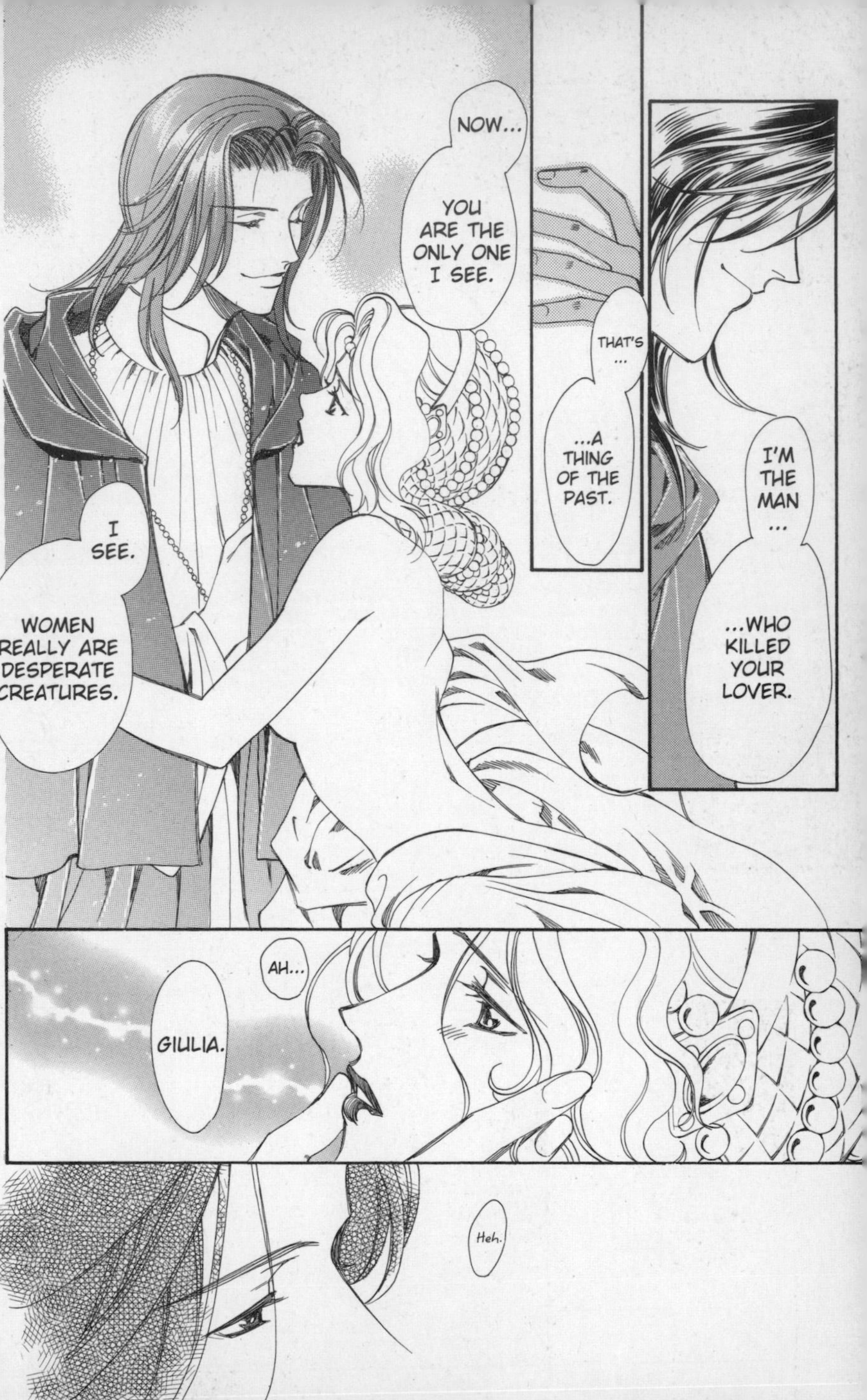
I'M THE MAN ...
...WHO KILLED YOUR LOVER.
THAT'S ...
...A THING OF THE PAST.
NOW...
YOU ARE THE ONLY ONE I SEE.
I SEE.
WOMEN REALLY ARE DESPERATE CREATURES.
AH...
GIULIA.
Heh.

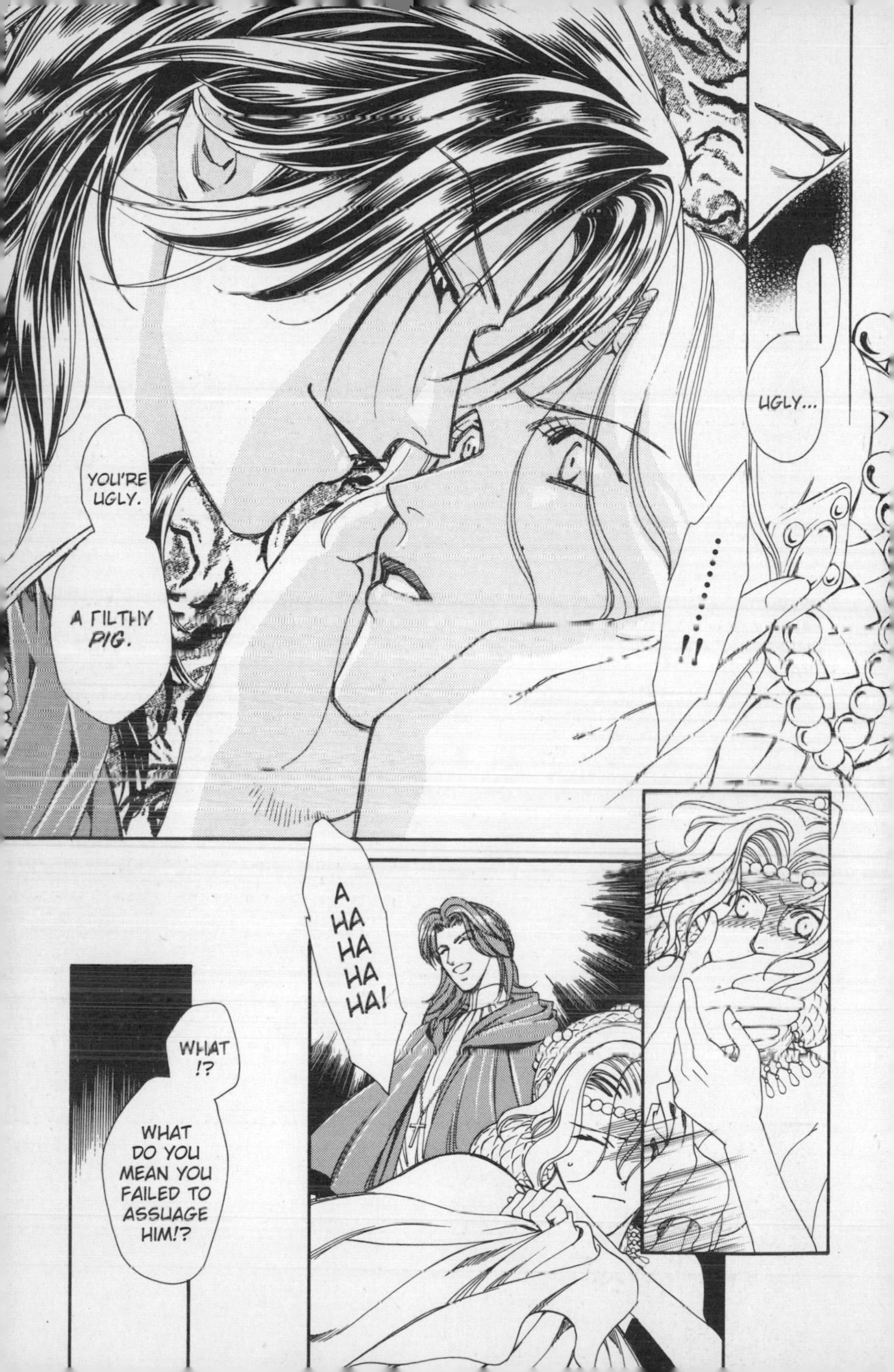
UGLY...
......!!
YOU'RE UGLY.
A FILTHY PIG.
A HA HA HA HA!
WHAT!?
WHAT DO YOU MEAN YOU FAILED TO ASSUAGE HIM!?

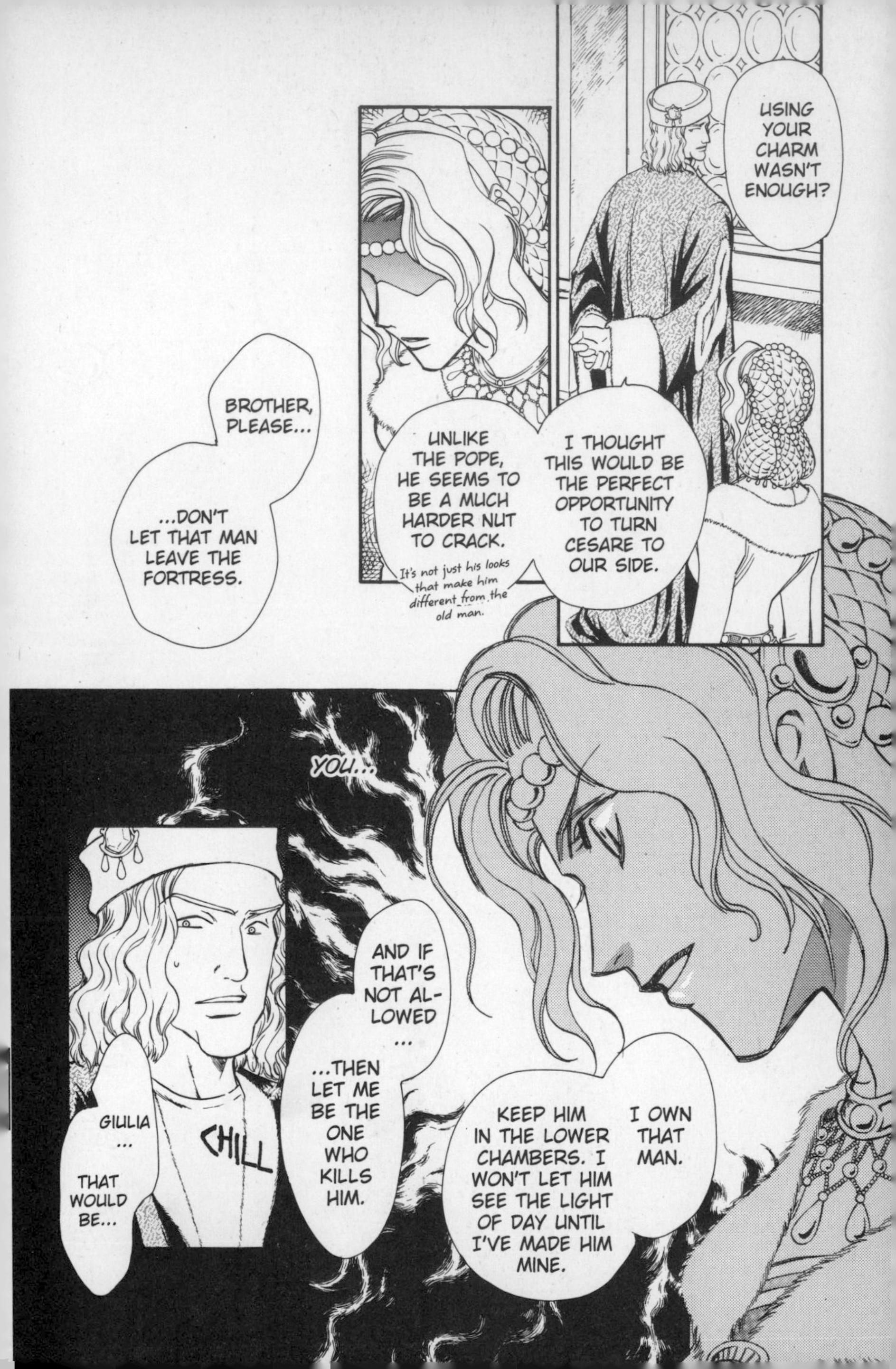
USING YOUR CHARM WASN'T ENOUGH?
I THOUGHT THIS WOULD BE THE PERFECT OPPORTUNITY TO TURN CESARE TO OUR SIDE.
UNLIKE THE POPE, HE SEEMS TO BE A MUCH HARDER NUT TO CRACK.
It's not just his looks that make him different from the old man.
BROTHER, PLEASE...
...DON'T LET THAT MAN LEAVE THE FORTRESS.
YOU...
I OWN THAT MAN.
KEEP HIM IN THE LOWER CHAMBERS. I WON'T LET HIM SEE THE LIGHT OF DAY UNTIL I'VE MADE HIM MINE.
AND IF THAT'S NOT AL-LOWED ...
...THEN LET ME BE THE ONE WHO KILLS HIM.
CHILL
GIULIA ...
THAT WOULD BE...

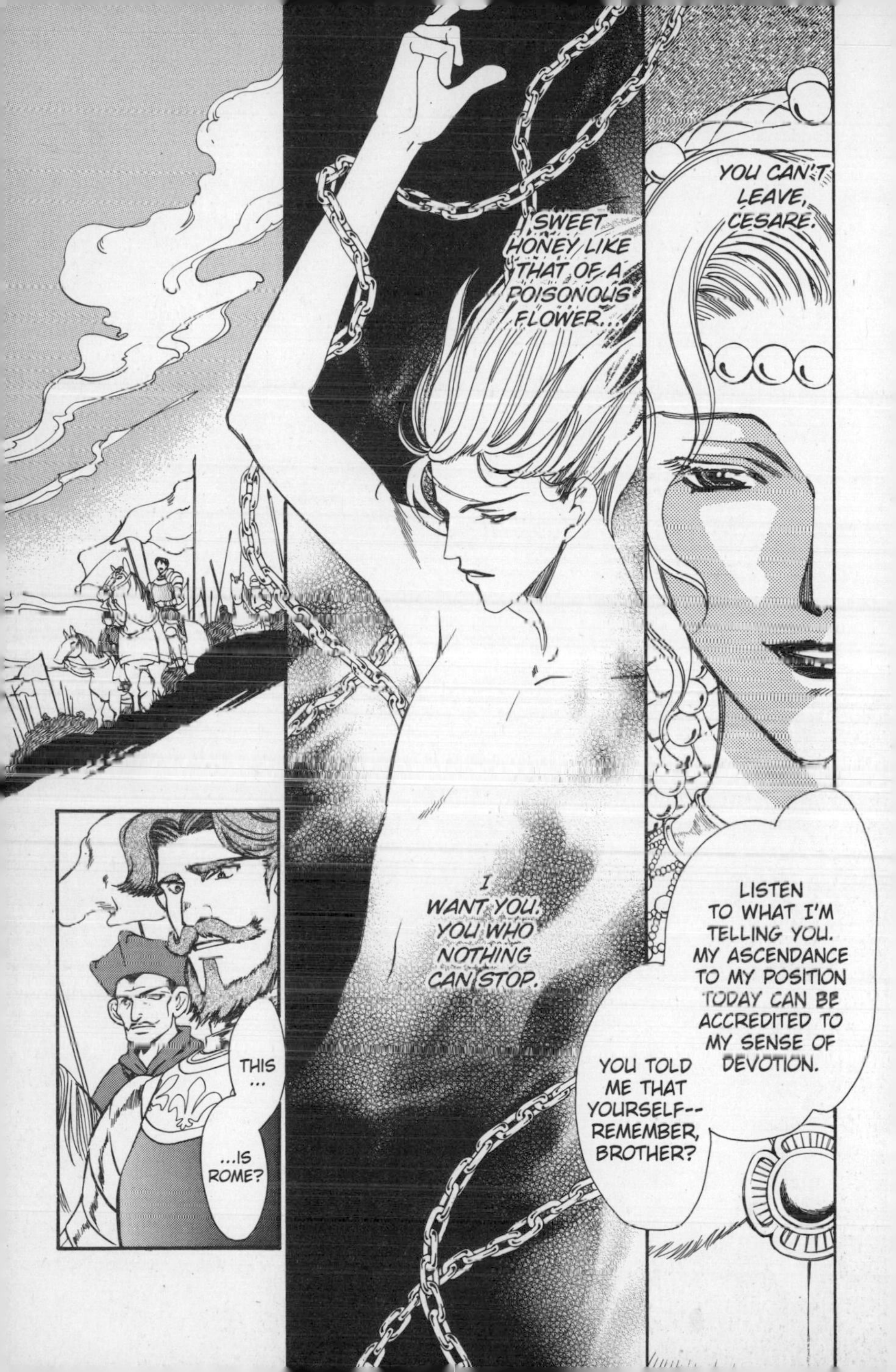
YOU CAN'T LEAVE, CESARE.
LISTEN TO WHAT I'M TELLING YOU. MY ASCENDANCE TO MY POSITION TODAY CAN BE ACCREDITED TO MY SENSE OF DEVOTION.
YOU TOLD ME THAT YOURSELF-- REMEMBER, BROTHER?
SWEET HONEY LIKE THAT OF A POISONOUS FLOWER...
I WANT YOU. YOU WHO NOTHING CAN STOP.
THIS ...
...IS ROME?

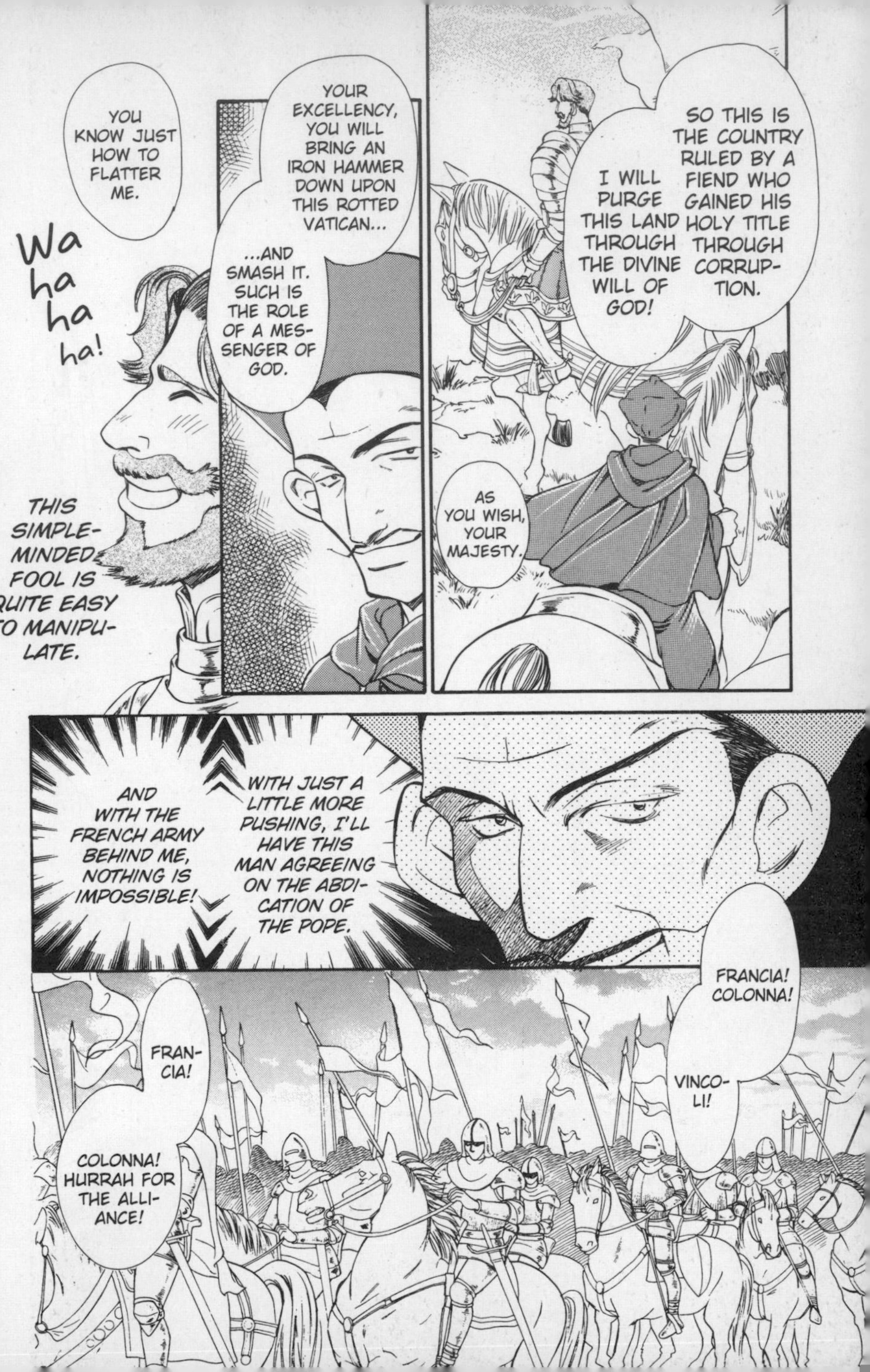
SO THIS IS THE COUNTRY RULED BY A FIEND WHO GAINED HIS HOLY TITLE THROUGH CORRUPTION.
I WILL PURGE THIS LAND THROUGH THE DIVINE WILL OF GOD!
AS YOU WISH, YOUR MAJESTY.
YOUR EXCELLENCY, YOU WILL BRING AN IRON HAMMER DOWN UPON THIS ROTTED VATICAN...
...AND SMASH IT. SUCH IS THE ROLE OF A MESSENGER OF GOD.
YOU KNOW JUST HOW TO FLATTER ME.
Wa ha ha ha!
THIS SIMPLE-MINDED FOOL IS QUITE EASY TO MANIPULATE.
WITH JUST A LITTLE MORE PUSHING, I'LL HAVE THIS MAN AGREEING ON THE ABDICATION OF THE POPE.
AND WITH THE FRENCH ARMY BEHIND ME, NOTHING IS IMPOSSIBLE!
FRANCIA! COLONNA!
VINCOLI!
FRANCIA!
COLONNA! HURRAH FOR THE ALLIANCE!

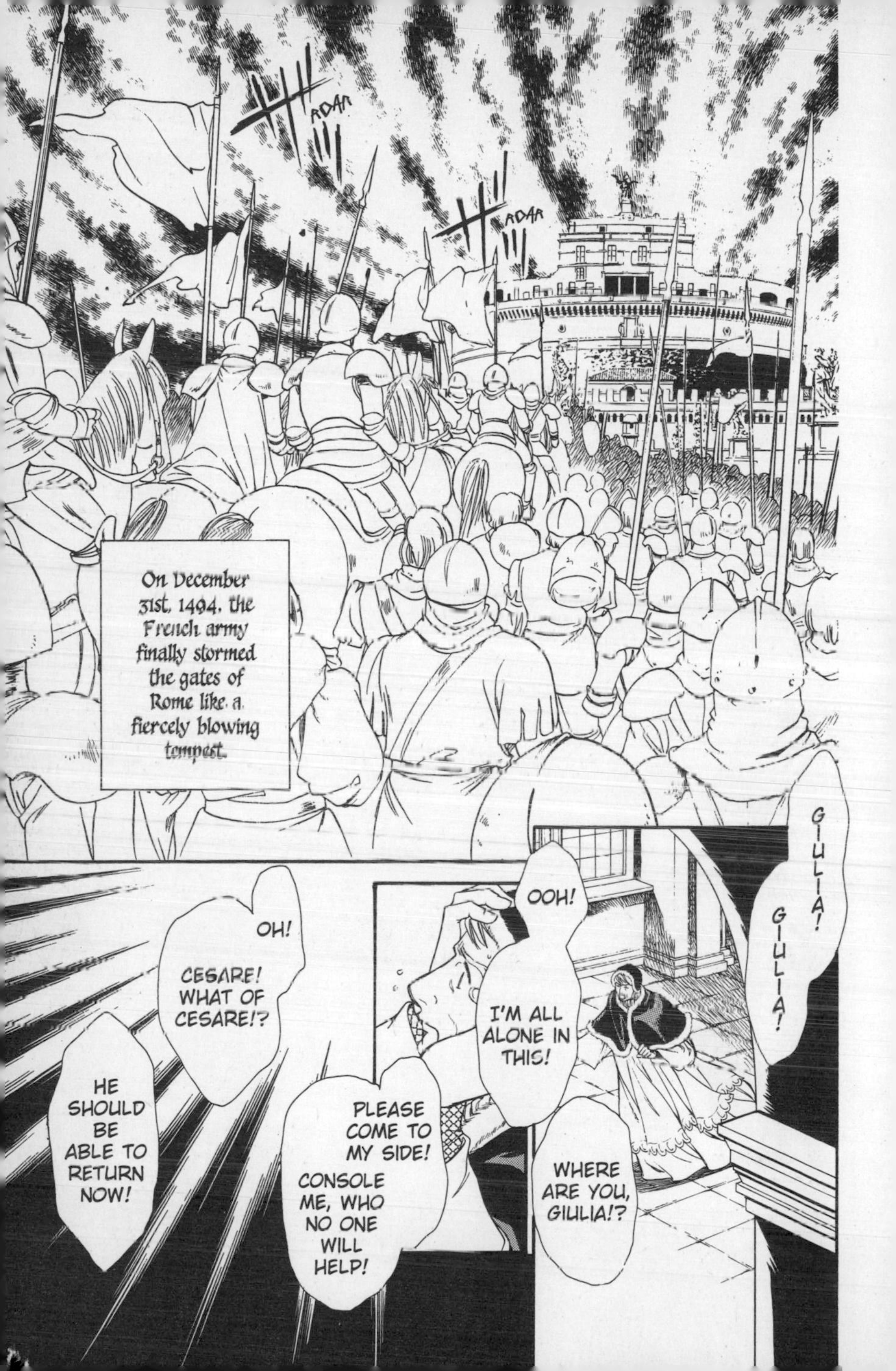
RDAR
RDAR
On December 31st, 1494, the French army finally stormed the gates of Rome like a fiercely blowing tempest.
GIULIA! GIULIA!
OOH!
I'M ALL ALONE IN THIS!
WHERE ARE YOU, GIULIA!?
PLEASE COME TO MY SIDE!
CONSOLE ME, WHO NO ONE WILL HELP!
OH!
CESARE! WHAT OF CESARE!?
HE SHOULD BE ABLE TO RETURN NOW!

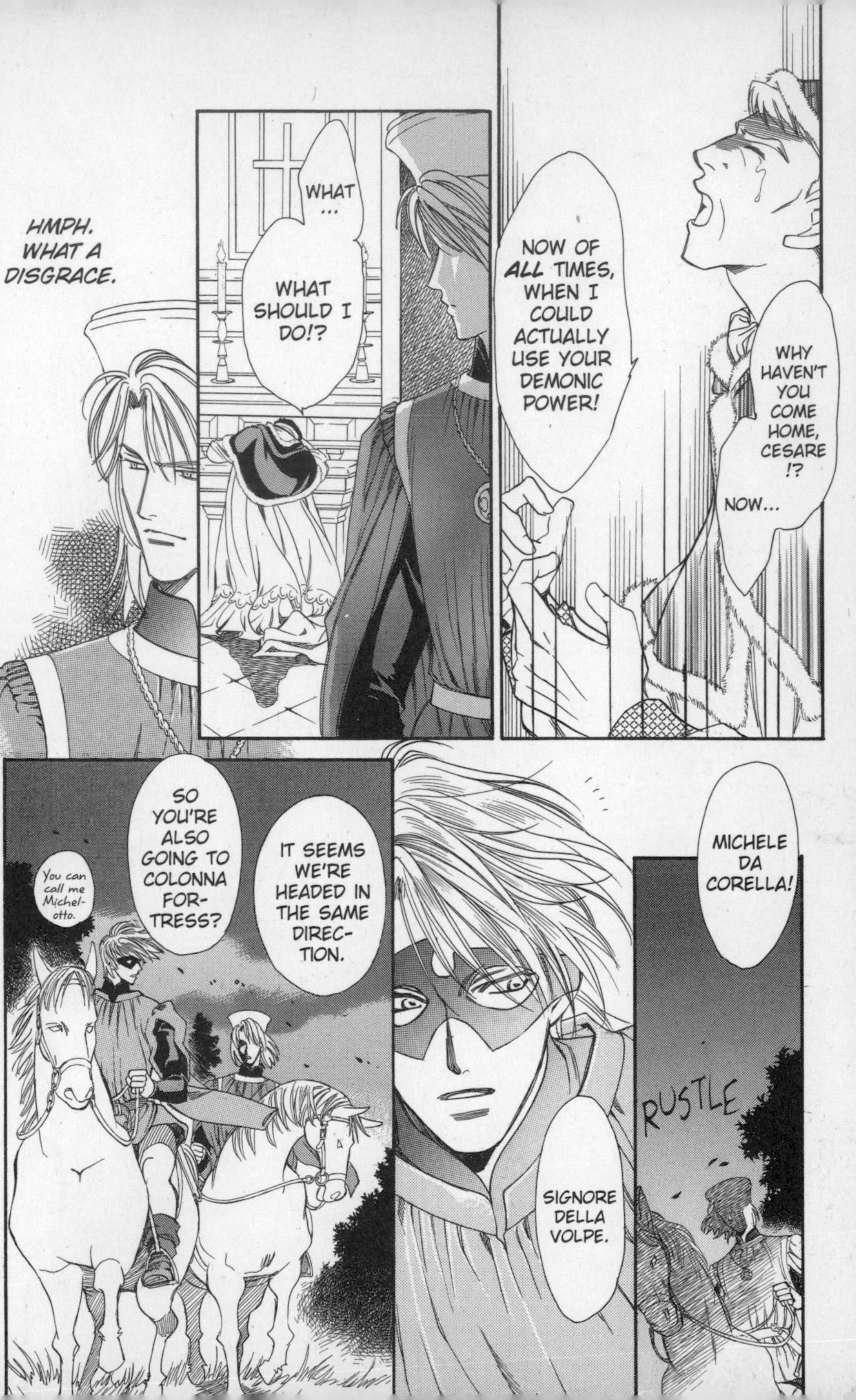
WHY HAVEN'T YOU COME HOME, CESARE!?
NOW...
NOW OF ALL TIMES, WHEN I COULD ACTUALLY USE YOUR DEMONIC POWER!
WHAT ...
WHAT SHOULD I DO!?
HMPH. WHAT A DISGRACE.
MICHELE DA CORELLA!
RUSTLE
SIGNORE DELLA VOLPE.
IT SEEMS WE'RE HEADED IN THE SAME DIREC-TION.
SO YOU'RE ALSO GOING TO COLONNA FOR-TRESS?
You can call me Michel-otto.

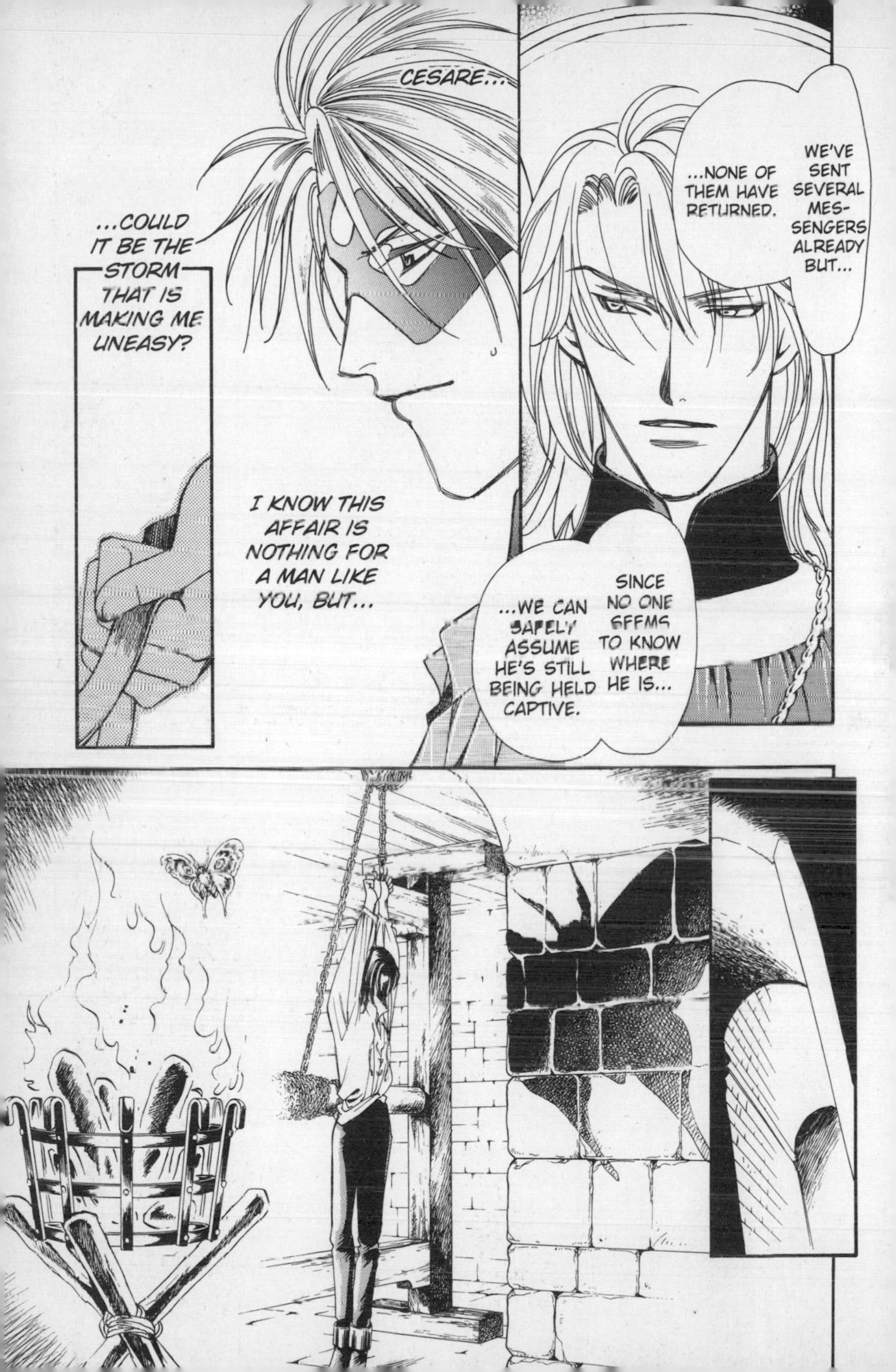
WE'VE SENT SEVERAL MES-SENGERS ALREADY BUT...
...NONE OF THEM HAVE RETURNED.
SINCE NO ONE SEEMS TO KNOW WHERE HE IS...
...WE CAN SAFELY ASSUME HE'S STILL BEING HELD CAPTIVE.
I KNOW THIS AFFAIR IS NOTHING FOR A MAN LIKE YOU, BUT...
CESARE...
...COULD IT BE THE STORM THAT IS MAKING ME UNEASY?

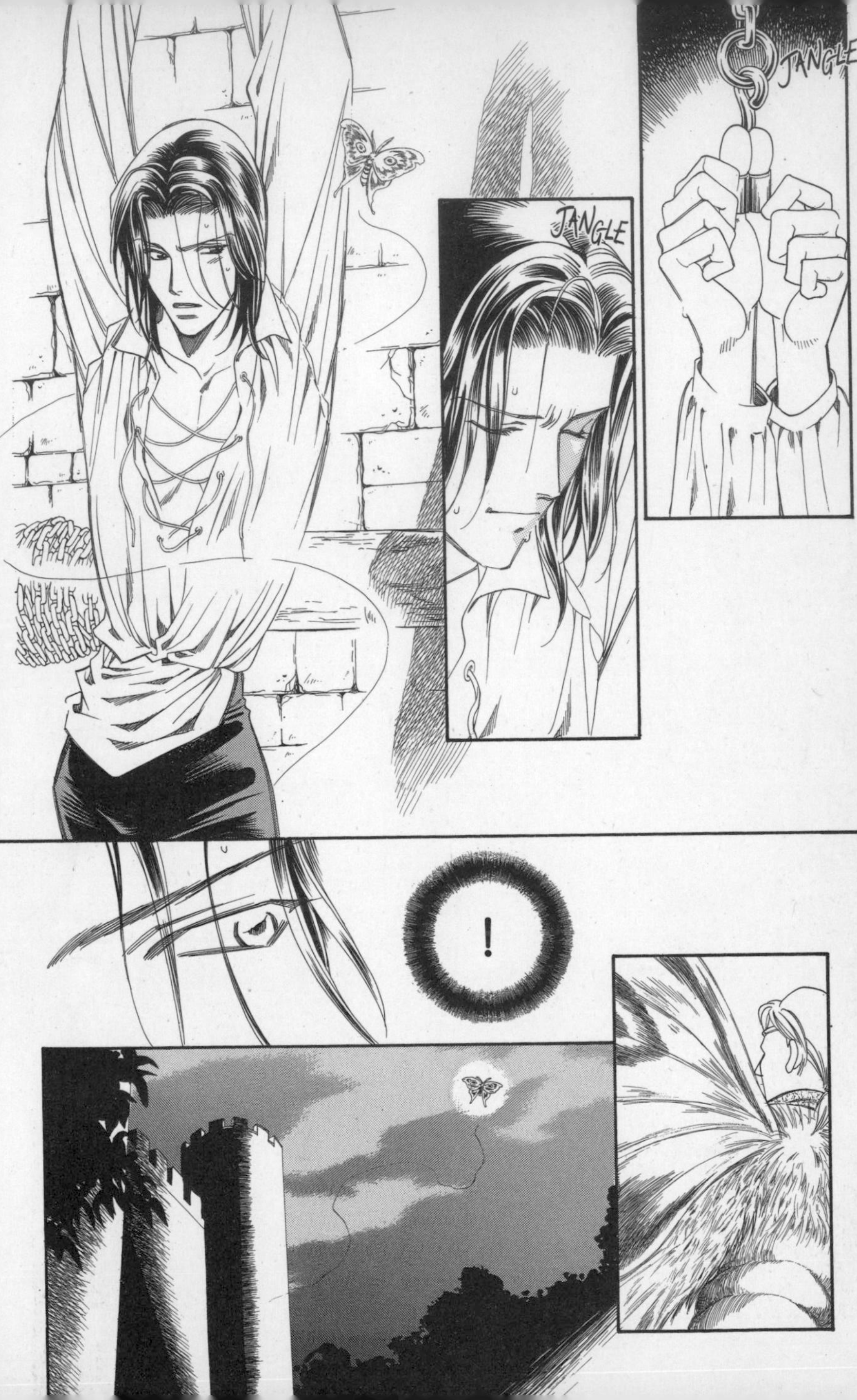
JANGLE
JANGLE
!

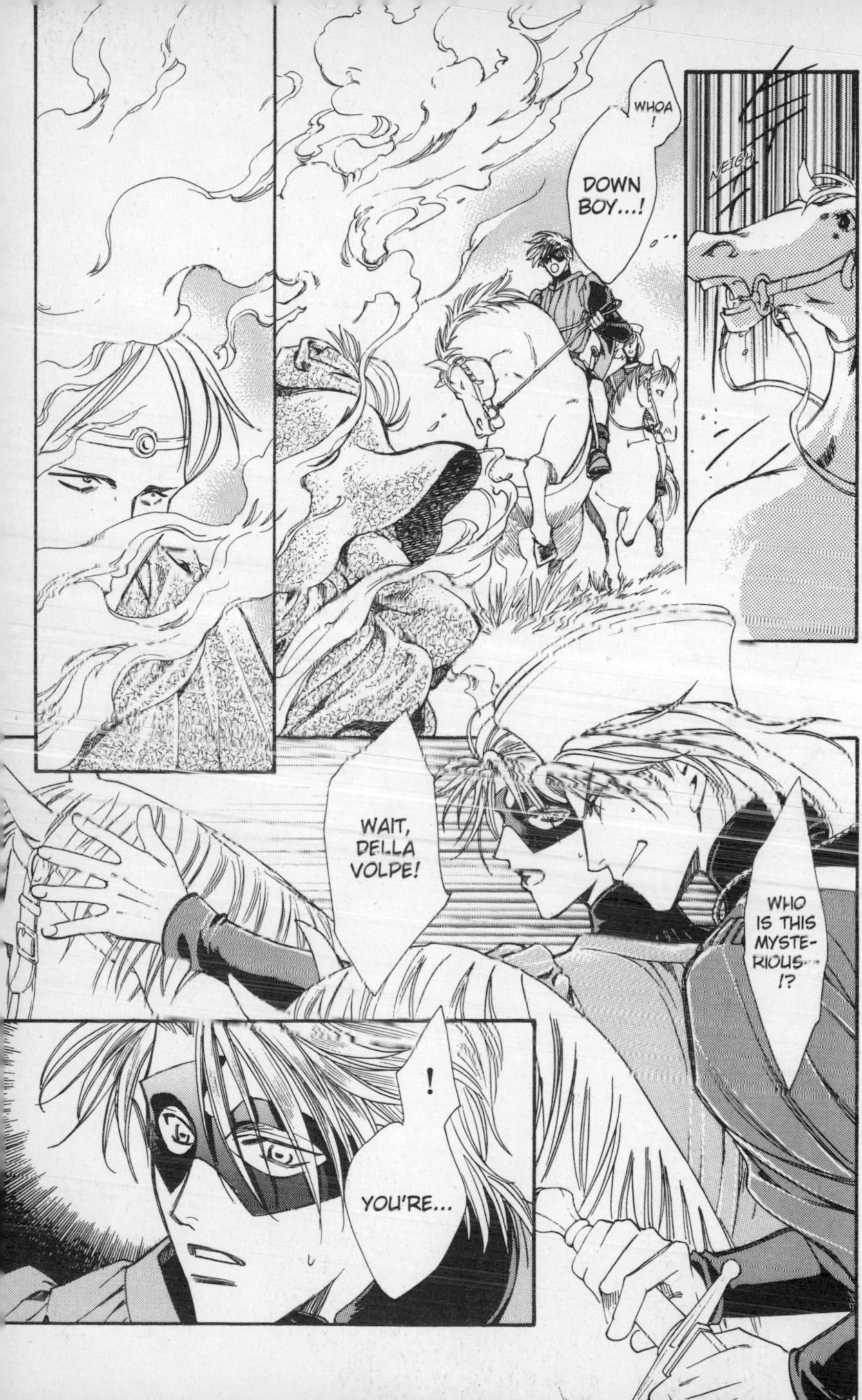
NEIGH
WHOA!
DOWN BOY...!
WHO IS THIS MYSTERIOUS--!?
WAIT, DELLA VOLPE!
!
YOU'RE...

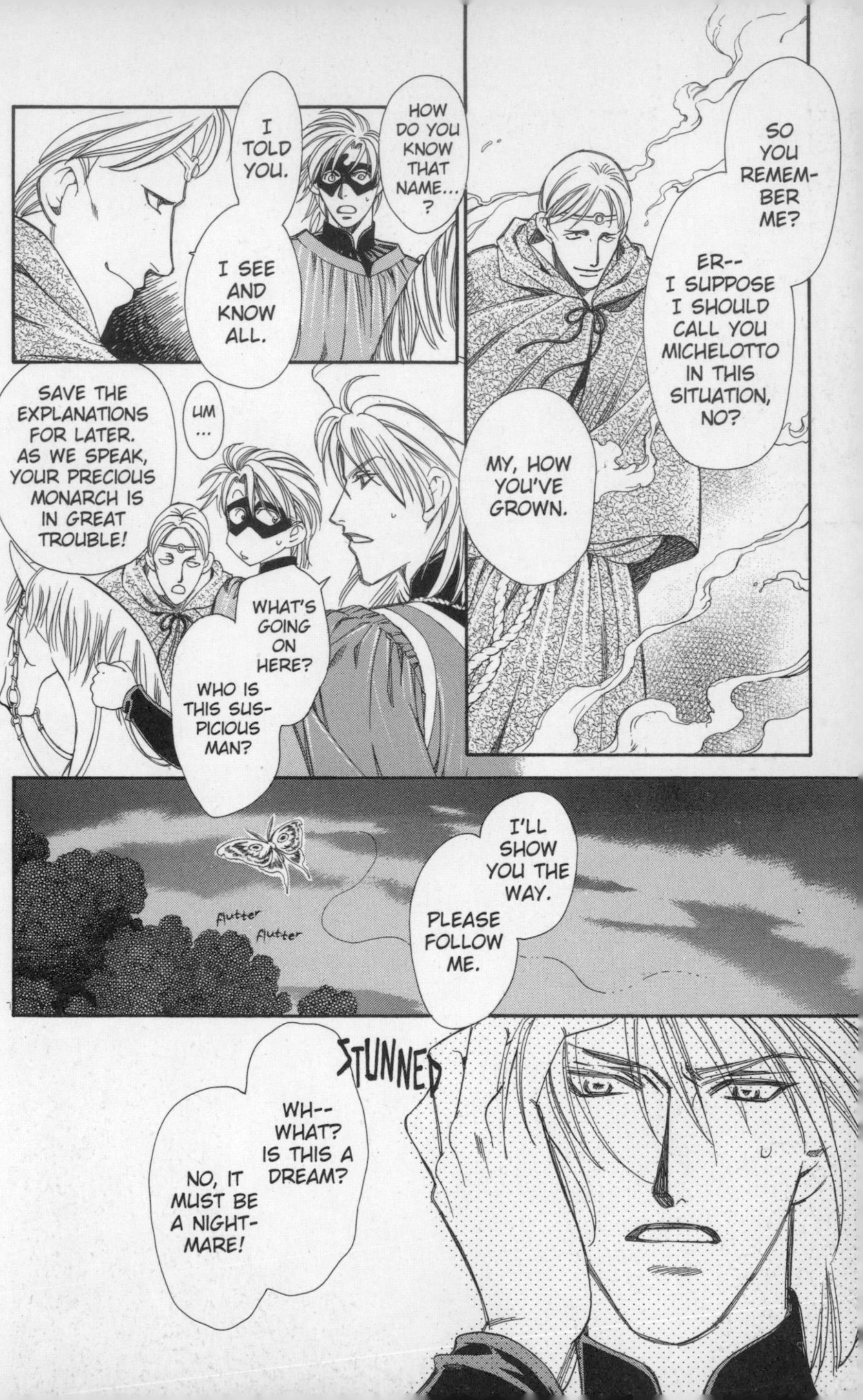
SO YOU REMEMBER ME?
ER-- I SUPPOSE I SHOULD CALL YOU MICHELOTTO IN THIS SITUATION, NO?
MY, HOW YOU'VE GROWN.
HOW DO YOU KNOW THAT NAME...?
I TOLD YOU.
I SEE AND KNOW ALL.
WHAT'S GOING ON HERE? WHO IS THIS SUSPICIOUS MAN?
UM...
SAVE THE EXPLANATIONS FOR LATER. AS WE SPEAK, YOUR PRECIOUS MONARCH IS IN GREAT TROUBLE!
I'LL SHOW YOU THE WAY. PLEASE FOLLOW ME.
flutter flutter
STUNNED
WH-- WHAT? IS THIS A DREAM? NO, IT MUST BE A NIGHTMARE!

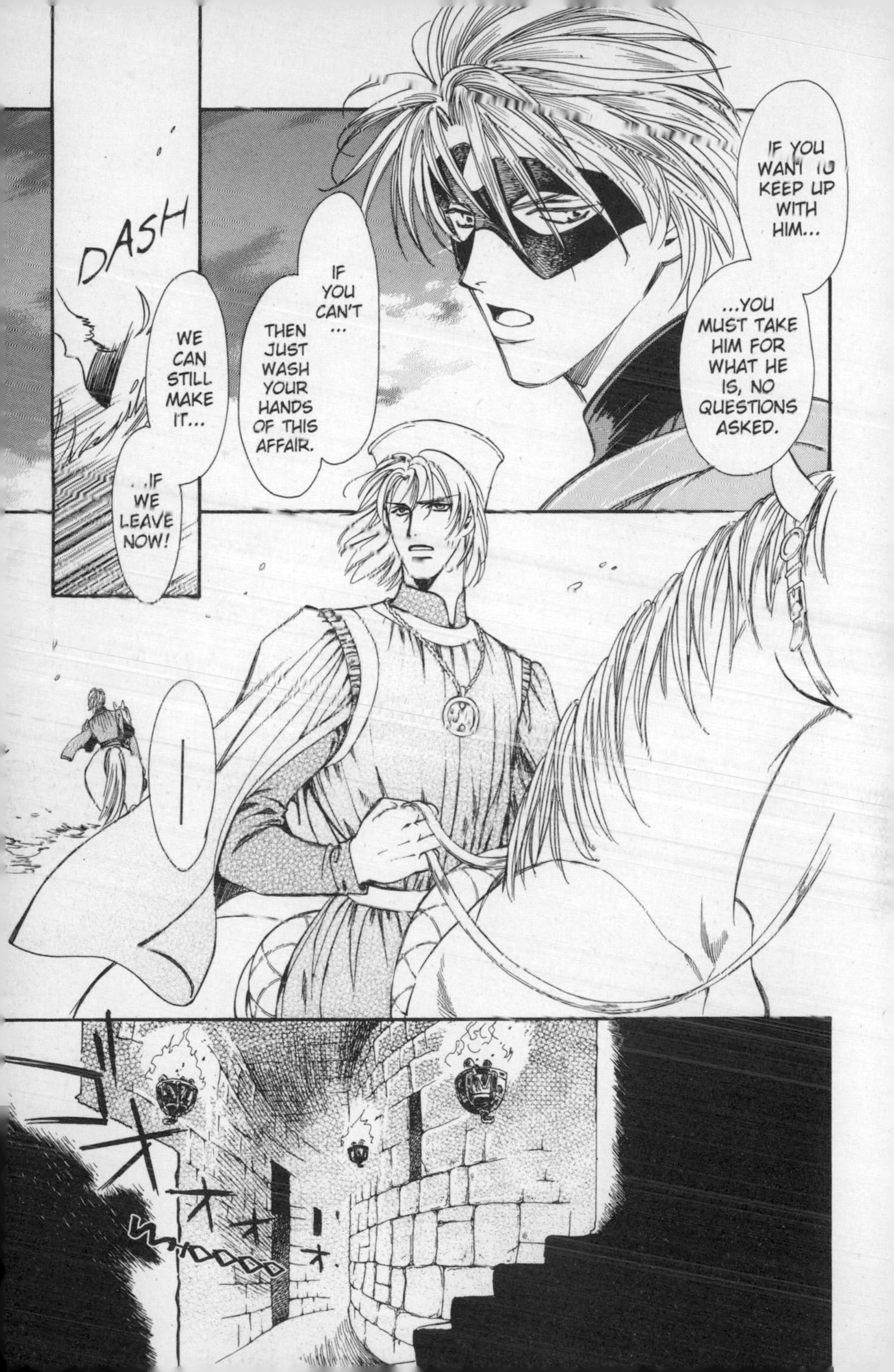
IF YOU WANT TO KEEP UP WITH HIM...
...YOU MUST TAKE HIM FOR WHAT HE IS, NO QUESTIONS ASKED.
IF YOU CAN'T ...
THEN JUST WASH YOUR HANDS OF THIS AFFAIR.
DASH
WE CAN STILL MAKE IT...
...IF WE LEAVE NOW!
—
WHOOOOO

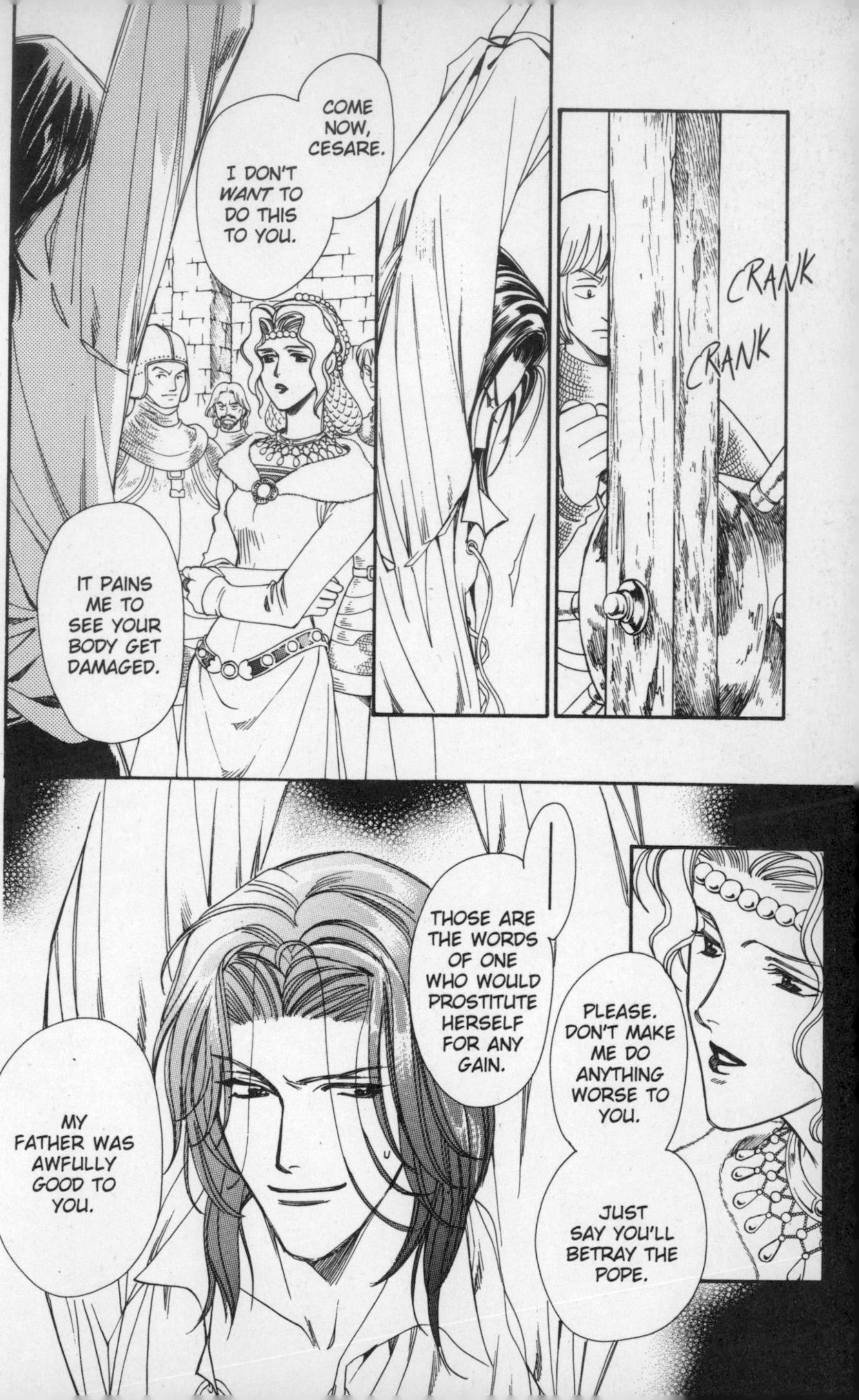
CRANK
CRANK
COME NOW, CESARE.
I DON'T *WANT* TO DO THIS TO YOU.
IT PAINS ME TO SEE YOUR BODY GET DAMAGED.
PLEASE. DON'T MAKE ME DO ANYTHING WORSE TO YOU.
JUST SAY YOU'LL BETRAY THE POPE.
THOSE ARE THE WORDS OF ONE WHO WOULD PROSTITUTE HERSELF FOR ANY GAIN.
MY FATHER WAS AWFULLY GOOD TO YOU.

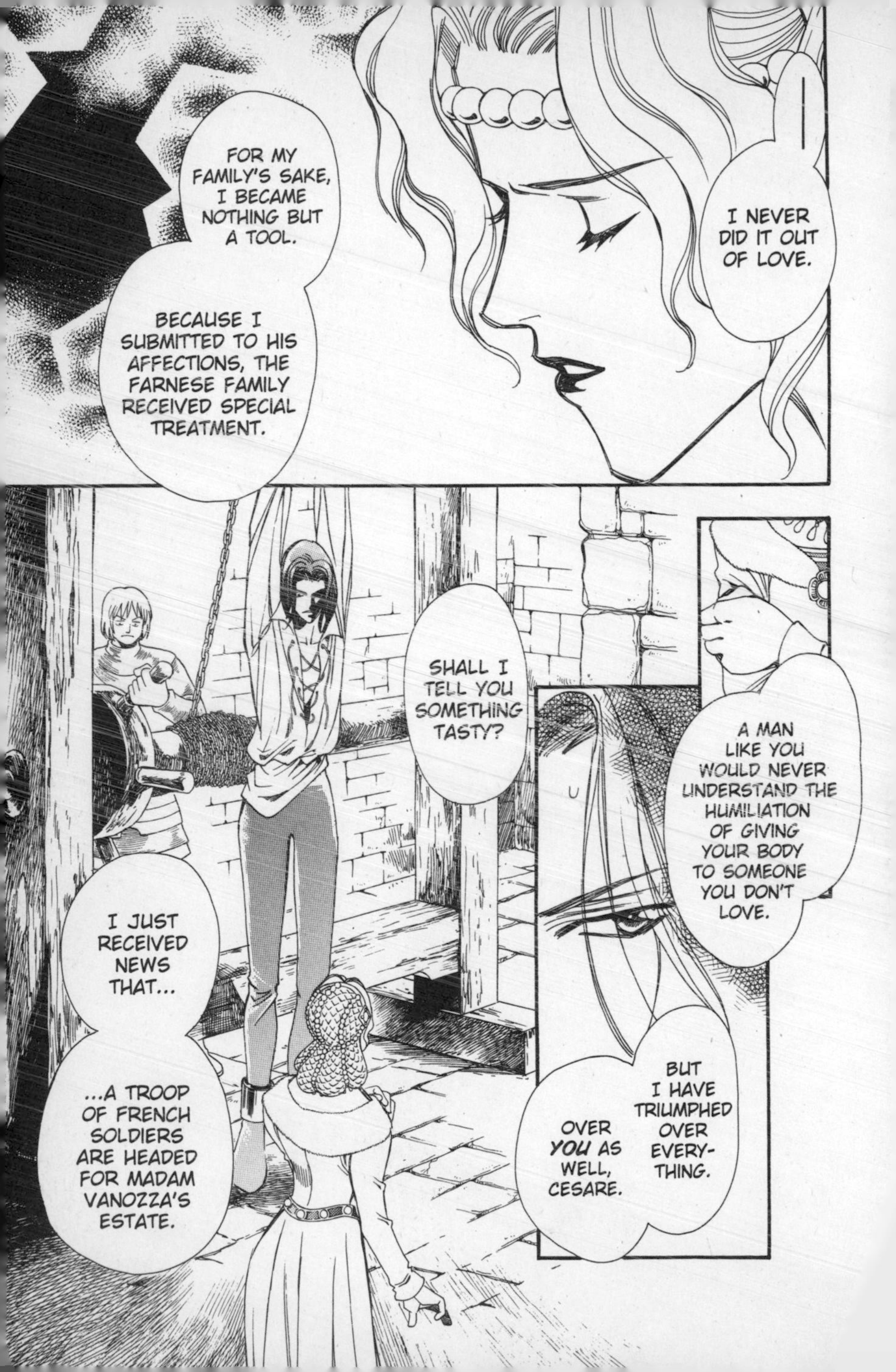
I NEVER DID IT OUT OF LOVE.
FOR MY FAMILY'S SAKE, I BECAME NOTHING BUT A TOOL.
BECAUSE I SUBMITTED TO HIS AFFECTIONS, THE FARNESE FAMILY RECEIVED SPECIAL TREATMENT.
A MAN LIKE YOU WOULD NEVER UNDERSTAND THE HUMILIATION OF GIVING YOUR BODY TO SOMEONE YOU DON'T LOVE.
BUT I HAVE TRIUMPHED OVER EVERYTHING.
OVER *YOU* AS WELL, CESARE.
SHALL I TELL YOU SOMETHING TASTY?
I JUST RECEIVED NEWS THAT...
...A TROOP OF FRENCH SOLDIERS ARE HEADED FOR MADAM VANOZZA'S ESTATE.

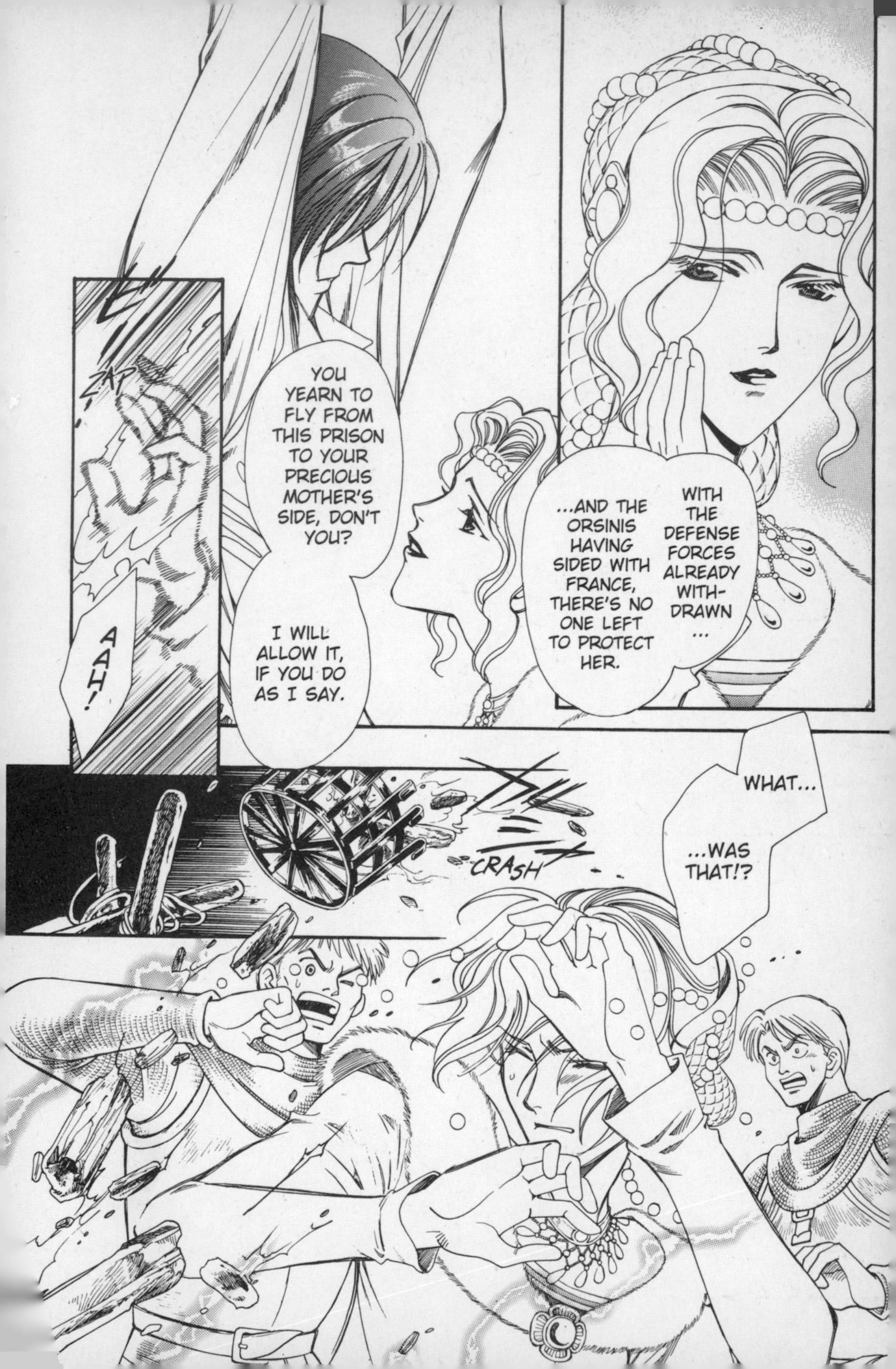
WITH THE DEFENSE FORCES ALREADY WITH-DRAWN ...
...AND THE ORSINIS HAVING SIDED WITH FRANCE, THERE'S NO ONE LEFT TO PROTECT HER.
YOU YEARN TO FLY FROM THIS PRISON TO YOUR PRECIOUS MOTHER'S SIDE, DON'T YOU?
I WILL ALLOW IT, IF YOU DO AS I SAY.
ZAP
AAH!
CRASH
WHAT...
...WAS THAT!?

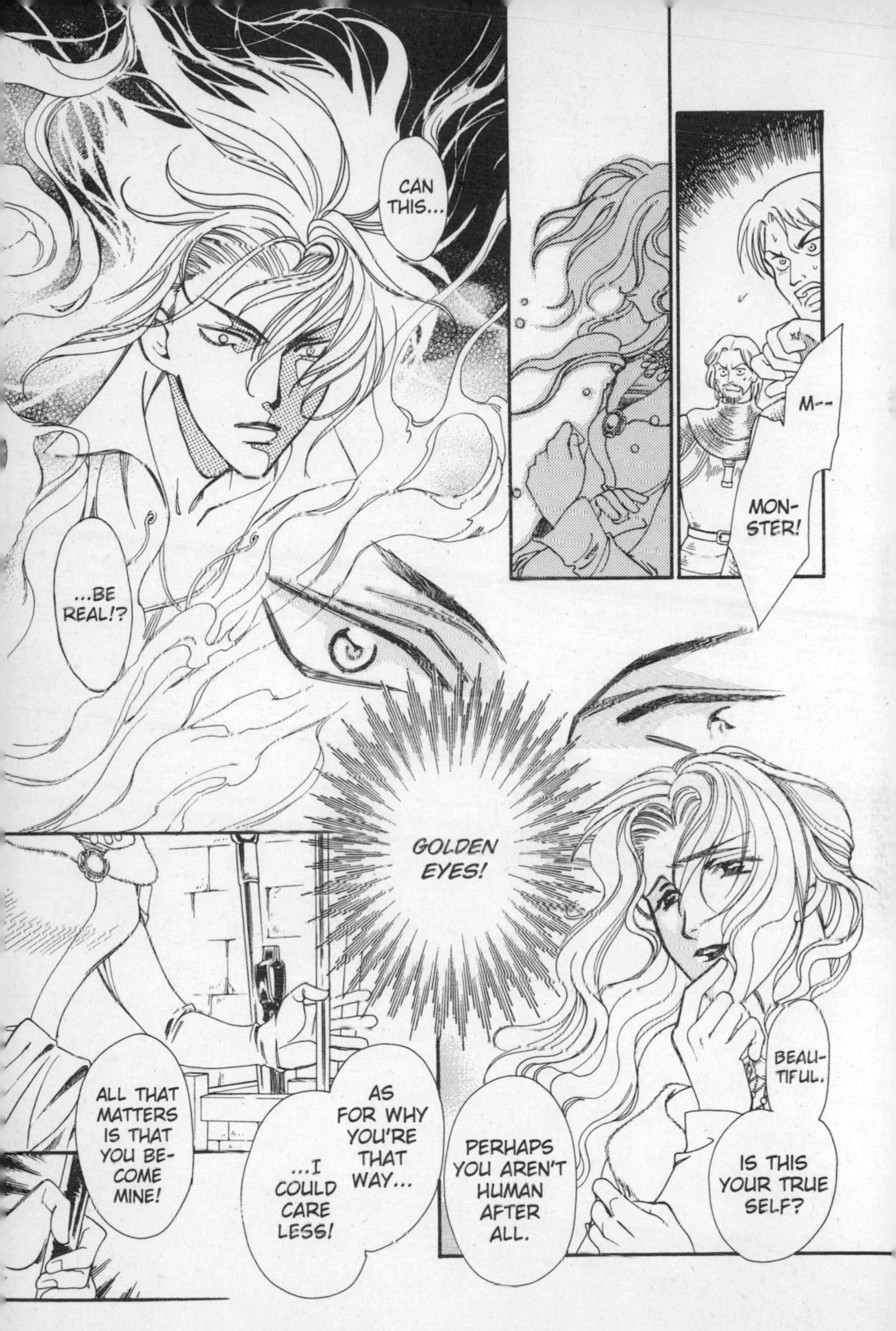
M--
MON-STER!
CAN THIS...
...BE REAL!?
GOLDEN EYES!
BEAU-TIFUL.
IS THIS YOUR TRUE SELF?
PERHAPS YOU AREN'T HUMAN AFTER ALL.
AS FOR WHY YOU'RE THAT WAY...
...I COULD CARE LESS!
ALL THAT MATTERS IS THAT YOU BE-COME MINE!

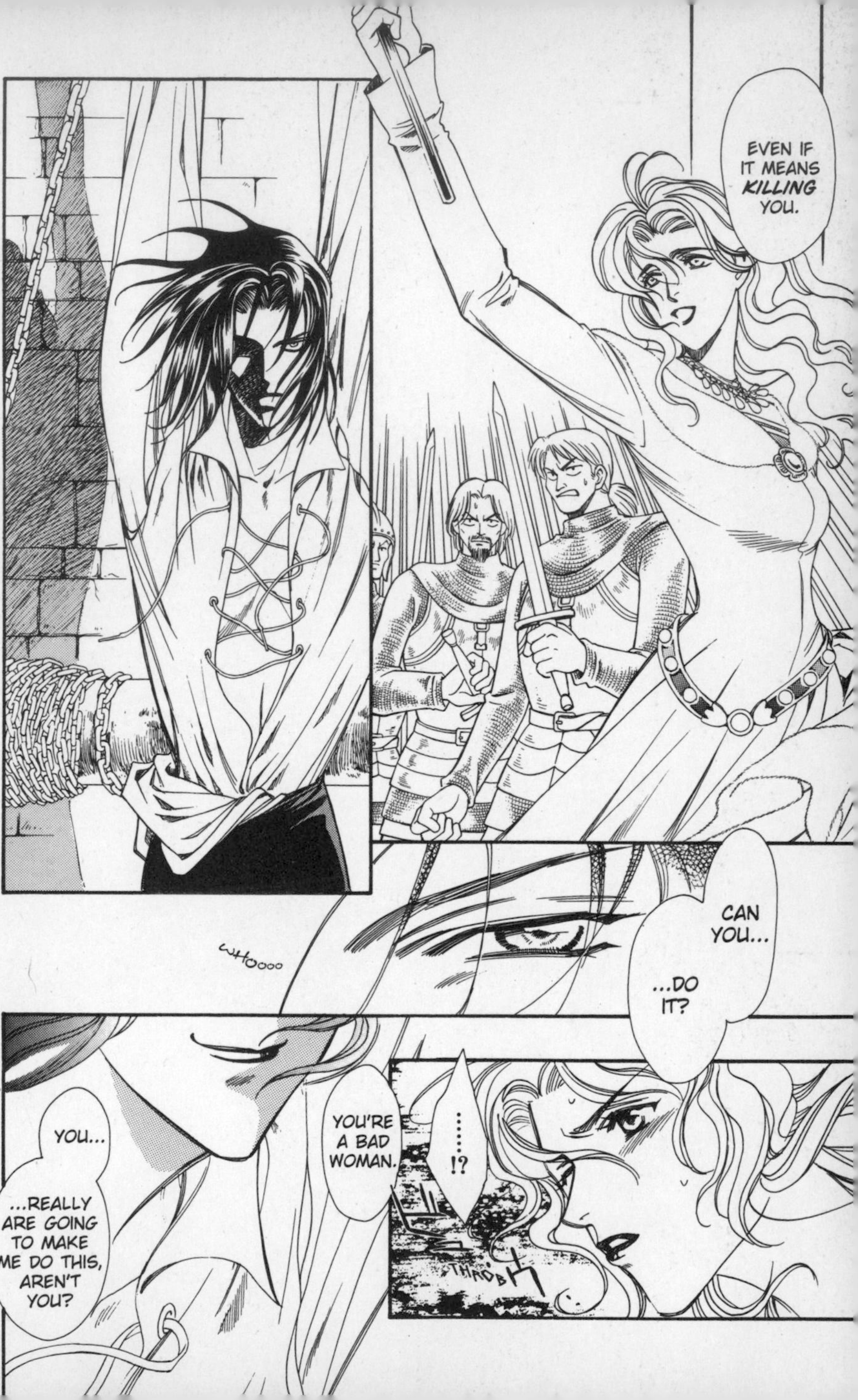
EVEN IF IT MEANS **KILLING** YOU.
CAN YOU...
...DO IT?
WHOOOO
......!?
THROB
YOU'RE A BAD WOMAN.
YOU...
...REALLY ARE GOING TO MAKE ME DO THIS, AREN'T YOU?

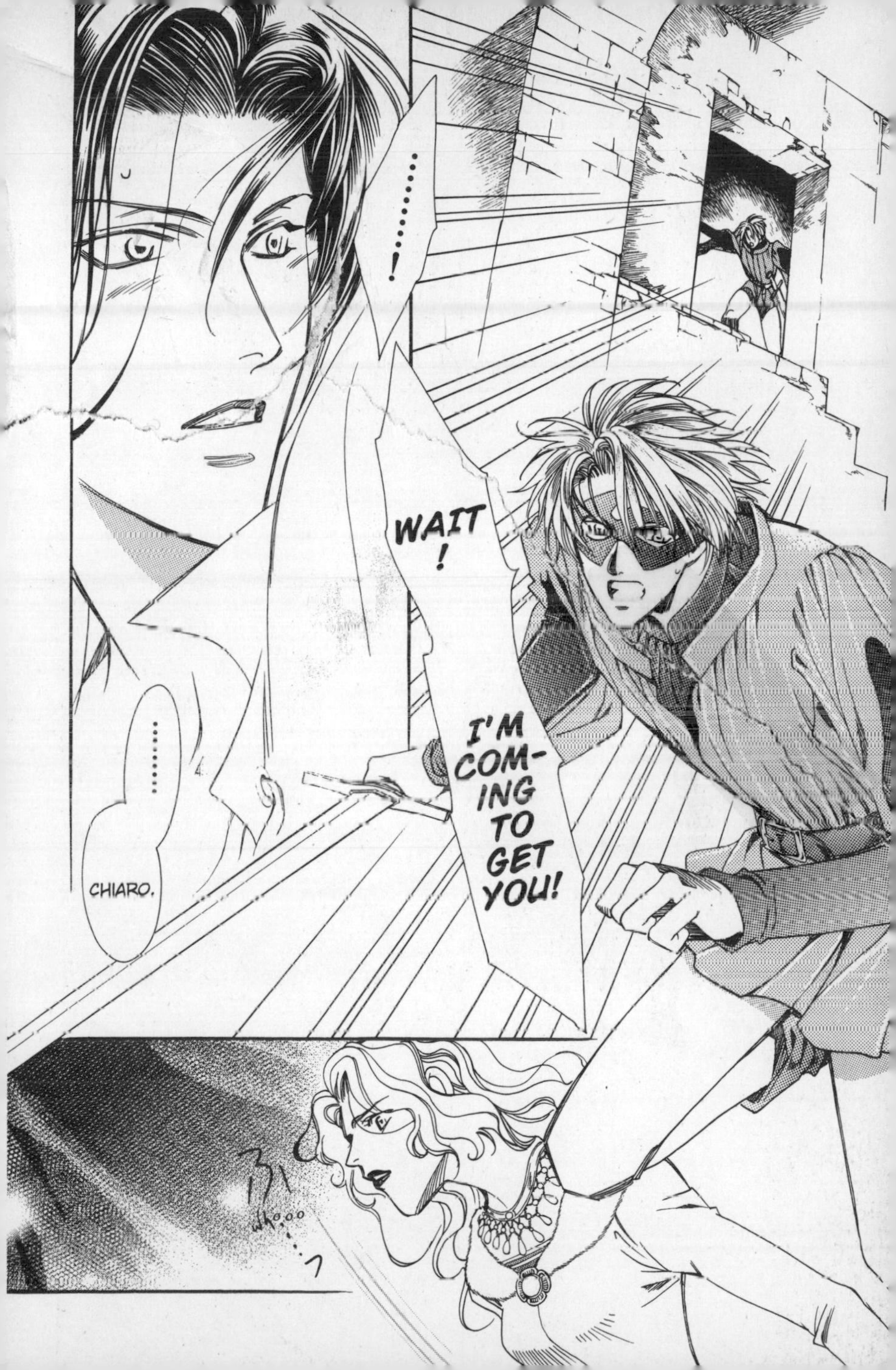
......!
WAIT!
I'M COMING TO GET YOU!
......
CHIARO.
whooo

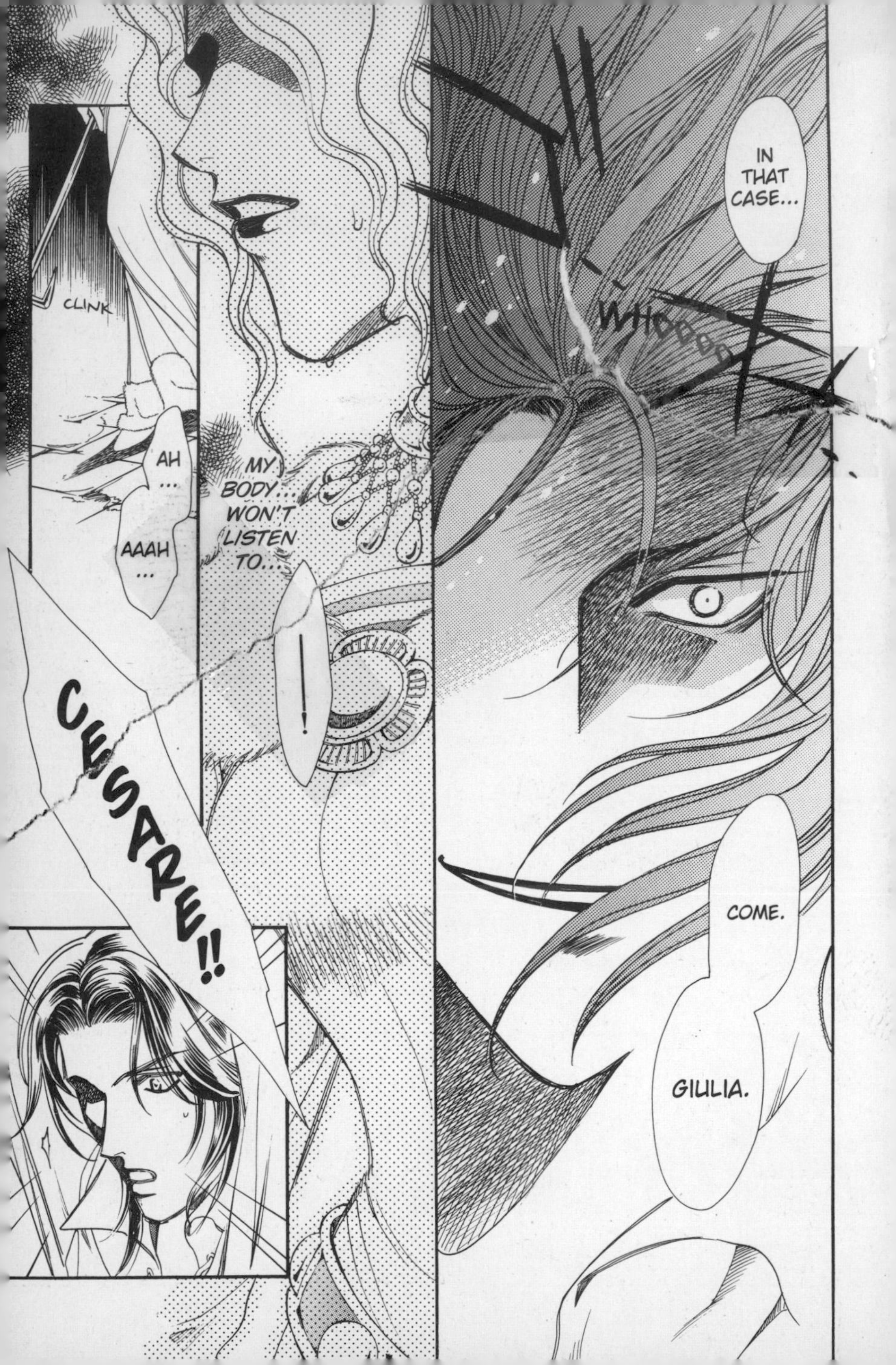
IN THAT CASE...
WHOOOO
COME.
GIULIA.
MY BODY... WON'T LISTEN TO...
!
CLINK
AH... AAAH...
CESARE!!

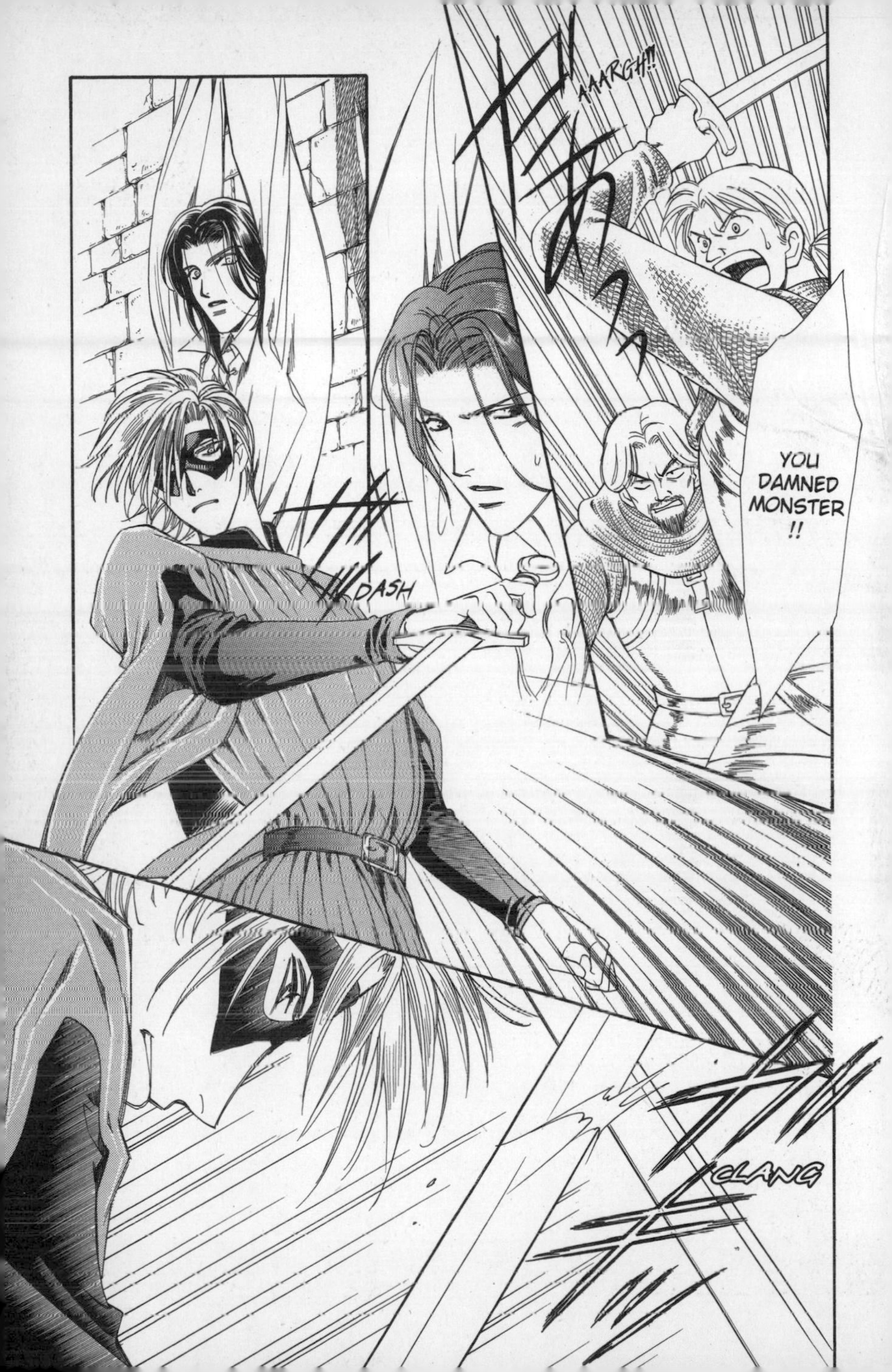
AAARGH!!
YOU DAMNED MONSTER !!
DASH
CLANG

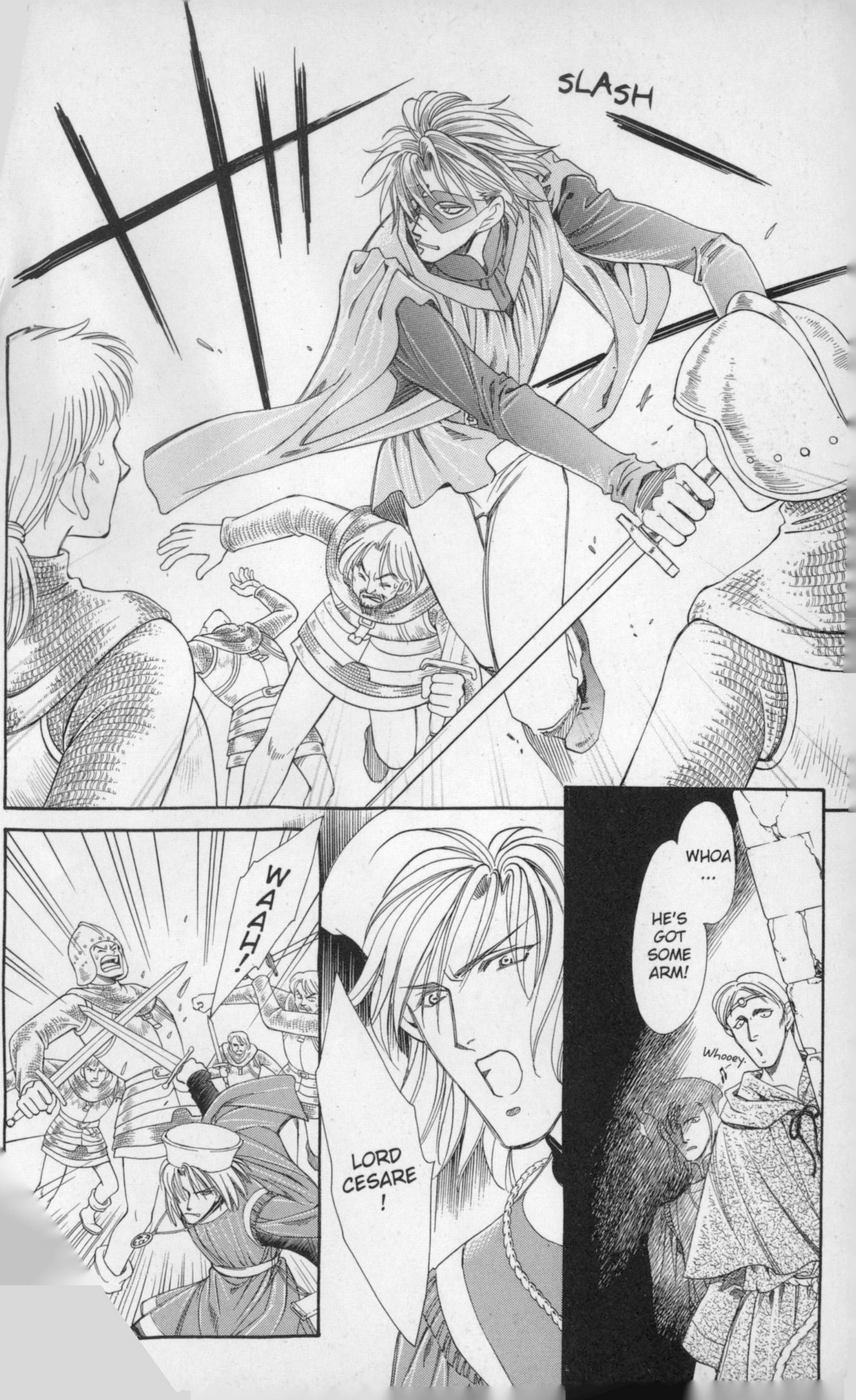
SLASH
WHOA ...
HE'S GOT SOME ARM!
Whooey.
LORD CESARE !
WAAAH!

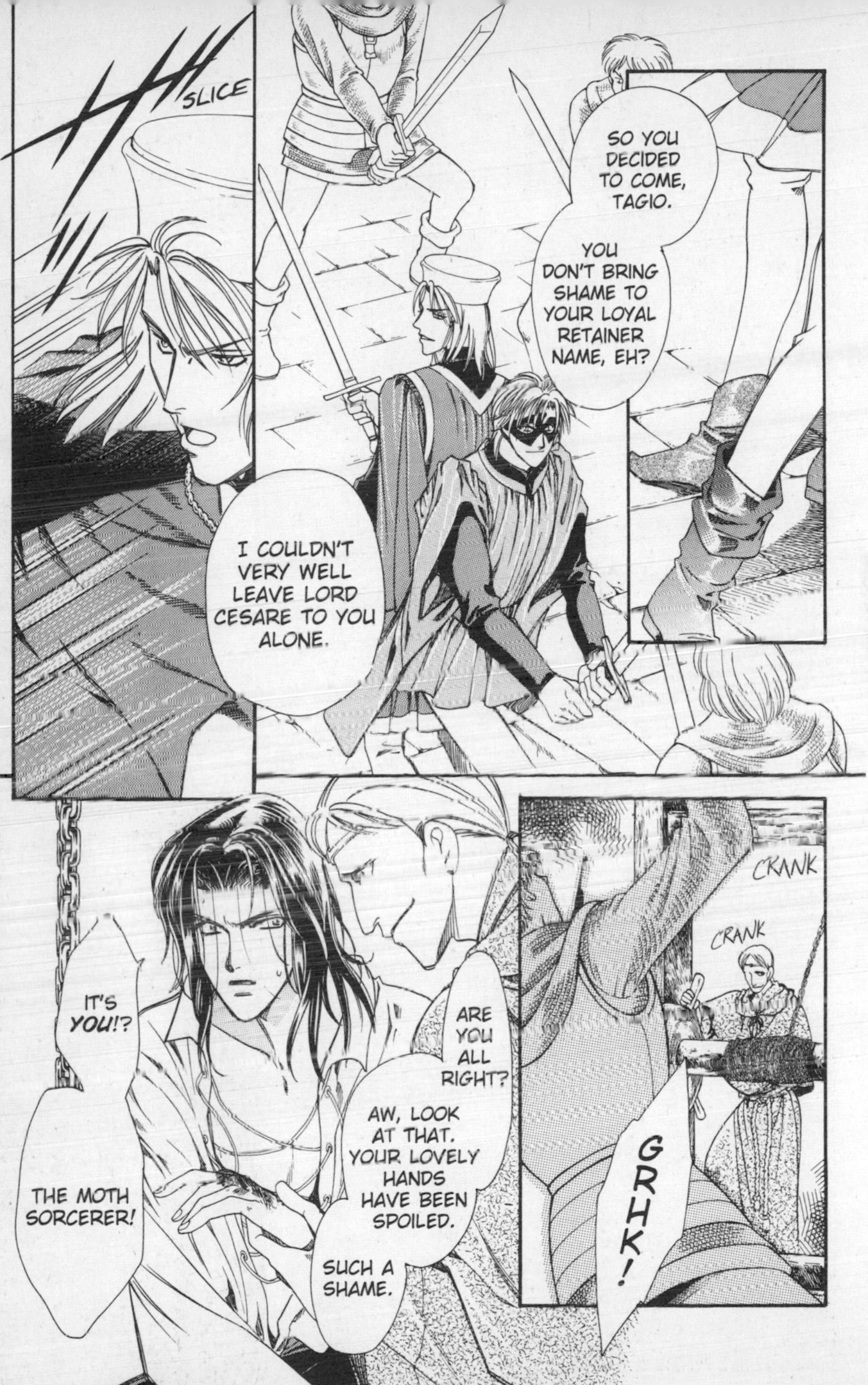
SO YOU DECIDED TO COME, TAGIO.
YOU DON'T BRING SHAME TO YOUR LOYAL RETAINER NAME, EH?
I COULDN'T VERY WELL LEAVE LORD CESARE TO YOU ALONE.
SLICE
CRANK
CRANK
GRHK!
ARE YOU ALL RIGHT?
AW, LOOK AT THAT. YOUR LOVELY HANDS HAVE BEEN SPOILED.
SUCH A SHAME.
IT'S *YOU*!?
THE MOTH SORCERER!

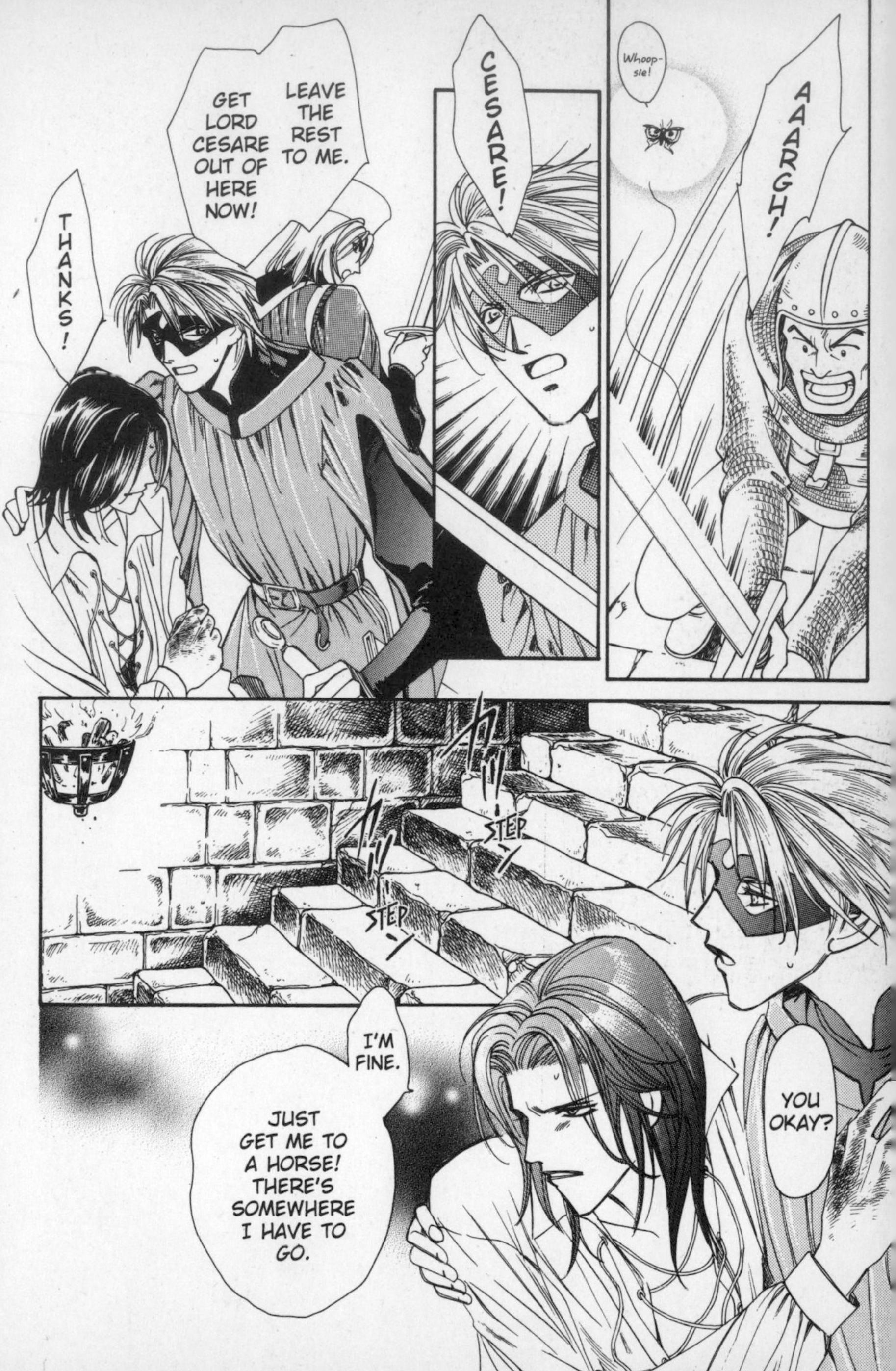

AAARGH!
Whoop-sie!
CESARE!
LEAVE THE REST TO ME.
GET LORD CESARE OUT OF HERE NOW!
THANKS!
STEP
STEP
YOU OKAY?
I'M FINE.
JUST GET ME TO A HORSE! THERE'S SOMEWHERE I HAVE TO GO.

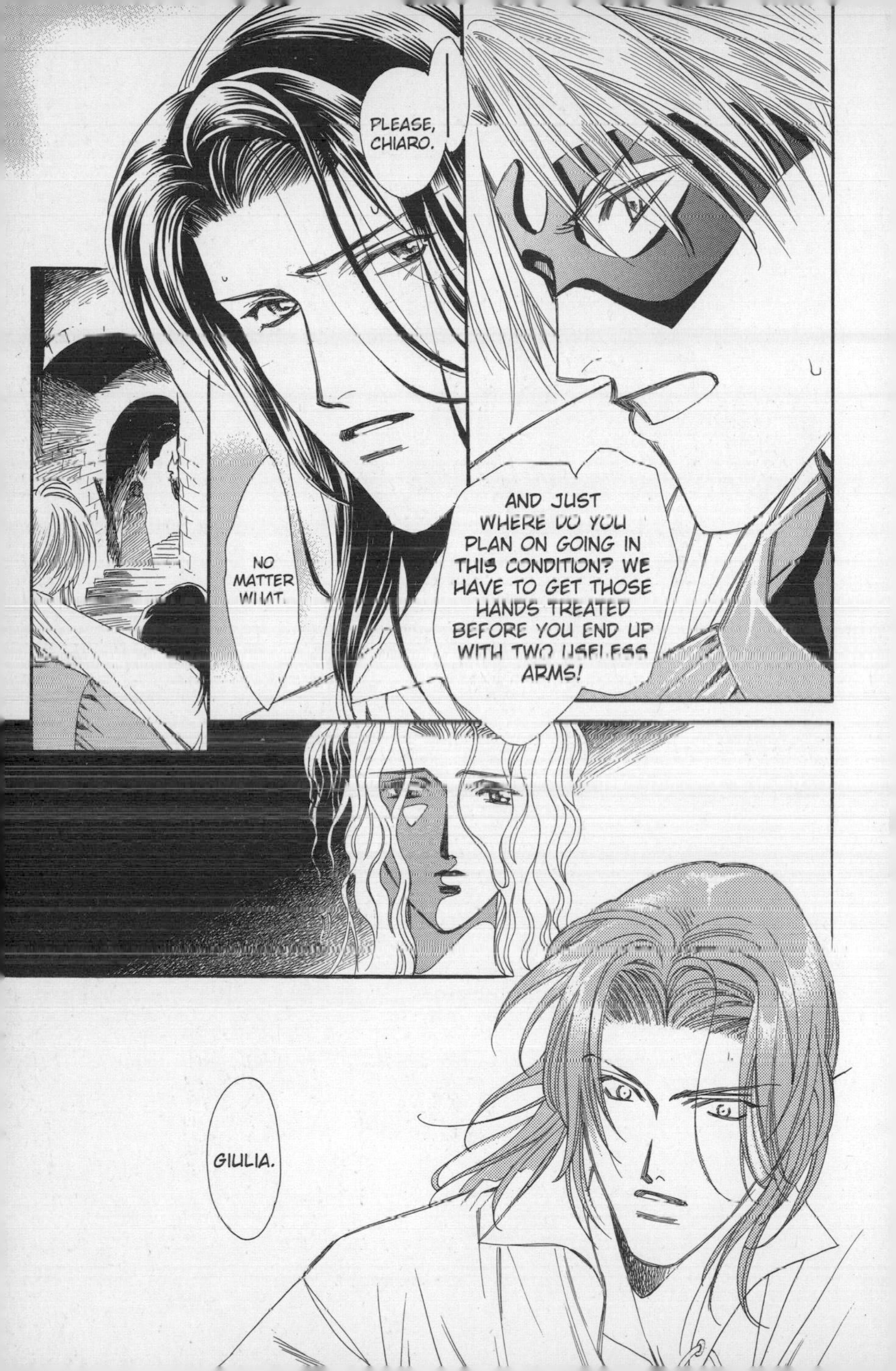
PLEASE, CHIARO.
NO MATTER WHAT.
AND JUST WHERE DO YOU PLAN ON GOING IN THIS CONDITION? WE HAVE TO GET THOSE HANDS TREATED BEFORE YOU END UP WITH TWO USELESS ARMS!
GIULIA.

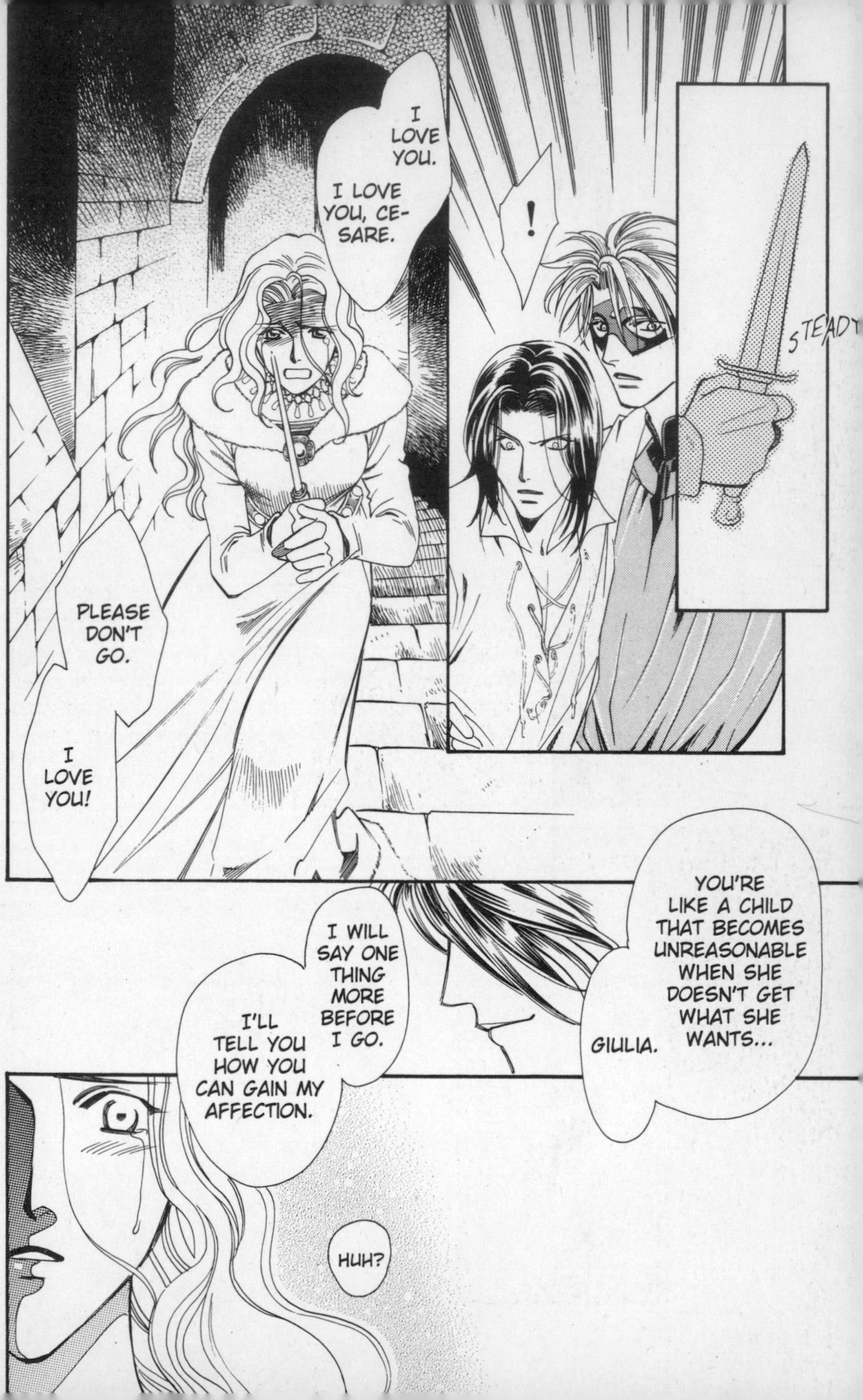
!
STEADY
I LOVE YOU.
I LOVE YOU, CE-SARE.
PLEASE DON'T GO.
I LOVE YOU!
YOU'RE LIKE A CHILD THAT BECOMES UNREASONABLE WHEN SHE DOESN'T GET WHAT SHE WANTS...
GIULIA.
I WILL SAY ONE THING MORE BEFORE I GO.
I'LL TELL YOU HOW YOU CAN GAIN MY AFFECTION.
HUH?

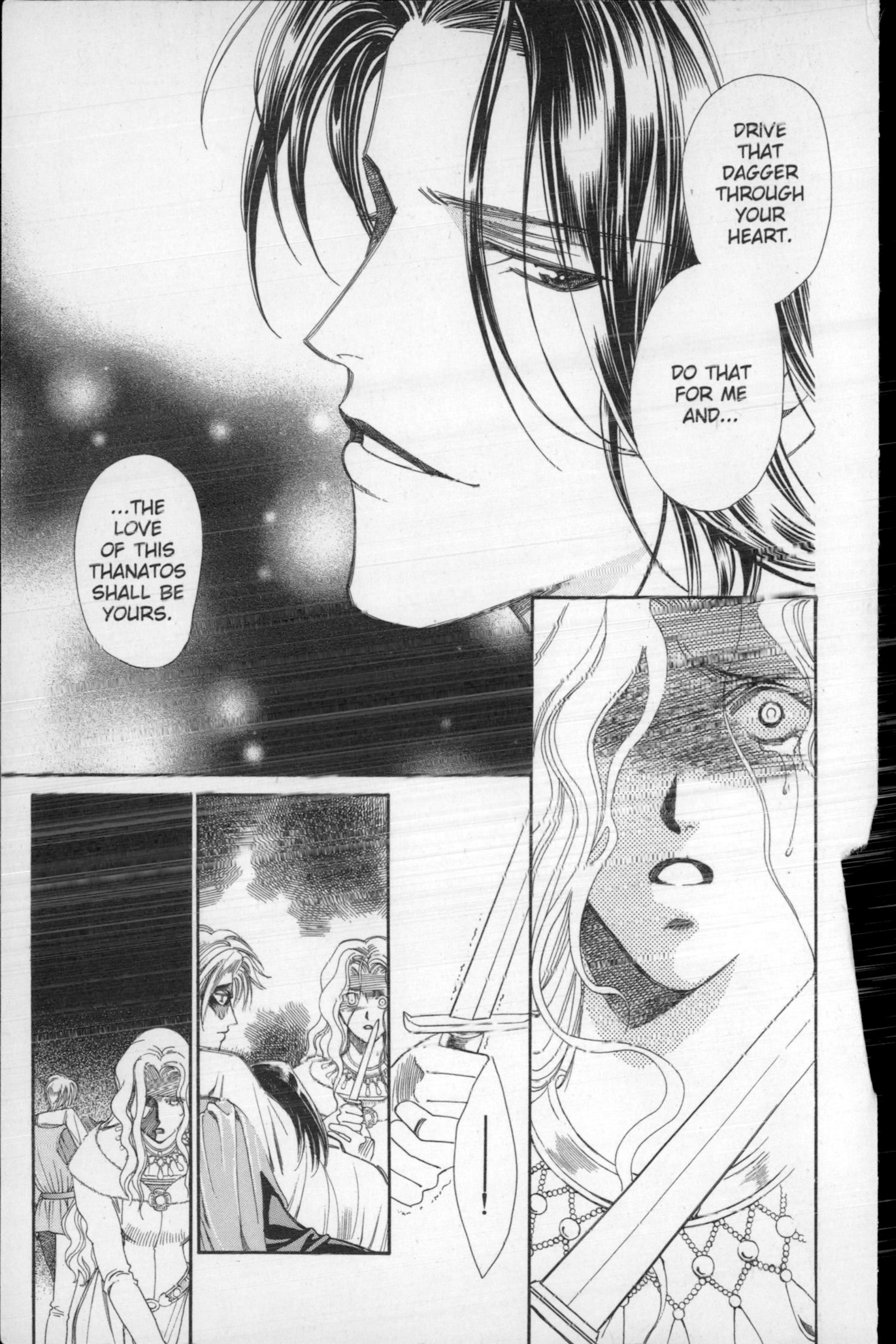
DRIVE THAT DAGGER THROUGH YOUR HEART.
DO THAT FOR ME AND...
...THE LOVE OF THIS THANATOS SHALL BE YOURS.
!

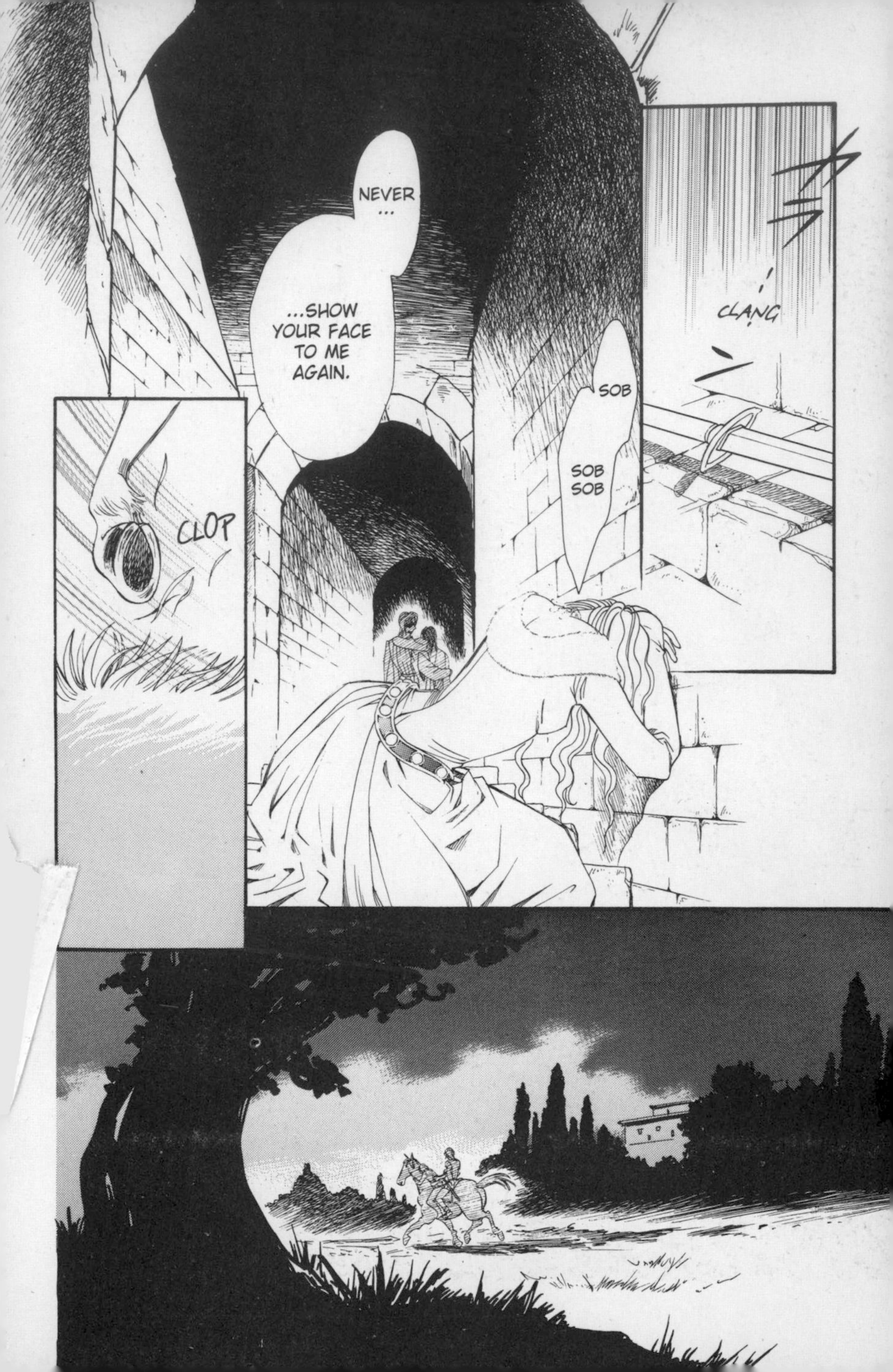
CLANG
NEVER ...
...SHOW YOUR FACE TO ME AGAIN.
SOB
SOB SOB
CLOP

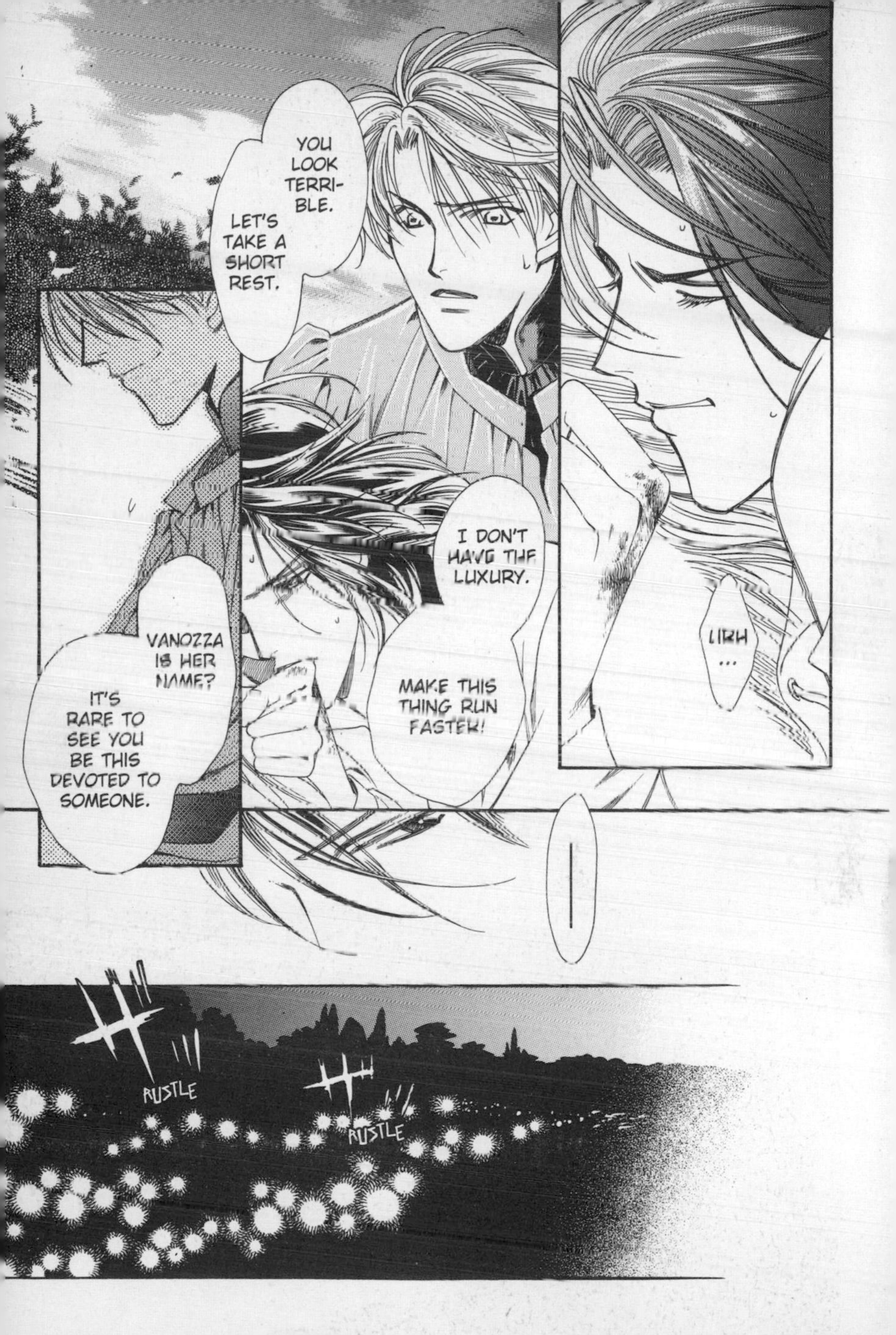

URH ...
YOU LOOK TERRIBLE.
LET'S TAKE A SHORT REST.
I DON'T HAVE THE LUXURY.
MAKE THIS THING RUN FASTER!
VANOZZA IS HER NAME?
IT'S RARE TO SEE YOU BE THIS DEVOTED TO SOMEONE.
RUSTLE
RUSTLE

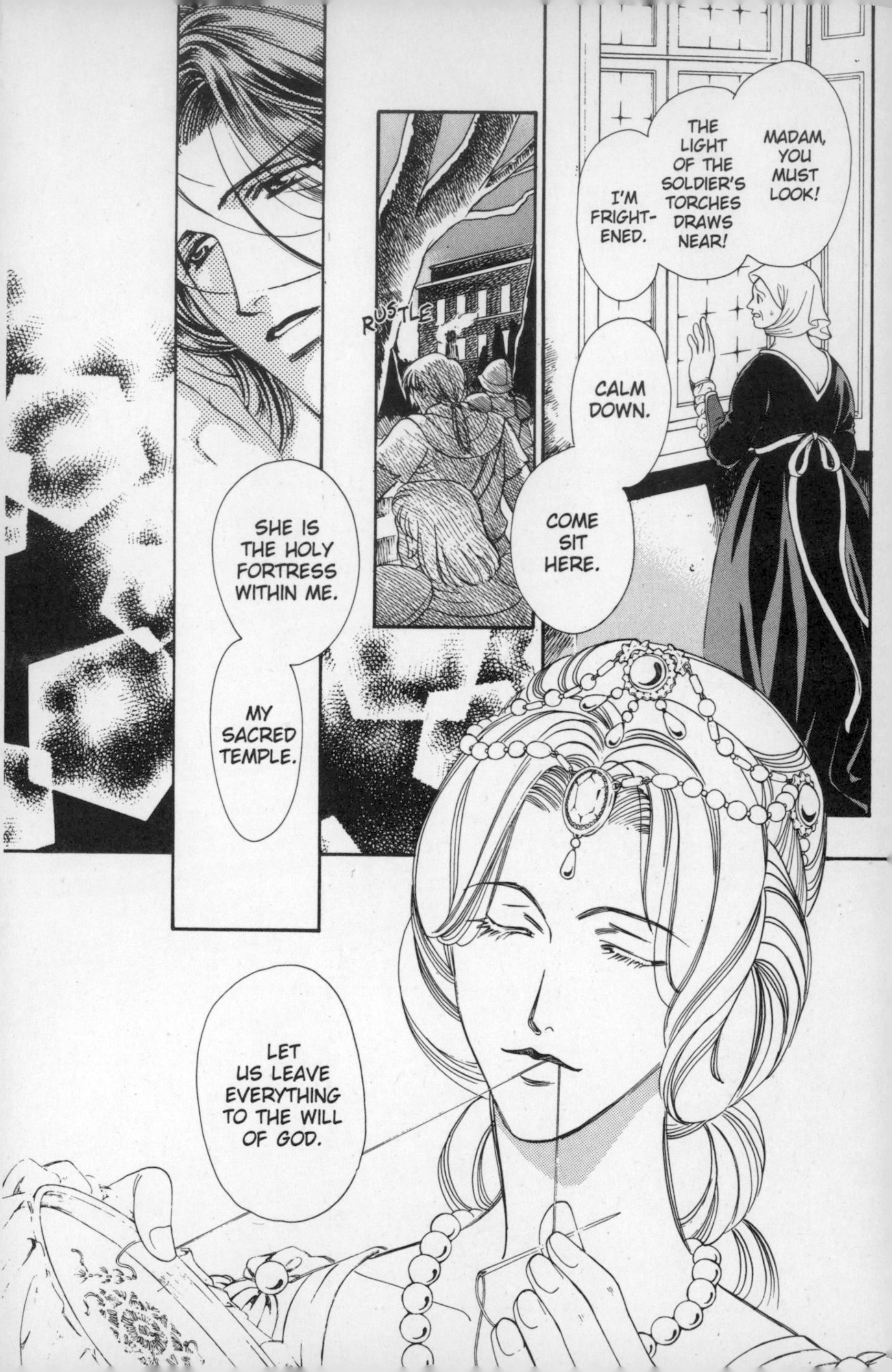
MADAM, YOU MUST LOOK!
THE LIGHT OF THE SOLDIER'S TORCHES DRAWS NEAR!
I'M FRIGHT-ENED.
CALM DOWN.
COME SIT HERE.
RUSTLE
SHE IS THE HOLY FORTRESS WITHIN ME.
MY SACRED TEMPLE.
LET US LEAVE EVERYTHING TO THE WILL OF GOD.

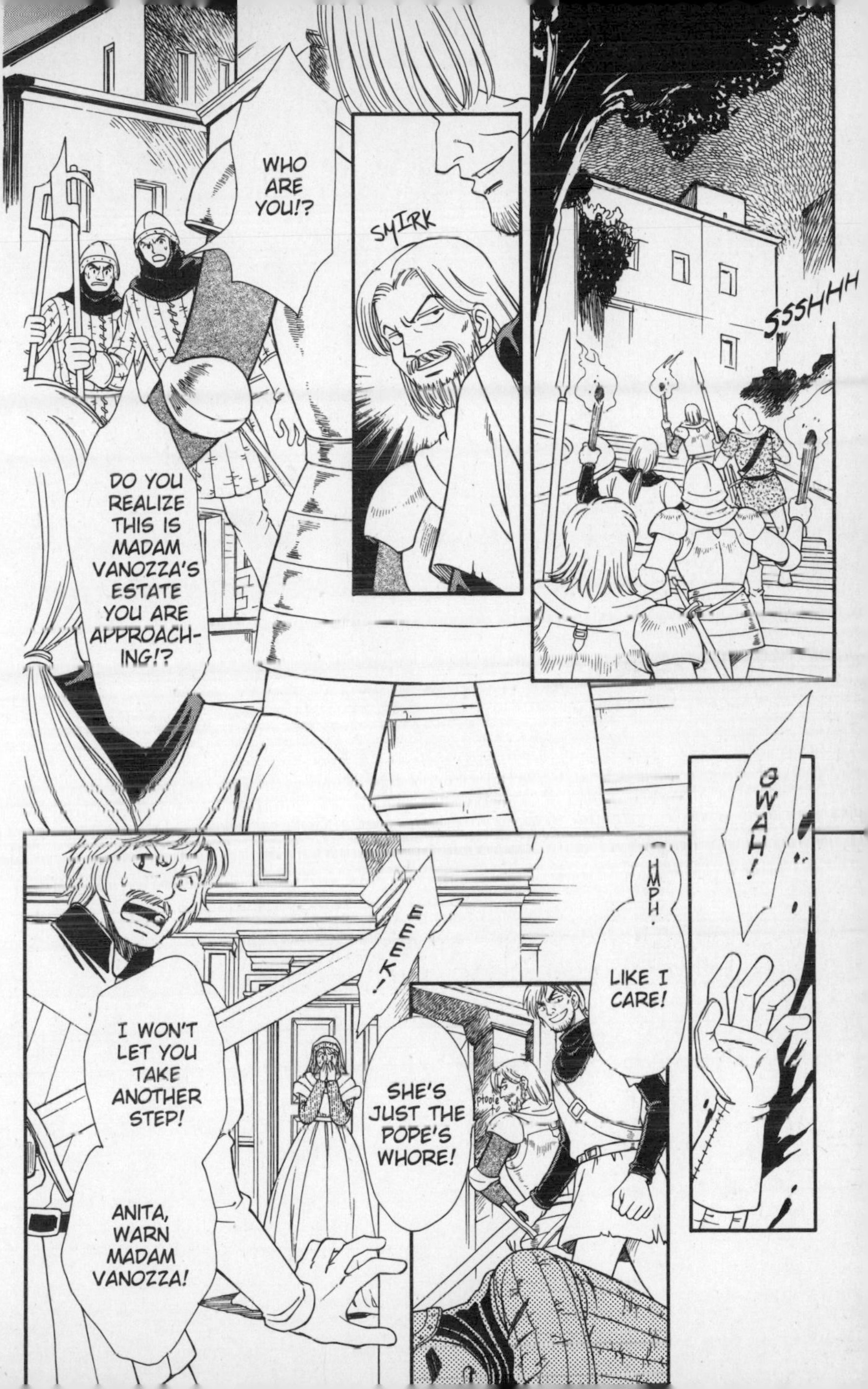
SSSHHH
SMIRK
WHO ARE YOU!?
DO YOU REALIZE THIS IS MADAM VANOZZA'S ESTATE YOU ARE APPROACH-ING!?
GWAH!
HMPH!
LIKE I CARE!
ptooie
SHE'S JUST THE POPE'S WHORE!
EEEEK!
I WON'T LET YOU TAKE ANOTHER STEP!
ANITA, WARN MADAM VANOZZA!

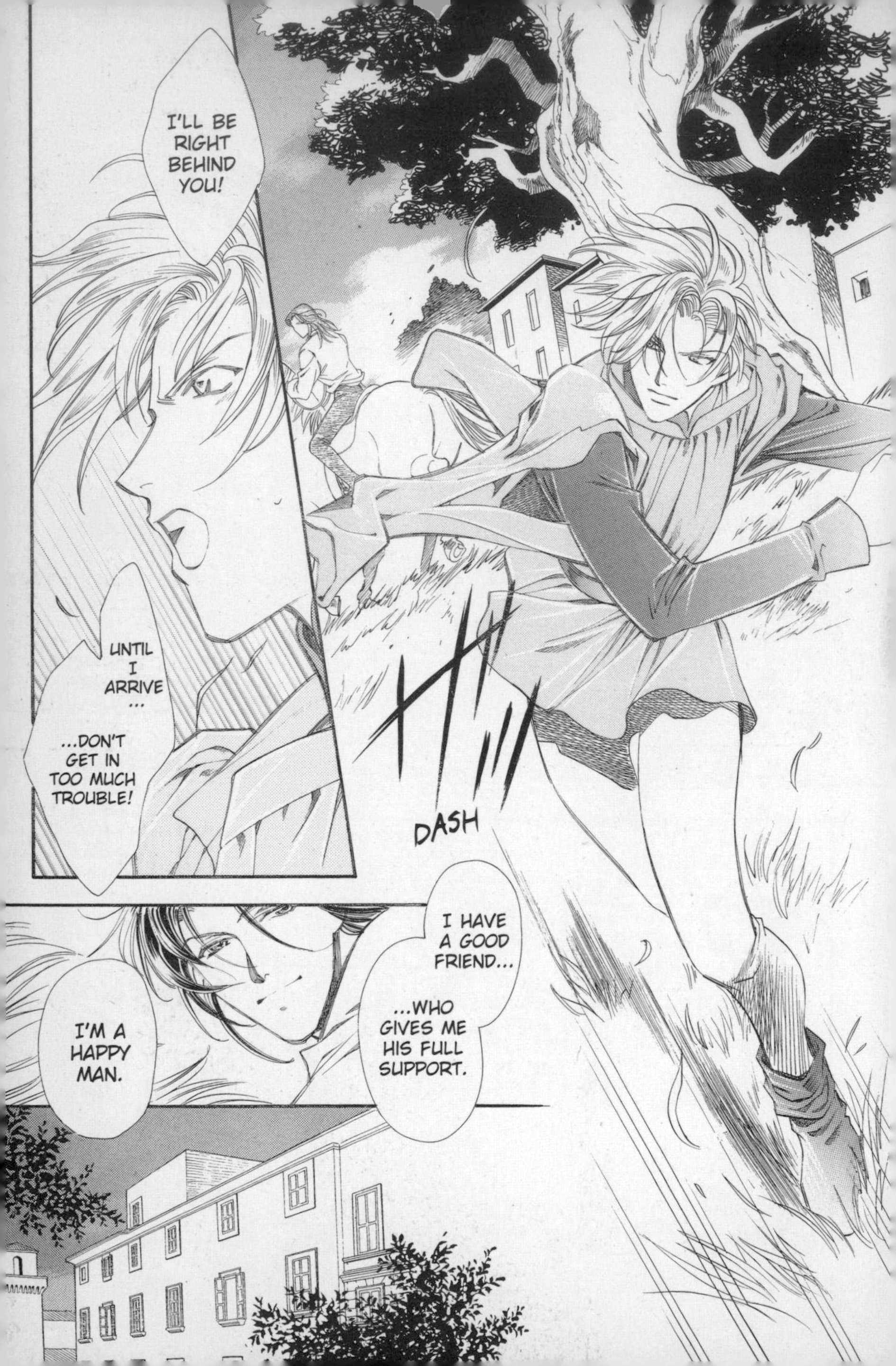
DASH
I'LL BE RIGHT BEHIND YOU!
UNTIL I ARRIVE...
...DON'T GET IN TOO MUCH TROUBLE!
I HAVE A GOOD FRIEND...
...WHO GIVES ME HIS FULL SUPPORT.
I'M A HAPPY MAN.

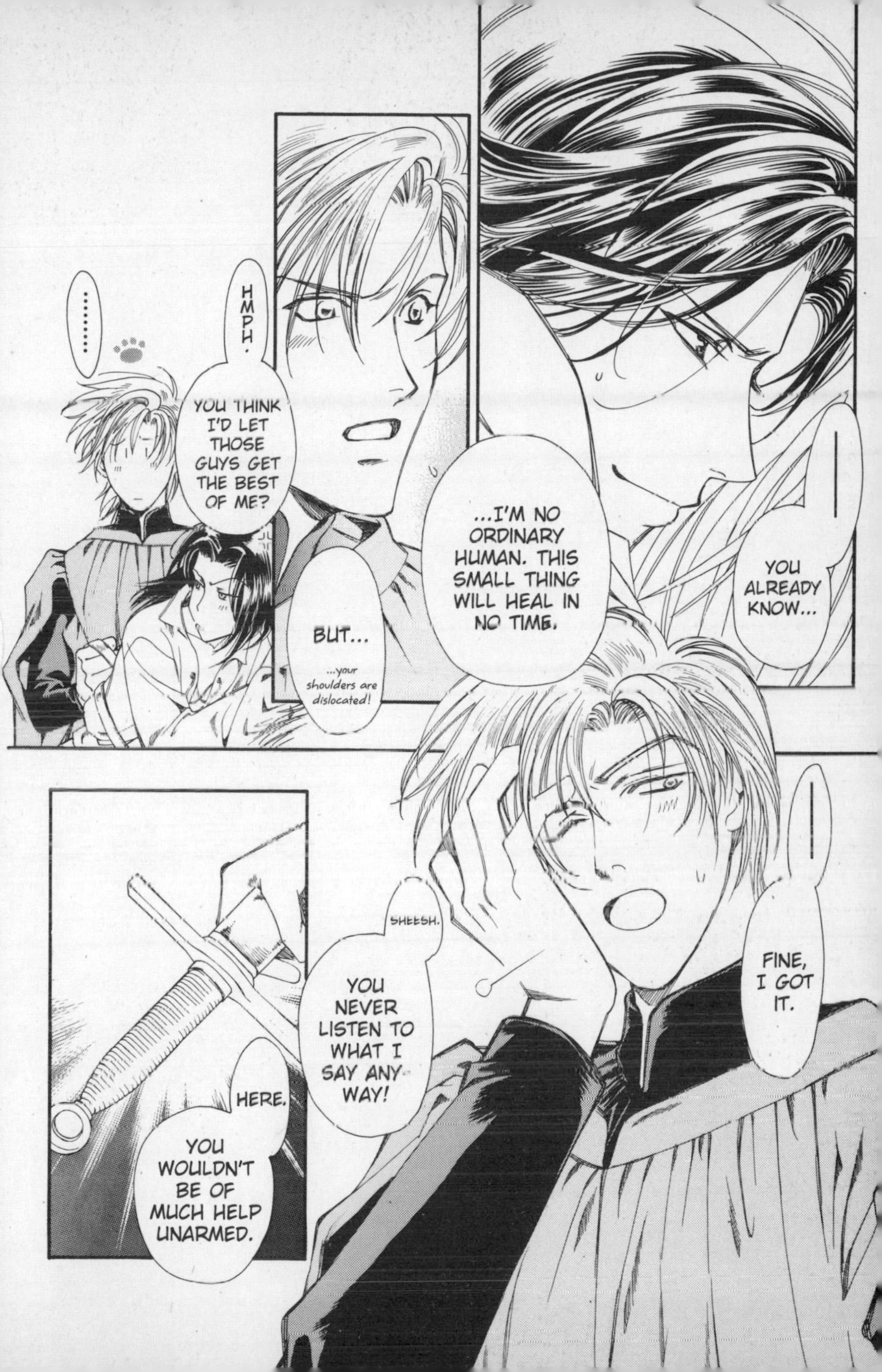
YOU ALREADY KNOW...
...I'M NO ORDINARY HUMAN. THIS SMALL THING WILL HEAL IN NO TIME.
BUT...
...your shoulders are dislocated!
HMPH.
YOU THINK I'D LET THOSE GUYS GET THE BEST OF ME?
....
FINE, I GOT IT.
SHEESH.
YOU NEVER LISTEN TO WHAT I SAY ANY WAY!
HERE.
YOU WOULDN'T BE OF MUCH HELP UNARMED.

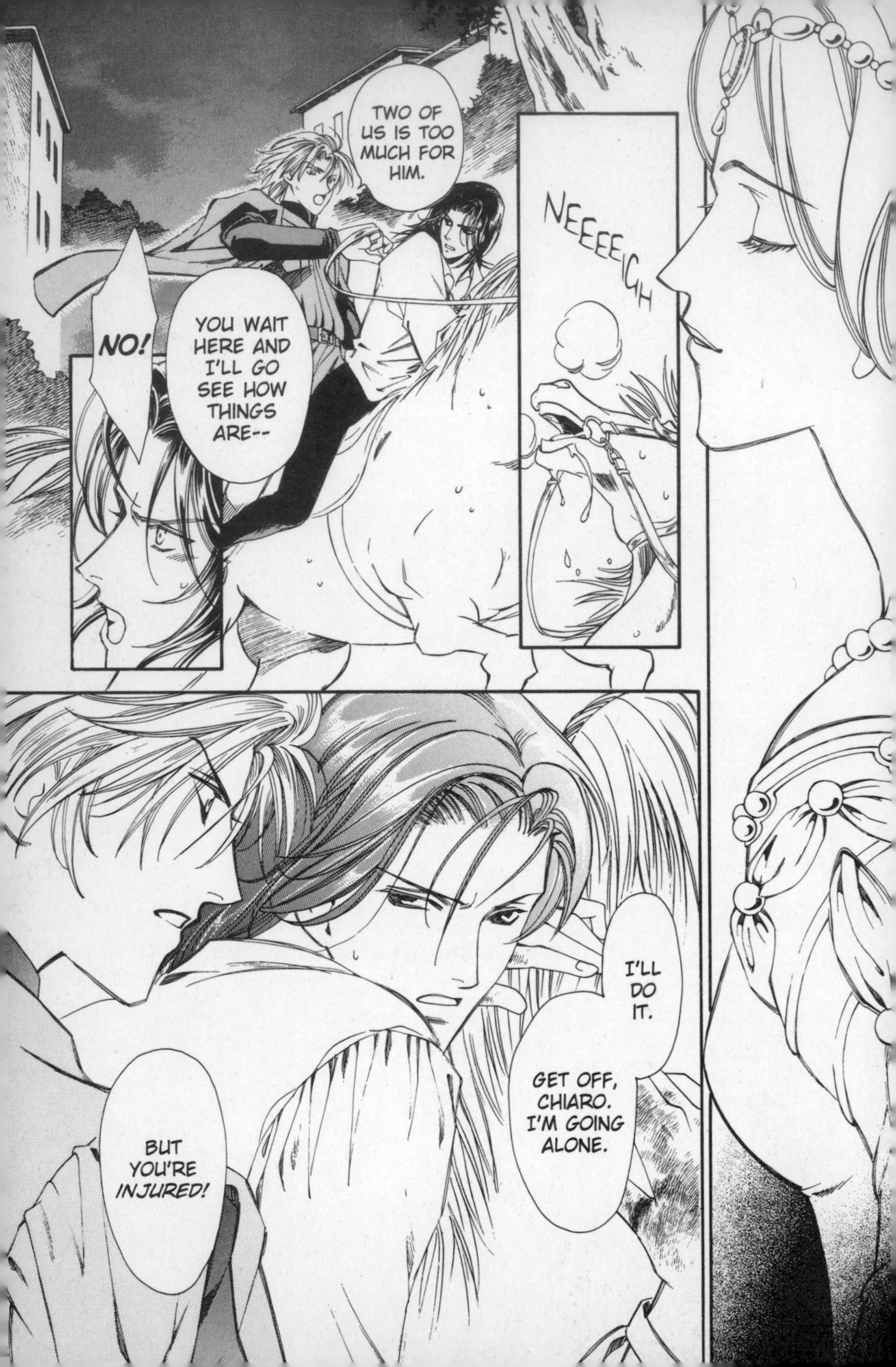
NEEEEICH
TWO OF US IS TOO MUCH FOR HIM.
YOU WAIT HERE AND I'LL GO SEE HOW THINGS ARE--
NO!
I'LL DO IT.
GET OFF, CHIARO. I'M GOING ALONE.
BUT YOU'RE INJURED!

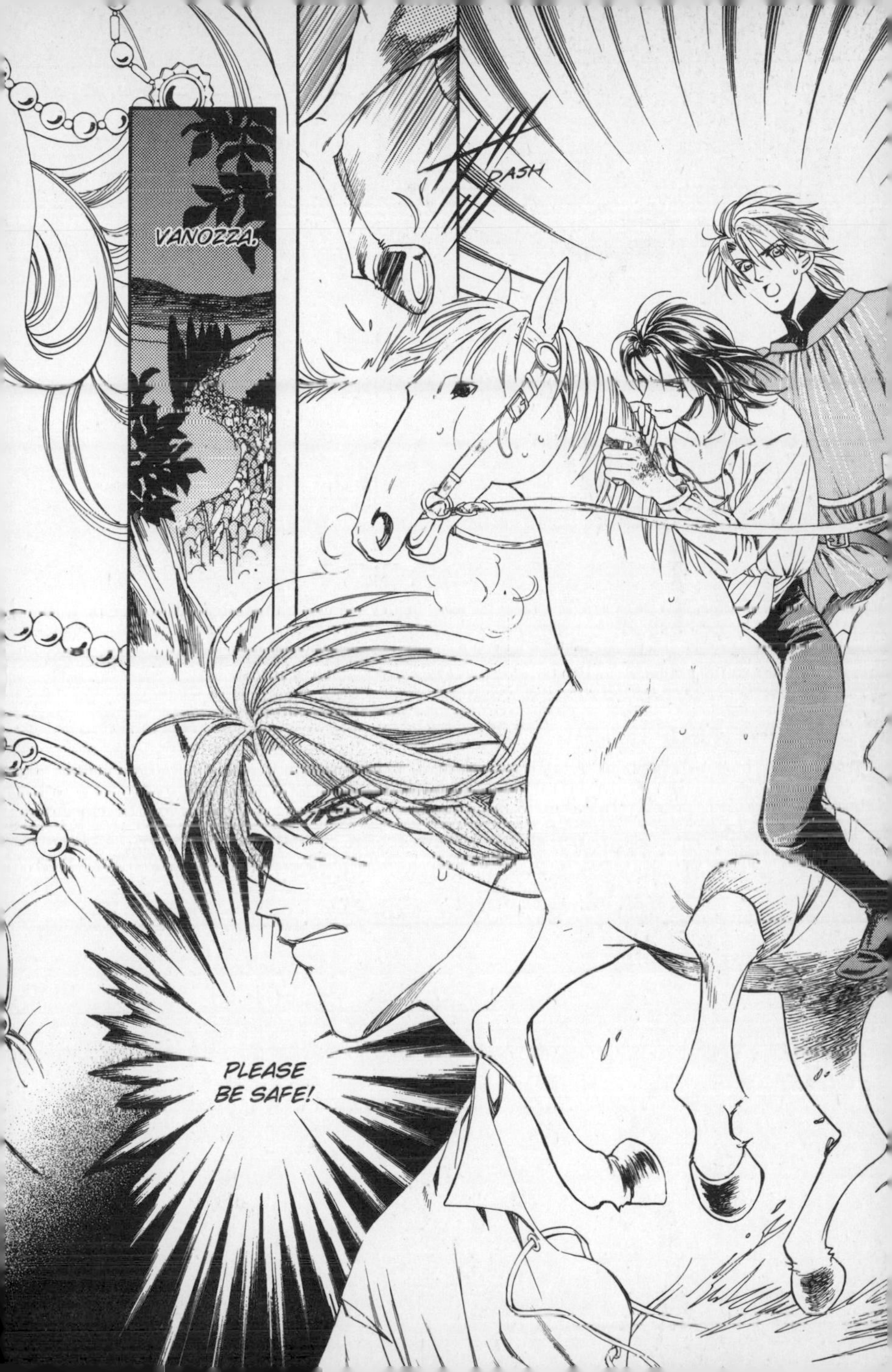
DASH
VANOZZA.
PLEASE BE SAFE!

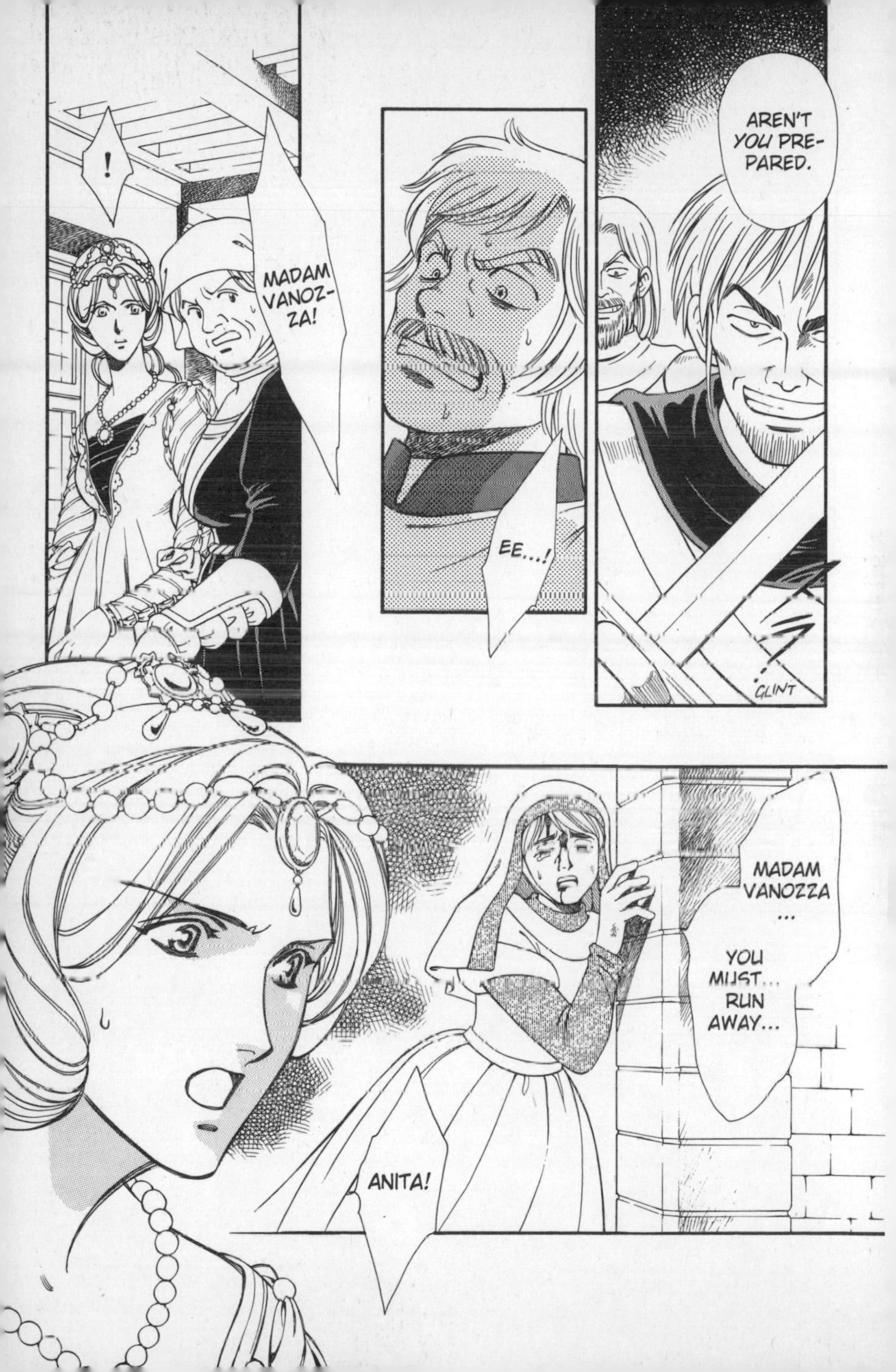
AREN'T YOU PRE-PARED.
GLINT
EE...!
!
MADAM VANOZ-ZA!
MADAM VANOZZA ...
YOU MUST... RUN AWAY...
ANITA!

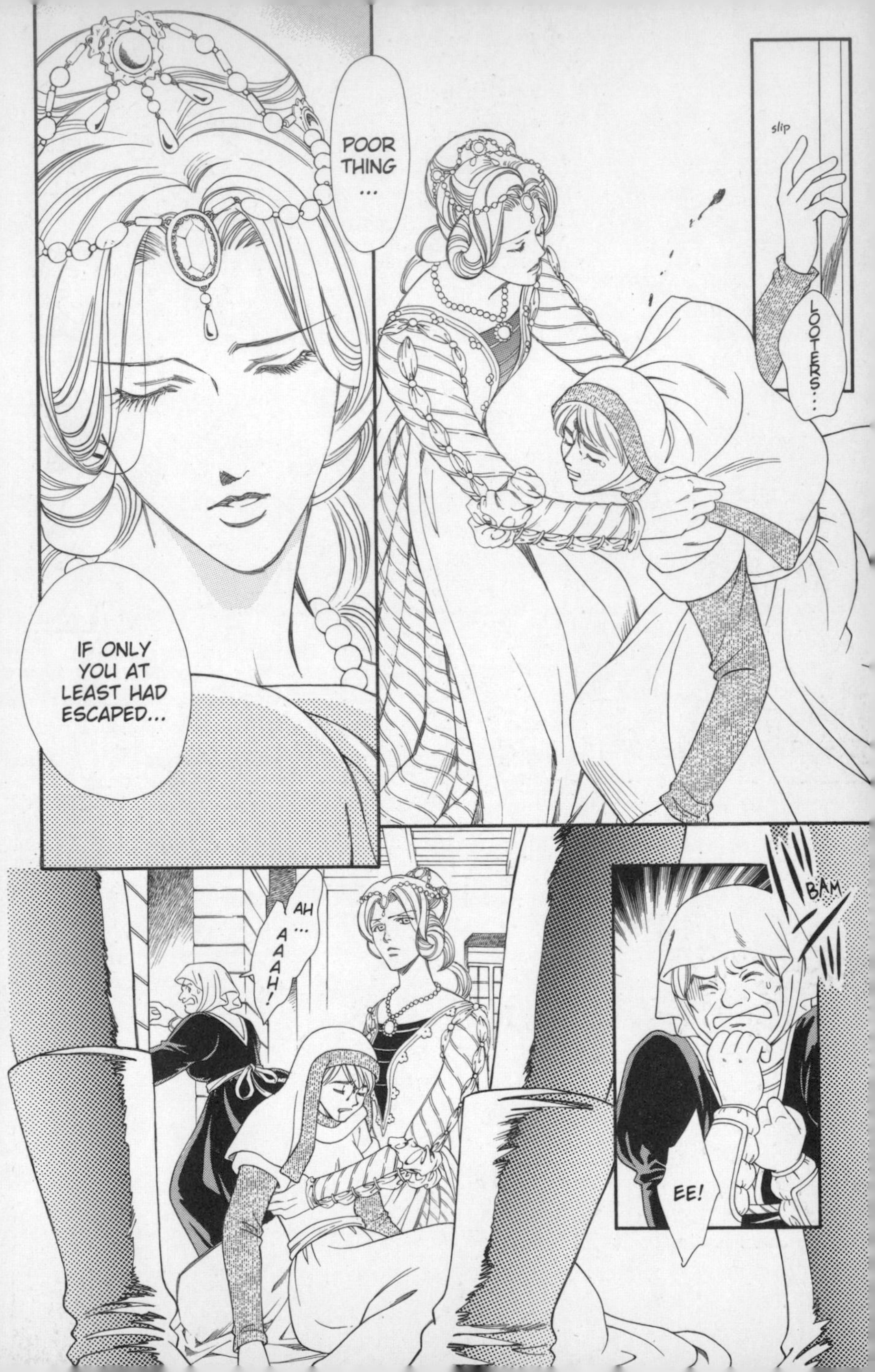
slip
LOOTERS...
POOR THING ...
IF ONLY YOU AT LEAST HAD ESCAPED...
BAM
EE!
AH ... AAAH!

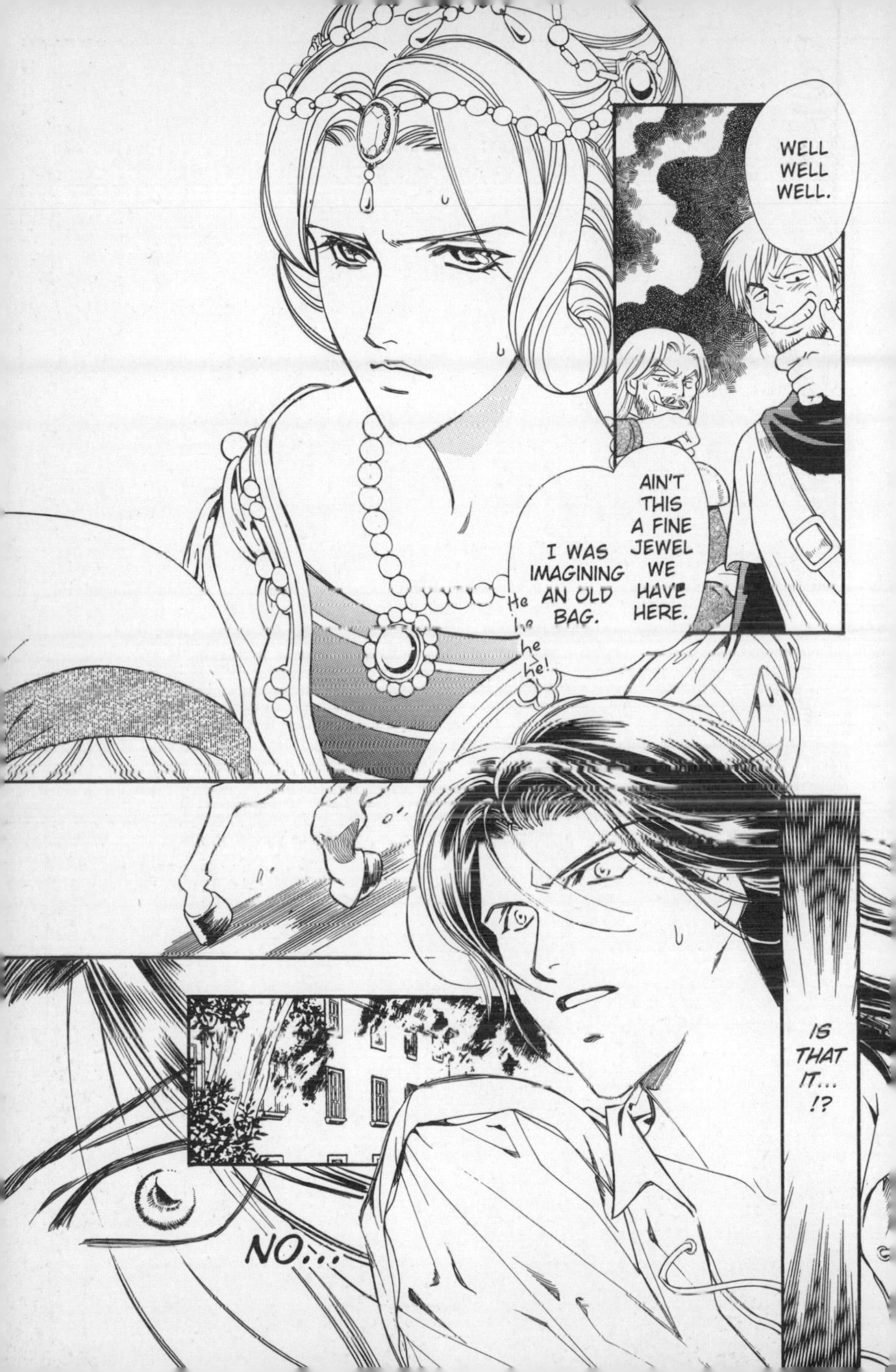
WELL WELL WELL.
AIN'T THIS A FINE JEWEL WE HAVE HERE.
I WAS IMAGINING AN OLD BAG.
He he he he!
IS THAT IT... !?
NO...

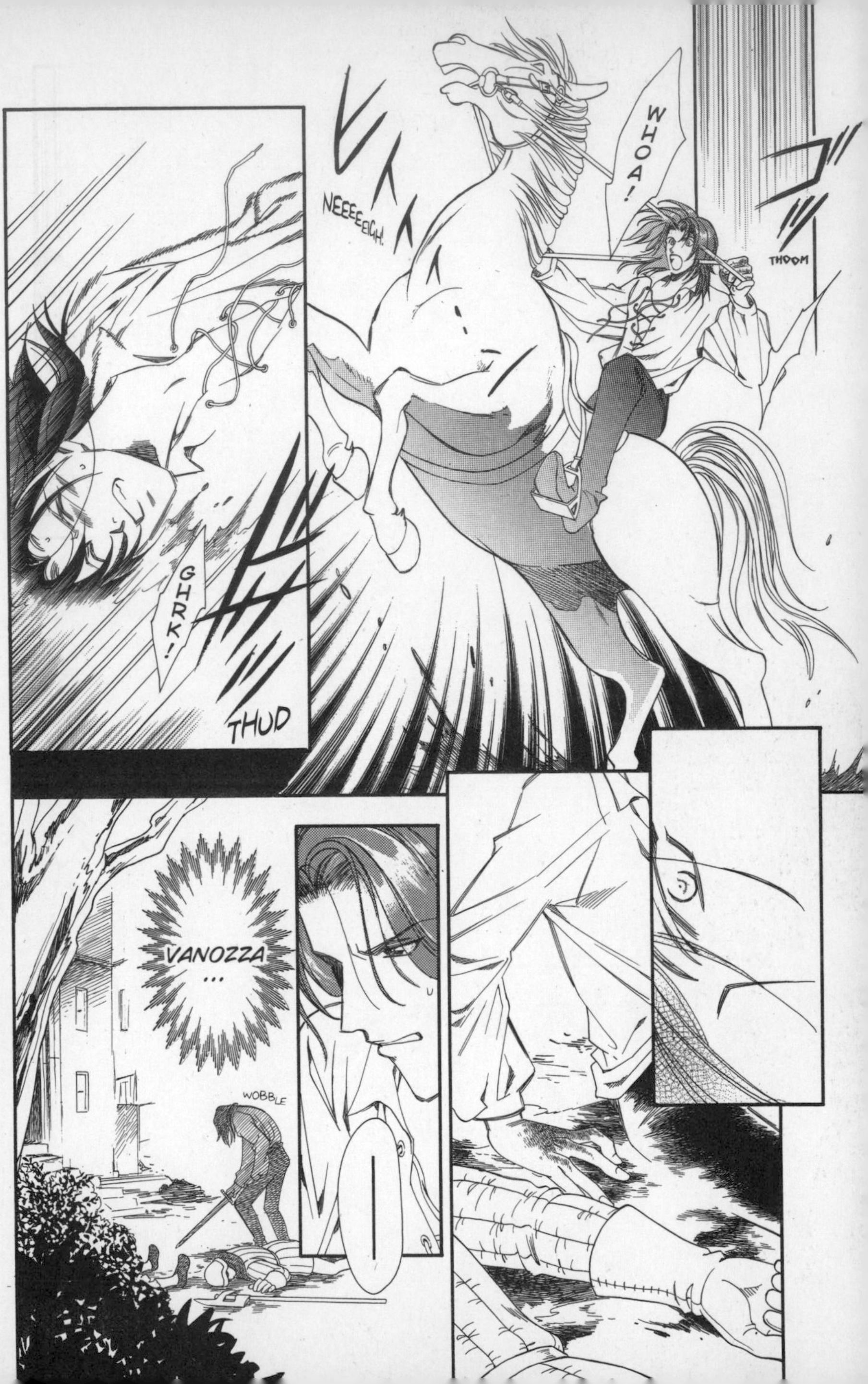

THOOM
WHOA!
NEEEEEIGH.
GHRK!
THUD
VANOZZA ...
WOBBLE

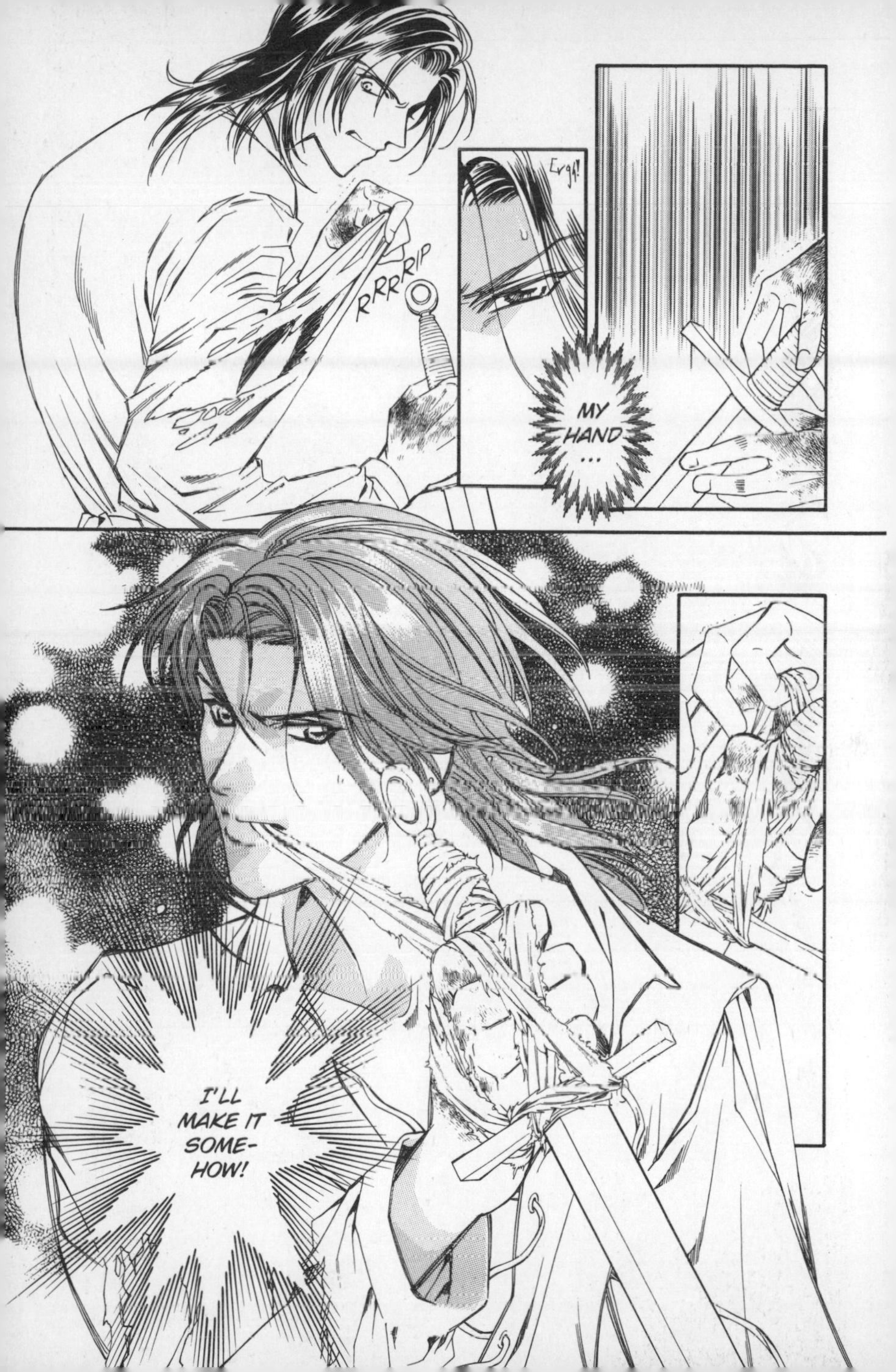
Ergh!
MY HAND ...
RRRRRIP
I'LL MAKE IT SOME-HOW!

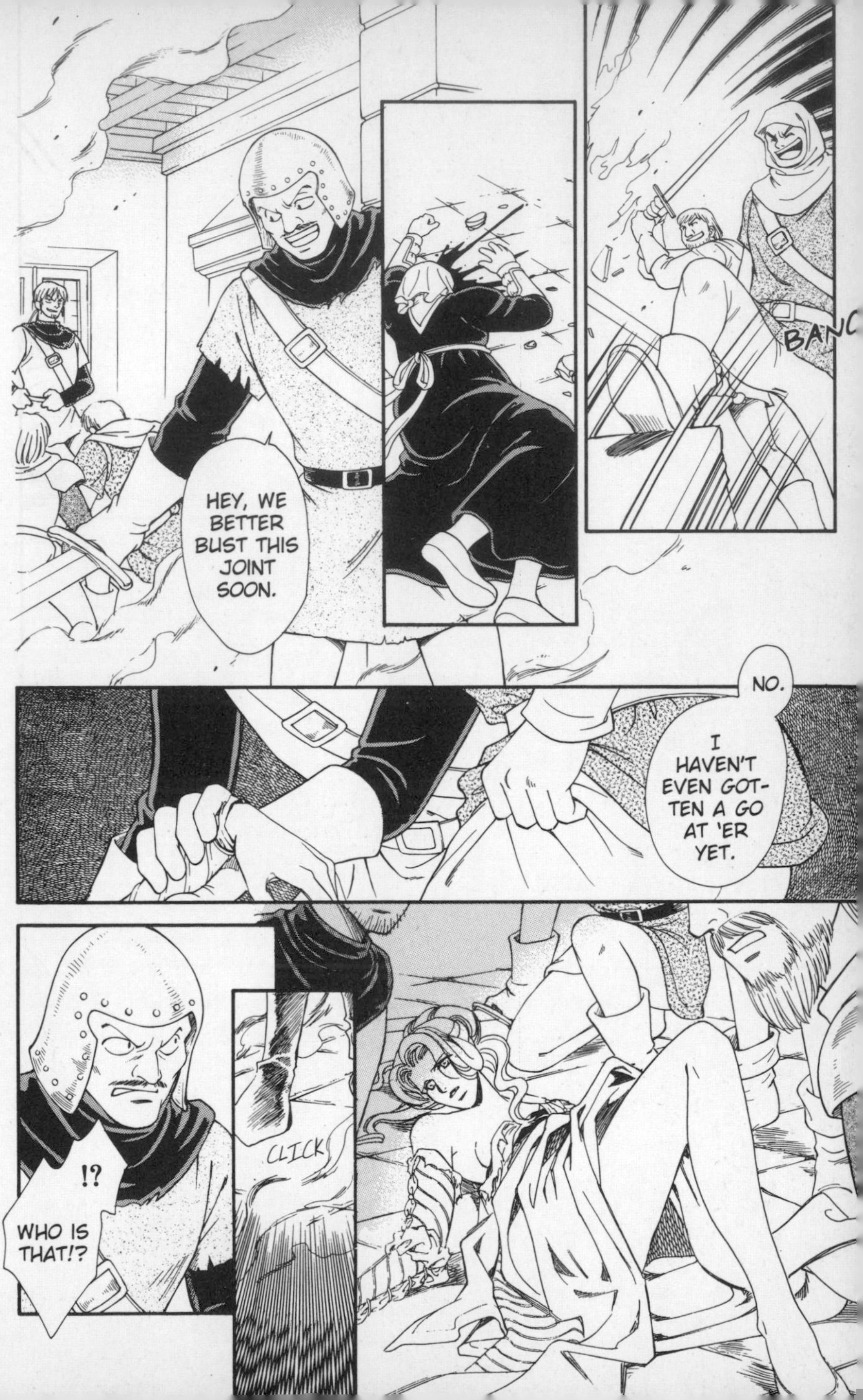
BAN
HEY, WE BETTER BUST THIS JOINT SOON.
NO.
I HAVEN'T EVEN GOT-TEN A GO AT 'ER YET.
CLICK
!?
WHO IS THAT!?

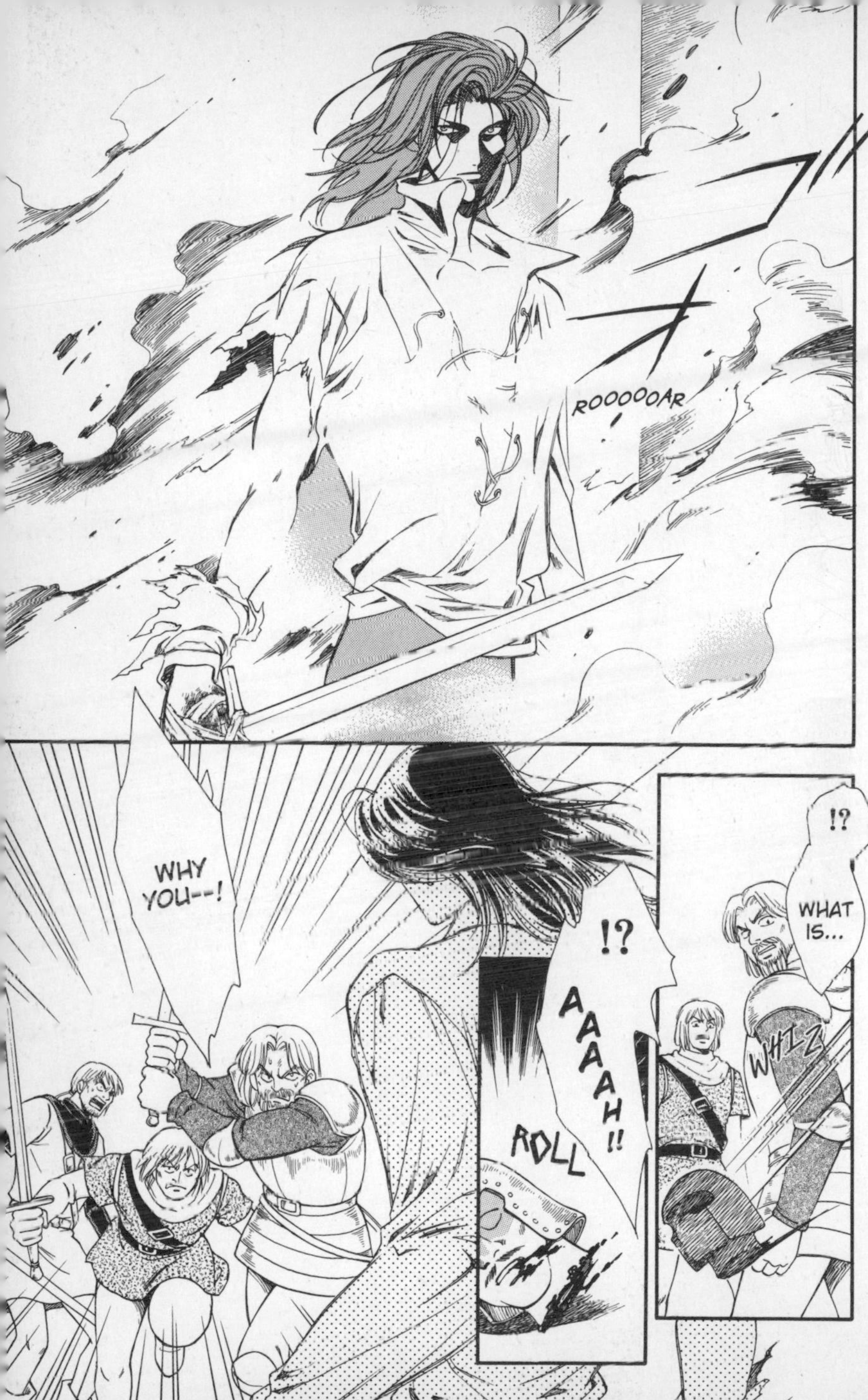
ROOOOOAR
!?
WHAT IS...
WHIZ
!?
AAAAAH!!
ROLL
WHY YOU--!

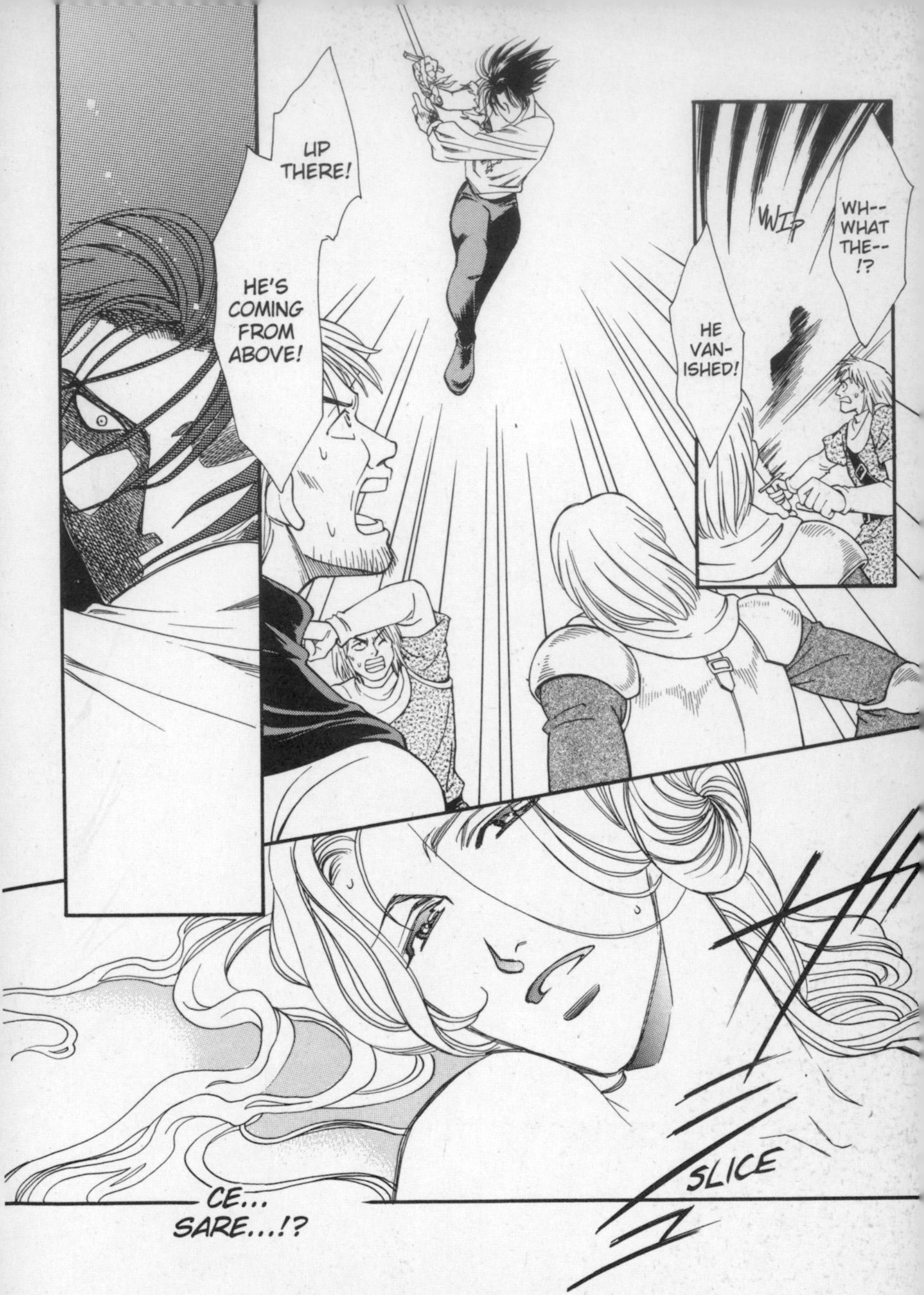
WH-- WHAT THE--!?
VWIP
HE VAN-ISHED!
UP THERE!
HE'S COMING FROM ABOVE!
SLICE
CE... SARE...!?

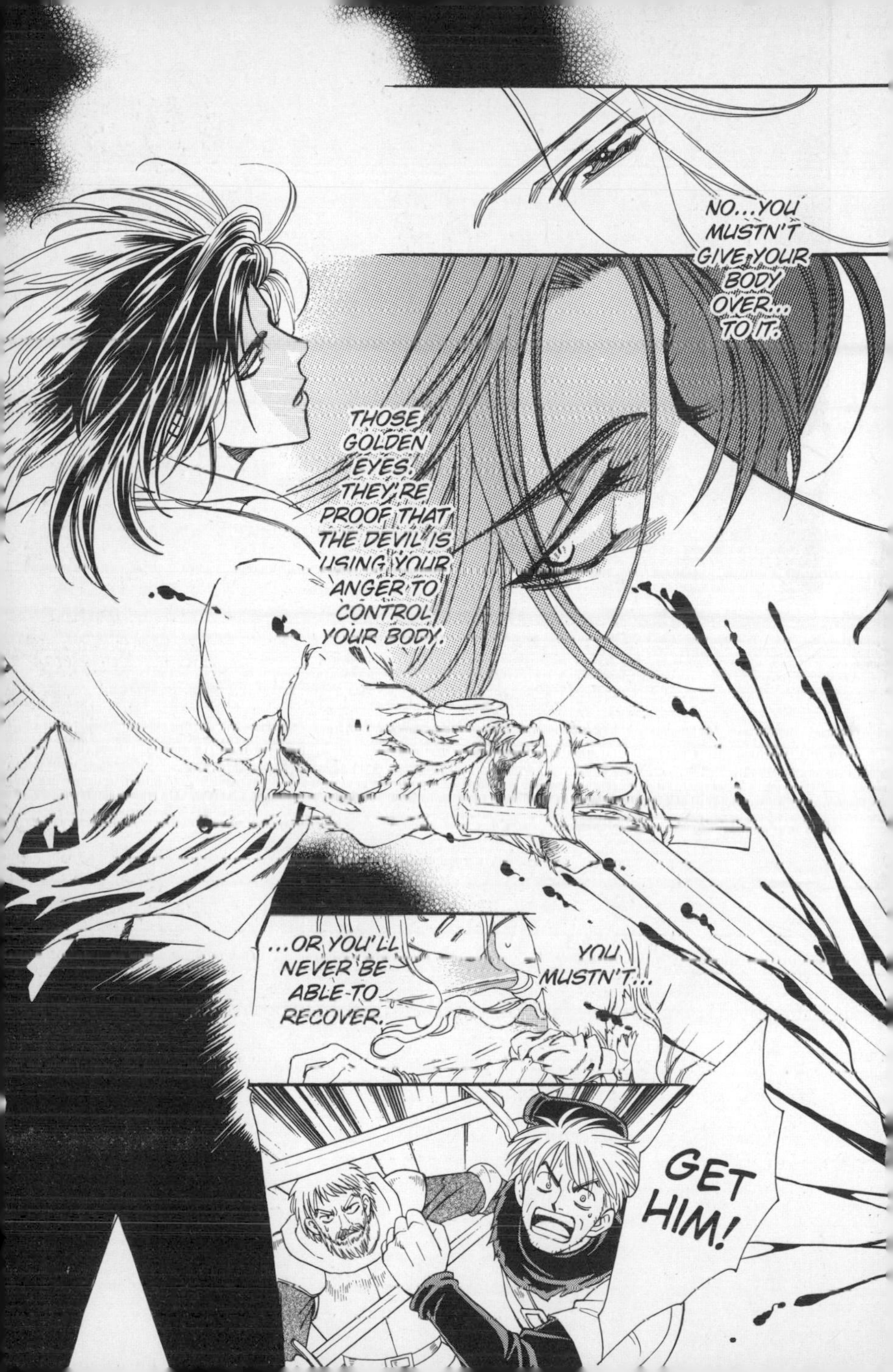
NO... YOU MUSTN'T GIVE YOUR BODY OVER... TO IT.
THOSE GOLDEN EYES. THEY'RE PROOF THAT THE DEVIL IS USING YOUR ANGER TO CONTROL YOUR BODY.
YOU MUSTN'T...
...OR YOU'LL NEVER BE ABLE TO RECOVER.
GET HIM!

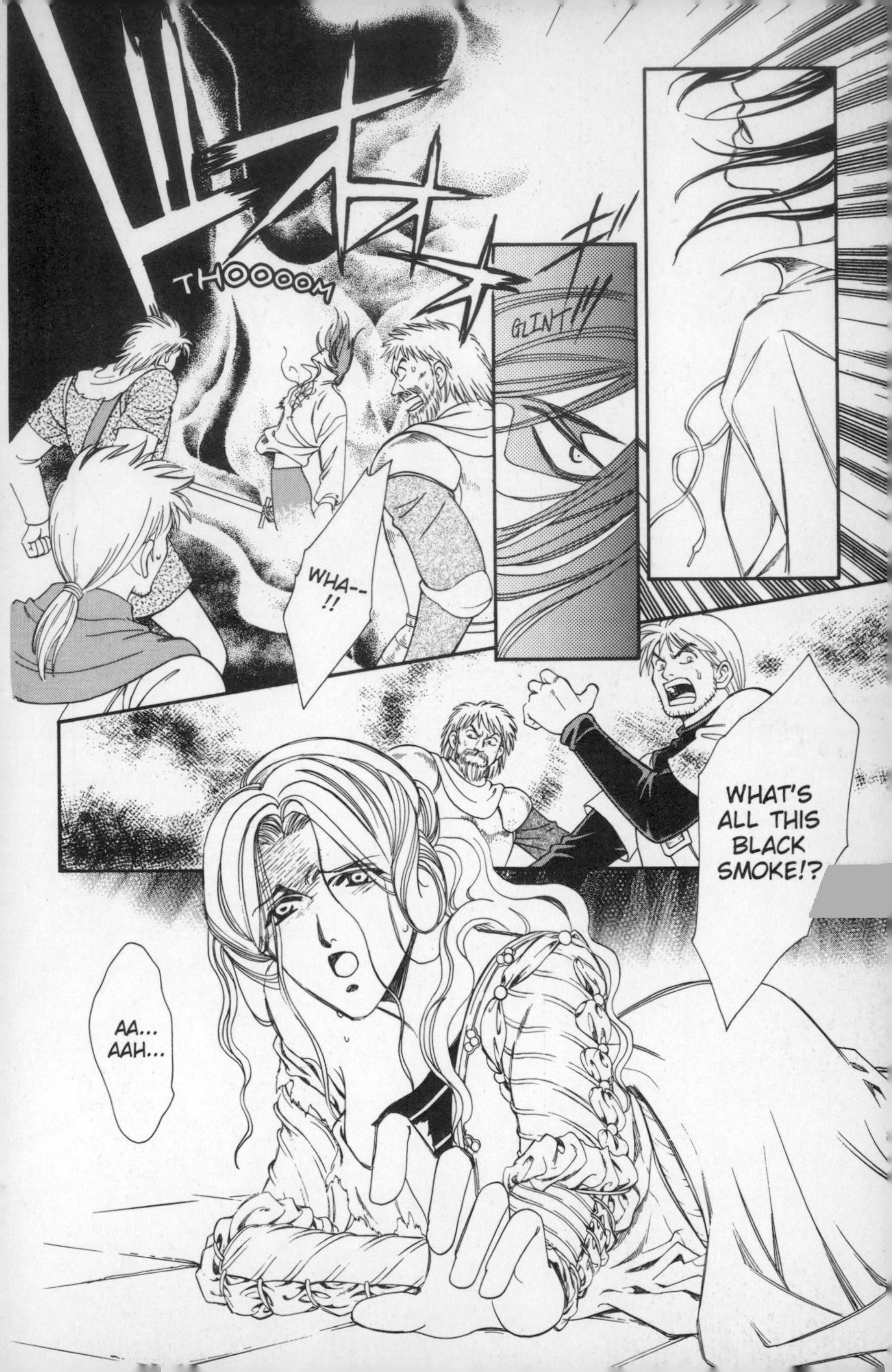
GLINT!!
THOOOOM
WHA-- !!
WHAT'S ALL THIS BLACK SMOKE!?
AA... AAH...

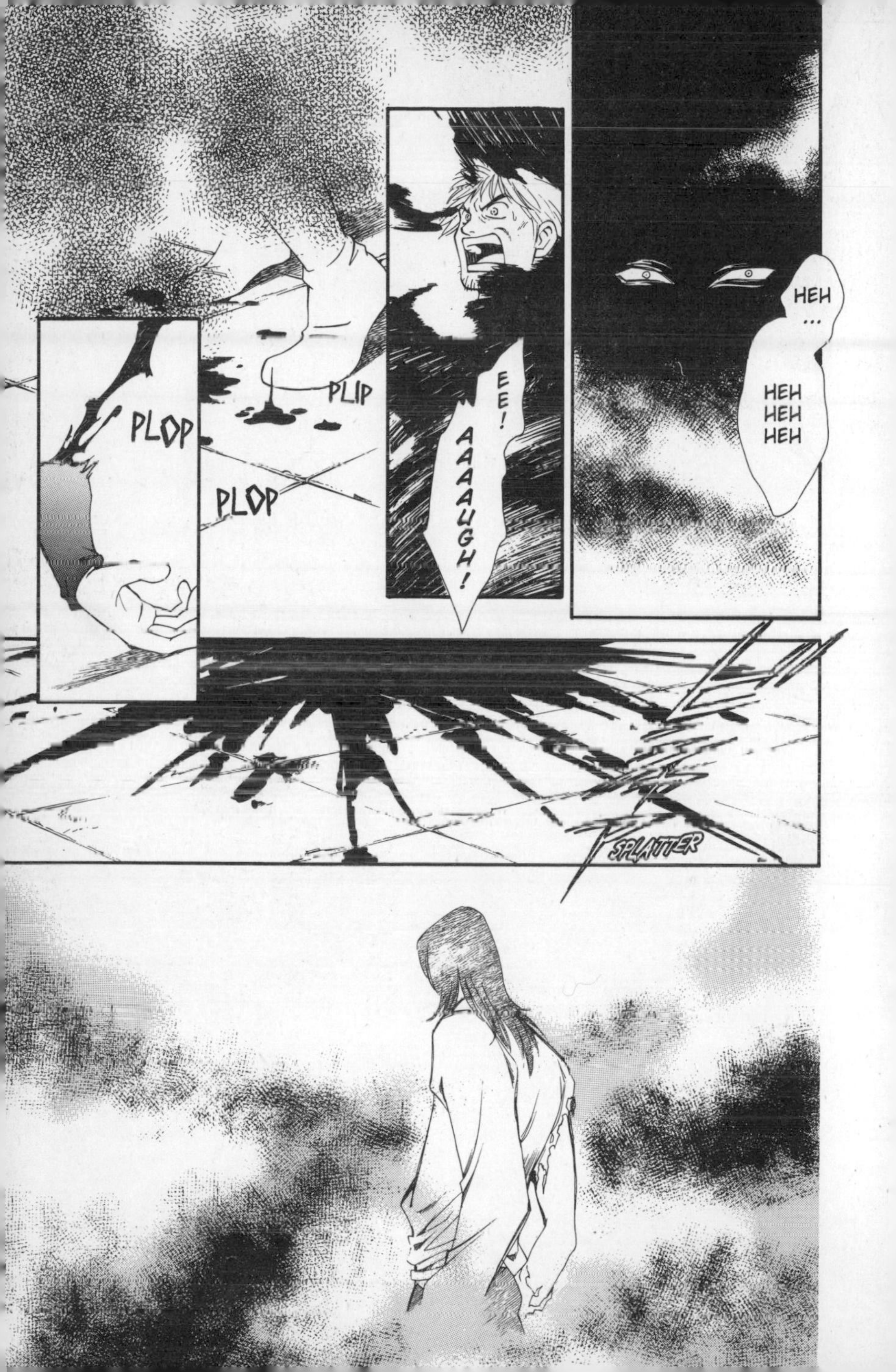
HEH ...
HEH HEH HEH
EE! AAAAAUGH!
PLIP
PLOP
PLOP
SPLATTER

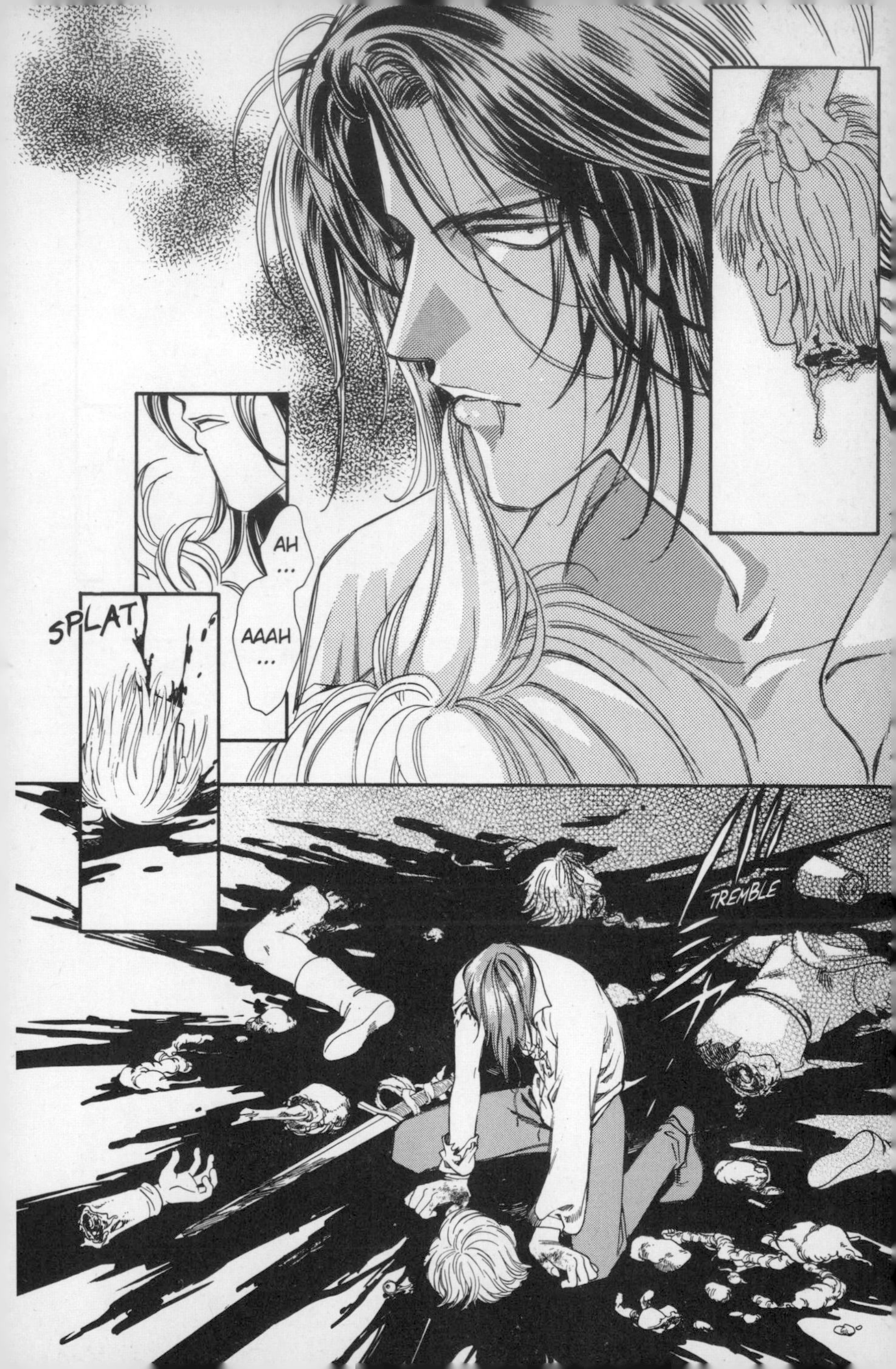
AH ...
AAAH ...
SPLAT
TREMBLE

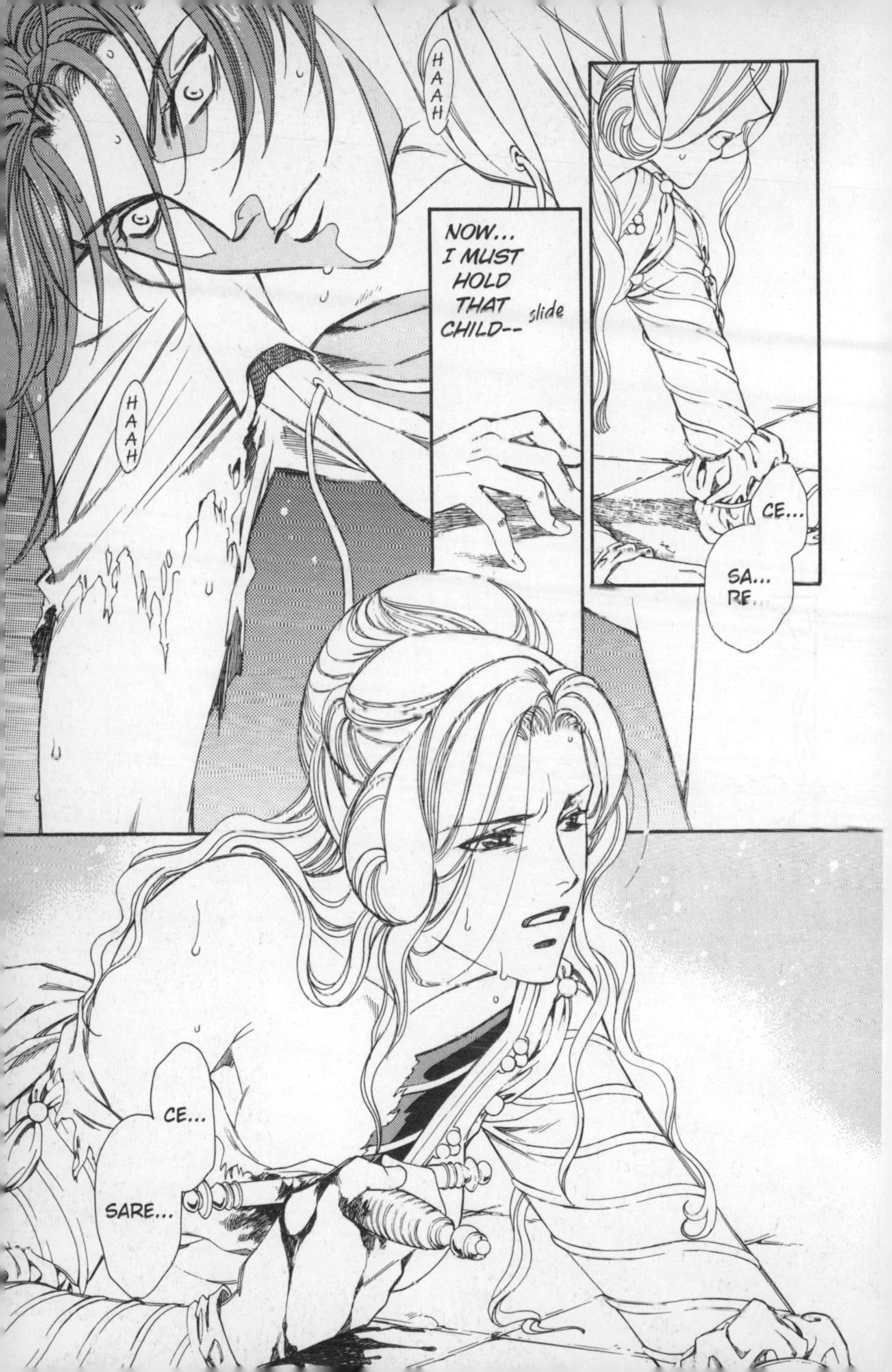
CE...
SA... RE...
HAAH
NOW... I MUST HOLD THAT CHILD--
slide
HAAH
CE...
SARE...

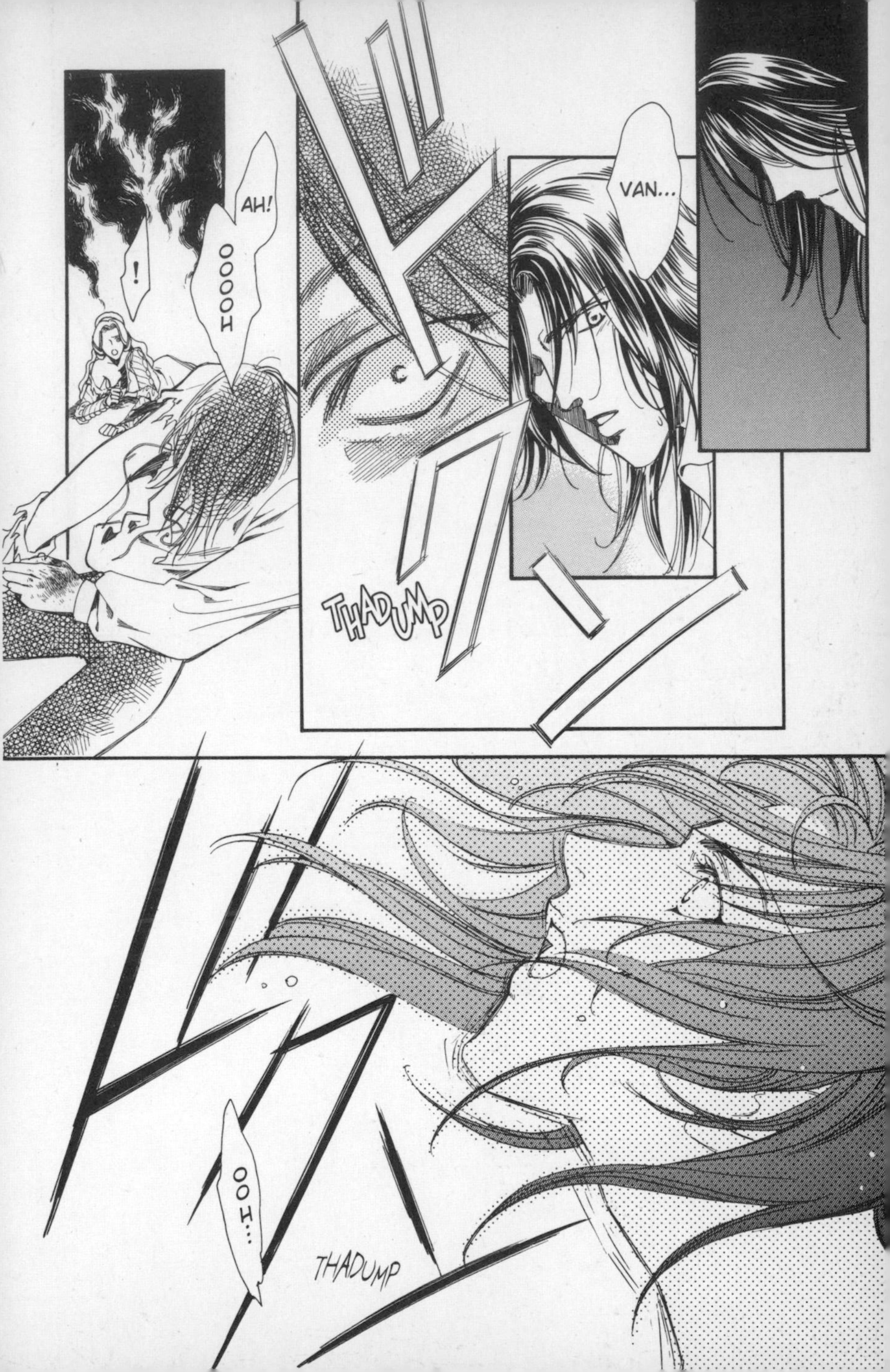

VAN...
THADUMP
AH!
OOOOH
!
OOH...
THADUMP

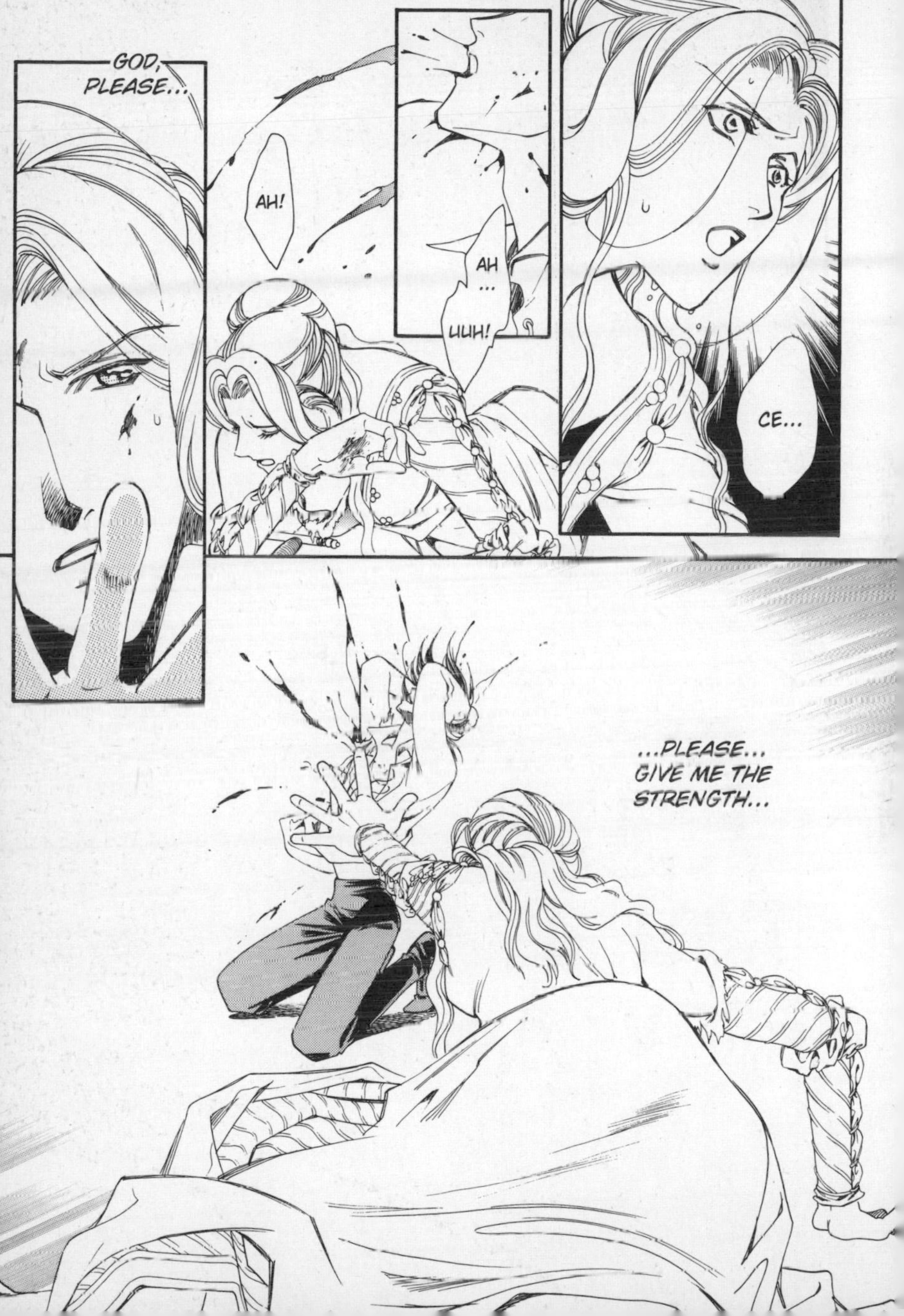
CE...
AH
...
UUH!
AH!
GOD, PLEASE...
...PLEASE... GIVE ME THE STRENGTH...

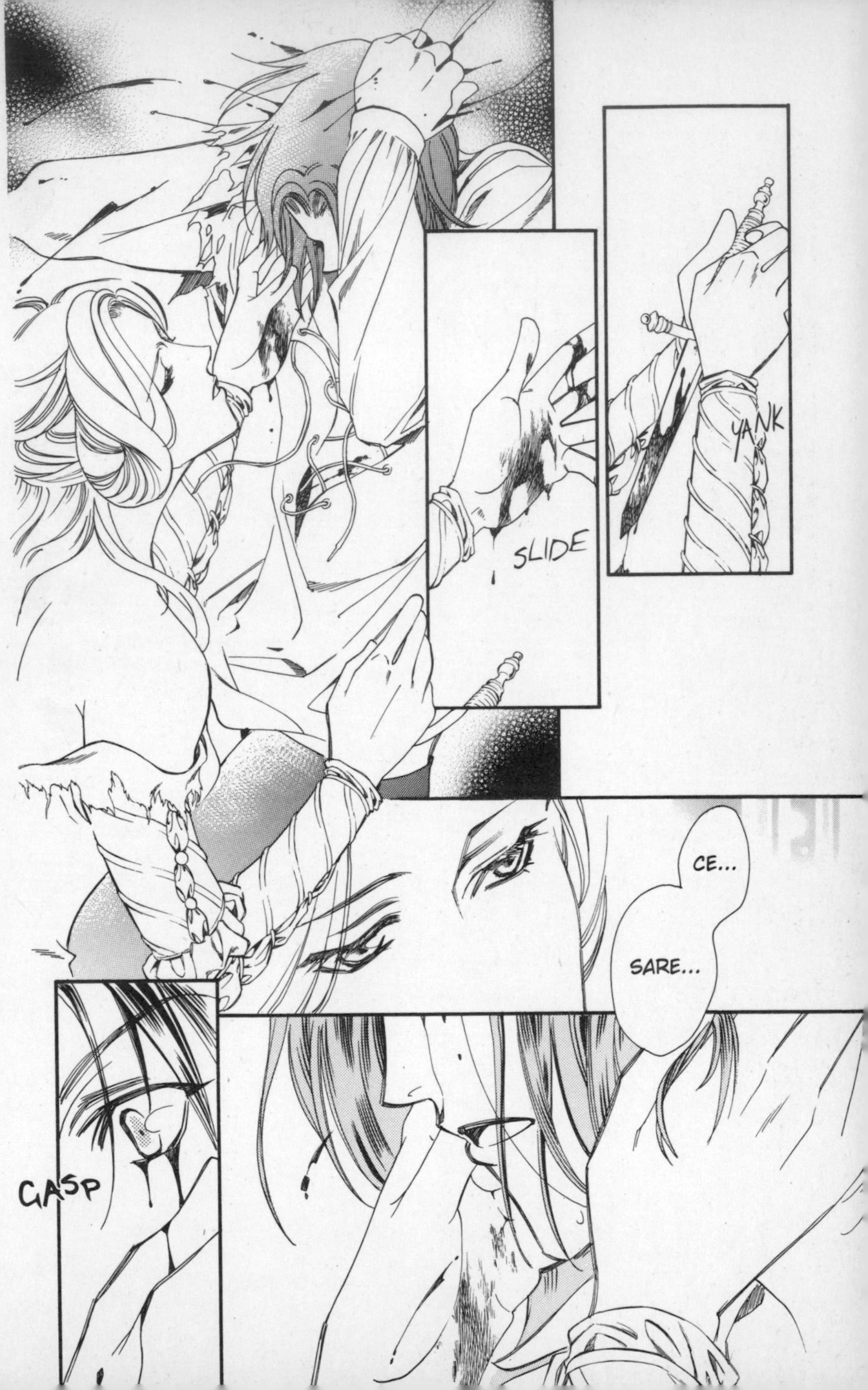
YANK
SLIDE
CE...
SARE...
GASP

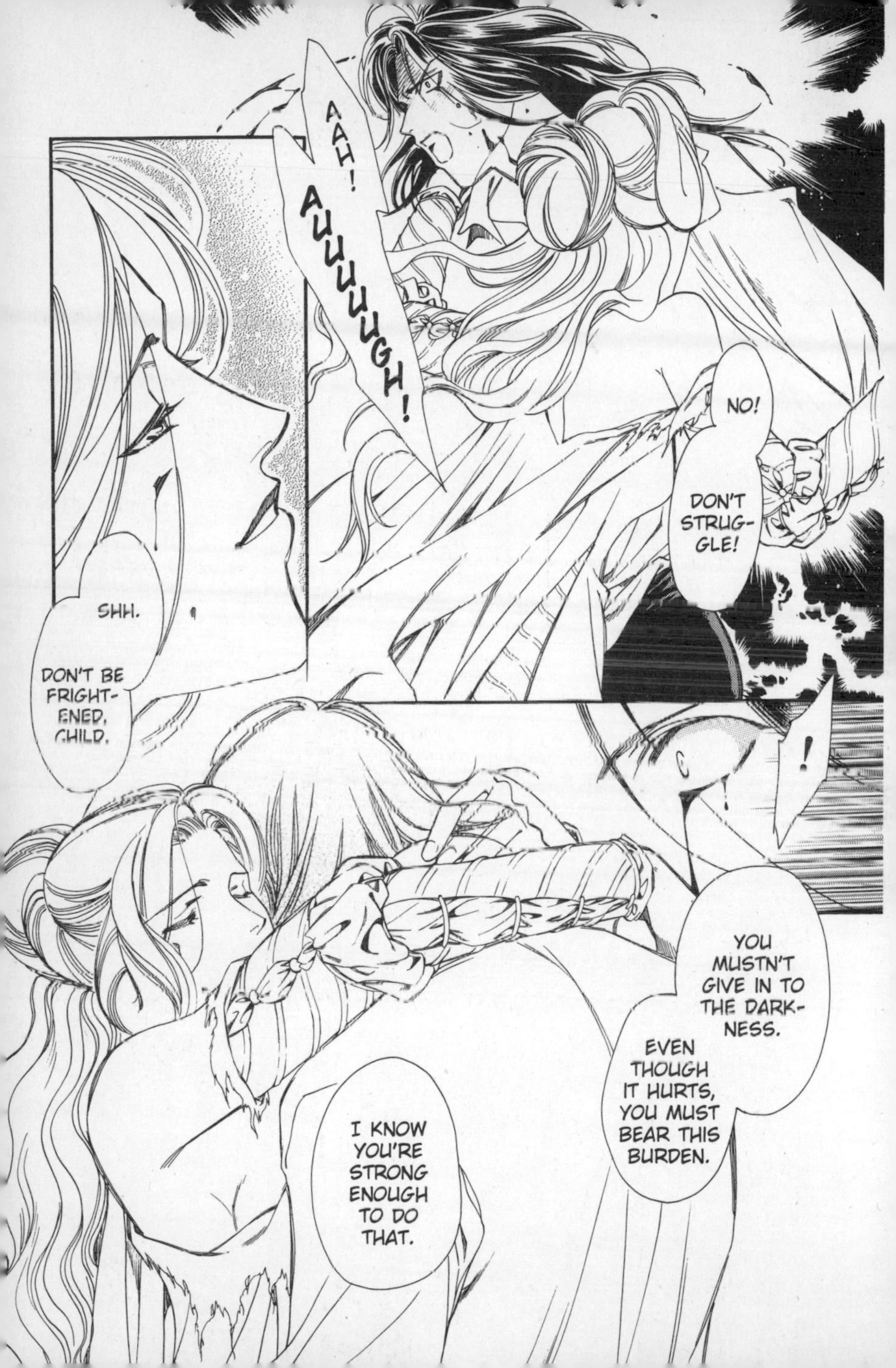
AAH!
AUUUUUGH!
NO!
DON'T STRUG-GLE!
!
SHH.
DON'T BE FRIGHT-ENED, CHILD.
YOU MUSTN'T GIVE IN TO THE DARK-NESS.
EVEN THOUGH IT HURTS, YOU MUST BEAR THIS BURDEN.
I KNOW YOU'RE STRONG ENOUGH TO DO THAT.

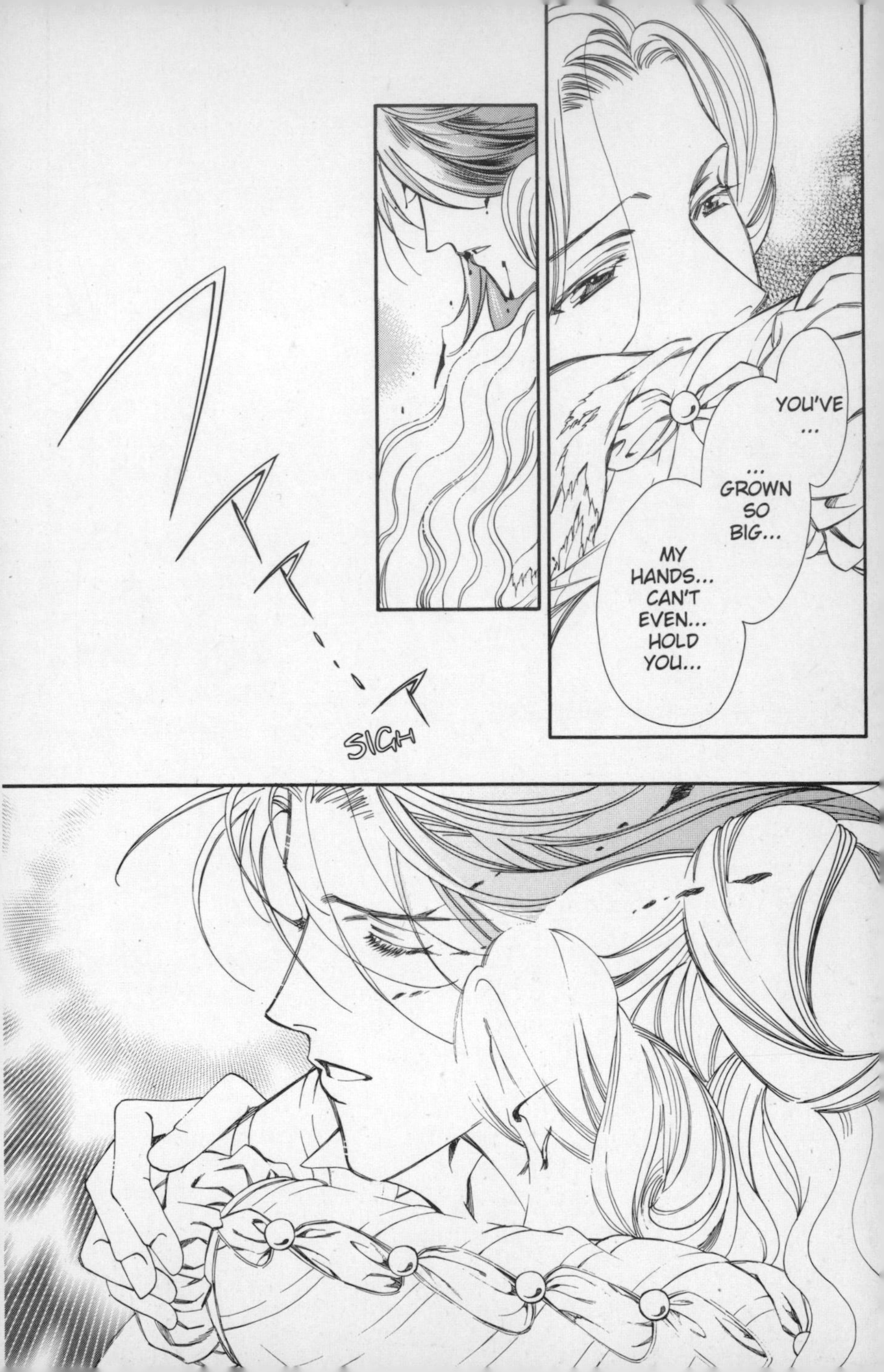

YOU'VE ...
... GROWN SO BIG...
MY HANDS... CAN'T EVEN... HOLD YOU...
SIGH
...

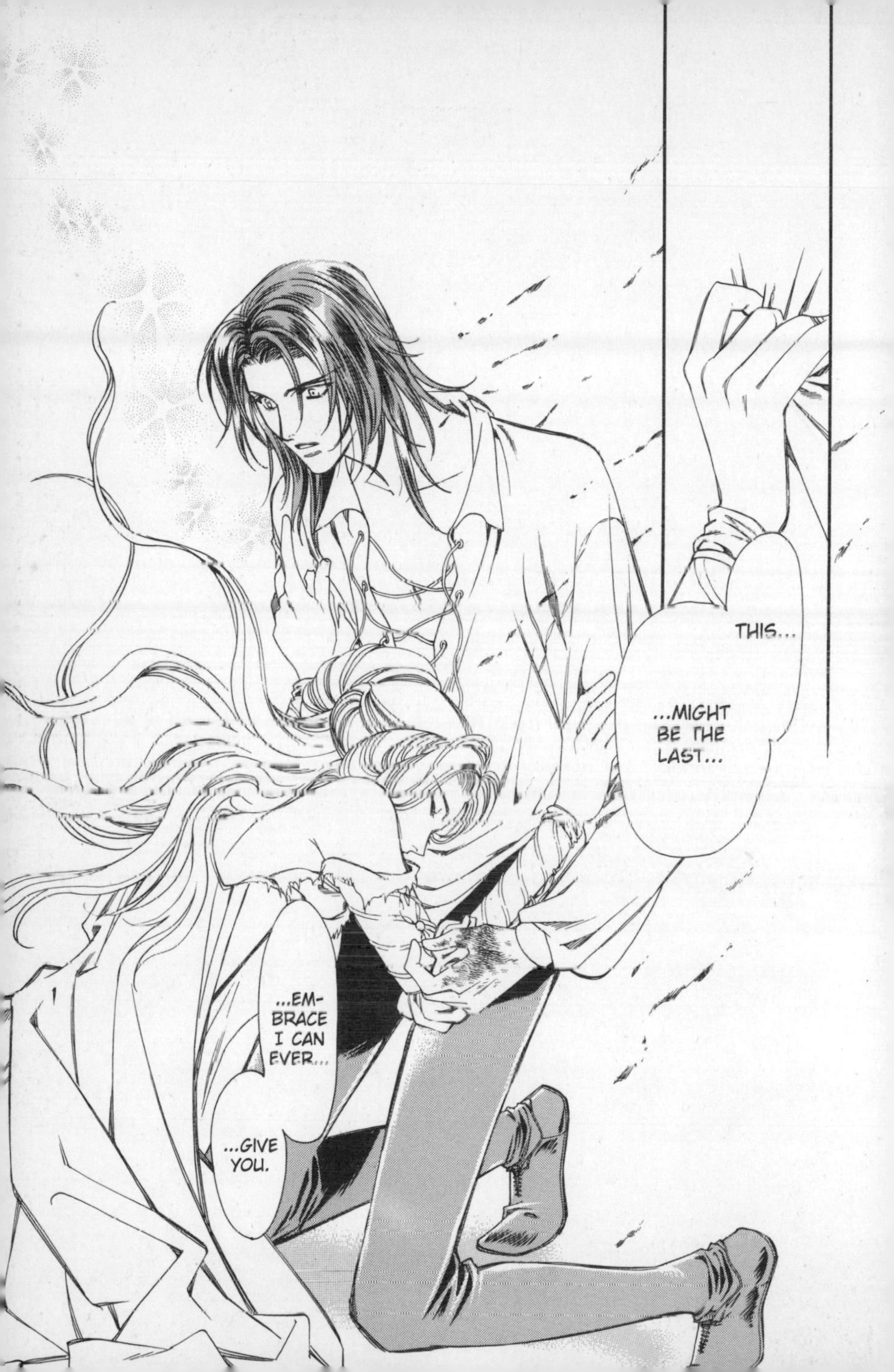
THIS...
...MIGHT BE THE LAST...
...EM-BRACE I CAN EVER...
...GIVE YOU.

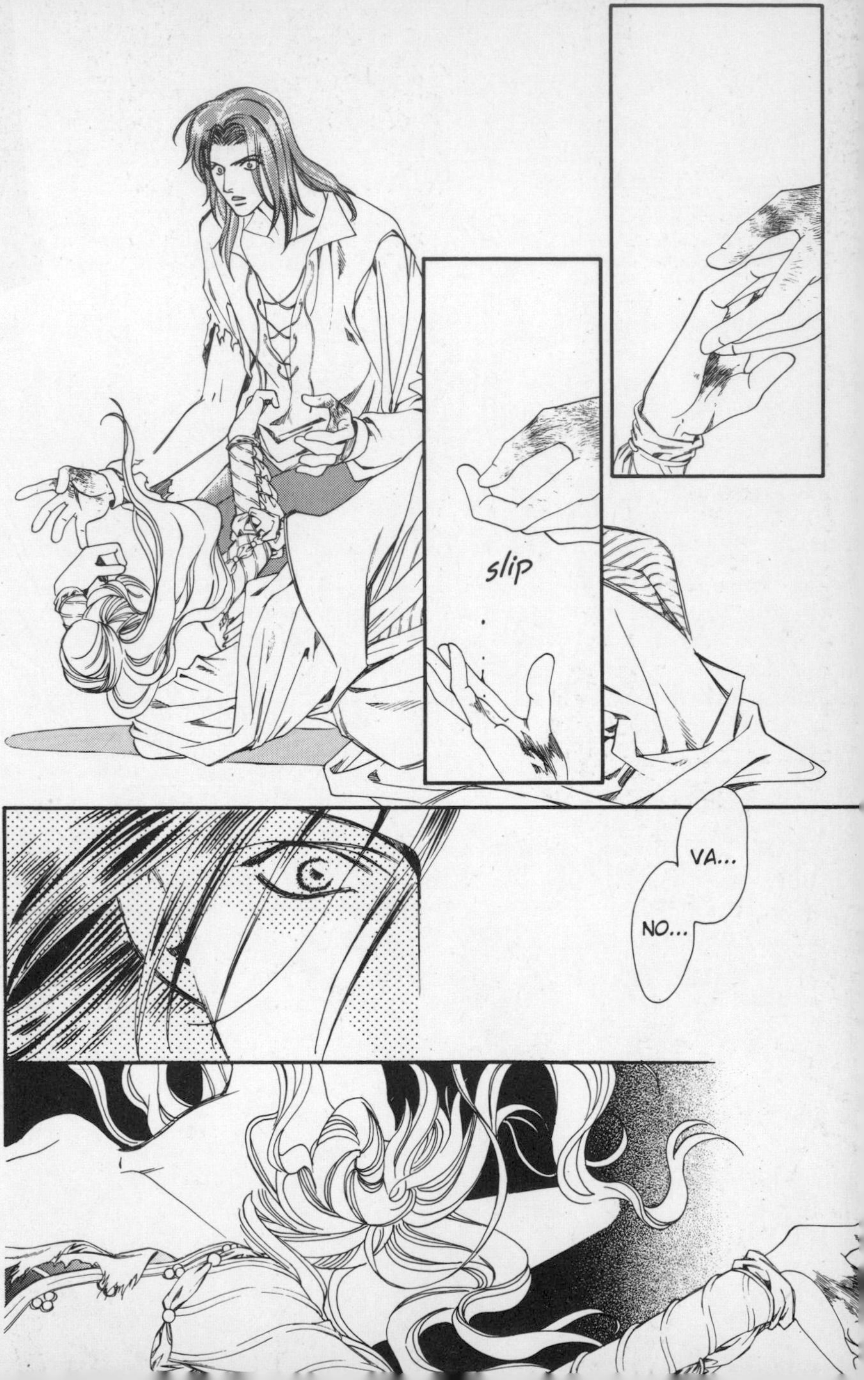
slip
VA... NO...

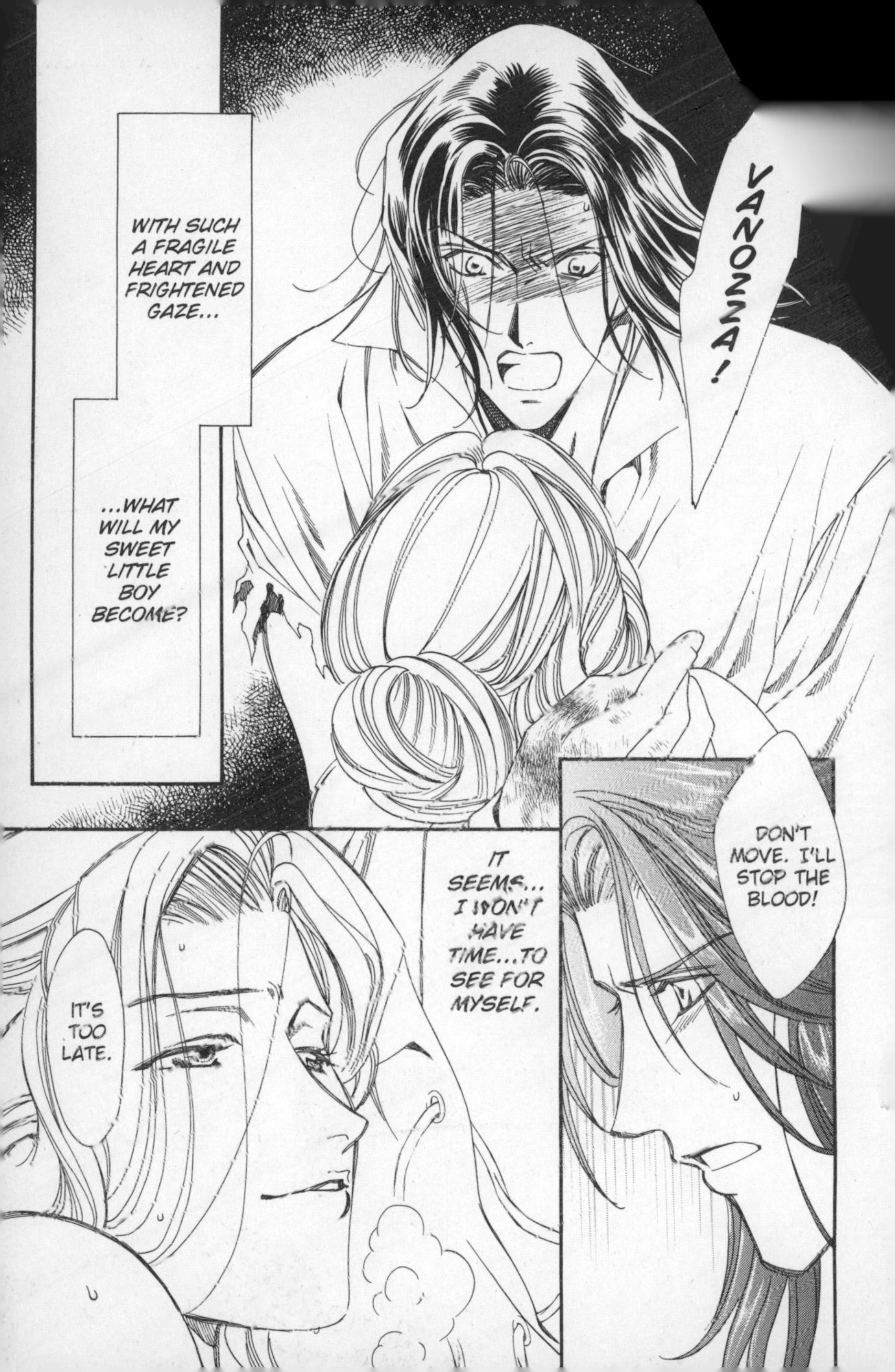
VANOZZA!
WITH SUCH A FRAGILE HEART AND FRIGHTENED GAZE...
...WHAT WILL MY SWEET LITTLE BOY BECOME?
DON'T MOVE. I'LL STOP THE BLOOD!
IT SEEMS... I WON'T HAVE TIME...TO SEE FOR MYSELF.
IT'S TOO LATE.

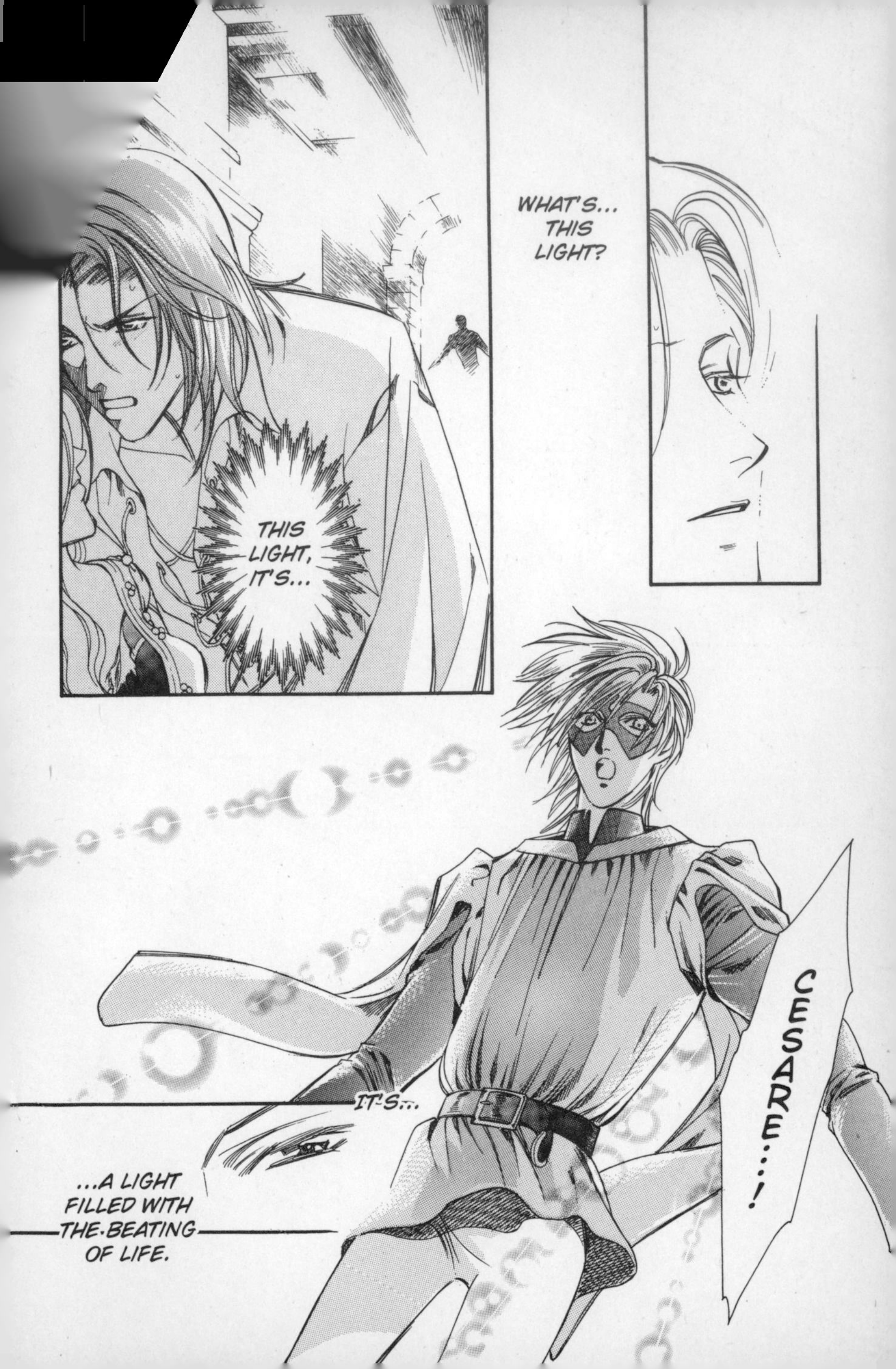
WHAT'S... THIS LIGHT?
THIS LIGHT, IT'S...
CESARE...!
IT'S...
...A LIGHT FILLED WITH THE BEATING OF LIFE.

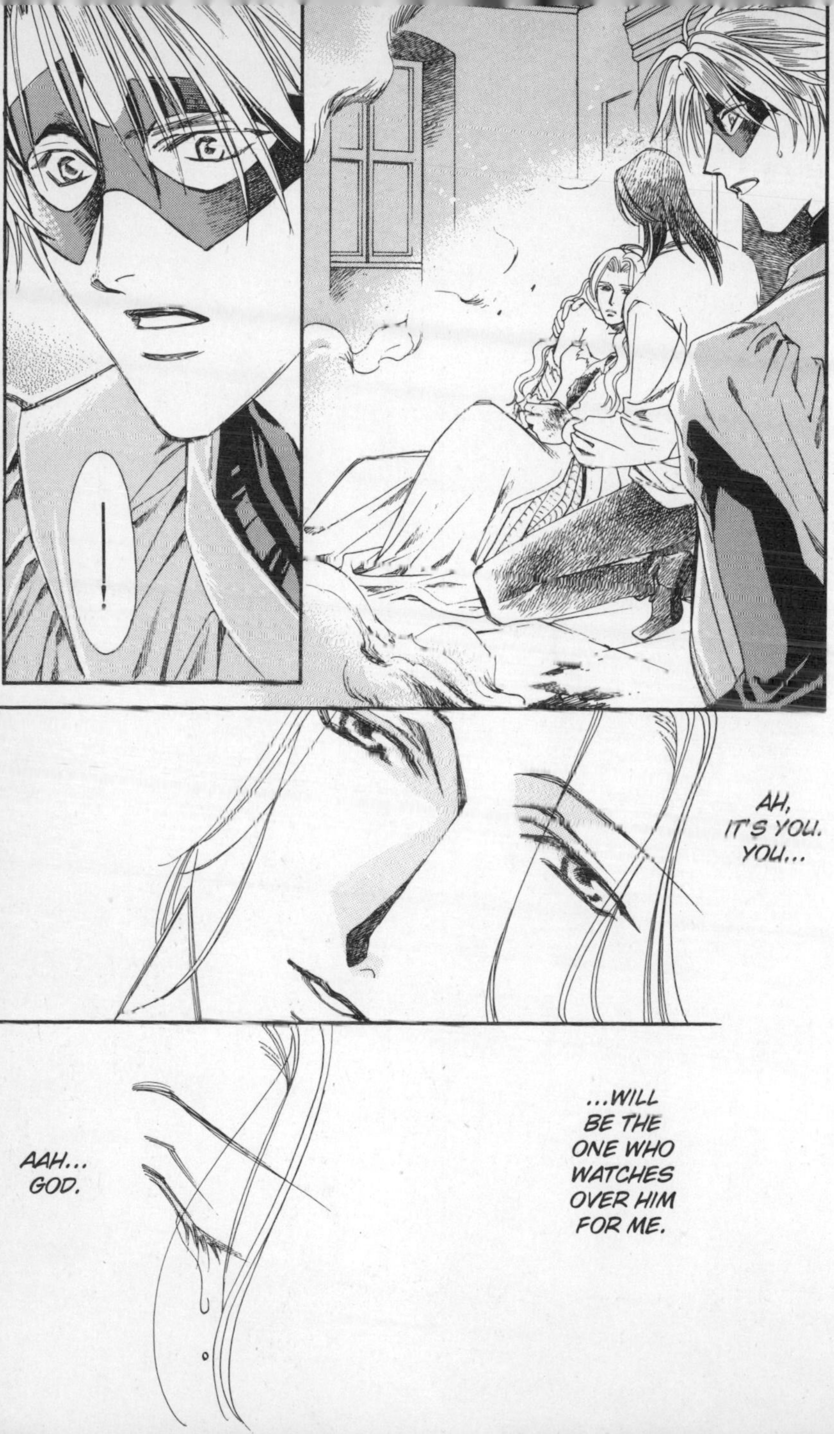
!
AH, IT'S YOU. YOU...
...WILL BE THE ONE WHO WATCHES OVER HIM FOR ME.
AAH... GOD.

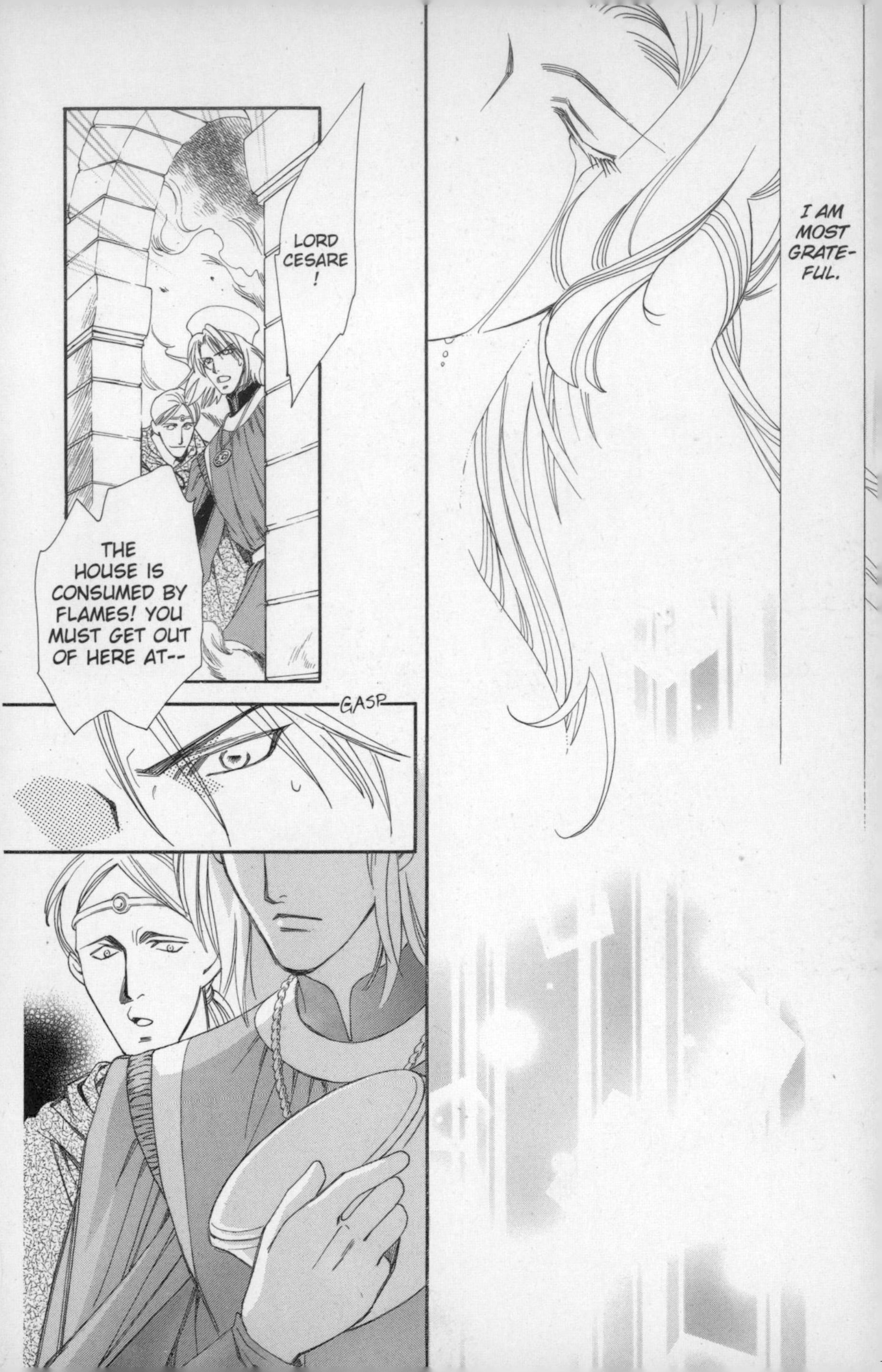
I AM MOST GRATE-FUL.
LORD CESARE!
THE HOUSE IS CONSUMED BY FLAMES! YOU MUST GET OUT OF HERE AT--
GASP

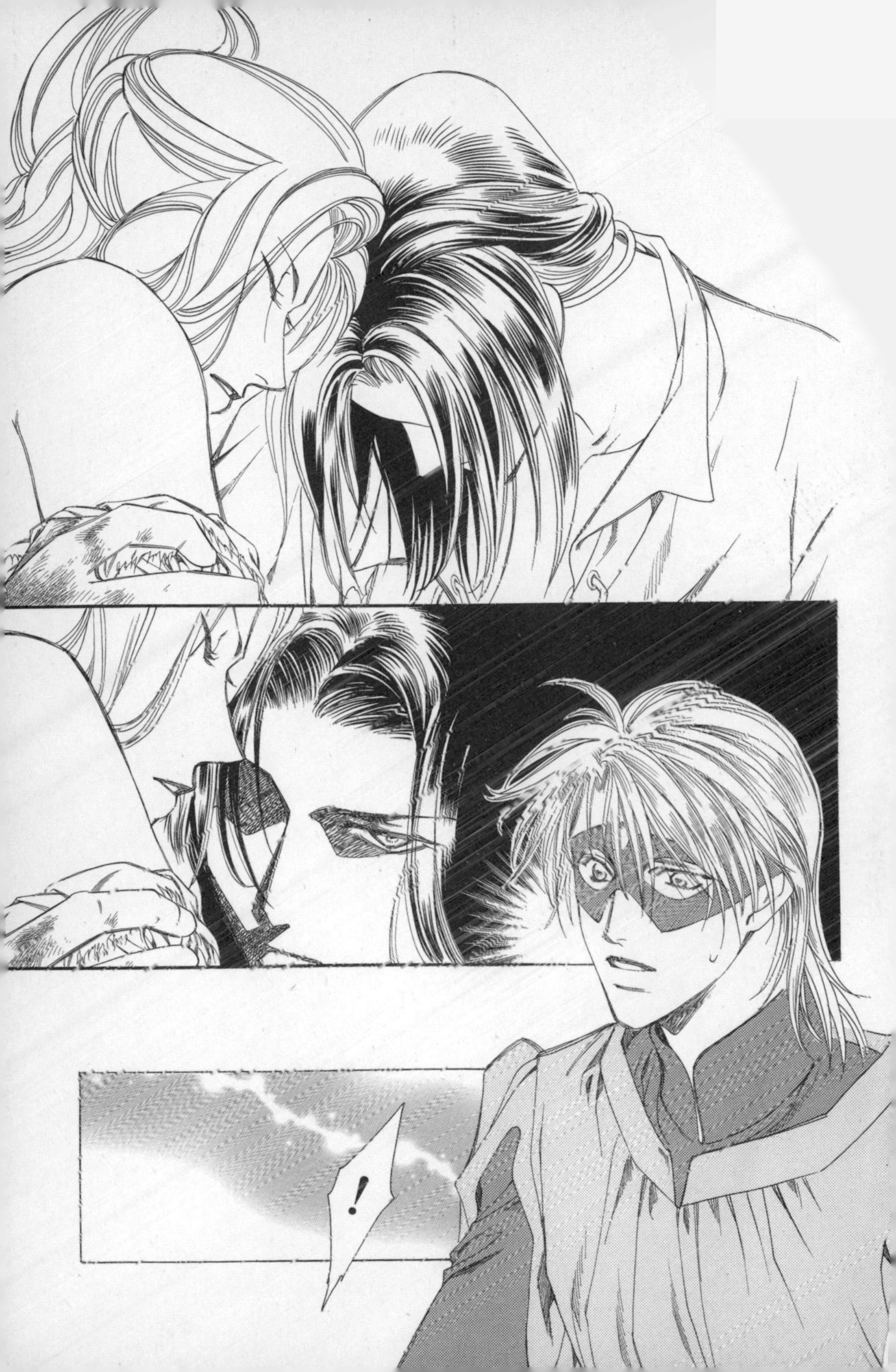
!

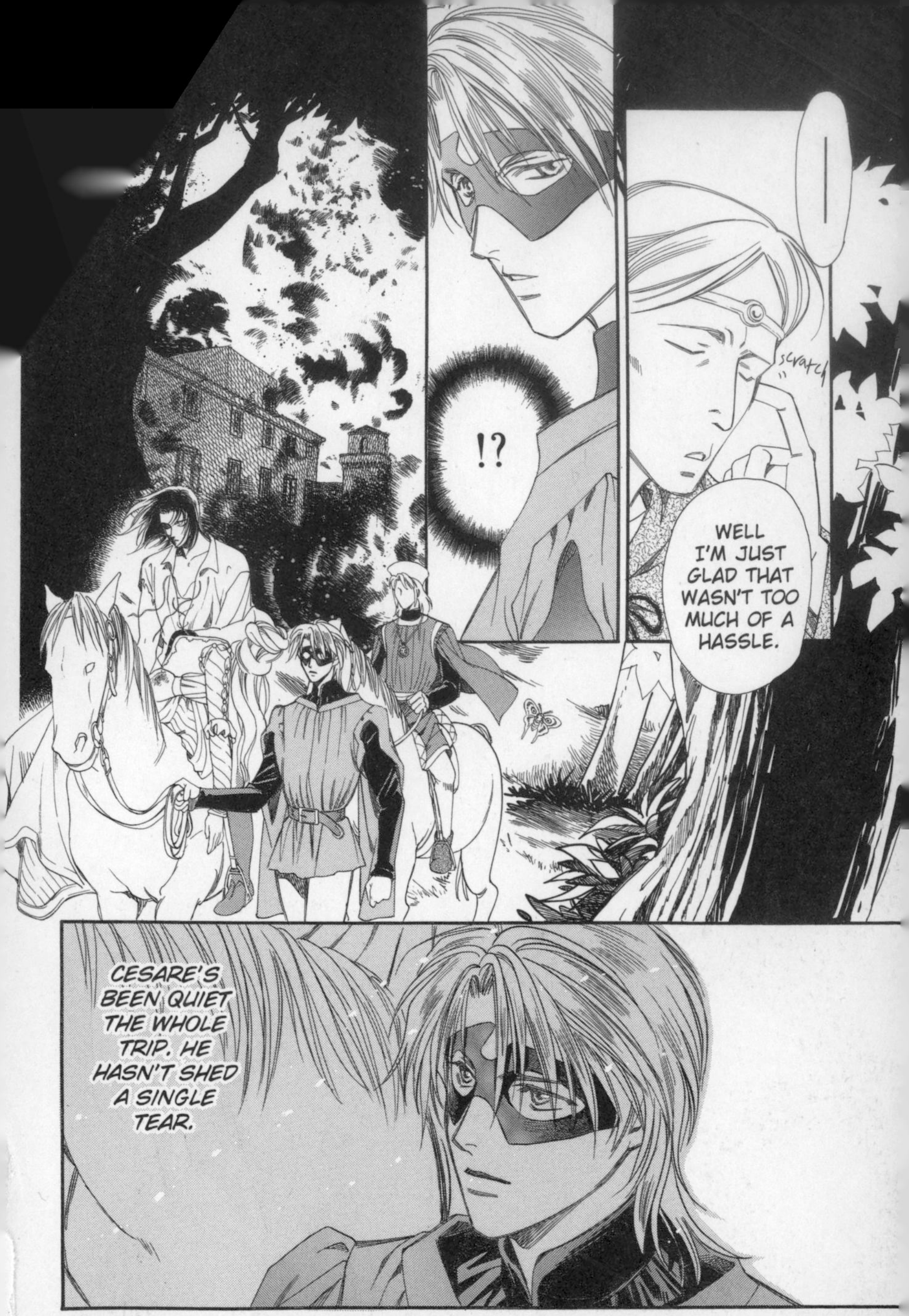
...
scratch
WELL I'M JUST GLAD THAT WASN'T TOO MUCH OF A HASSLE.
!?
CESARE'S BEEN QUIET THE WHOLE TRIP. HE HASN'T SHED A SINGLE TEAR.

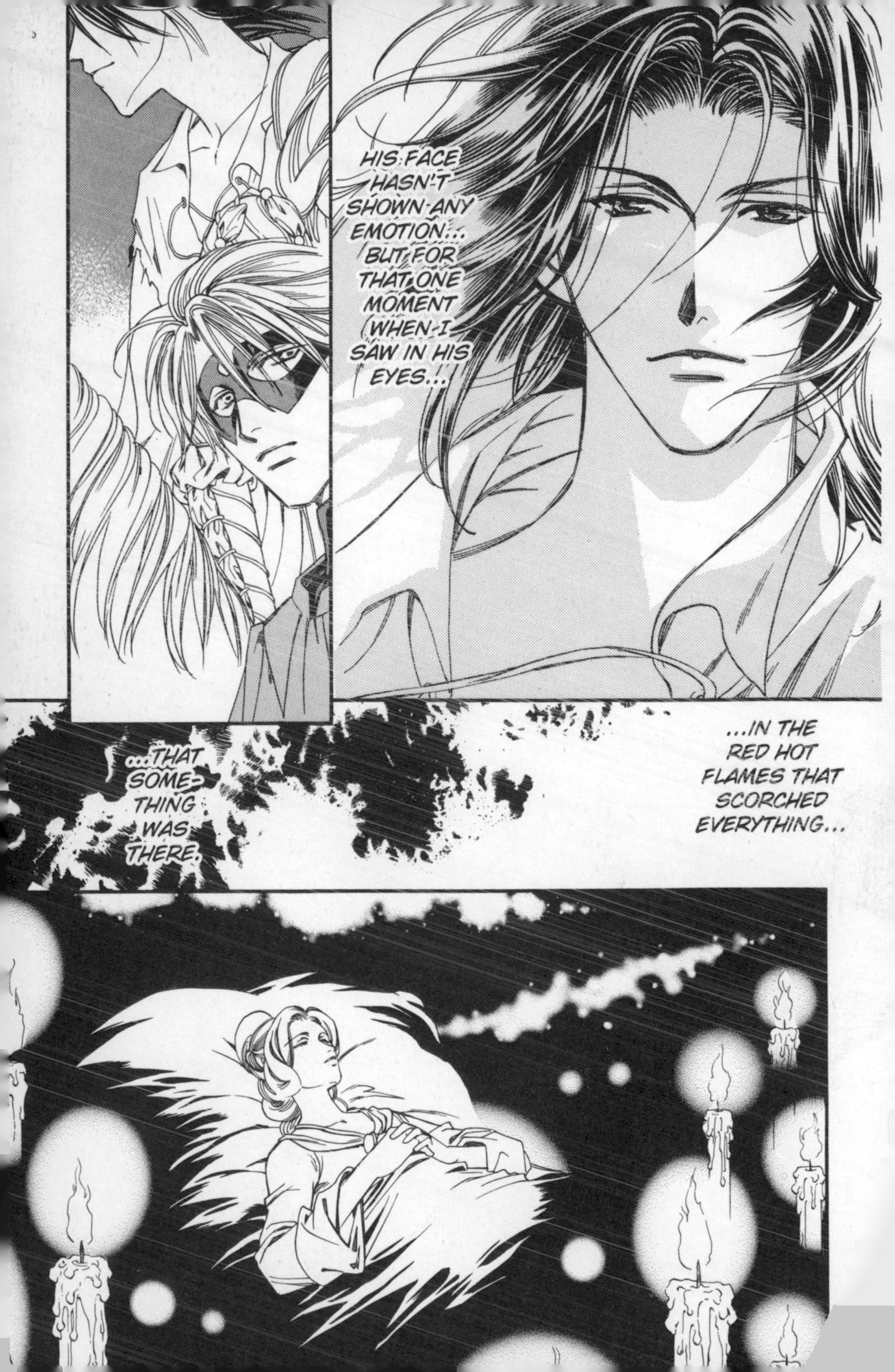
HIS FACE HASN'T SHOWN ANY EMOTION... BUT FOR THAT ONE MOMENT WHEN I SAW IN HIS EYES...
...IN THE RED HOT FLAMES THAT SCORCHED EVERYTHING...
...THAT SOME-THING WAS THERE.

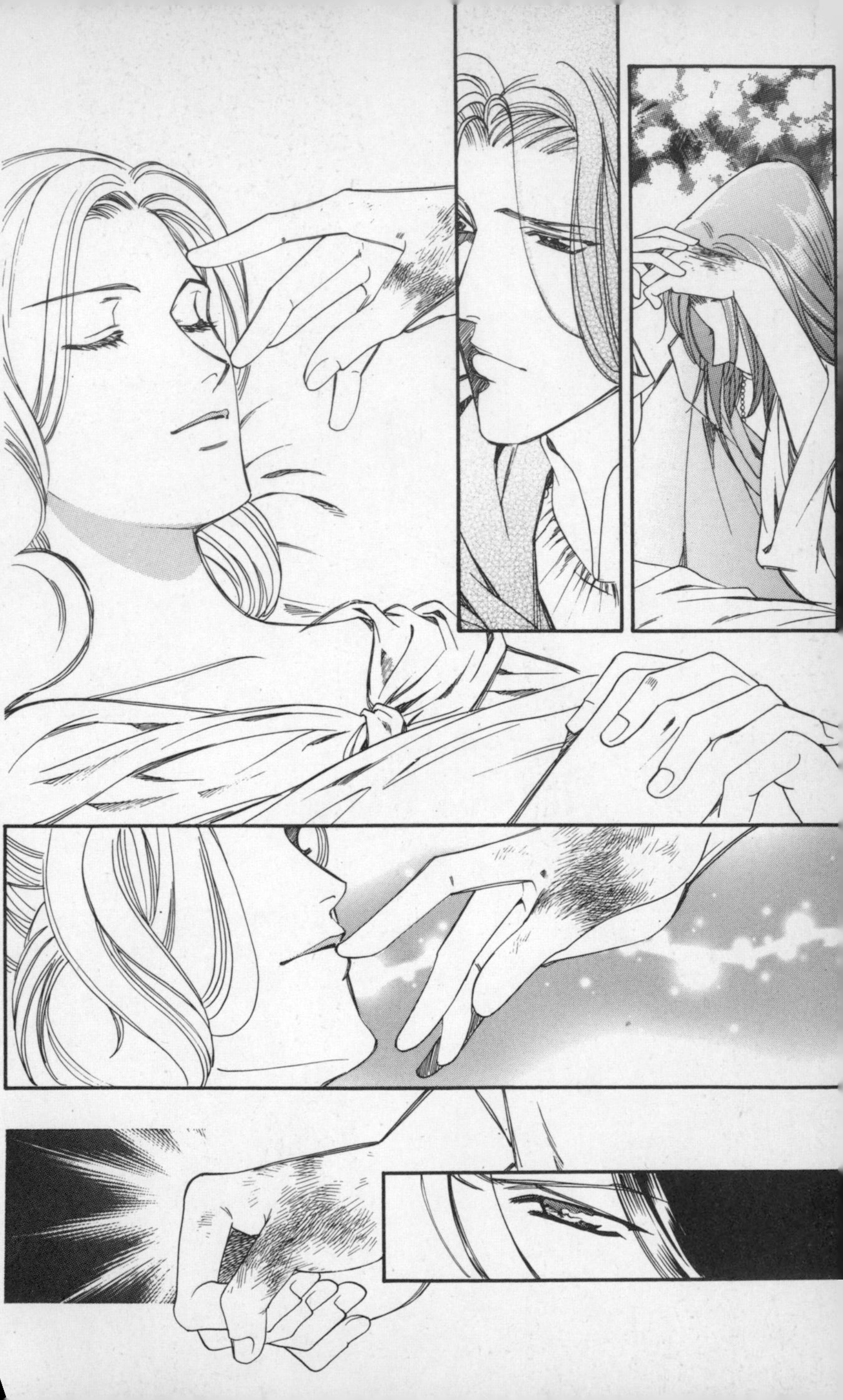

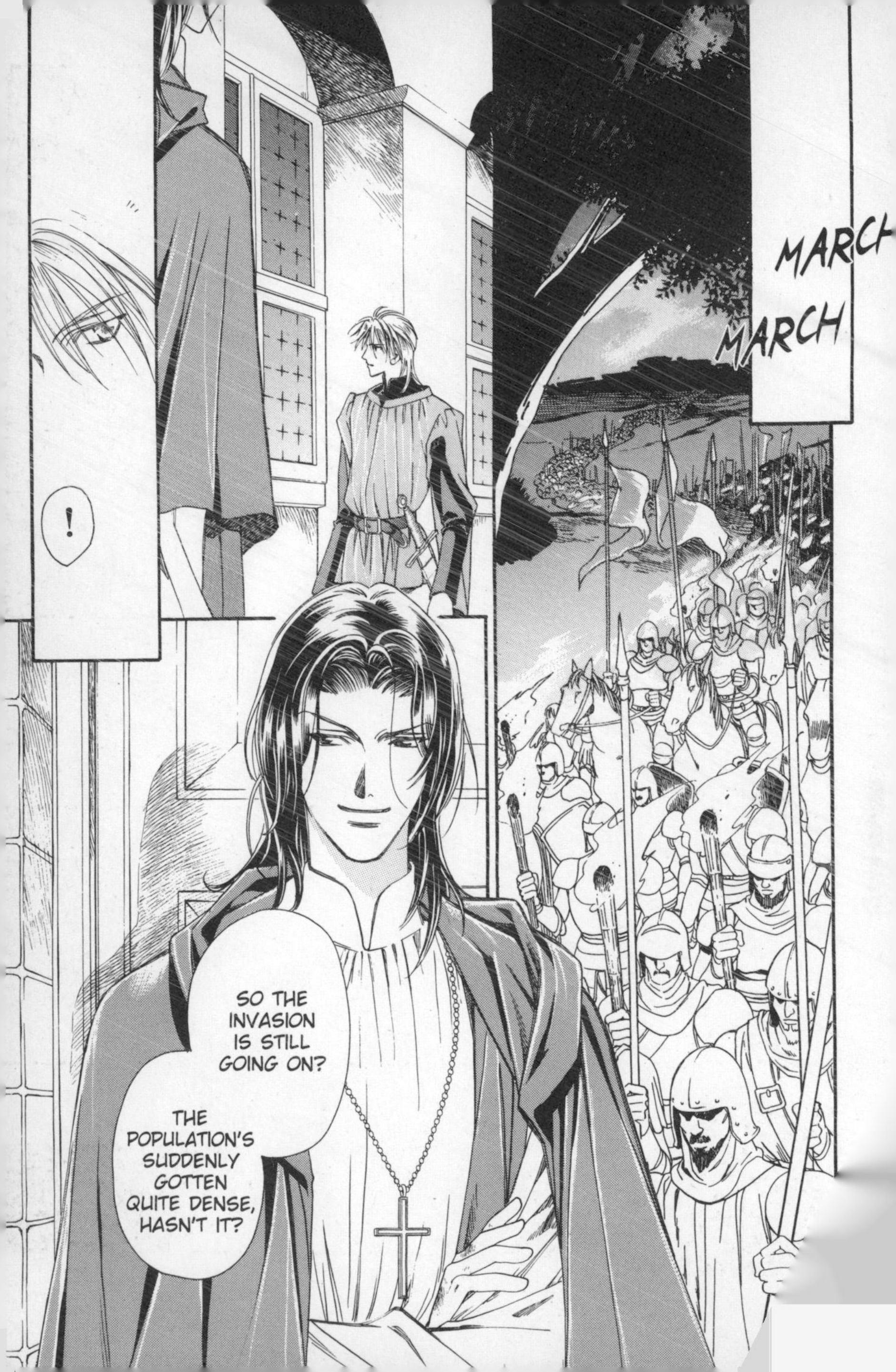
MARCH
MARCH
!
SO THE INVASION IS STILL GOING ON?
THE POPULATION'S SUDDENLY GOTTEN QUITE DENSE, HASN'T IT?

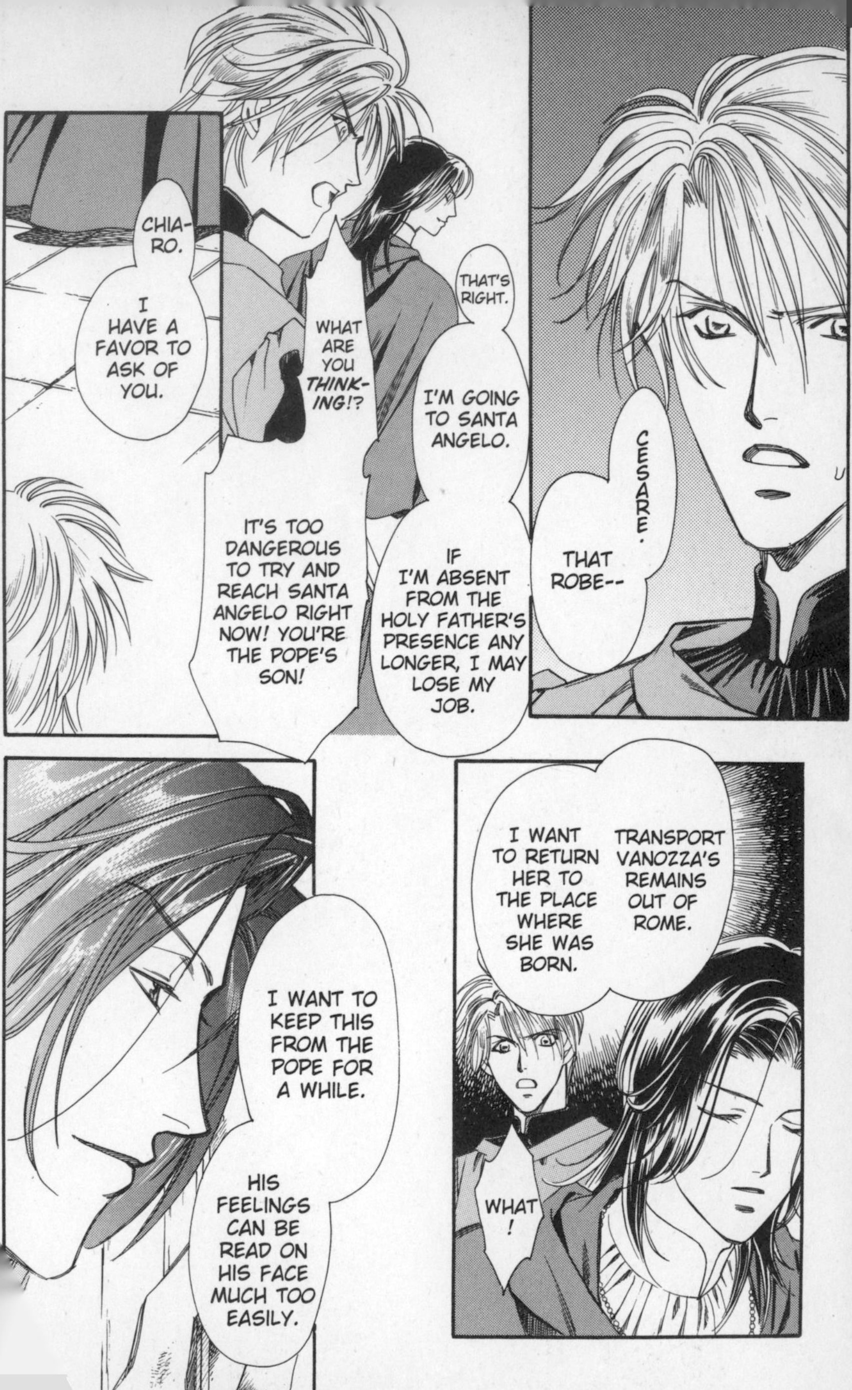
CESARE.
THAT ROBE--
THAT'S RIGHT.
I'M GOING TO SANTA ANGELO.
IF I'M ABSENT FROM THE HOLY FATHER'S PRESENCE ANY LONGER, I MAY LOSE MY JOB.
WHAT ARE YOU *THINKING*!?
IT'S TOO DANGEROUS TO TRY AND REACH SANTA ANGELO RIGHT NOW! YOU'RE THE POPE'S SON!
CHIARO.
I HAVE A FAVOR TO ASK OF YOU.
TRANSPORT VANOZZA'S REMAINS OUT OF ROME.
I WANT TO RETURN HER TO THE PLACE WHERE SHE WAS BORN.
WHAT!
I WANT TO KEEP THIS FROM THE POPE FOR A WHILE.
HIS FEELINGS CAN BE READ ON HIS FACE MUCH TOO EASILY.

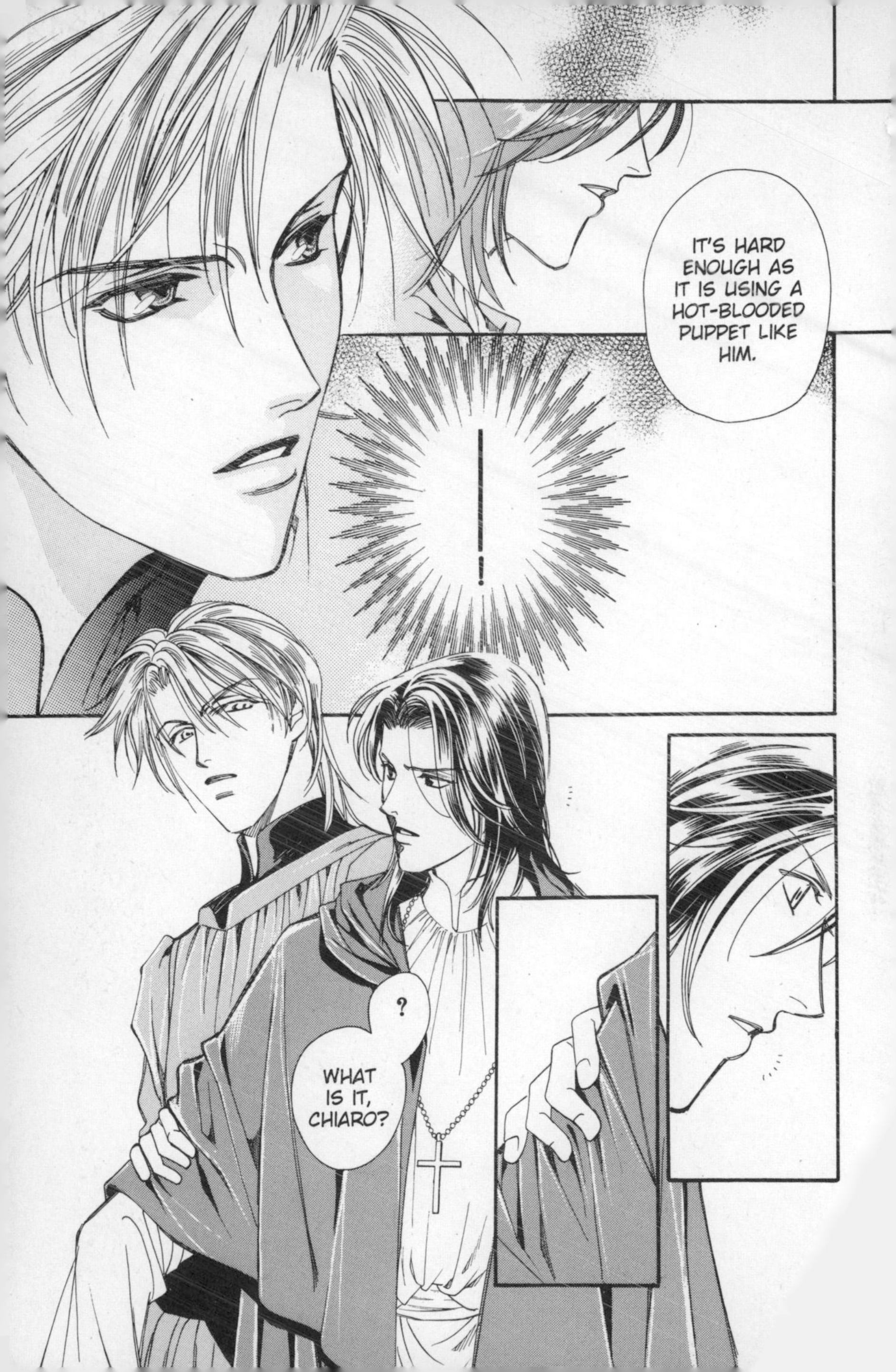
IT'S HARD ENOUGH AS IT IS USING A HOT-BLOODED PUPPET LIKE HIM.
!
?
WHAT IS IT, CHIARO?

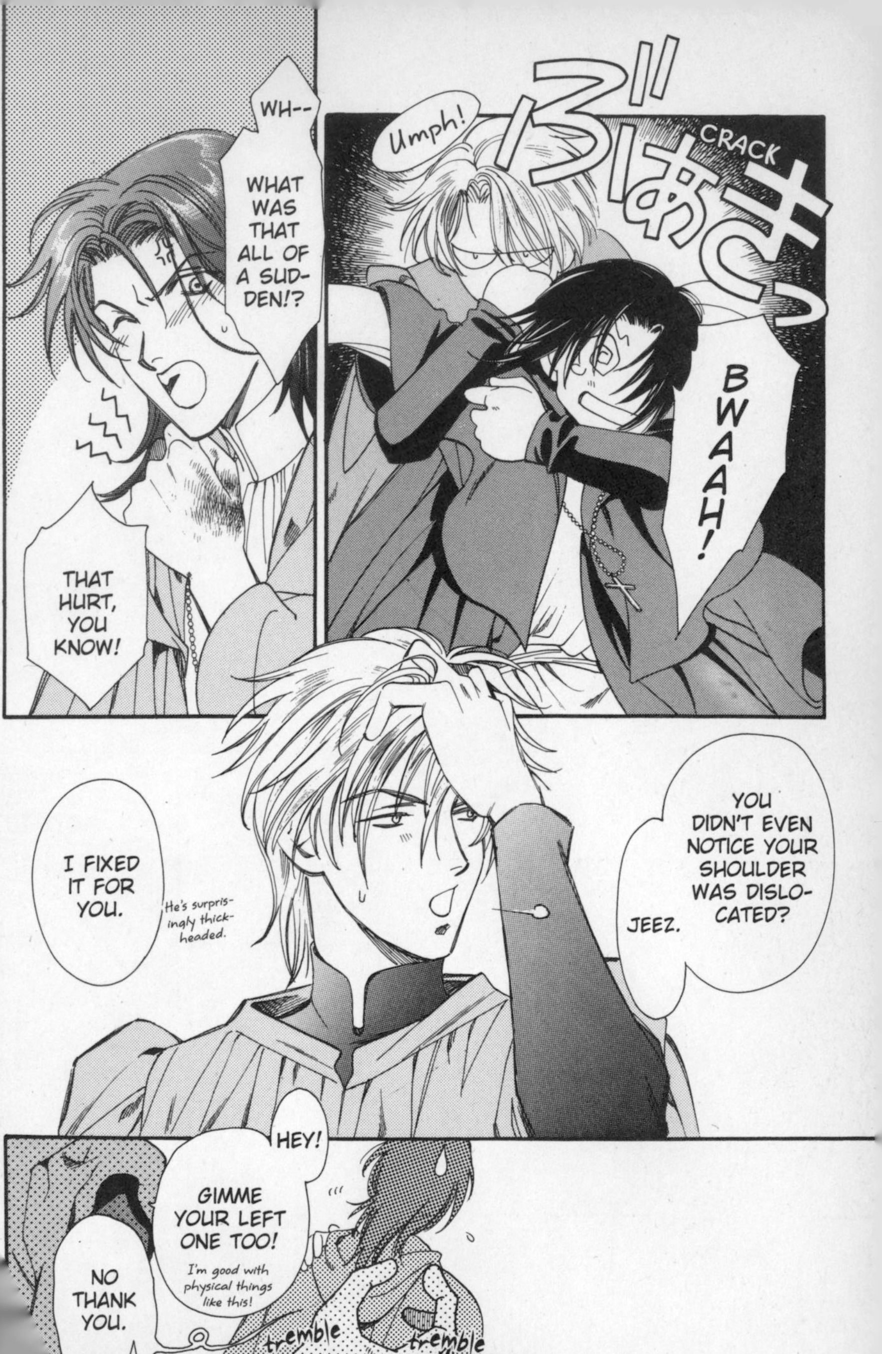
Umph!
CRACK
BWAAAH!
WH--
WHAT WAS THAT ALL OF A SUDDEN!?
THAT HURT, YOU KNOW!
YOU DIDN'T EVEN NOTICE YOUR SHOULDER WAS DISLOCATED?
JEEZ.
I FIXED IT FOR YOU.
He's surprisingly thickheaded.
HEY!
GIMME YOUR LEFT ONE TOO!
I'm good with physical things like this!
tremble
tremble
NO THANK YOU.

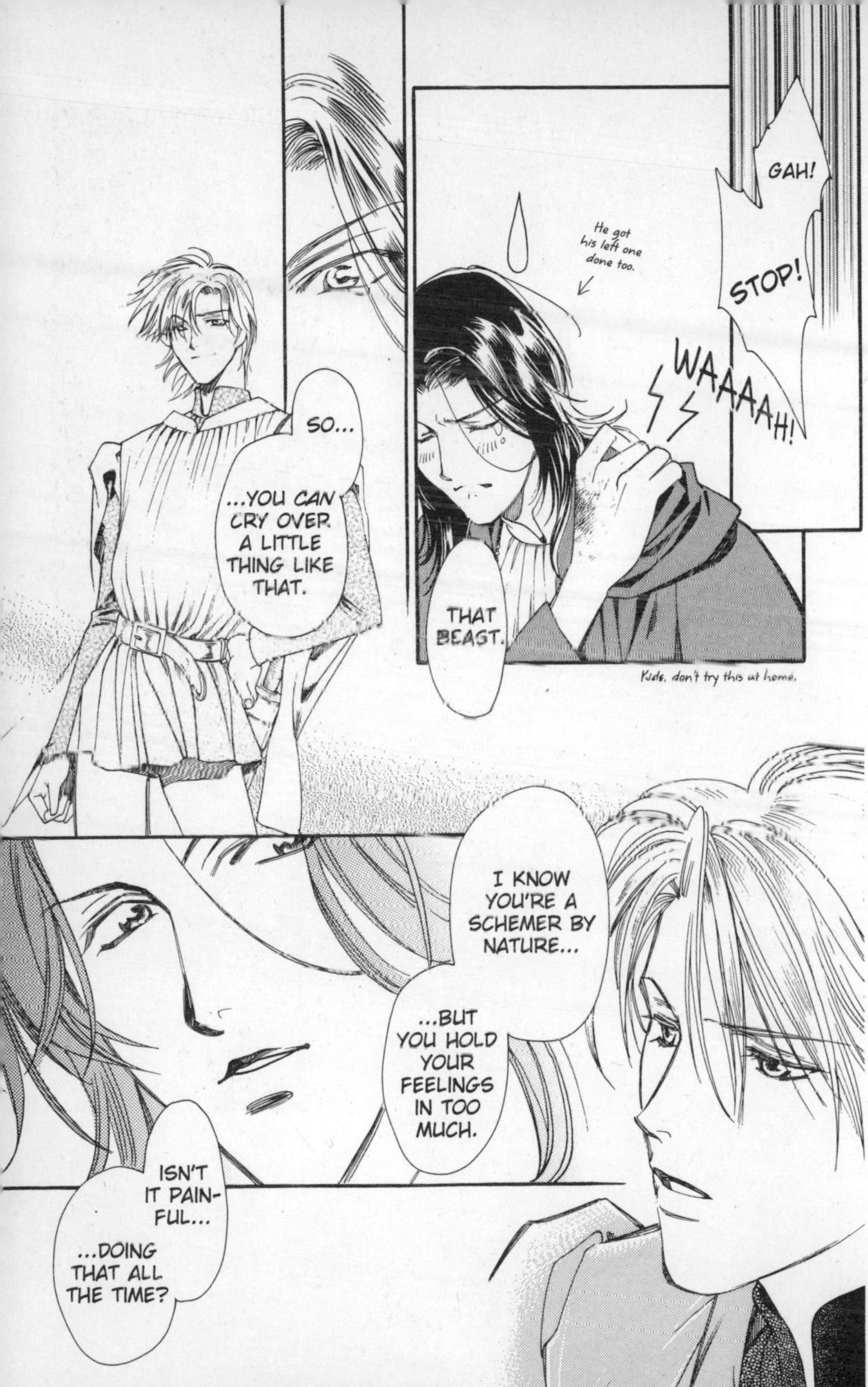
GAH!
STOP!
WAAAAAH!
He got his left one done too.
THAT BEAST.
Kids, don't try this at home.
SO...
...YOU CAN CRY OVER A LITTLE THING LIKE THAT.
I KNOW YOU'RE A SCHEMER BY NATURE...
...BUT YOU HOLD YOUR FEELINGS IN TOO MUCH.
ISN'T IT PAIN-FUL...
...DOING THAT ALL THE TIME?

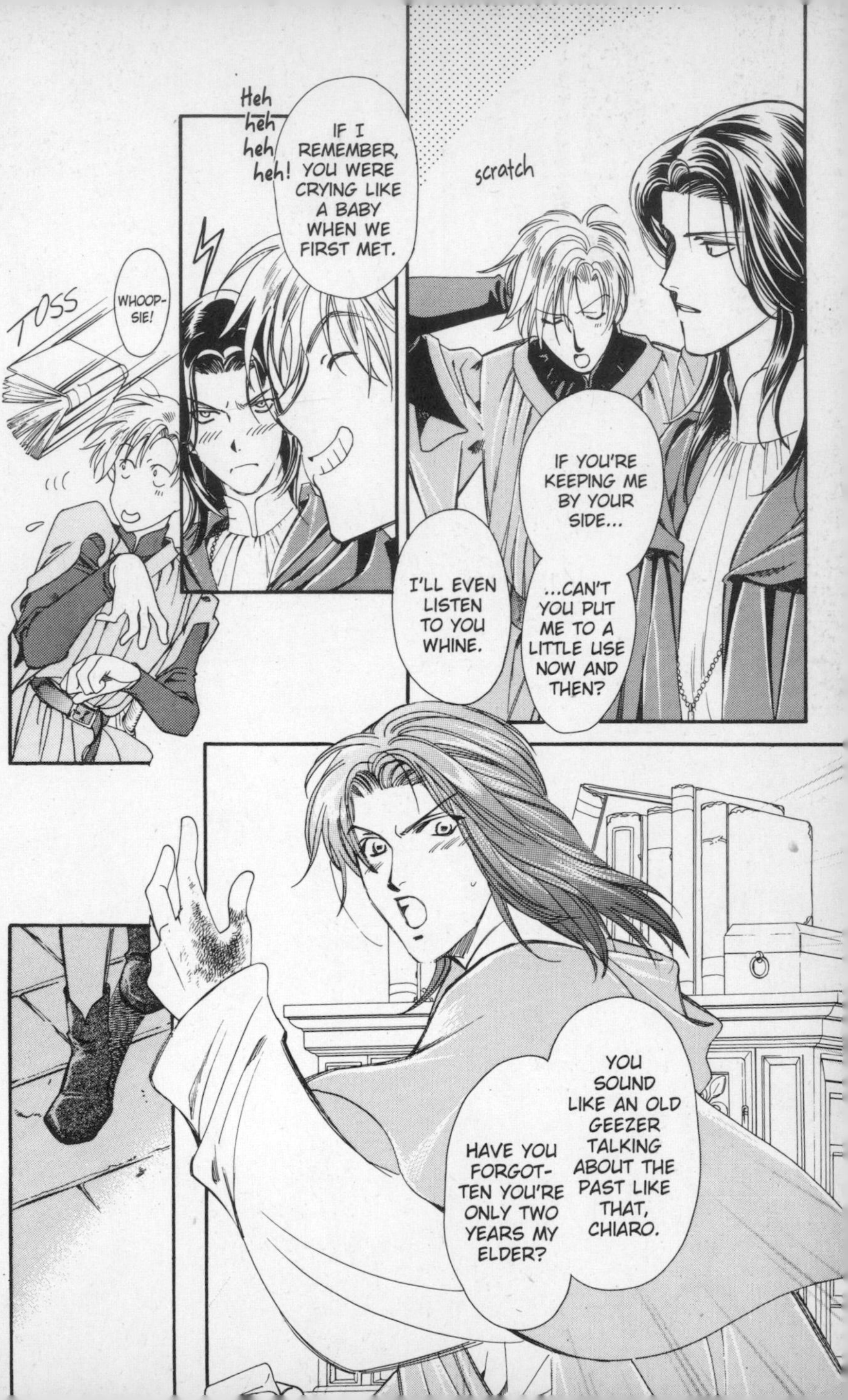
scratch
IF YOU'RE KEEPING ME BY YOUR SIDE...
...CAN'T YOU PUT ME TO A LITTLE USE NOW AND THEN?
I'LL EVEN LISTEN TO YOU WHINE.
Heh heh heh heh!
IF I REMEMBER, YOU WERE CRYING LIKE A BABY WHEN WE FIRST MET.
TOSS
WHOOP-SIE!
YOU SOUND LIKE AN OLD GEEZER TALKING ABOUT THE PAST LIKE THAT, CHIARO.
HAVE YOU FORGOT-TEN YOU'RE ONLY TWO YEARS MY ELDER?

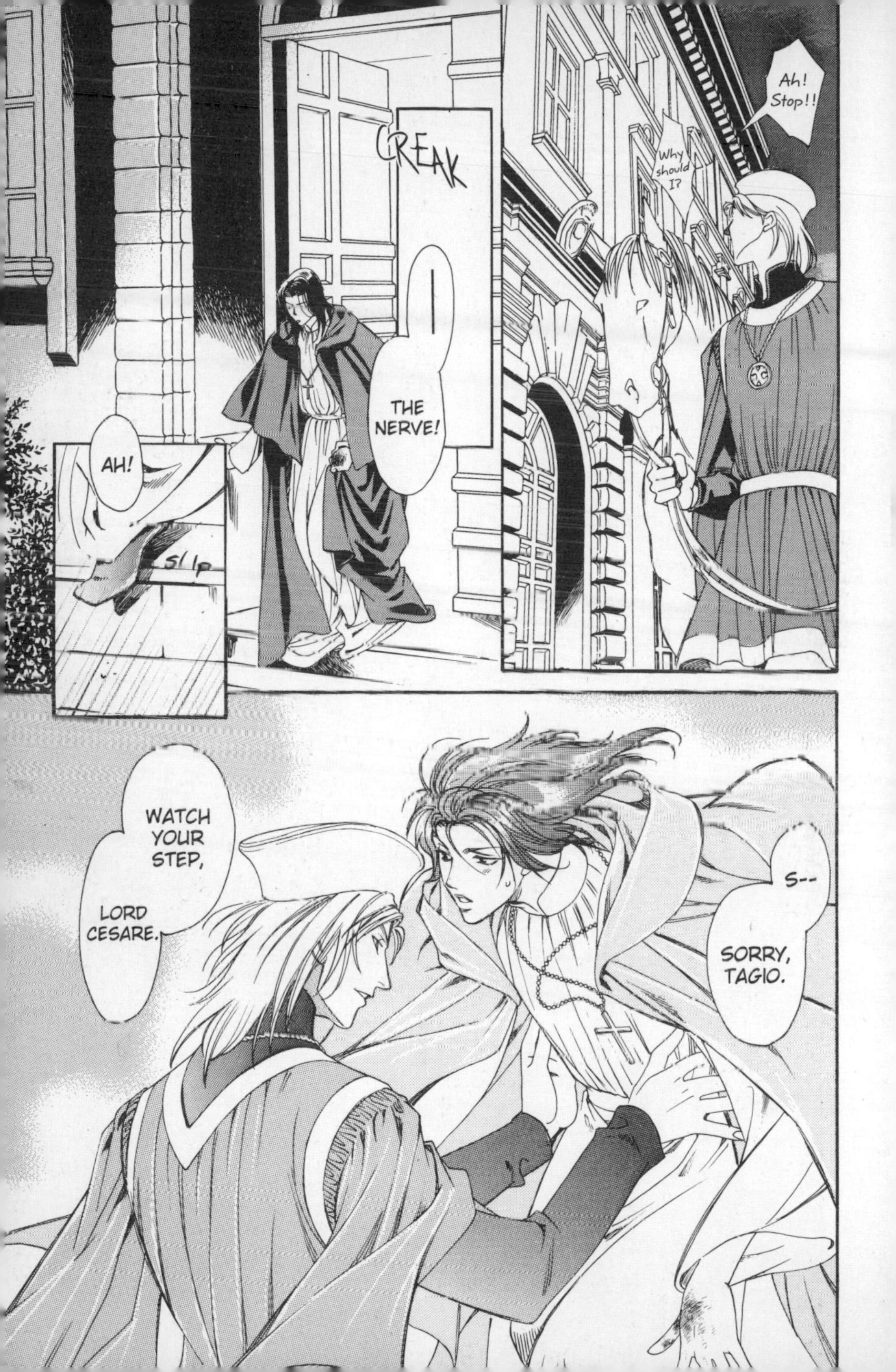

Ah! Stop!!
Why should I?
CREAK
THE NERVE!
AH!
slip
S--
SORRY, TAGIO.
WATCH YOUR STEP,
LORD CESARE.

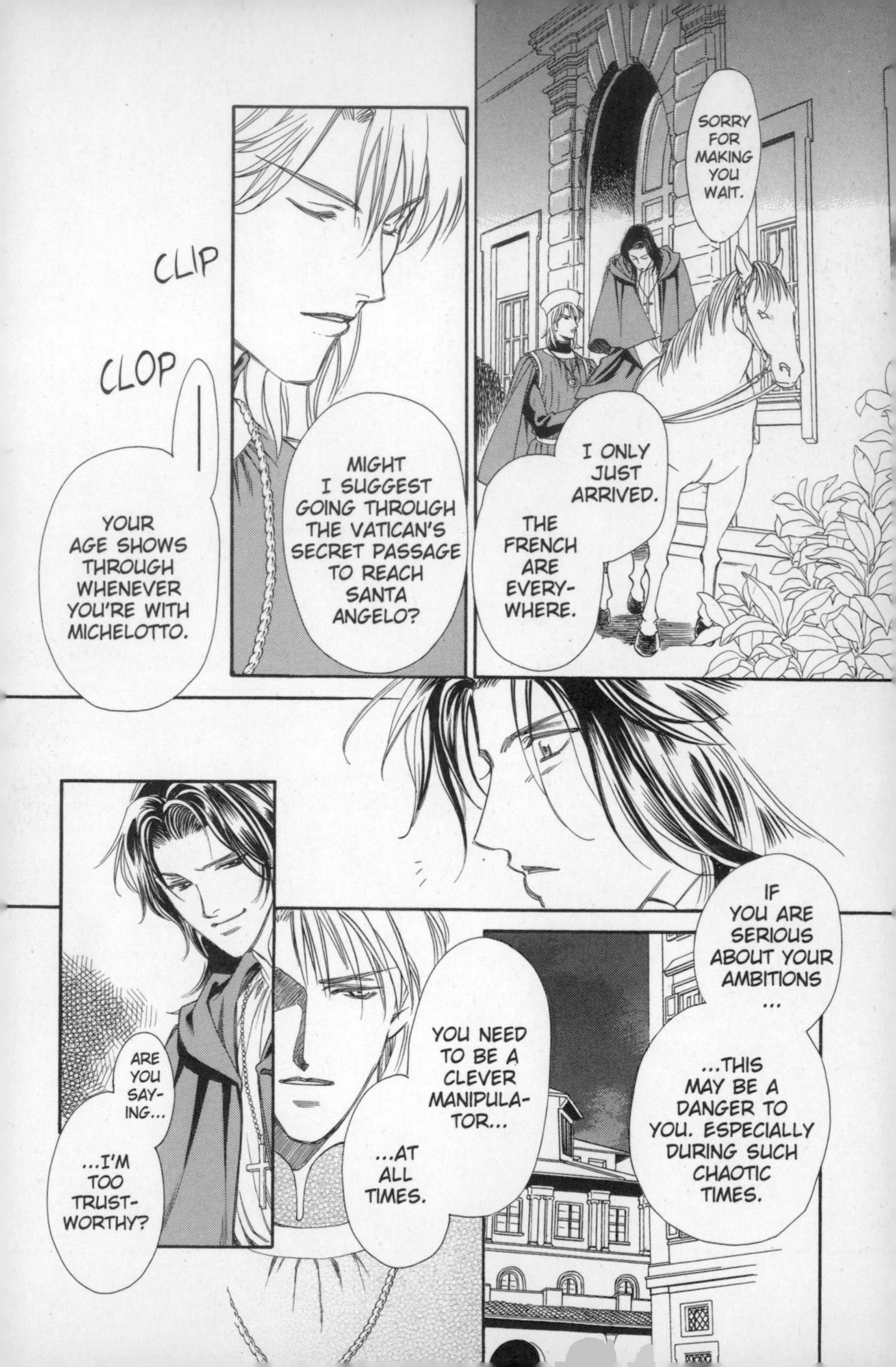
SORRY FOR MAKING YOU WAIT.
I ONLY JUST ARRIVED.
THE FRENCH ARE EVERY-WHERE.
MIGHT I SUGGEST GOING THROUGH THE VATICAN'S SECRET PASSAGE TO REACH SANTA ANGELO?
CLIP
CLOP
YOUR AGE SHOWS THROUGH WHENEVER YOU'RE WITH MICHELOTTO.
IF YOU ARE SERIOUS ABOUT YOUR AMBITIONS ...
...THIS MAY BE A DANGER TO YOU. ESPECIALLY DURING SUCH CHAOTIC TIMES.
YOU NEED TO BE A CLEVER MANIPULA-TOR...
...AT ALL TIMES.
ARE YOU SAY-ING...
...I'M TOO TRUST-WORTHY?

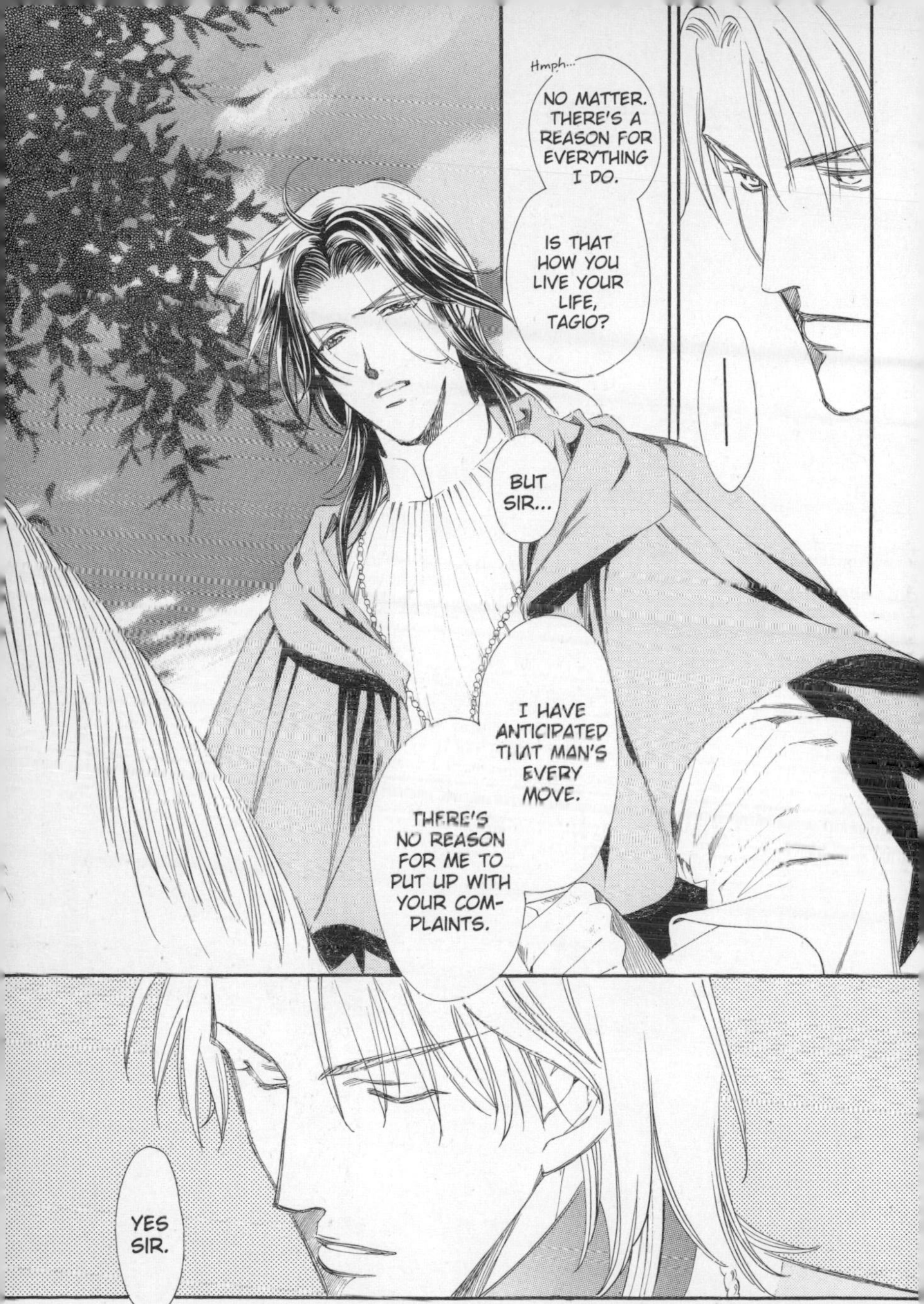
Hmph...
NO MATTER. THERE'S A REASON FOR EVERYTHING I DO.
IS THAT HOW YOU LIVE YOUR LIFE, TAGIO?
BUT SIR...
I HAVE ANTICIPATED THAT MAN'S EVERY MOVE.
THERE'S NO REASON FOR ME TO PUT UP WITH YOUR COM-PLAINTS.
YES SIR.

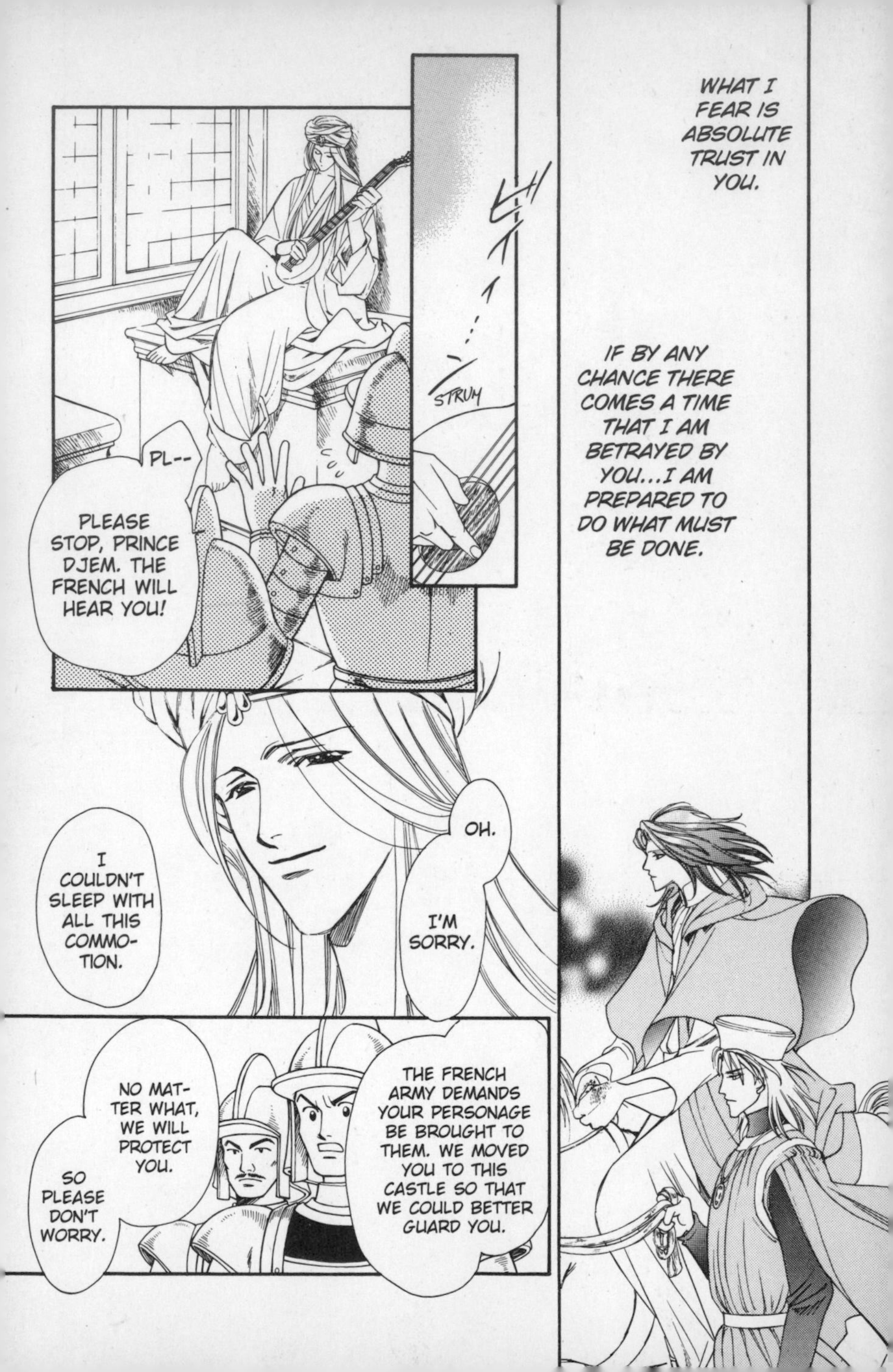
WHAT I FEAR IS ABSOLUTE TRUST IN YOU.
IF BY ANY CHANCE THERE COMES A TIME THAT I AM BETRAYED BY YOU...I AM PREPARED TO DO WHAT MUST BE DONE.
STRUM
PL--
PLEASE STOP, PRINCE DJEM. THE FRENCH WILL HEAR YOU!
OH.
I'M SORRY.
I COULDN'T SLEEP WITH ALL THIS COMMOTION.
THE FRENCH ARMY DEMANDS YOUR PERSONAGE BE BROUGHT TO THEM. WE MOVED YOU TO THIS CASTLE SO THAT WE COULD BETTER GUARD YOU.
NO MATTER WHAT, WE WILL PROTECT YOU.
SO PLEASE DON'T WORRY.

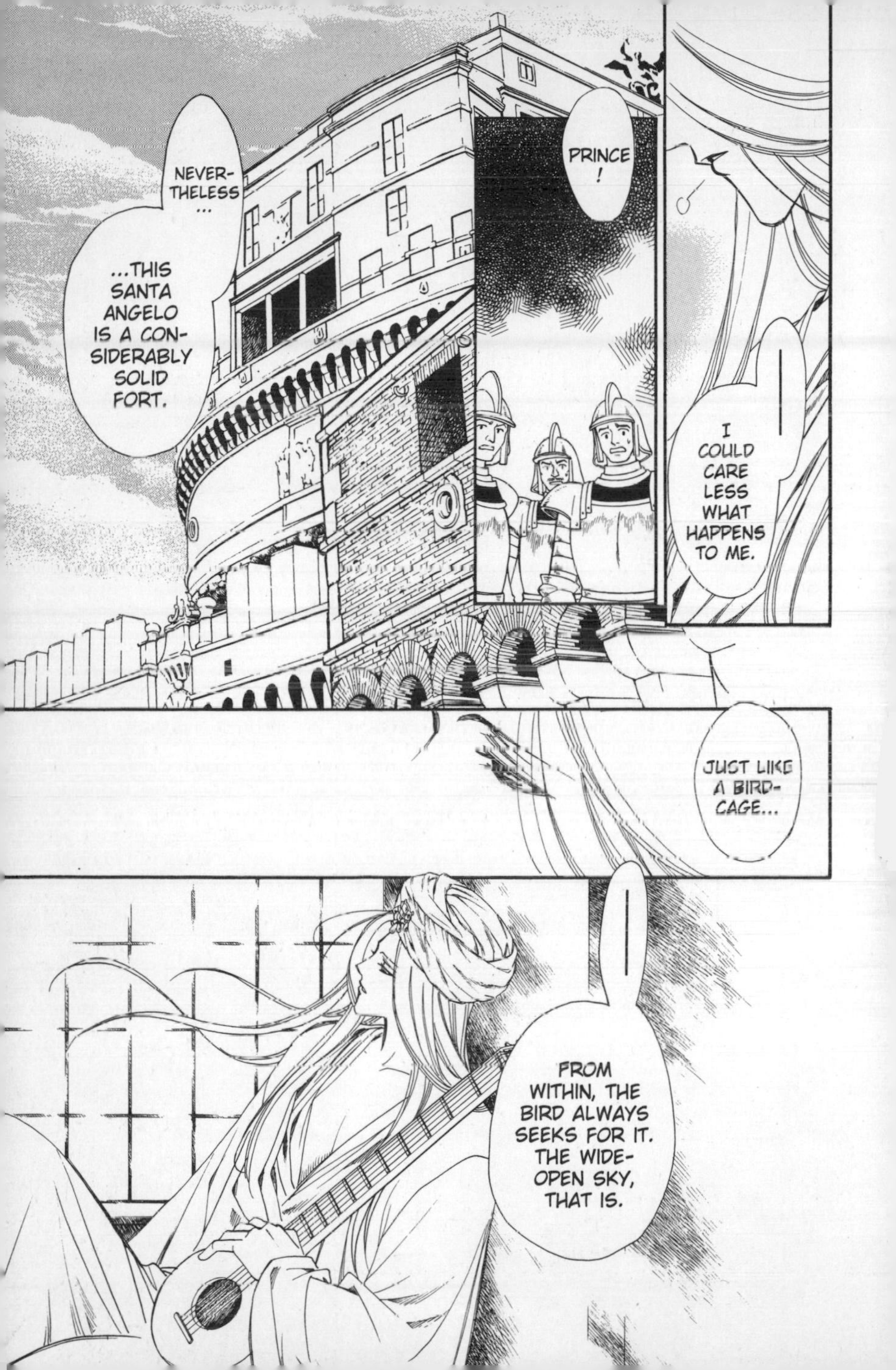
I COULD CARE LESS WHAT HAPPENS TO ME.
PRINCE!
NEVER-THELESS...
...THIS SANTA ANGELO IS A CON-SIDERABLY SOLID FORT.
JUST LIKE A BIRD-CAGE...
FROM WITHIN, THE BIRD ALWAYS SEEKS FOR IT. THE WIDE-OPEN SKY, THAT IS.

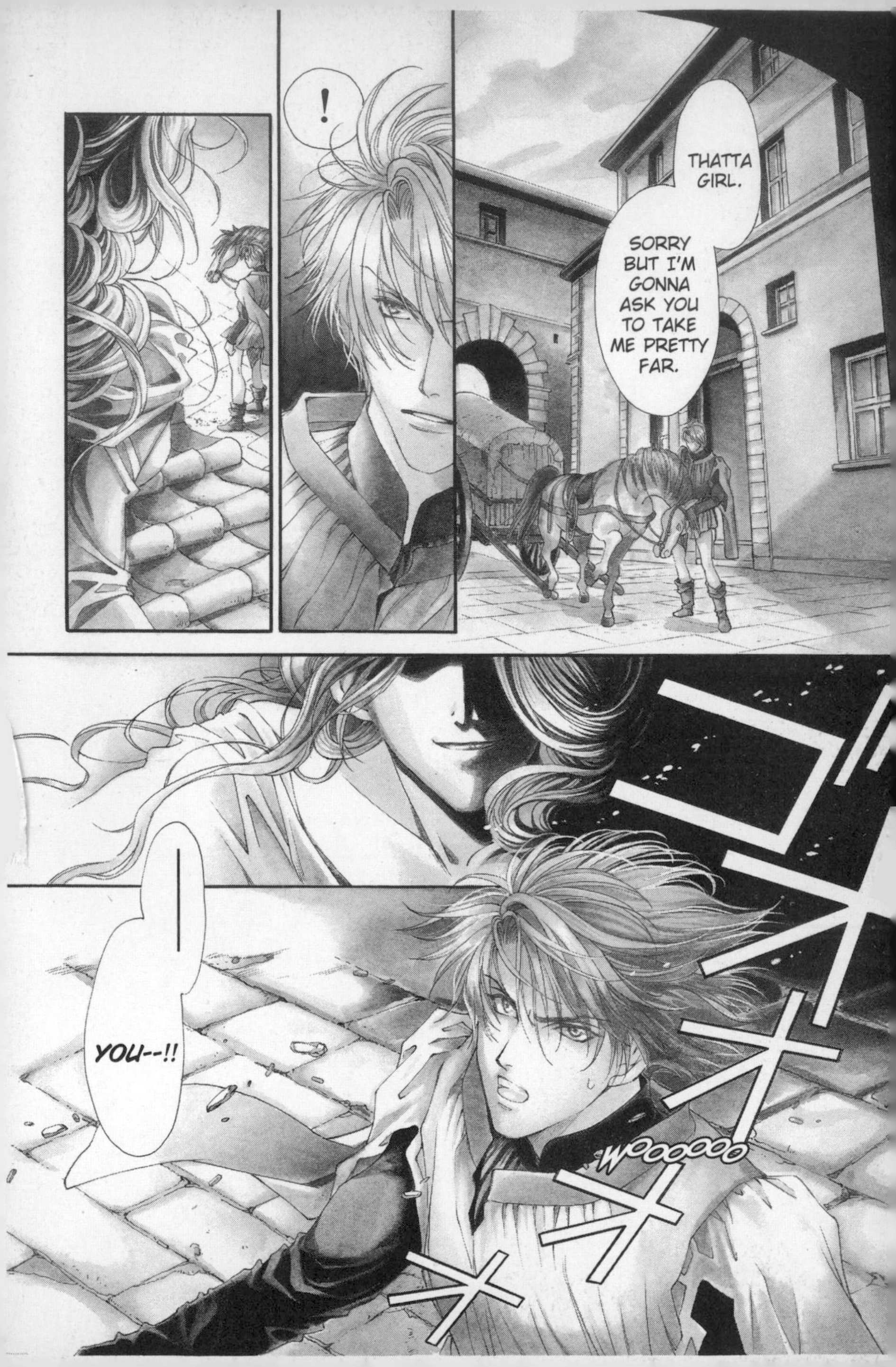
THATTA GIRL.
SORRY BUT I'M GONNA ASK YOU TO TAKE ME PRETTY FAR.
!
—
YOU--!!
WOOOOOO

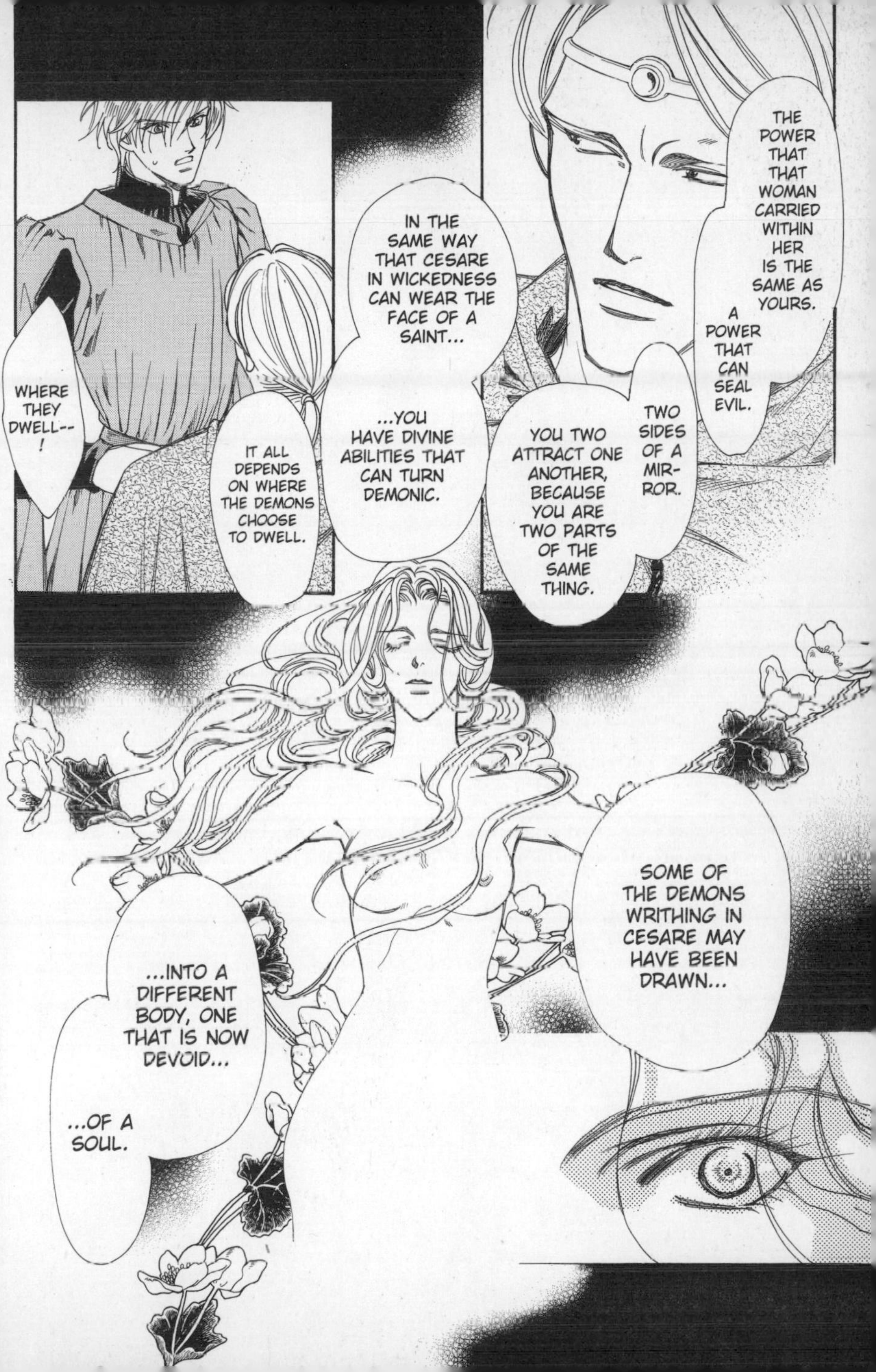
THE POWER THAT THAT WOMAN CARRIED WITHIN HER IS THE SAME AS YOURS.
A POWER THAT CAN SEAL EVIL.
TWO SIDES OF A MIR-ROR.
YOU TWO ATTRACT ONE ANOTHER, BECAUSE YOU ARE TWO PARTS OF THE SAME THING.
IN THE SAME WAY THAT CESARE IN WICKEDNESS CAN WEAR THE FACE OF A SAINT...
...YOU HAVE DIVINE ABILITIES THAT CAN TURN DEMONIC.
IT ALL DEPENDS ON WHERE THE DEMONS CHOOSE TO DWELL.
WHERE THEY DWELL--!
SOME OF THE DEMONS WRITHING IN CESARE MAY HAVE BEEN DRAWN...
...INTO A DIFFERENT BODY, ONE THAT IS NOW DEVOID...
...OF A SOUL.

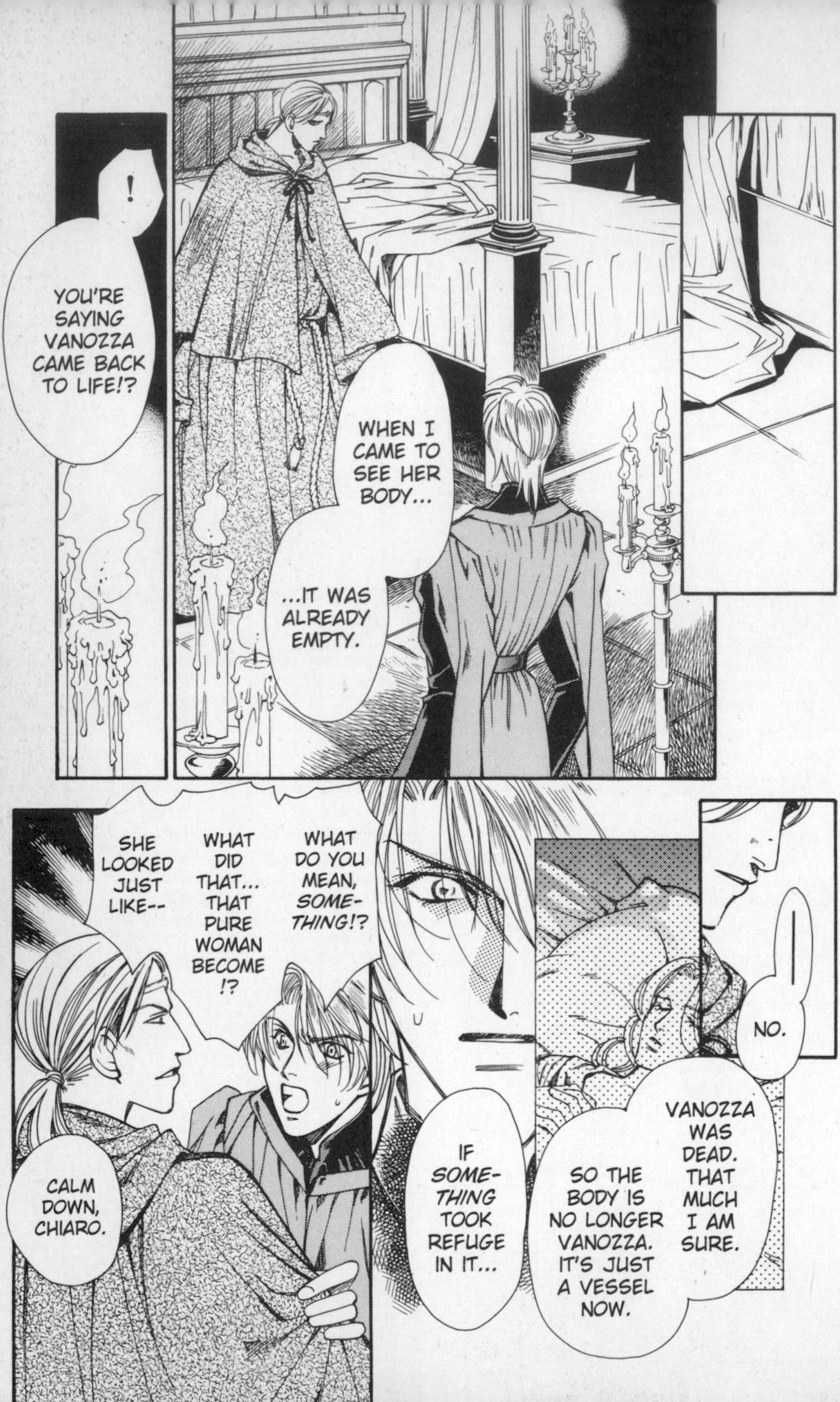
WHEN I CAME TO SEE HER BODY...
...IT WAS ALREADY EMPTY.
!
YOU'RE SAYING VANOZZA CAME BACK TO LIFE!?
NO.
VANOZZA WAS DEAD. THAT MUCH I AM SURE.
SO THE BODY IS NO LONGER VANOZZA. IT'S JUST A VESSEL NOW.
IF *SOMETHING* TOOK REFUGE IN IT...
WHAT DO YOU MEAN, *SOMETHING*!?
WHAT DID THAT... THAT PURE WOMAN BECOME!?
SHE LOOKED JUST LIKE--
CALM DOWN, CHIARO.

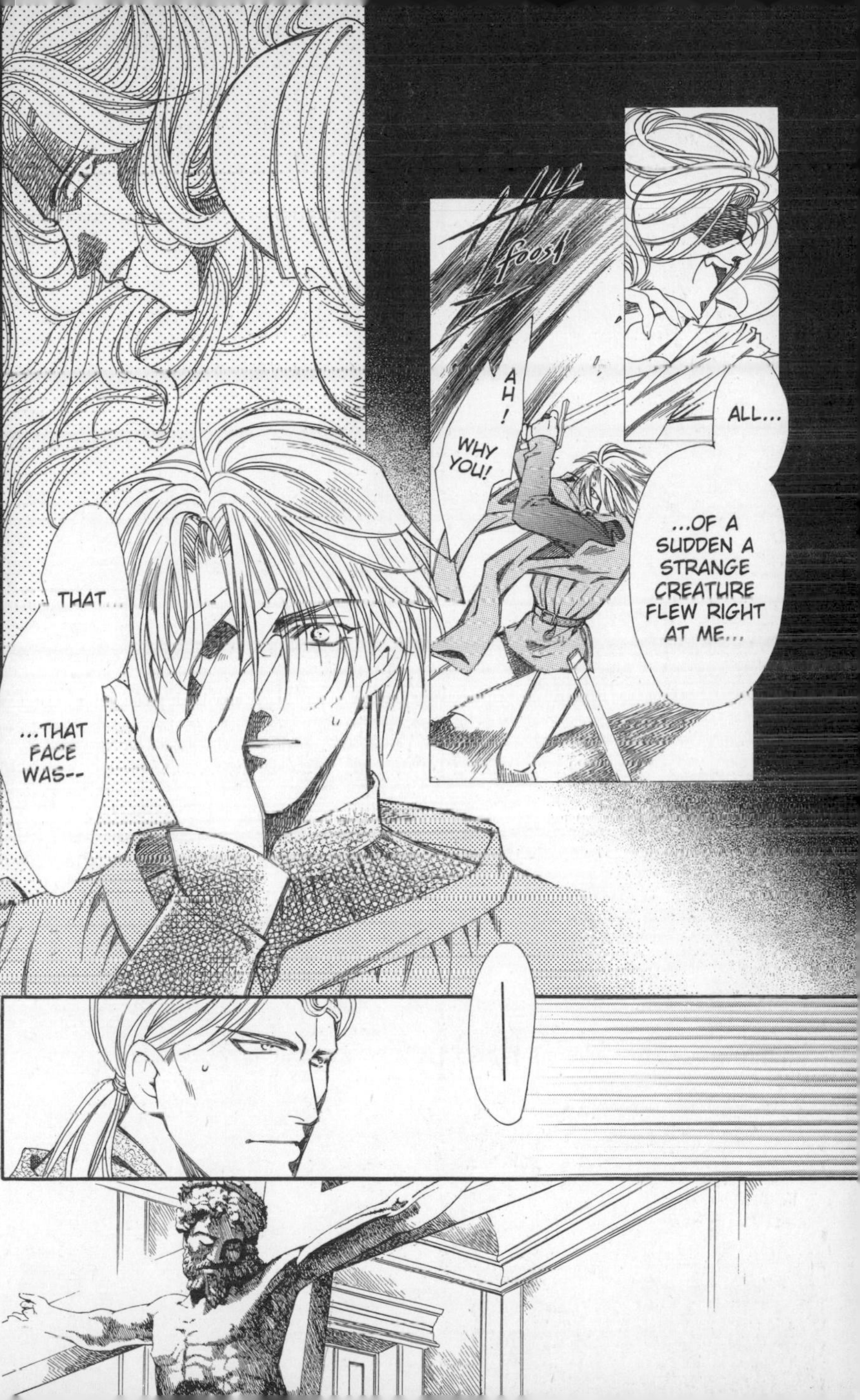

ALL...
...OF A SUDDEN A STRANGE CREATURE FLEW RIGHT AT ME...
foosh
!
AH! WHY YOU!
THAT...
...THAT FACE WAS--
—

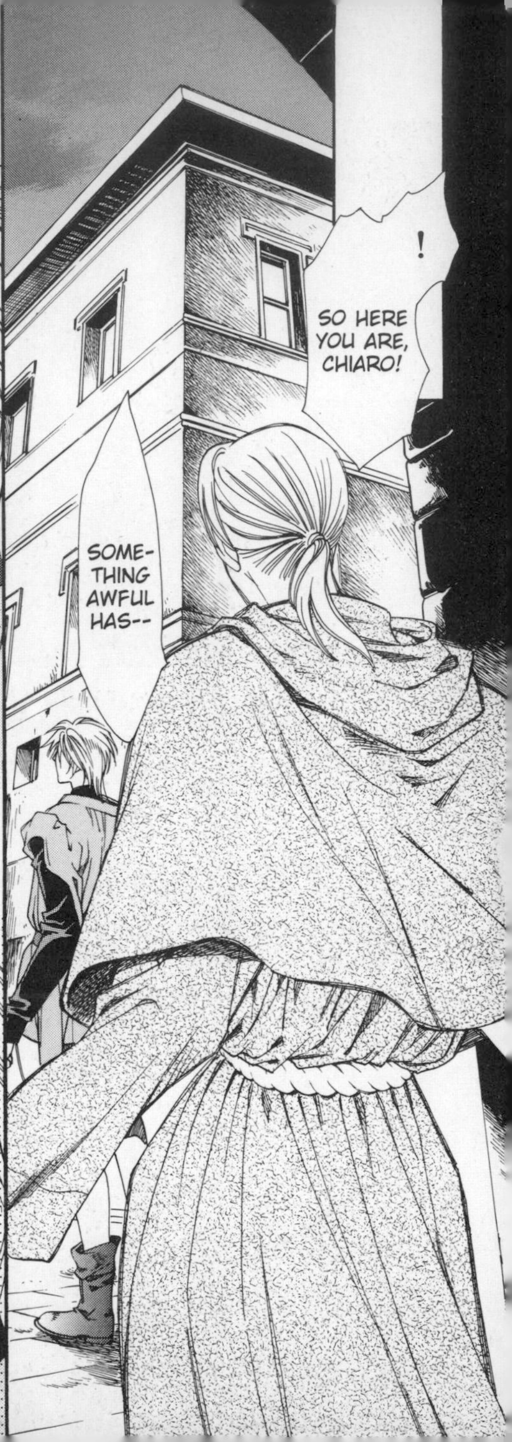
!
SO HERE YOU ARE, CHIARO!
SOME-THING AWFUL HAS--
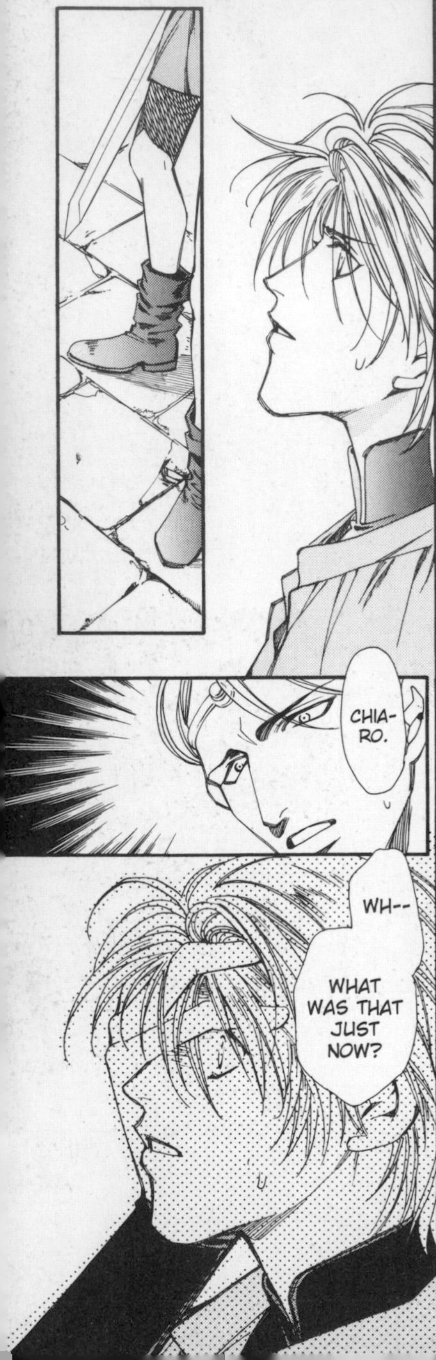
CHIA-RO.
WH--
WHAT WAS THAT JUST NOW?

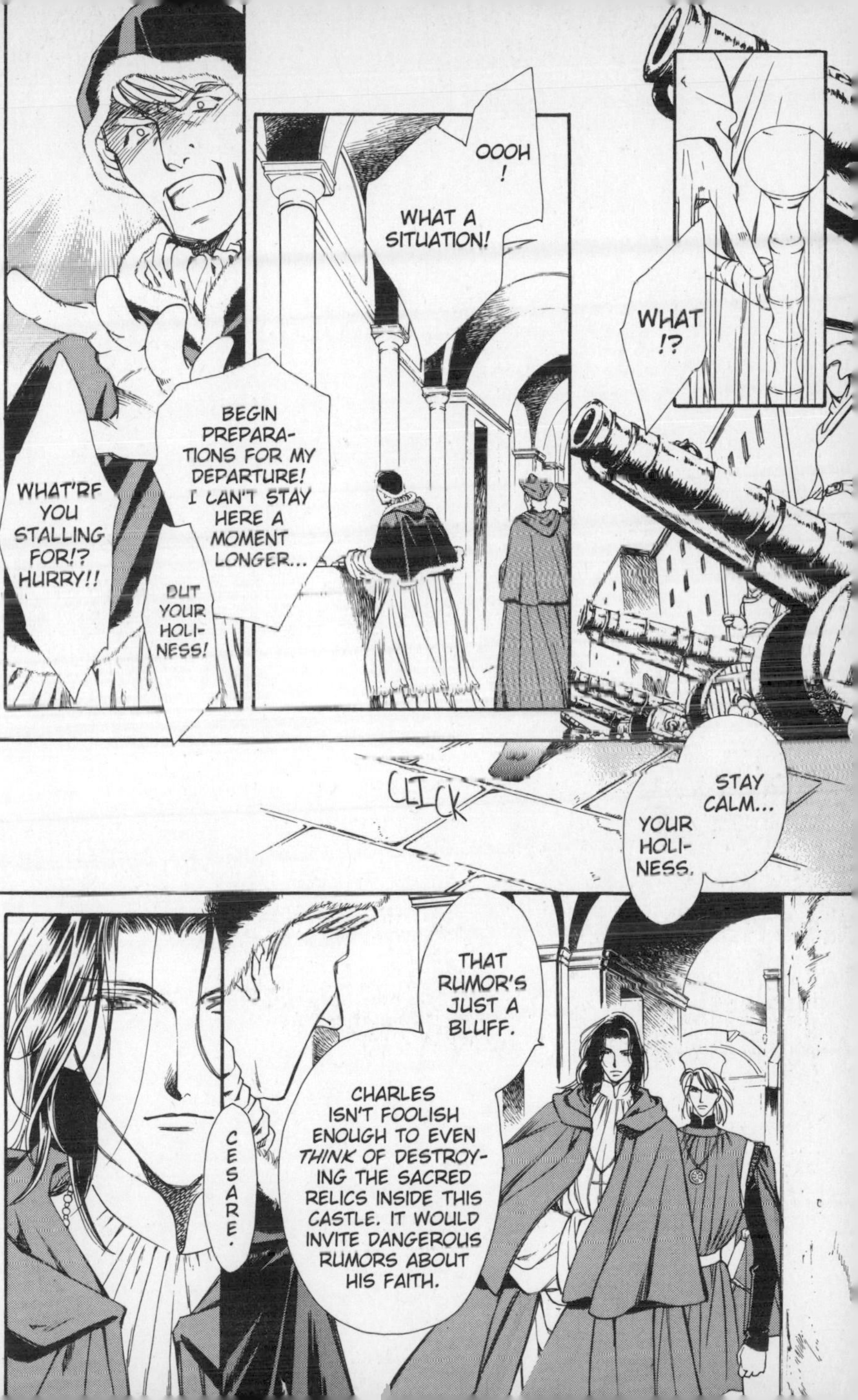
WHAT !?
OOOH !
WHAT A SITUATION!
BEGIN PREPARATIONS FOR MY DEPARTURE! I CAN'T STAY HERE A MOMENT LONGER...
BUT YOUR HOLINESS!
WHAT'RE YOU STALLING FOR!? HURRY!!
CLICK
STAY CALM...
YOUR HOLINESS.
THAT RUMOR'S JUST A BLUFF.
CHARLES ISN'T FOOLISH ENOUGH TO EVEN *THINK* OF DESTROYING THE SACRED RELICS INSIDE THIS CASTLE. IT WOULD INVITE DANGEROUS RUMORS ABOUT HIS FAITH.
CESARE.

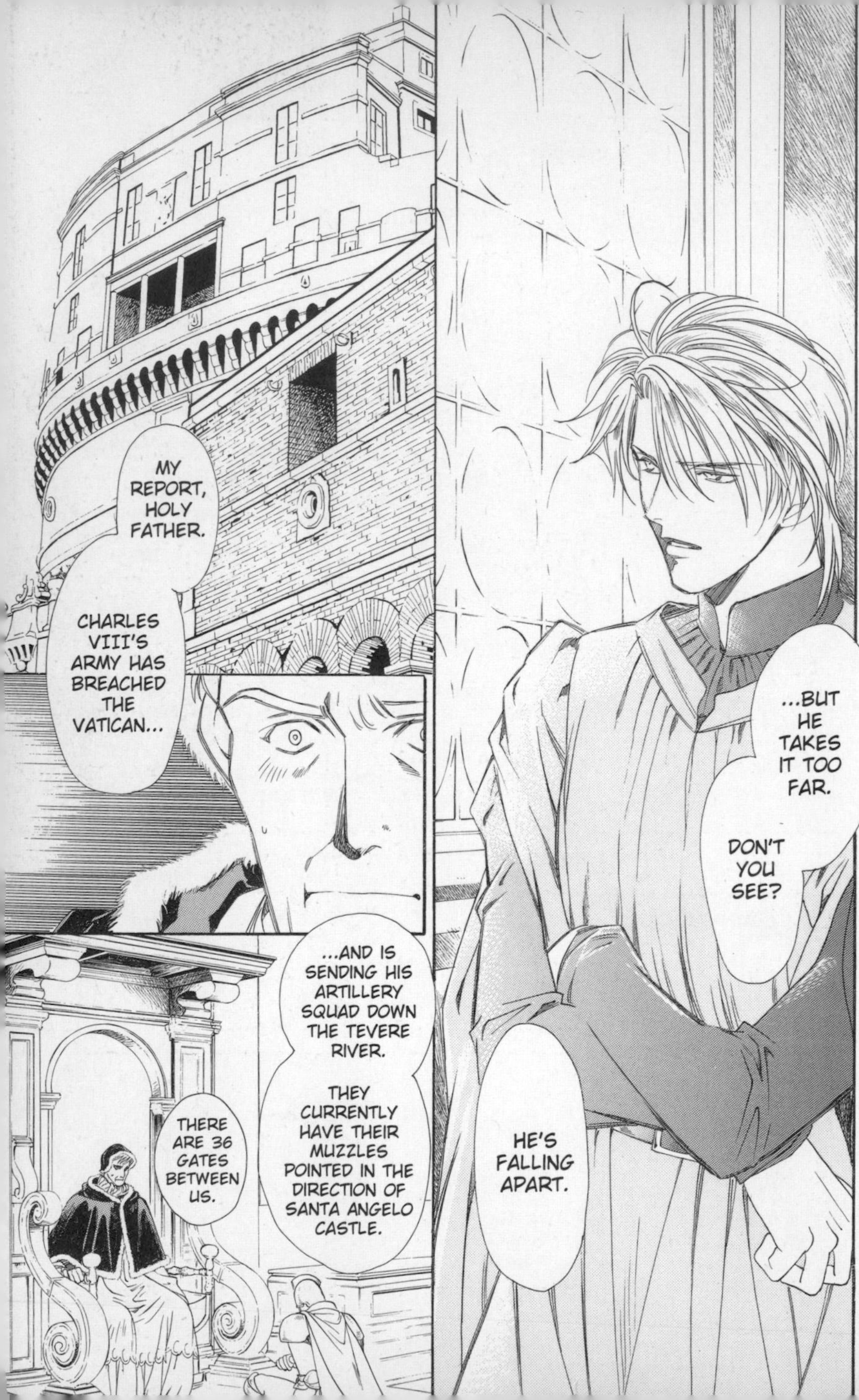
...BUT HE TAKES IT TOO FAR.
DON'T YOU SEE?
HE'S FALLING APART.
MY REPORT, HOLY FATHER.
CHARLES VIII'S ARMY HAS BREACHED THE VATICAN...
...AND IS SENDING HIS ARTILLERY SQUAD DOWN THE TEVERE RIVER.
THEY CURRENTLY HAVE THEIR MUZZLES POINTED IN THE DIRECTION OF SANTA ANGELO CASTLE.
THERE ARE 36 GATES BETWEEN US.

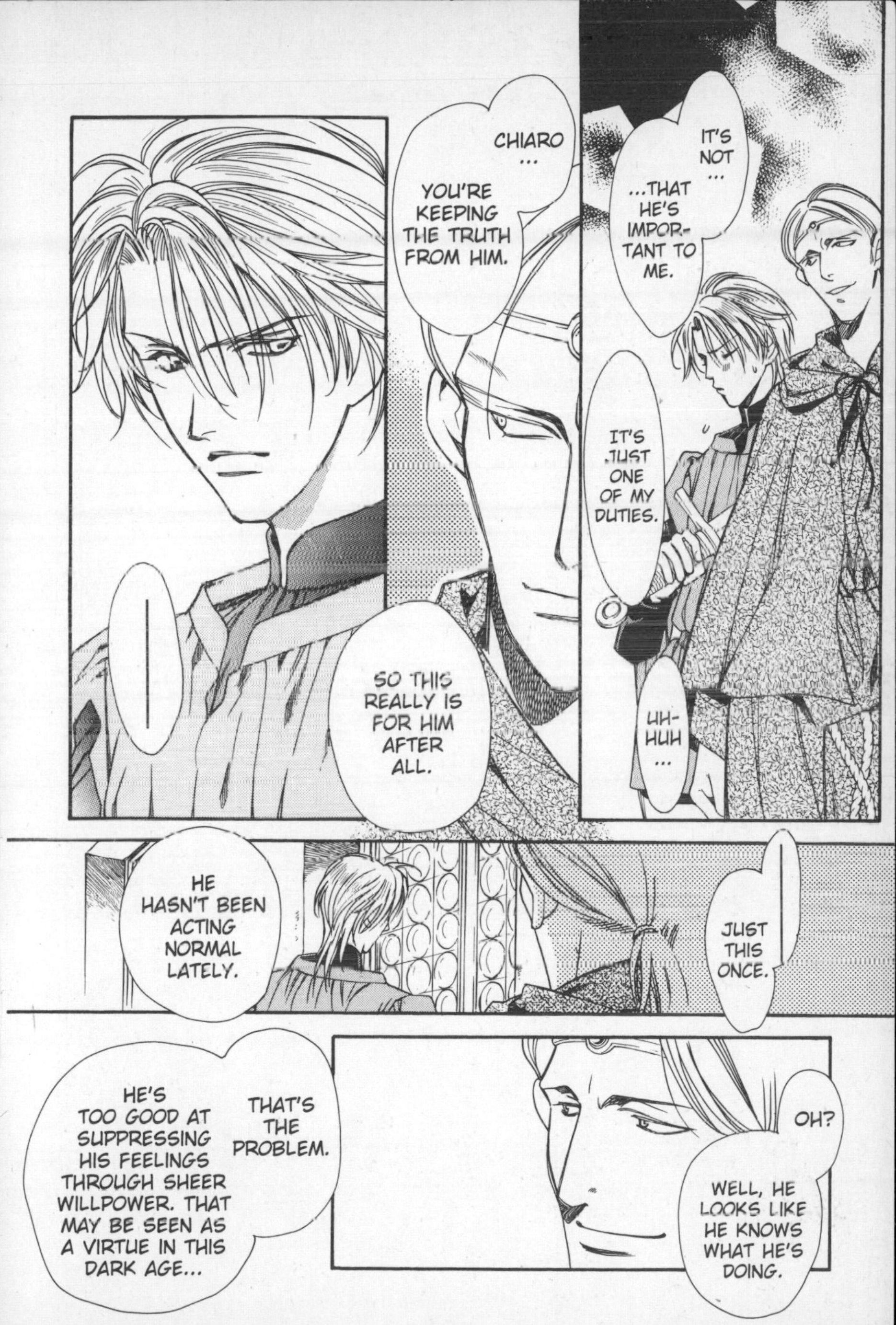
CHIARO ...
YOU'RE KEEPING THE TRUTH FROM HIM.
IT'S NOT ...
...THAT HE'S IMPOR-TANT TO ME.
IT'S JUST ONE OF MY DUTIES.
UH-HUH ...
SO THIS REALLY IS FOR HIM AFTER ALL.
JUST THIS ONCE.
HE HASN'T BEEN ACTING NORMAL LATELY.
OH?
WELL, HE LOOKS LIKE HE KNOWS WHAT HE'S DOING.
THAT'S THE PROBLEM.
HE'S TOO GOOD AT SUPPRESSING HIS FEELINGS THROUGH SHEER WILLPOWER. THAT MAY BE SEEN AS A VIRTUE IN THIS DARK AGE...

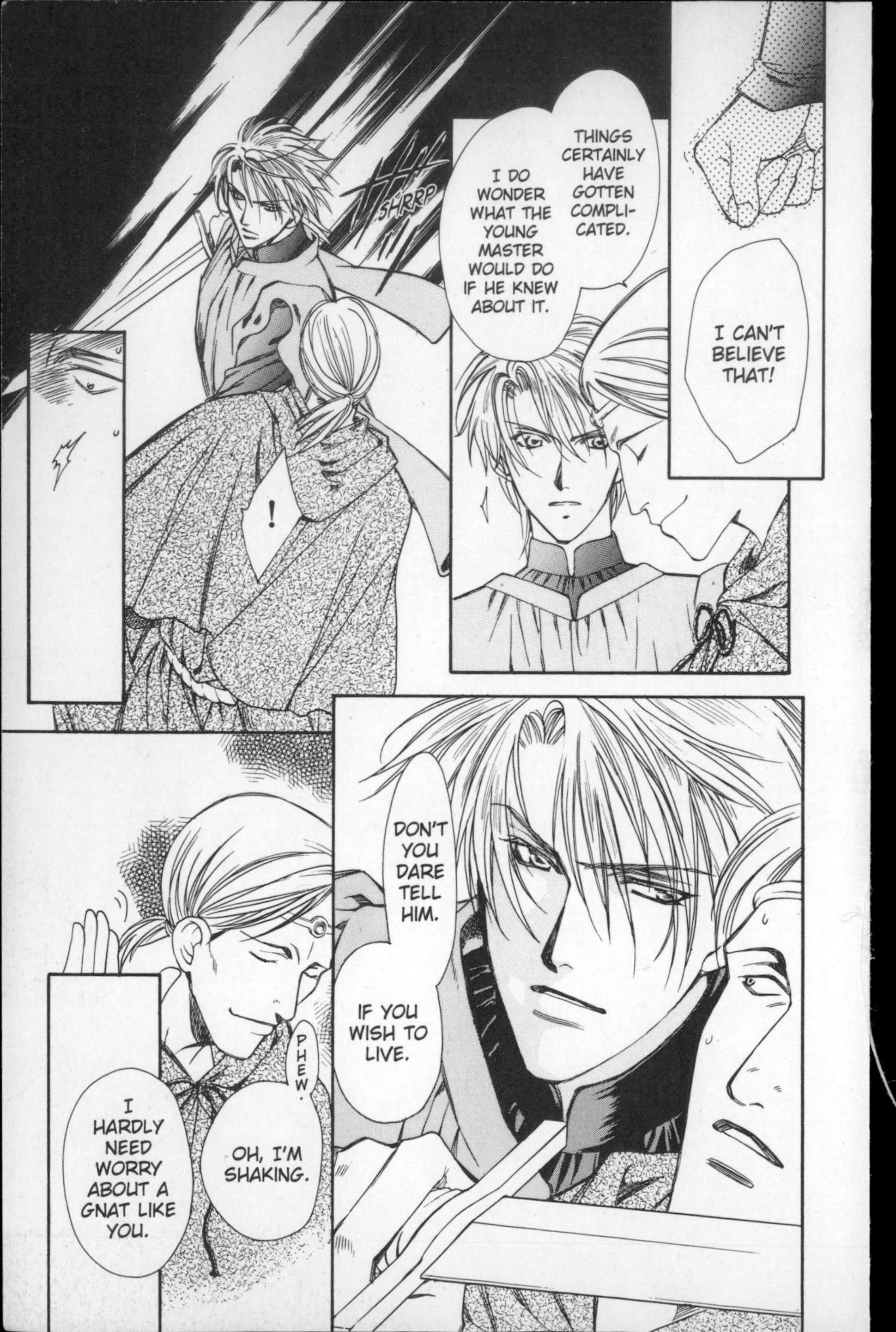
I CAN'T BELIEVE THAT!
THINGS CERTAINLY HAVE GOTTEN COMPLICATED.
I DO WONDER WHAT THE YOUNG MASTER WOULD DO IF HE KNEW ABOUT IT.
SHRRP
!
DON'T YOU DARE TELL HIM.
IF YOU WISH TO LIVE.
PHEW.
OH, I'M SHAKING.
I HARDLY NEED WORRY ABOUT A GNAT LIKE YOU.

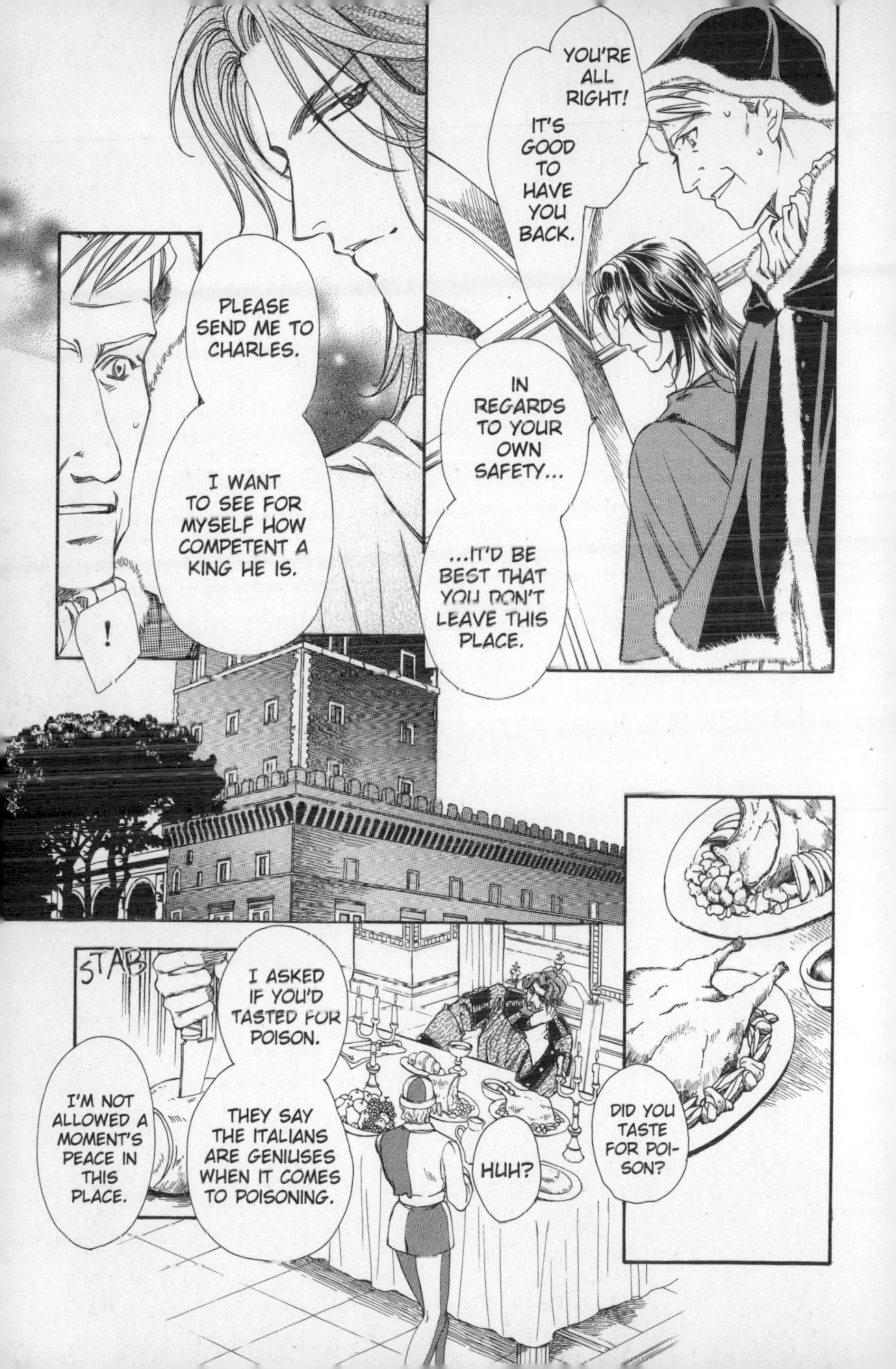
YOU'RE ALL RIGHT!
IT'S GOOD TO HAVE YOU BACK.
IN REGARDS TO YOUR OWN SAFETY...
...IT'D BE BEST THAT YOU DON'T LEAVE THIS PLACE.
PLEASE SEND ME TO CHARLES.
I WANT TO SEE FOR MYSELF HOW COMPETENT A KING HE IS.
!
DID YOU TASTE FOR POI- SON?
HUH?
I ASKED IF YOU'D TASTED FOR POISON.
THEY SAY THE ITALIANS ARE GENIUSES WHEN IT COMES TO POISONING.
STAB
I'M NOT ALLOWED A MOMENT'S PEACE IN THIS PLACE.

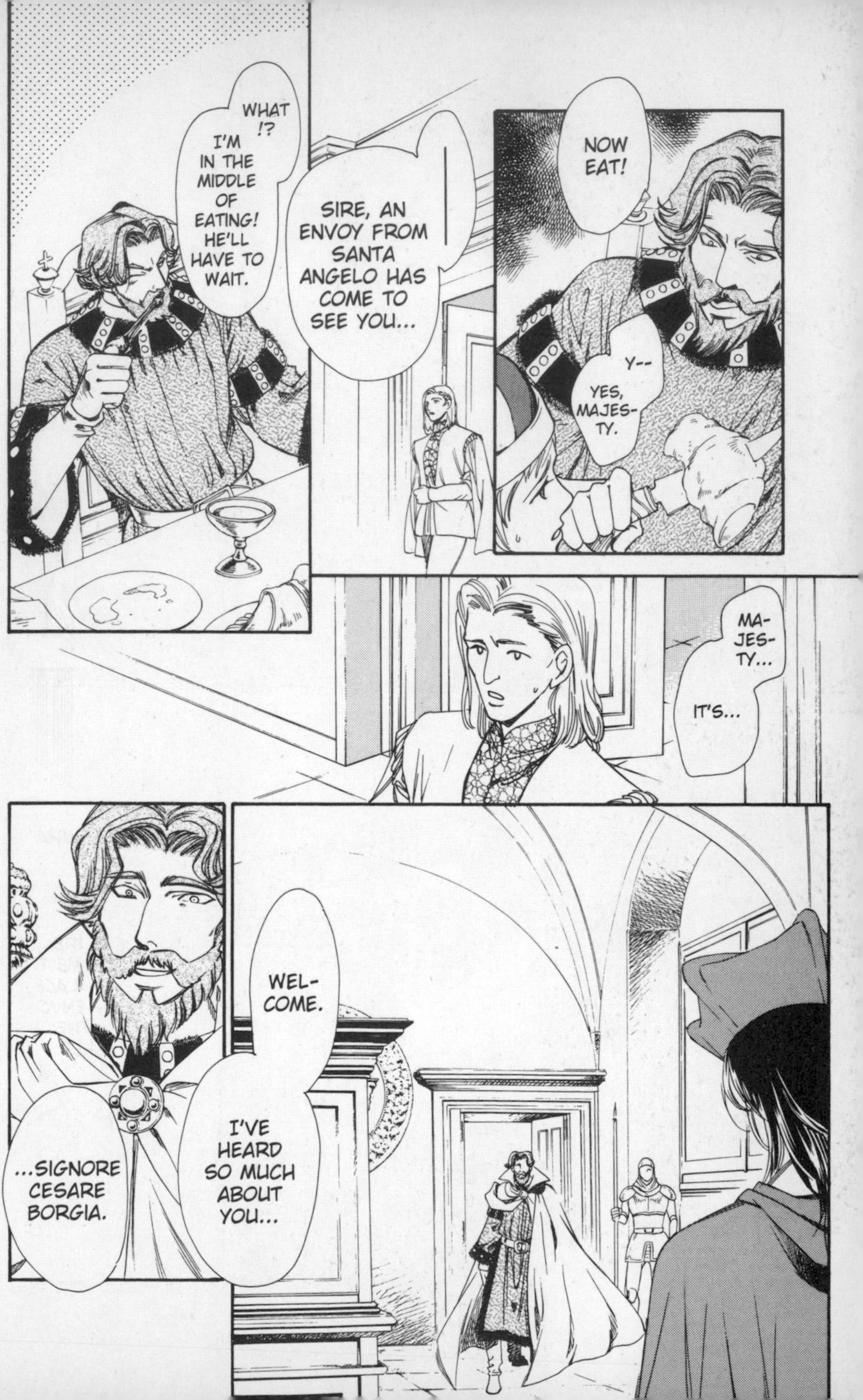
NOW EAT!
Y-- YES, MAJESTY.
SIRE, AN ENVOY FROM SANTA ANGELO HAS COME TO SEE YOU...
WHAT!? I'M IN THE MIDDLE OF EATING! HE'LL HAVE TO WAIT.
MAJESTY...
IT'S...
WELCOME.
I'VE HEARD SO MUCH ABOUT YOU...
...SIGNORE CESARE BORGIA.

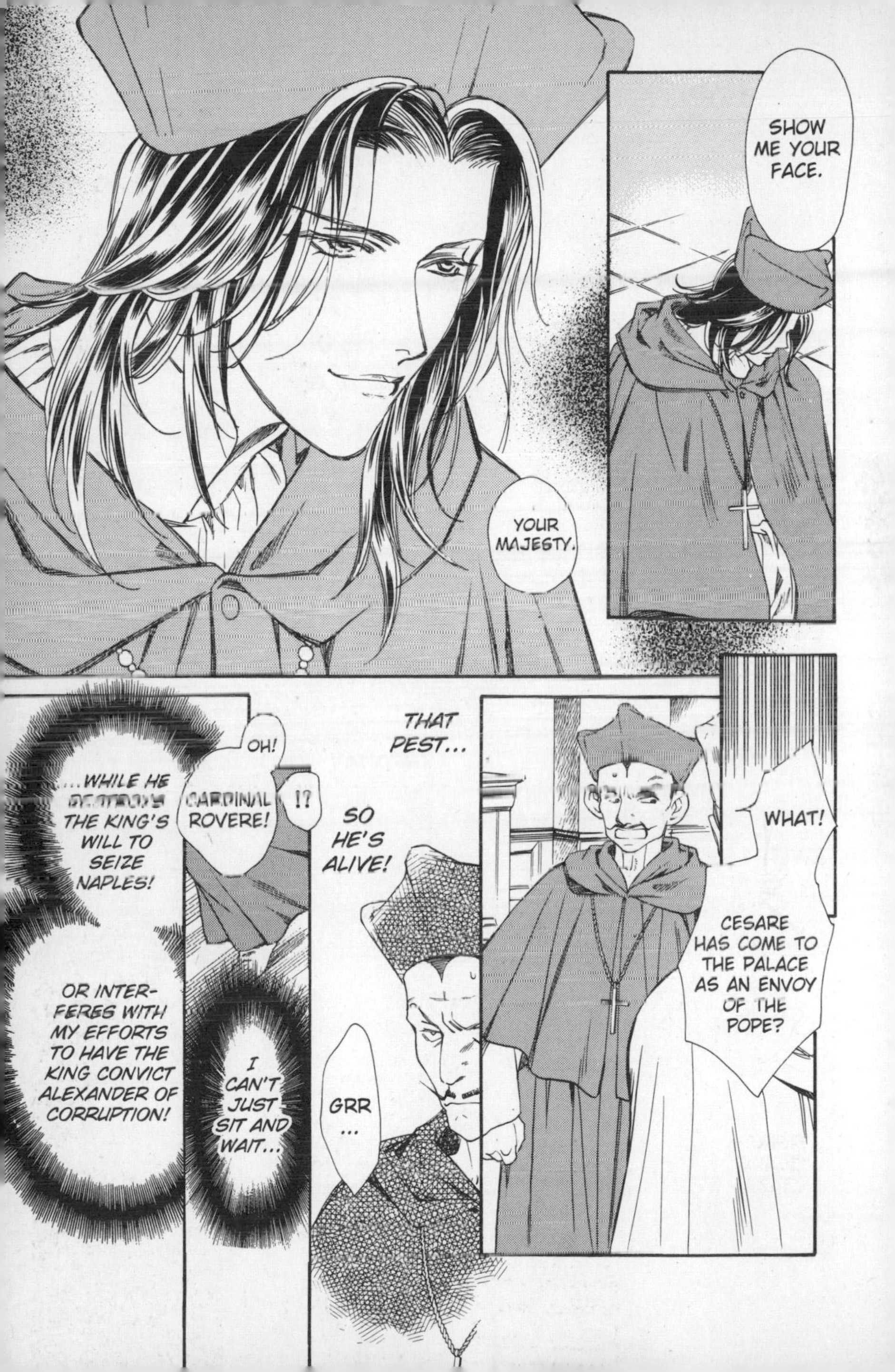
SHOW ME YOUR FACE.
YOUR MAJESTY.
WHAT!
CESARE HAS COME TO THE PALACE AS AN ENVOY OF THE POPE?
THAT PEST...
SO HE'S ALIVE!
GRR ...
OH!
CARDINAL ROVERE!
!?
...WHILE HE DESTROYS THE KING'S WILL TO SEIZE NAPLES!
OR INTERFERES WITH MY EFFORTS TO HAVE THE KING CONVICT ALEXANDER OF CORRUPTION!
I CAN'T JUST SIT AND WAIT...

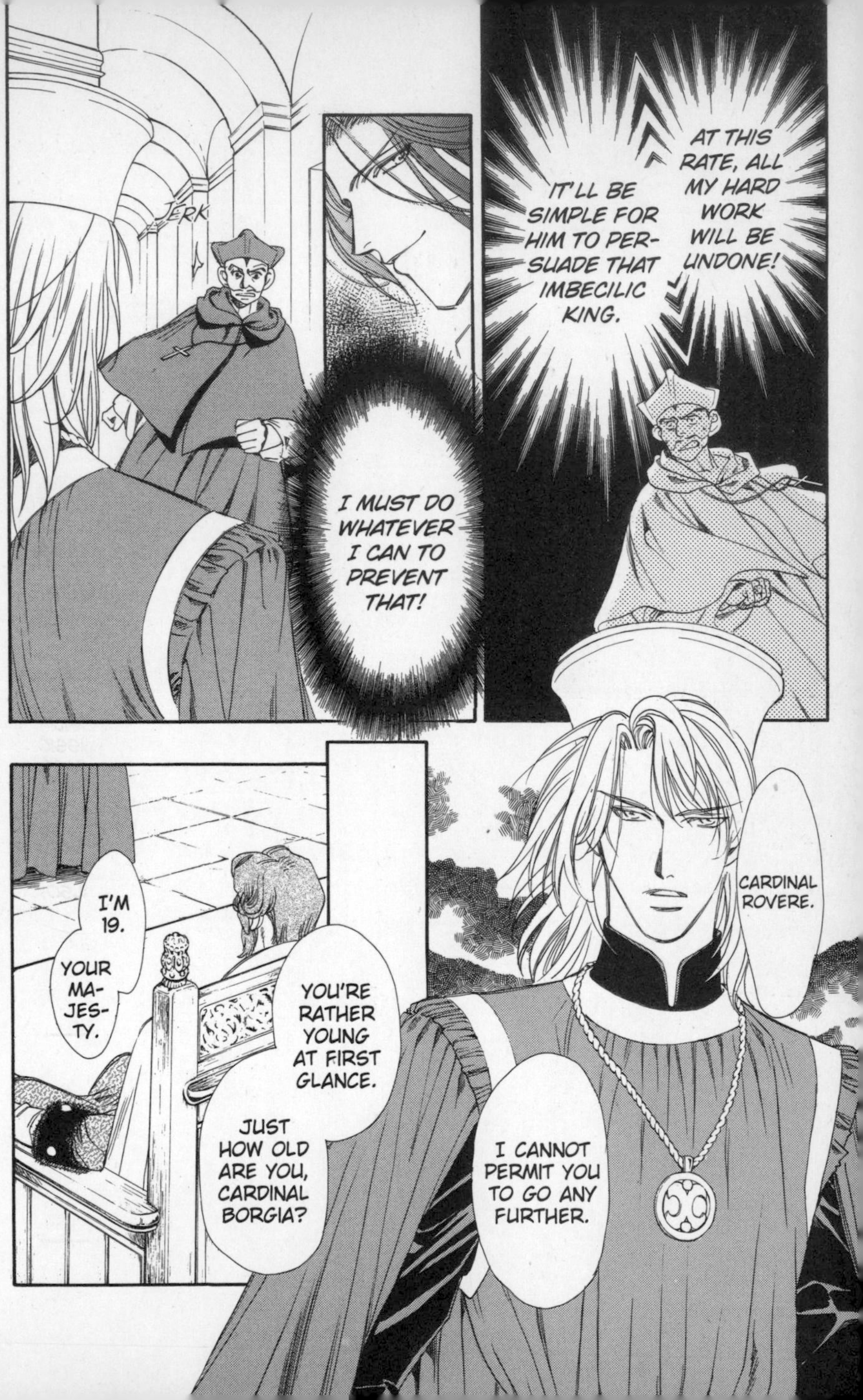
AT THIS RATE, ALL MY HARD WORK WILL BE UNDONE!
IT'LL BE SIMPLE FOR HIM TO PERSUADE THAT IMBECILIC KING.
I MUST DO WHATEVER I CAN TO PREVENT THAT!
JERK
CARDINAL ROVERE.
I CANNOT PERMIT YOU TO GO ANY FURTHER.
YOU'RE RATHER YOUNG AT FIRST GLANCE.
JUST HOW OLD ARE YOU, CARDINAL BORGIA?
I'M 19.
YOUR MAJESTY.

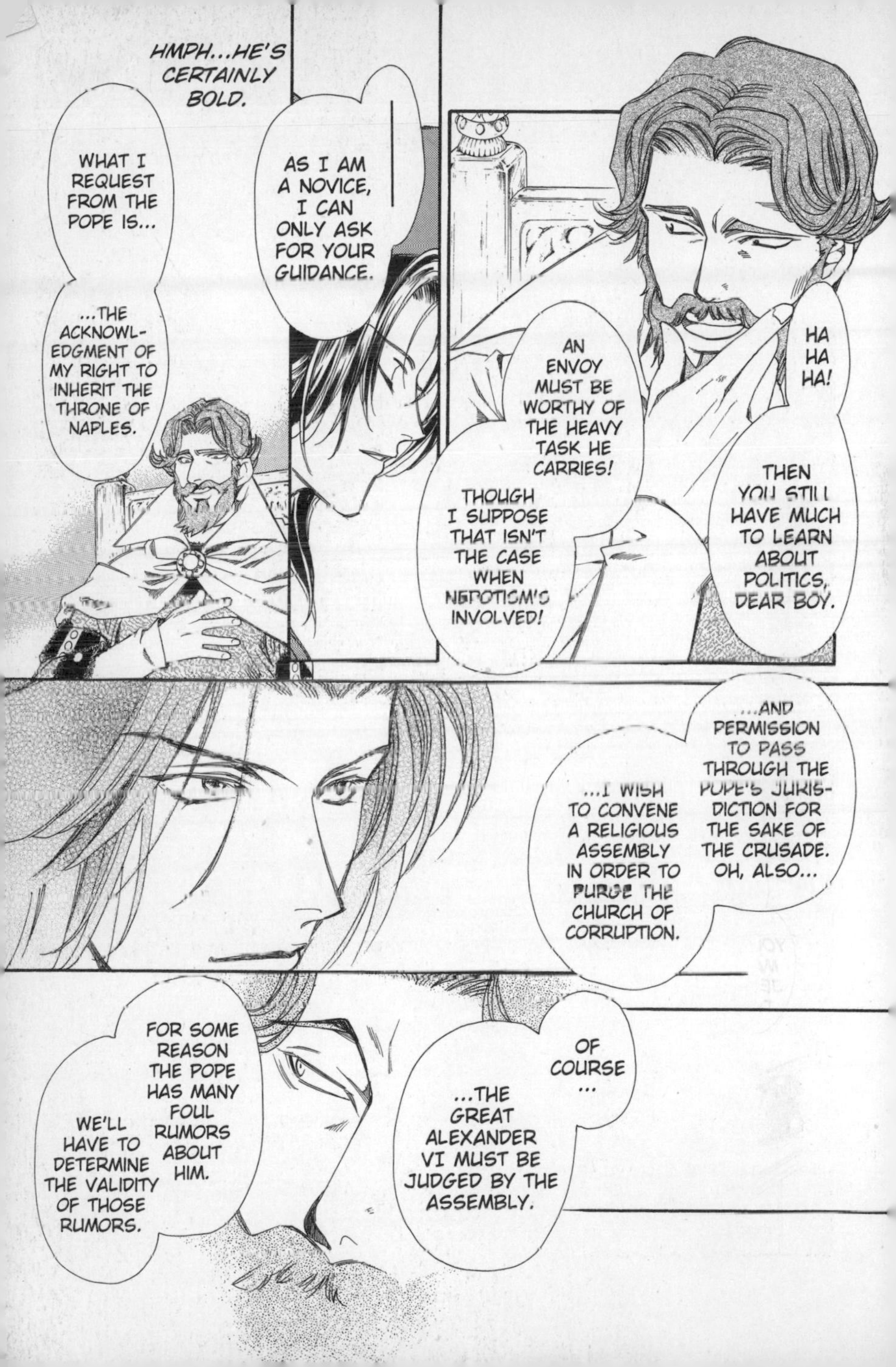
HA HA HA!
THEN YOU STILL HAVE MUCH TO LEARN ABOUT POLITICS, DEAR BOY.
AN ENVOY MUST BE WORTHY OF THE HEAVY TASK HE CARRIES!
THOUGH I SUPPOSE THAT ISN'T THE CASE WHEN NEPOTISM'S INVOLVED!
AS I AM A NOVICE, I CAN ONLY ASK FOR YOUR GUIDANCE.
HMPH...HE'S CERTAINLY BOLD.
WHAT I REQUEST FROM THE POPE IS...
...THE ACKNOWL-EDGMENT OF MY RIGHT TO INHERIT THE THRONE OF NAPLES.
...AND PERMISSION TO PASS THROUGH THE POPE'S JURIS-DICTION FOR THE SAKE OF THE CRUSADE. OH, ALSO...
...I WISH TO CONVENE A RELIGIOUS ASSEMBLY IN ORDER TO PURGE THE CHURCH OF CORRUPTION.
OF COURSE...
...THE GREAT ALEXANDER VI MUST BE JUDGED BY THE ASSEMBLY.
FOR SOME REASON THE POPE HAS MANY FOUL RUMORS ABOUT HIM.
WE'LL HAVE TO DETERMINE THE VALIDITY OF THOSE RUMORS.

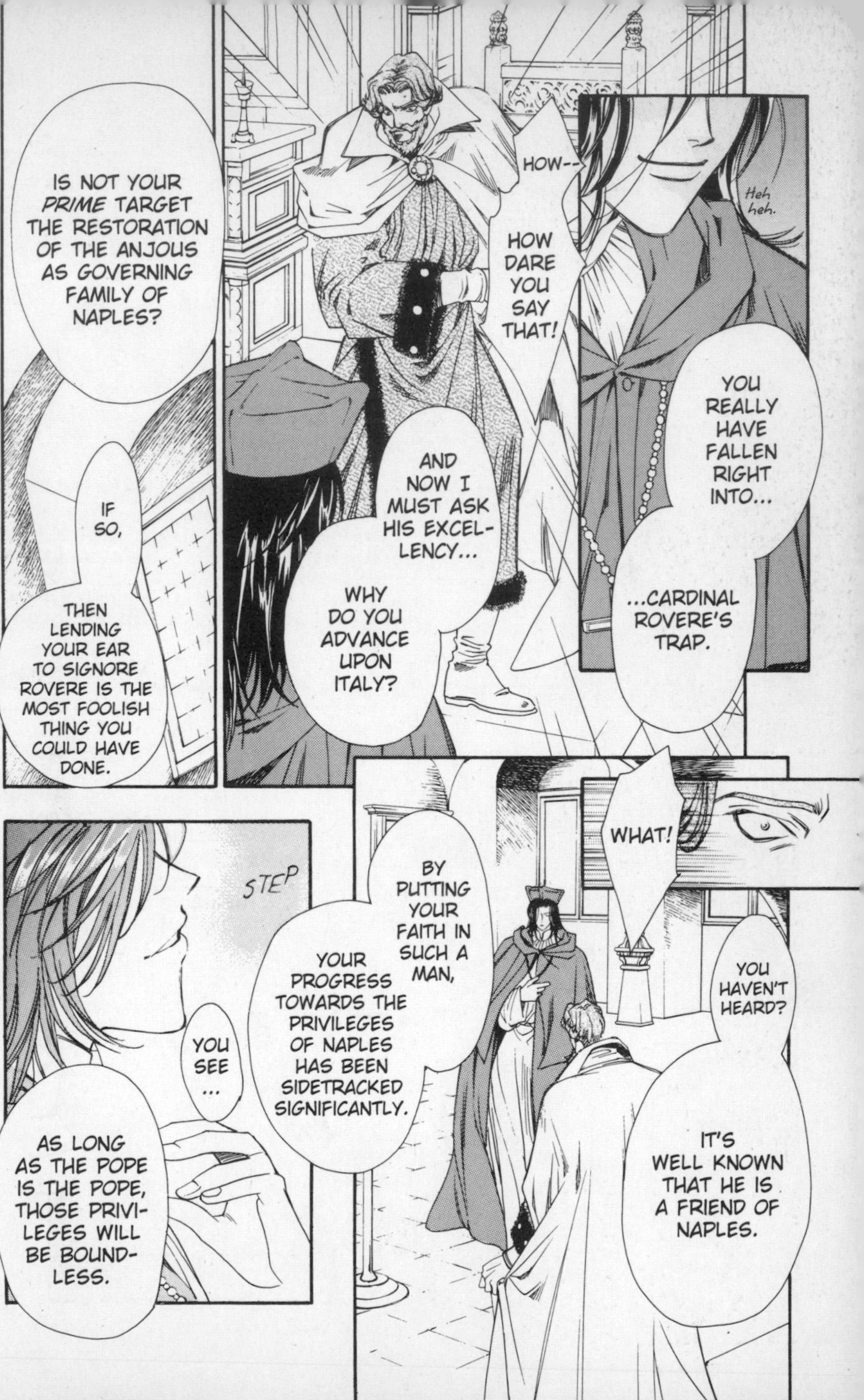
HOW--
Heh heh.
YOU REALLY HAVE FALLEN RIGHT INTO...
...CARDINAL ROVERE'S TRAP.
HOW DARE YOU SAY THAT!
AND NOW I MUST ASK HIS EXCELLENCY...
WHY DO YOU ADVANCE UPON ITALY?
IS NOT YOUR *PRIME* TARGET THE RESTORATION OF THE ANJOUS AS GOVERNING FAMILY OF NAPLES?
IF SO,
THEN LENDING YOUR EAR TO SIGNORE ROVERE IS THE MOST FOOLISH THING YOU COULD HAVE DONE.
WHAT!
YOU HAVEN'T HEARD?
IT'S WELL KNOWN THAT HE IS A FRIEND OF NAPLES.
BY PUTTING YOUR FAITH IN SUCH A MAN,
YOUR PROGRESS TOWARDS THE PRIVILEGES OF NAPLES HAS BEEN SIDETRACKED SIGNIFICANTLY.
STEP
YOU SEE...
AS LONG AS THE POPE IS THE POPE, THOSE PRIVILEGES WILL BE BOUNDLESS.

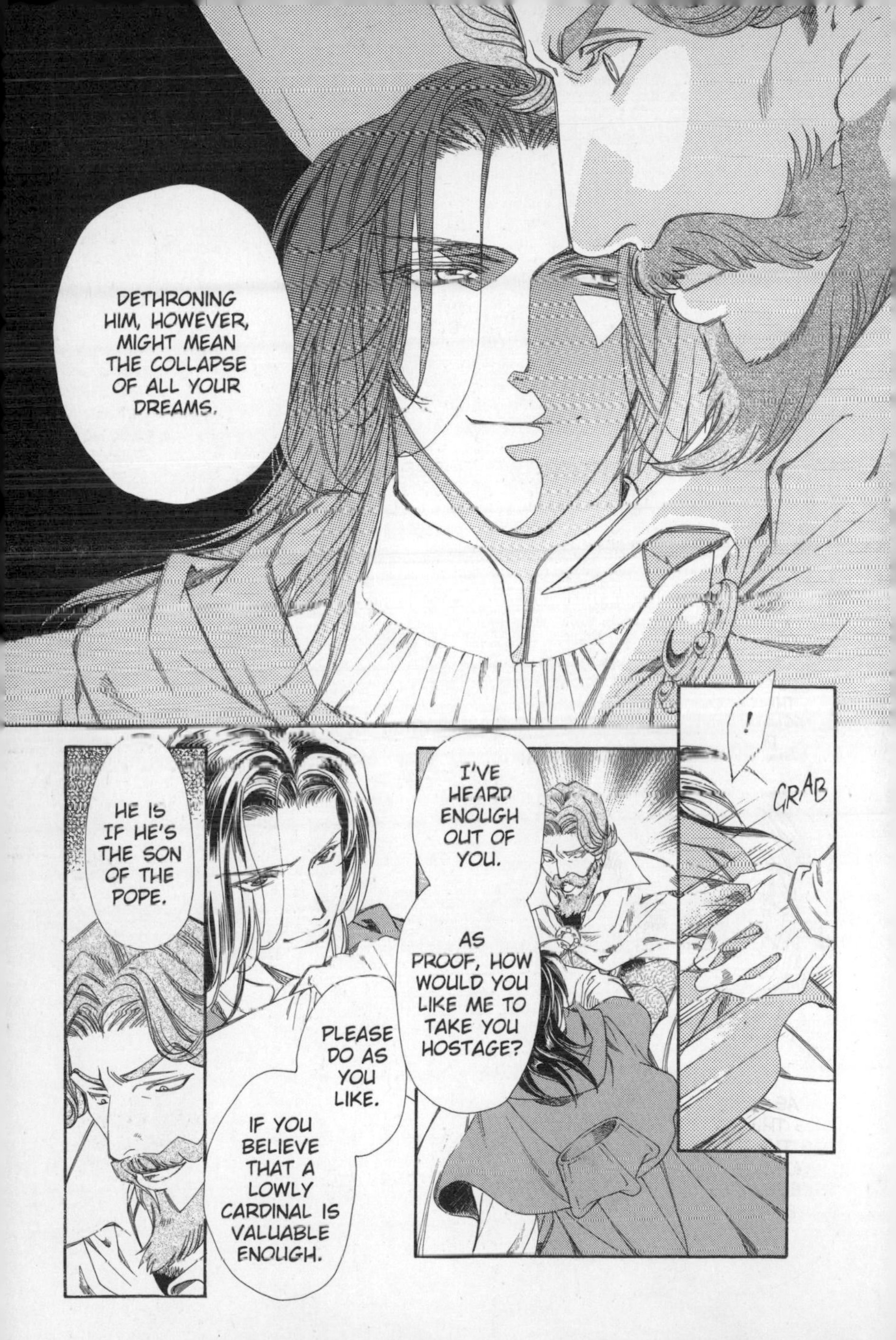
DETHRONING HIM, HOWEVER, MIGHT MEAN THE COLLAPSE OF ALL YOUR DREAMS.
!
GRAB
I'VE HEARD ENOUGH OUT OF YOU.
AS PROOF, HOW WOULD YOU LIKE ME TO TAKE YOU HOSTAGE?
HE IS IF HE'S THE SON OF THE POPE.
PLEASE DO AS YOU LIKE.
IF YOU BELIEVE THAT A LOWLY CARDINAL IS VALUABLE ENOUGH.

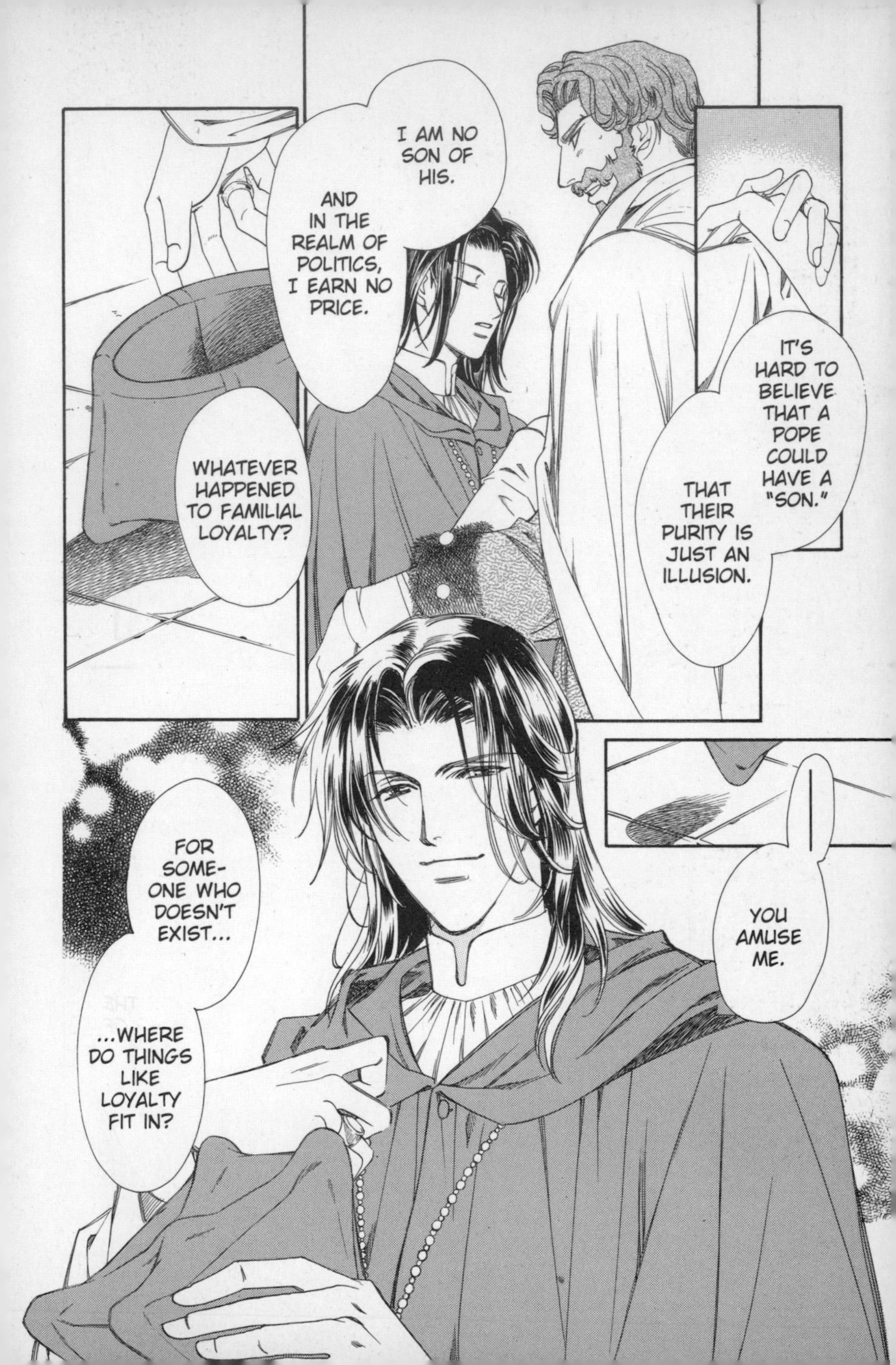
IT'S HARD TO BELIEVE THAT A POPE COULD HAVE A "SON."
THAT THEIR PURITY IS JUST AN ILLUSION.
I AM NO SON OF HIS.
AND IN THE REALM OF POLITICS, I EARN NO PRICE.
WHATEVER HAPPENED TO FAMILIAL LOYALTY?
!
YOU AMUSE ME.
FOR SOME-ONE WHO DOESN'T EXIST...
...WHERE DO THINGS LIKE LOYALTY FIT IN?

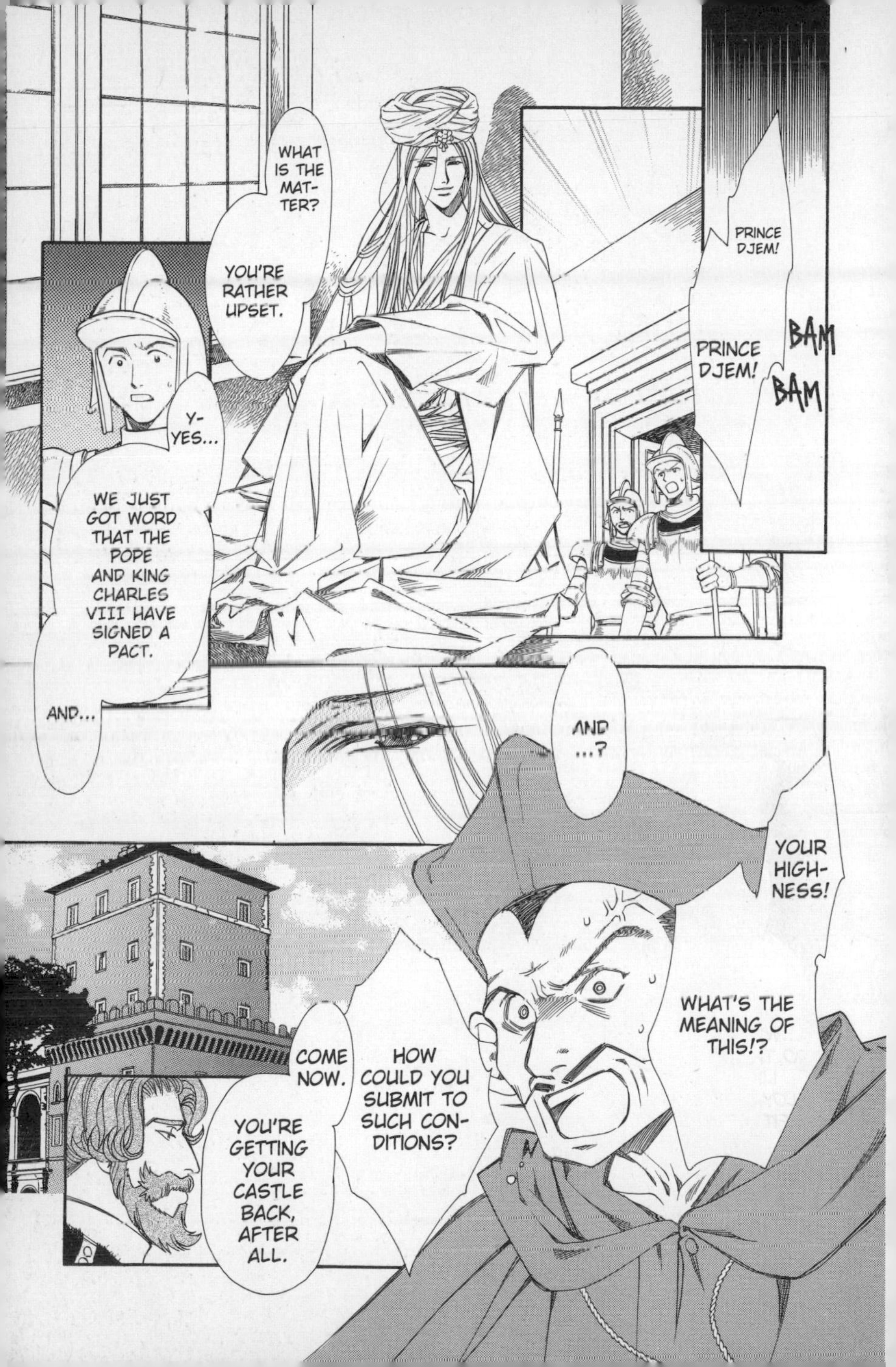
PRINCE DJEM!
BAM
PRINCE DJEM!
BAM
WHAT IS THE MATTER?
YOU'RE RATHER UPSET.
Y-YES...
WE JUST GOT WORD THAT THE POPE AND KING CHARLES VIII HAVE SIGNED A PACT.
AND...
AND ...?
YOUR HIGHNESS!
WHAT'S THE MEANING OF THIS!?
HOW COULD YOU SUBMIT TO SUCH CONDITIONS?
COME NOW.
YOU'RE GETTING YOUR CASTLE BACK, AFTER ALL.

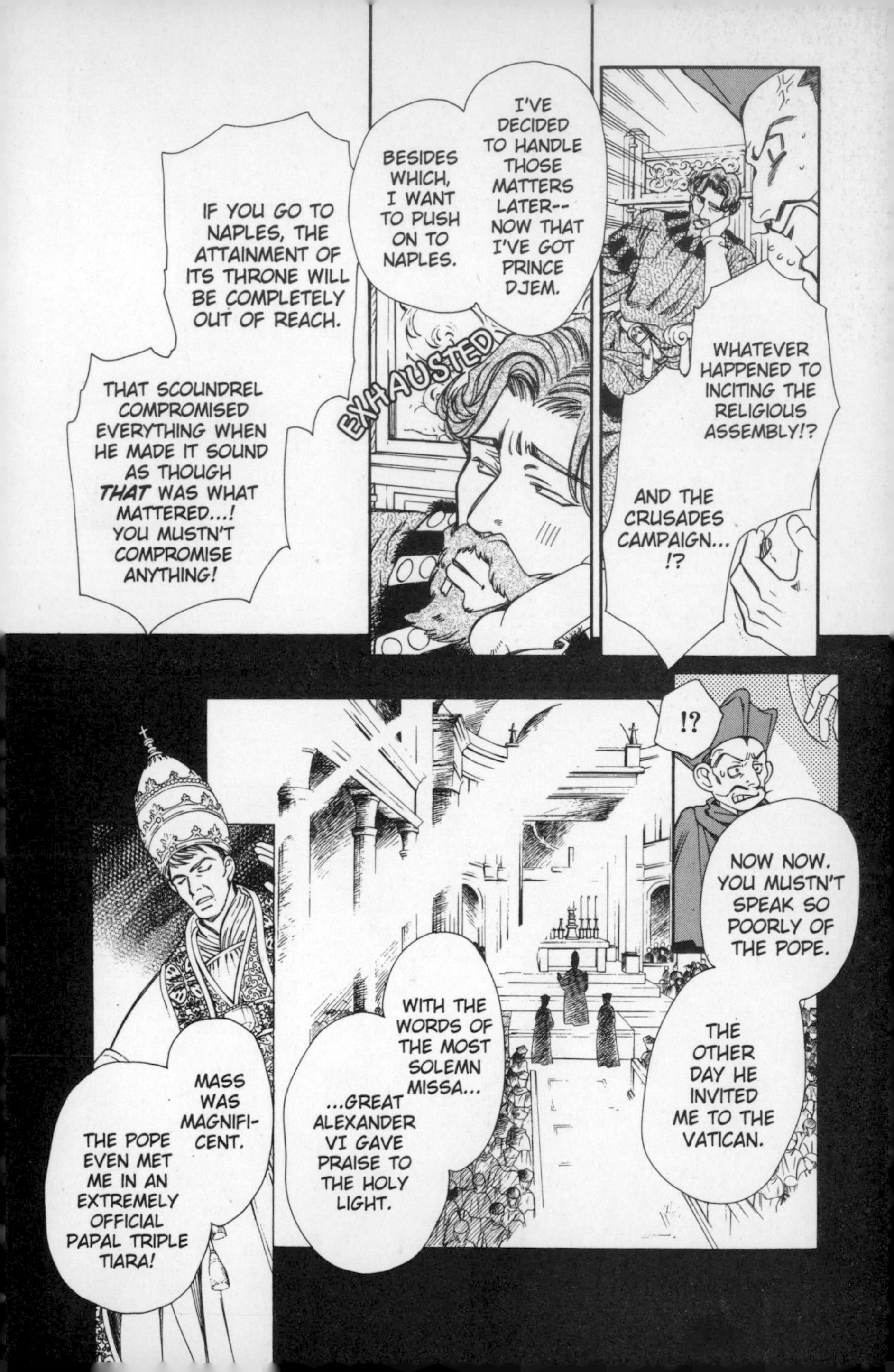
WHATEVER HAPPENED TO INCITING THE RELIGIOUS ASSEMBLY!?
AND THE CRUSADES CAMPAIGN... !?
I'VE DECIDED TO HANDLE THOSE MATTERS LATER-- NOW THAT I'VE GOT PRINCE DJEM.
BESIDES WHICH, I WANT TO PUSH ON TO NAPLES.
EXHAUSTED
IF YOU GO TO NAPLES, THE ATTAINMENT OF ITS THRONE WILL BE COMPLETELY OUT OF REACH.
THAT SCOUNDREL COMPROMISED EVERYTHING WHEN HE MADE IT SOUND AS THOUGH *THAT* WAS WHAT MATTERED...! YOU MUSTN'T COMPROMISE ANYTHING!
!?
NOW NOW. YOU MUSTN'T SPEAK SO POORLY OF THE POPE.
THE OTHER DAY HE INVITED ME TO THE VATICAN.
WITH THE WORDS OF THE MOST SOLEMN MISSA...
...GREAT ALEXANDER VI GAVE PRAISE TO THE HOLY LIGHT.
MASS WAS MAGNIFI-CENT.
THE POPE EVEN MET ME IN AN EXTREMELY OFFICIAL PAPAL TRIPLE TIARA!

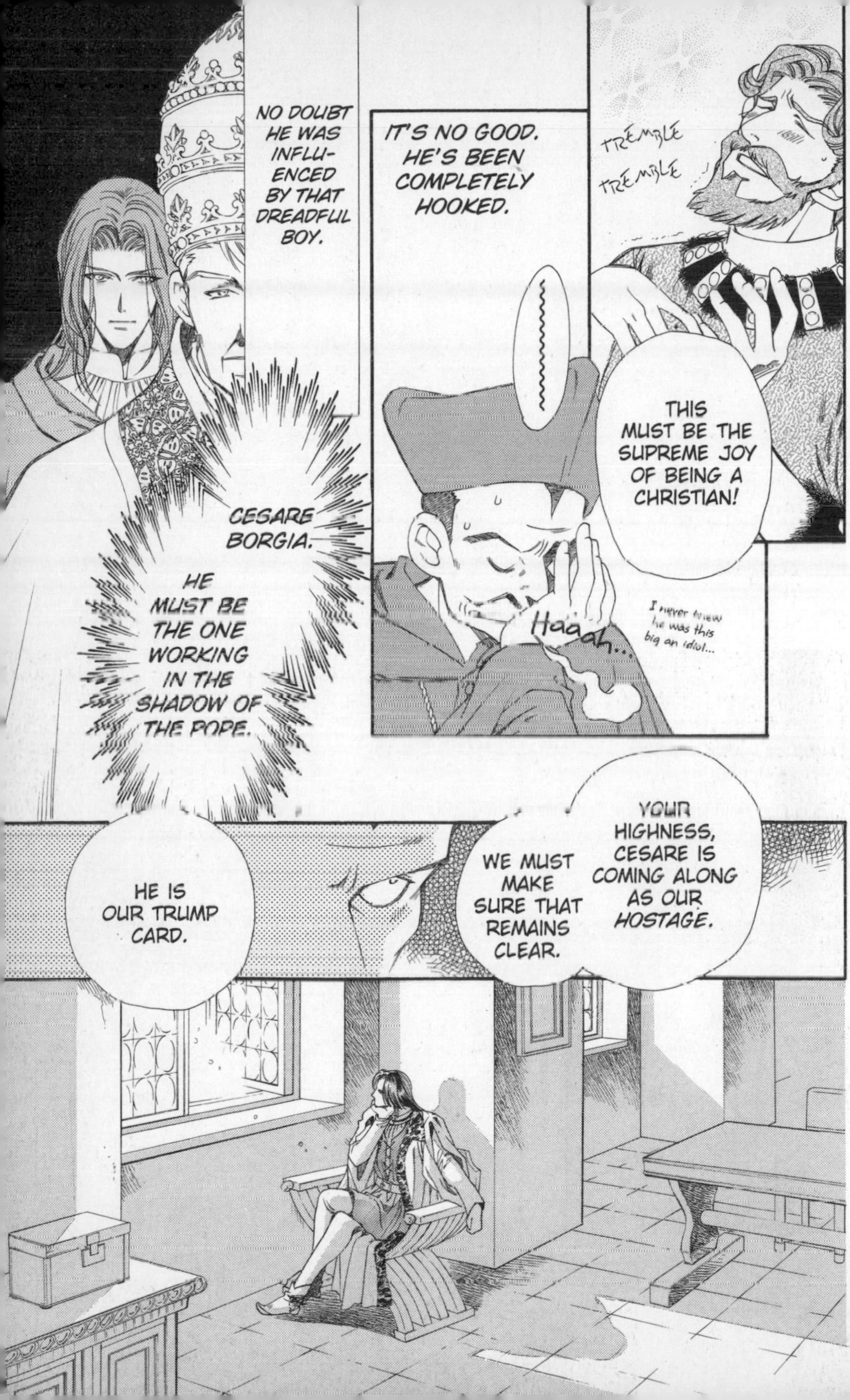
TREMBLE
TREMBLE
THIS MUST BE THE SUPREME JOY OF BEING A CHRISTIAN!
IT'S NO GOOD. HE'S BEEN COMPLETELY HOOKED.
Haaah...
I never knew he was this big an idiot...
NO DOUBT HE WAS INFLUENCED BY THAT DREADFUL BOY.
CESARE BORGIA.
HE MUST BE THE ONE WORKING IN THE SHADOW OF THE POPE.
YOUR HIGHNESS, CESARE IS COMING ALONG AS OUR HOSTAGE.
WE MUST MAKE SURE THAT REMAINS CLEAR.
HE IS OUR TRUMP CARD.

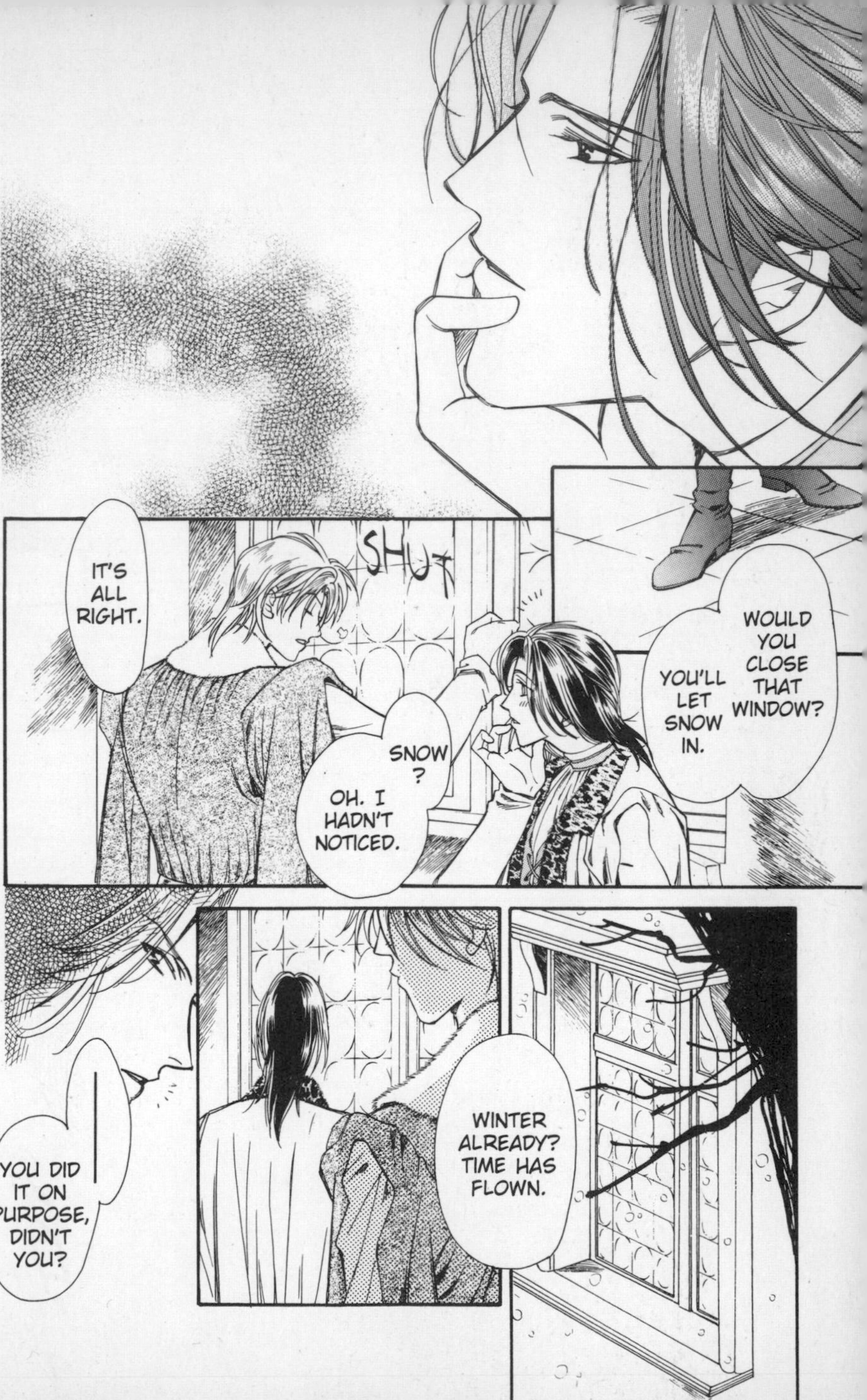
WOULD YOU CLOSE THAT WINDOW?
YOU'LL LET SNOW IN.
SHUT
SNOW?
OH. I HADN'T NOTICED.
IT'S ALL RIGHT.
WINTER ALREADY? TIME HAS FLOWN.
YOU DID IT ON PURPOSE, DIDN'T YOU?

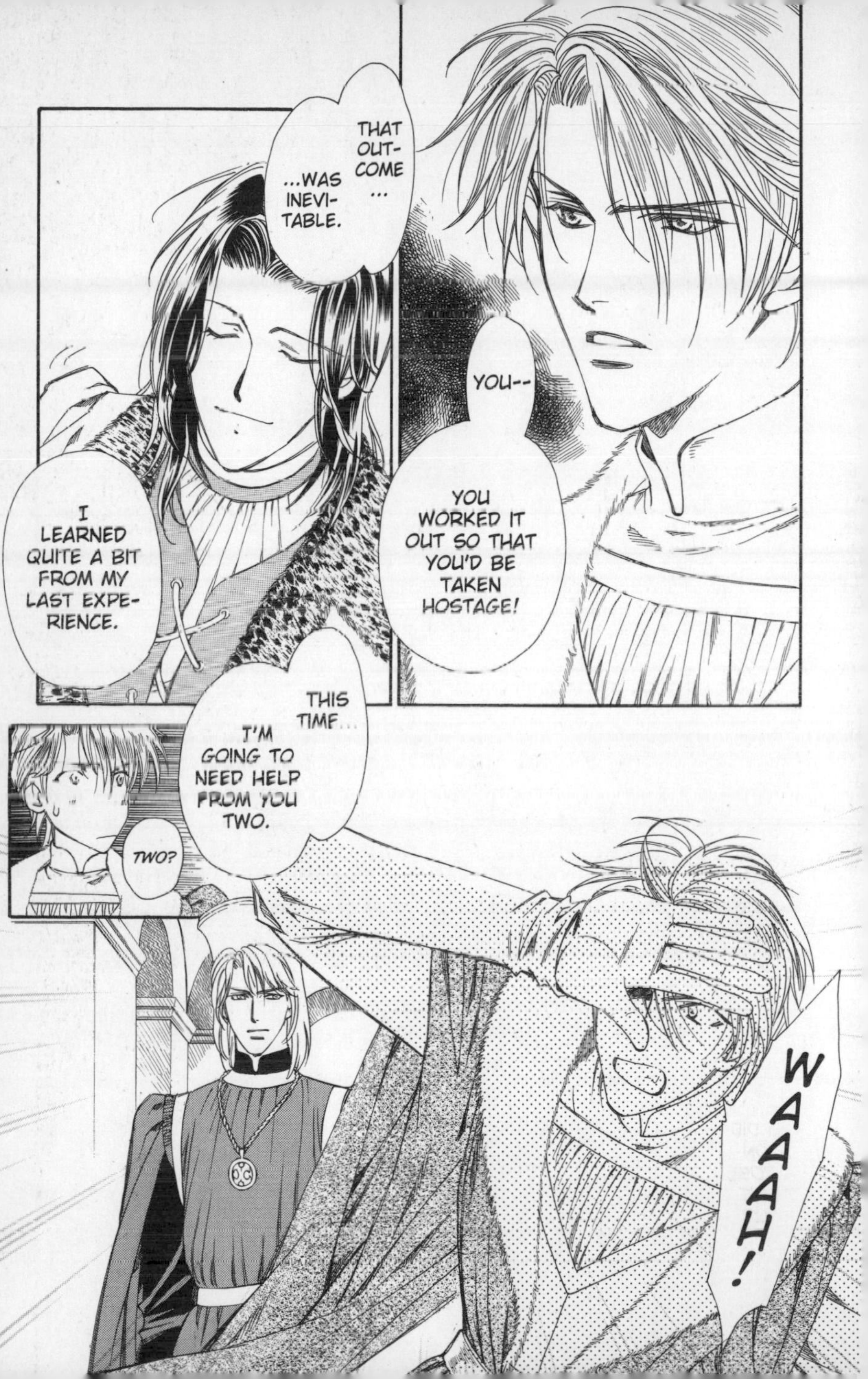
YOU--
YOU WORKED IT OUT SO THAT YOU'D BE TAKEN HOSTAGE!
THAT OUT-COME ...
...WAS INEVI-TABLE.
I LEARNED QUITE A BIT FROM MY LAST EXPE-RIENCE.
THIS TIME...
I'M GOING TO NEED HELP FROM YOU TWO.
WAAAH!
TWO?

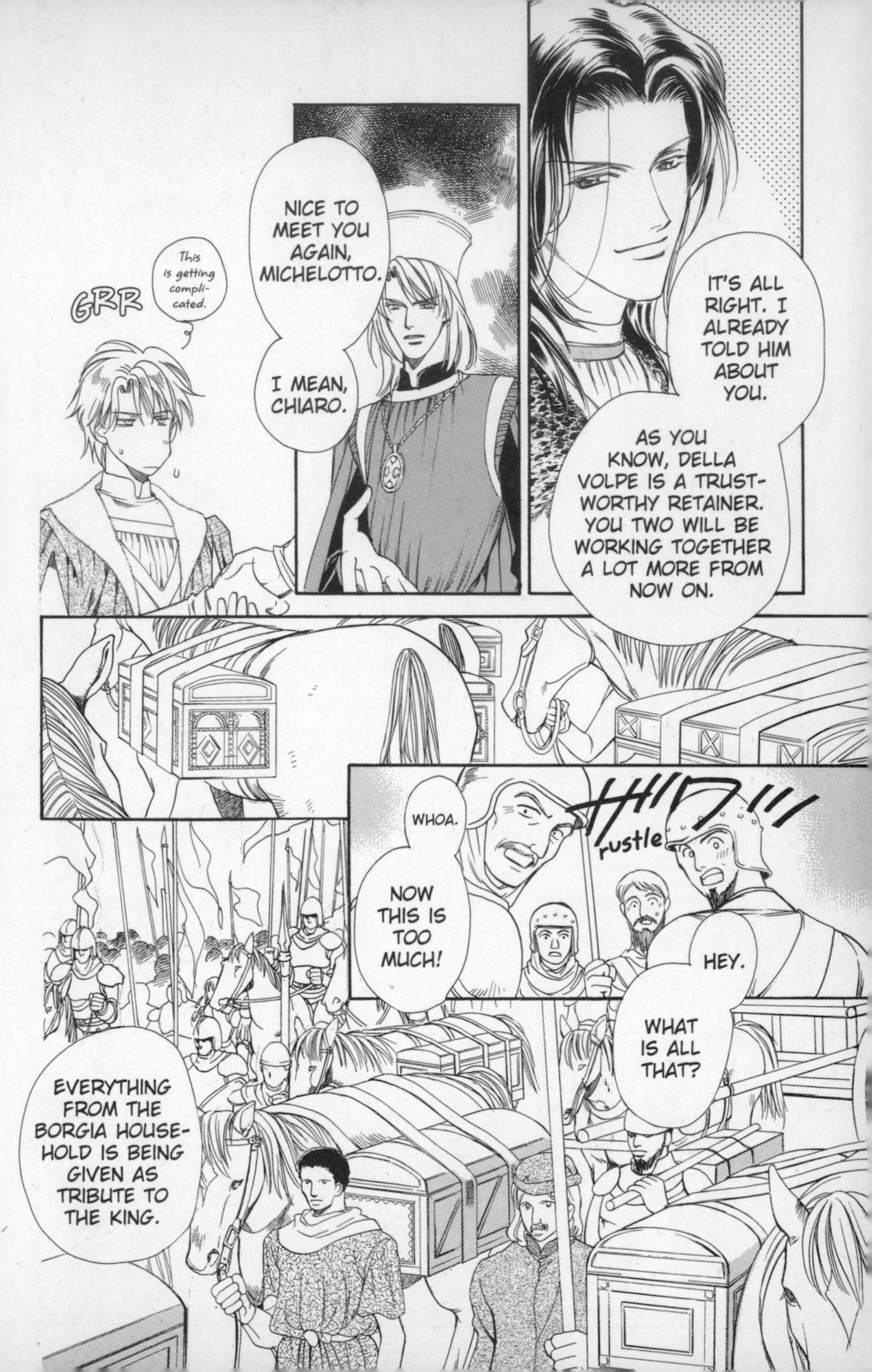
IT'S ALL RIGHT. I ALREADY TOLD HIM ABOUT YOU.
AS YOU KNOW, DELLA VOLPE IS A TRUST-WORTHY RETAINER. YOU TWO WILL BE WORKING TOGETHER A LOT MORE FROM NOW ON.
NICE TO MEET YOU AGAIN, MICHELOTTO.
I MEAN, CHIARO.
This is getting compli-cated.
GRR
rustle
WHOA.
NOW THIS IS TOO MUCH!
HEY.
WHAT IS ALL THAT?
EVERYTHING FROM THE BORGIA HOUSE-HOLD IS BEING GIVEN AS TRIBUTE TO THE KING.

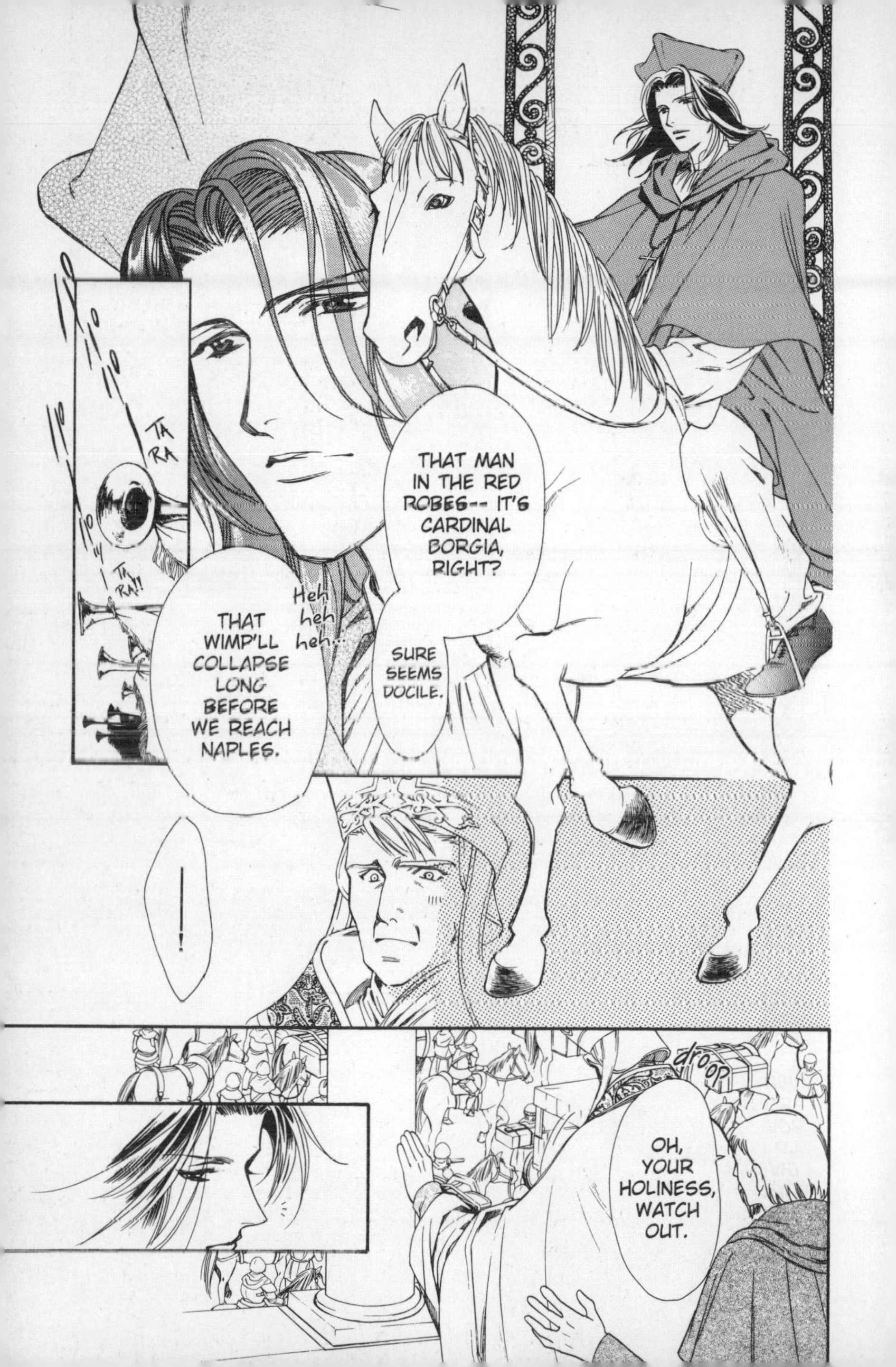
THAT MAN IN THE RED ROBES-- IT'S CARDINAL BORGIA, RIGHT?
SURE SEEMS DOCILE.
Heh heh heh...
THAT WIMP'LL COLLAPSE LONG BEFORE WE REACH NAPLES.
TA RA
TA RA!!
!
droop
OH, YOUR HOLINESS, WATCH OUT.

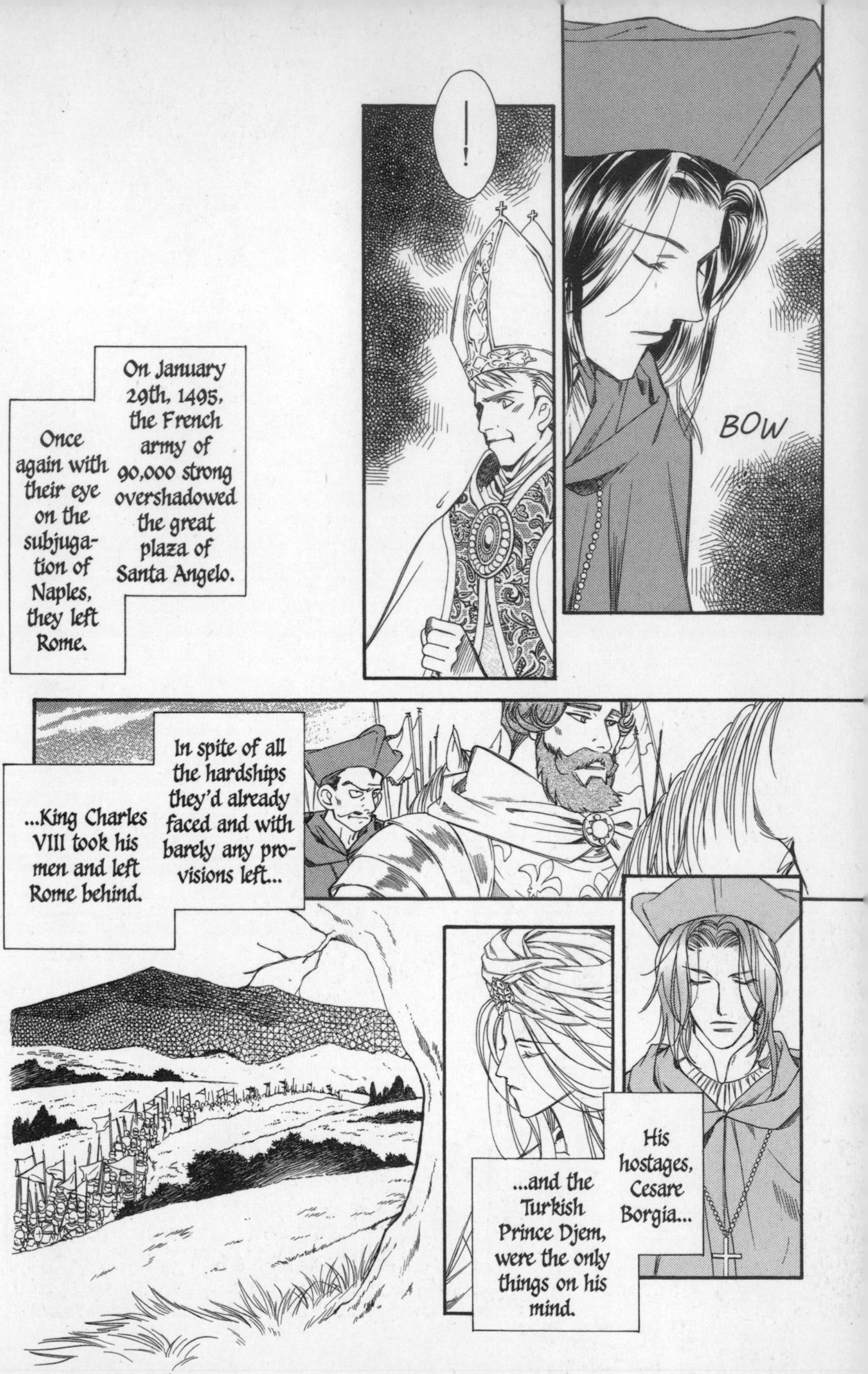
BOW
!
On January 29th, 1495, the French army of 90,000 strong overshadowed the great plaza of Santa Angelo.
Once again with their eye on the subjugation of Naples, they left Rome.
In spite of all the hardships they'd already faced and with barely any provisions left...
...King Charles VIII took his men and left Rome behind.
His hostages, Cesare Borgia...
...and the Turkish Prince Djem, were the only things on his mind.

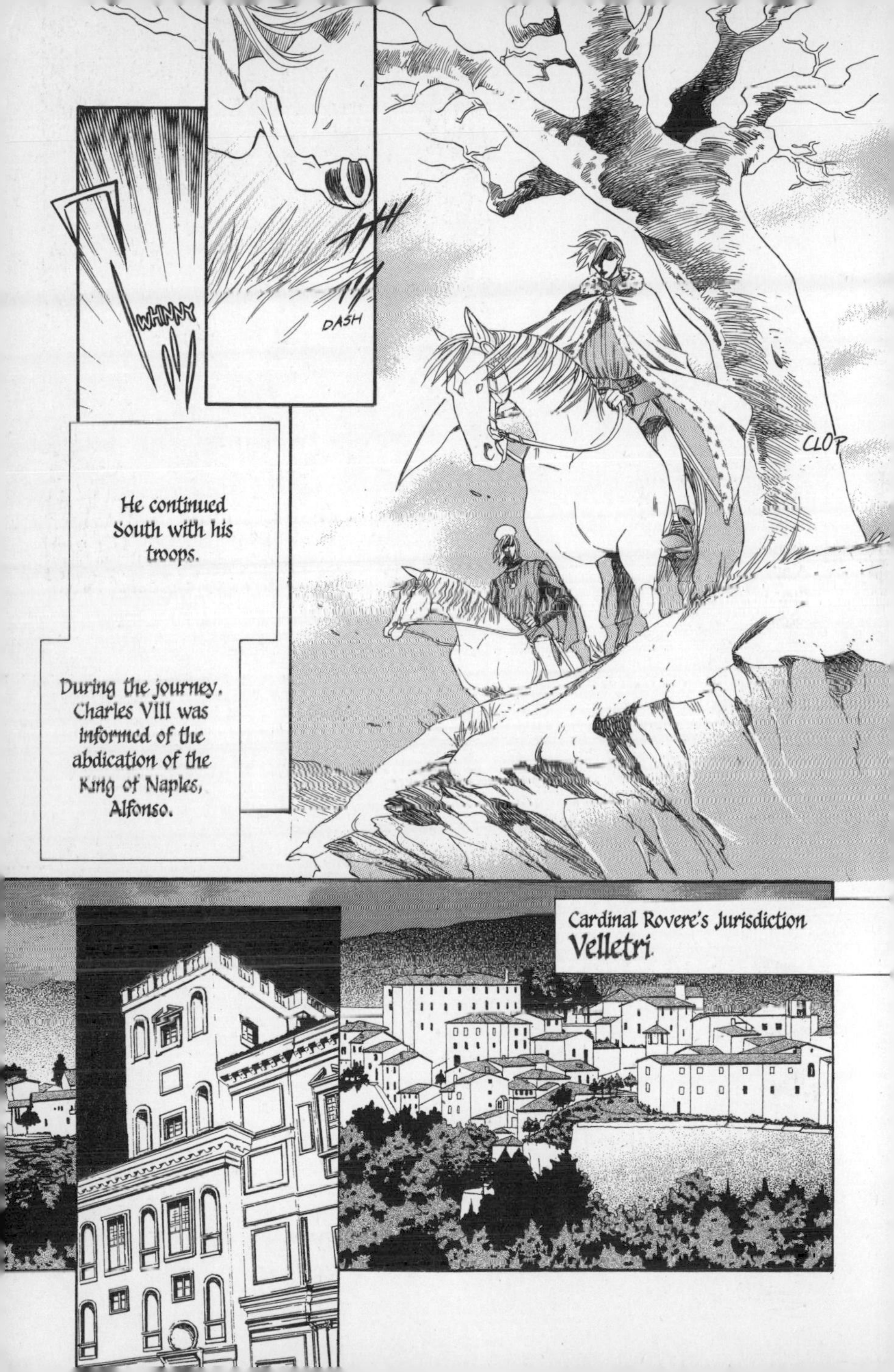
CLOP
DASH
WHNNY
He continued South with his troops.
During the journey, Charles VIII was informed of the abdication of the King of Naples, Alfonso.
Cardinal Rovere's Jurisdiction
Velletri

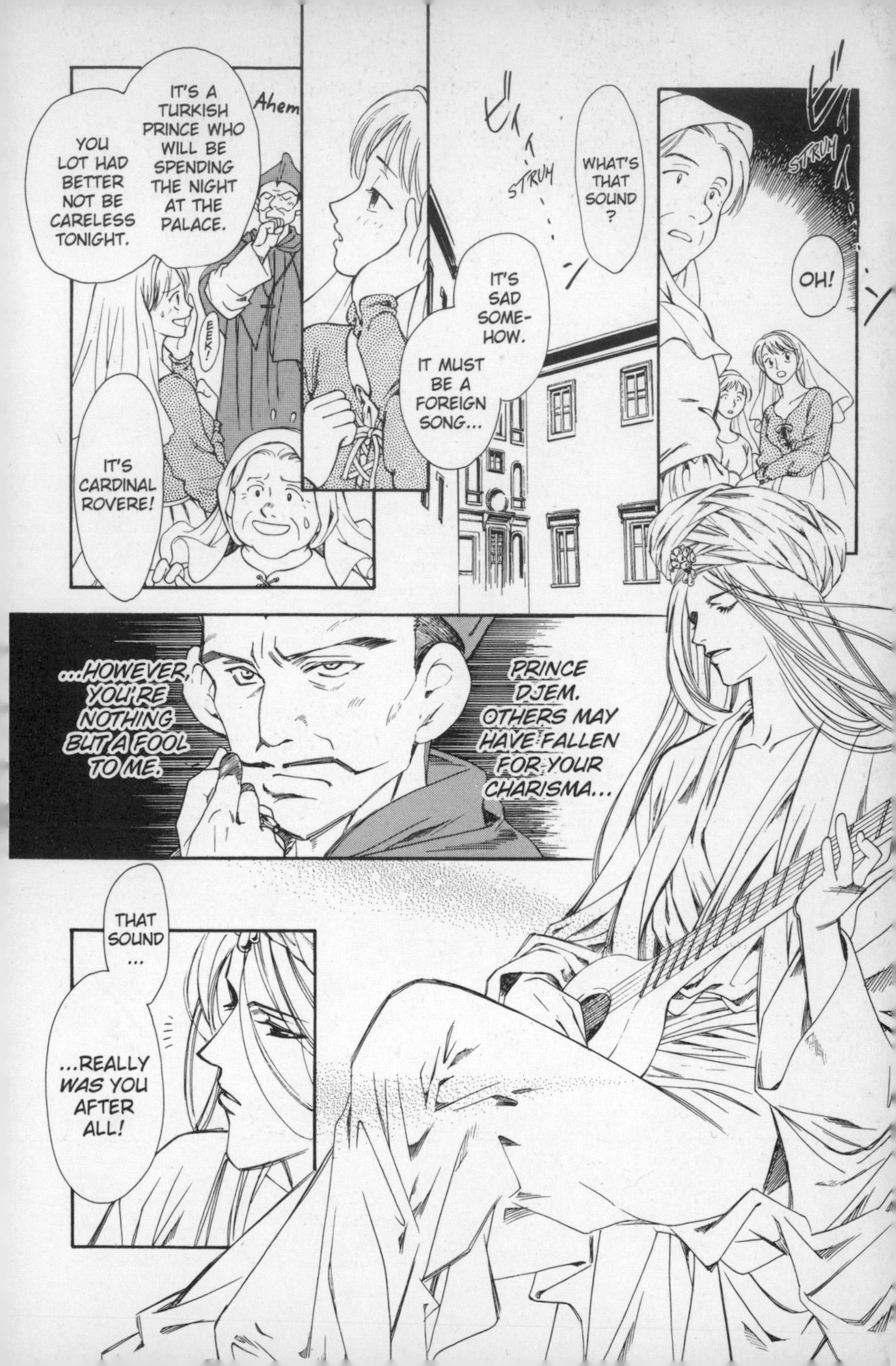
STRUM
OH!
STRUM
WHAT'S THAT SOUND?
IT'S SAD SOMEHOW.
IT MUST BE A FOREIGN SONG...
IT'S A TURKISH PRINCE WHO WILL BE SPENDING THE NIGHT AT THE PALACE.
Ahem
YOU LOT HAD BETTER NOT BE CARELESS TONIGHT.
EEK!
IT'S CARDINAL ROVERE!
PRINCE DJEM. OTHERS MAY HAVE FALLEN FOR YOUR CHARISMA...
...HOWEVER, YOU'RE NOTHING BUT A FOOL TO ME.
THAT SOUND...
...REALLY WAS YOU AFTER ALL!

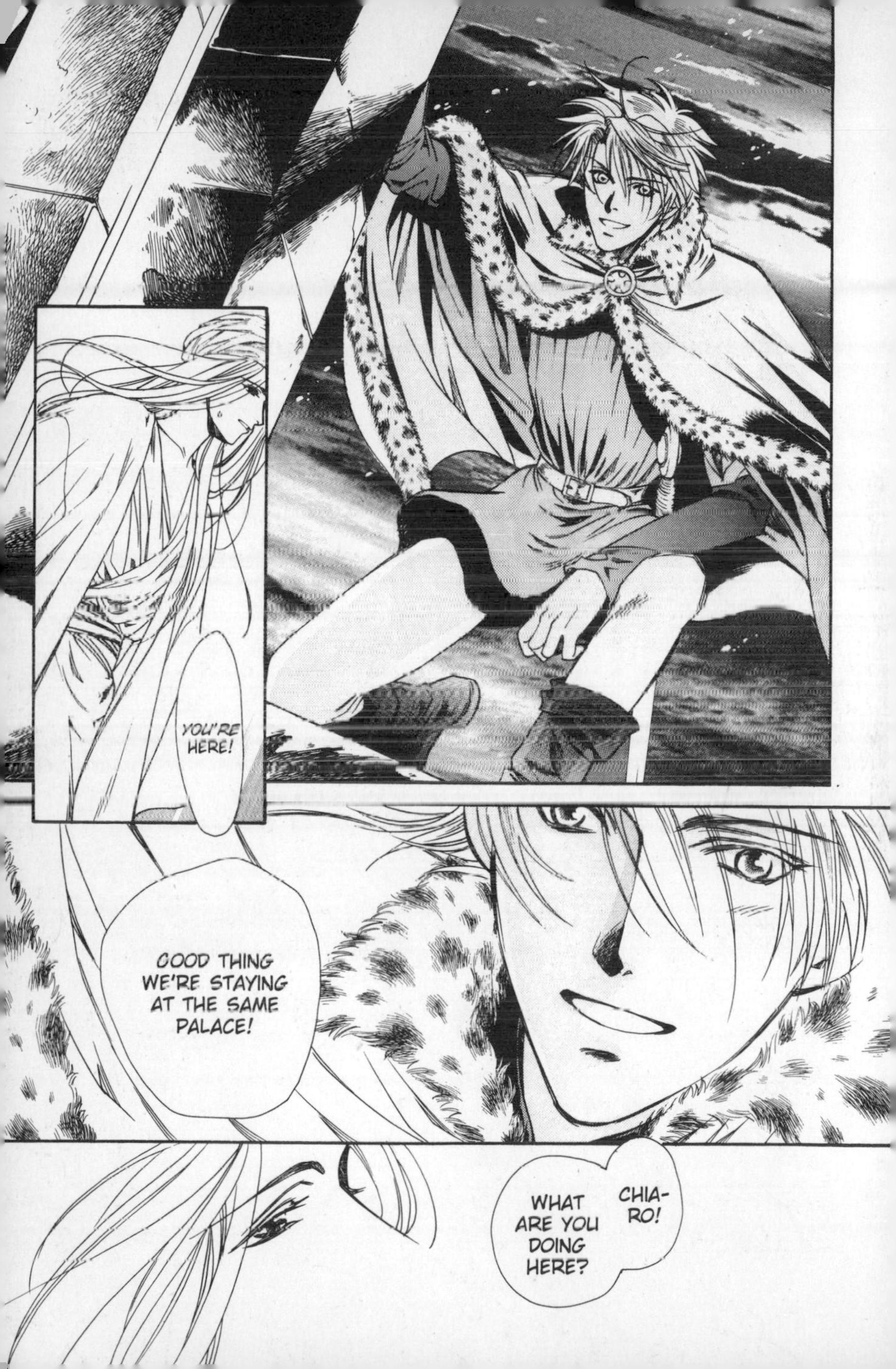
YOU'RE HERE!
GOOD THING WE'RE STAYING AT THE SAME PALACE!
CHIA-RO!
WHAT ARE YOU DOING HERE?

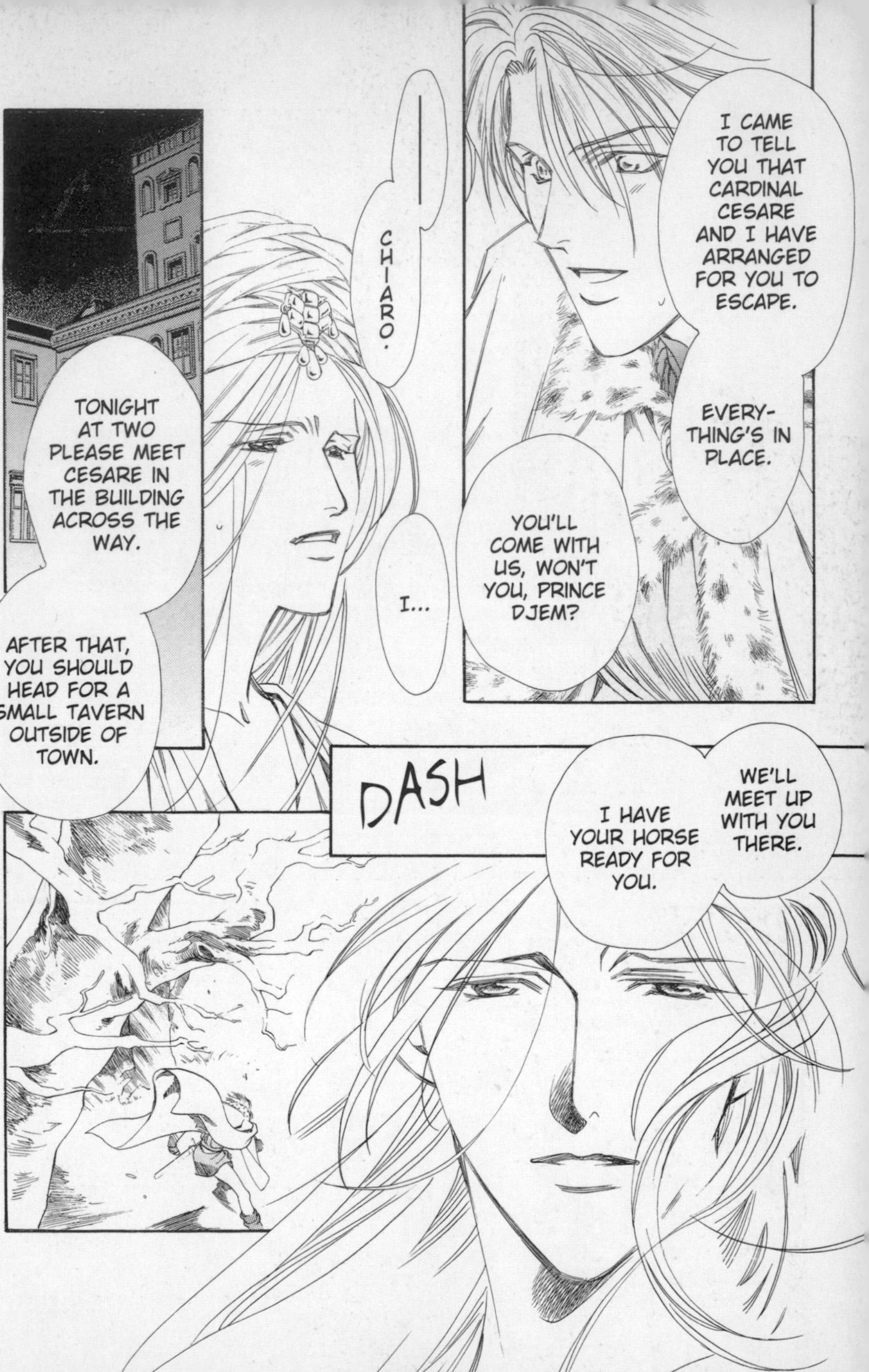
I CAME TO TELL YOU THAT CARDINAL CESARE AND I HAVE ARRANGED FOR YOU TO ESCAPE.
EVERY-THING'S IN PLACE.
YOU'LL COME WITH US, WON'T YOU, PRINCE DJEM?
—CHIARO.
I...
TONIGHT AT TWO PLEASE MEET CESARE IN THE BUILDING ACROSS THE WAY.
AFTER THAT, YOU SHOULD HEAD FOR A SMALL TAVERN OUTSIDE OF TOWN.
WE'LL MEET UP WITH YOU THERE.
I HAVE YOUR HORSE READY FOR YOU.
DASH

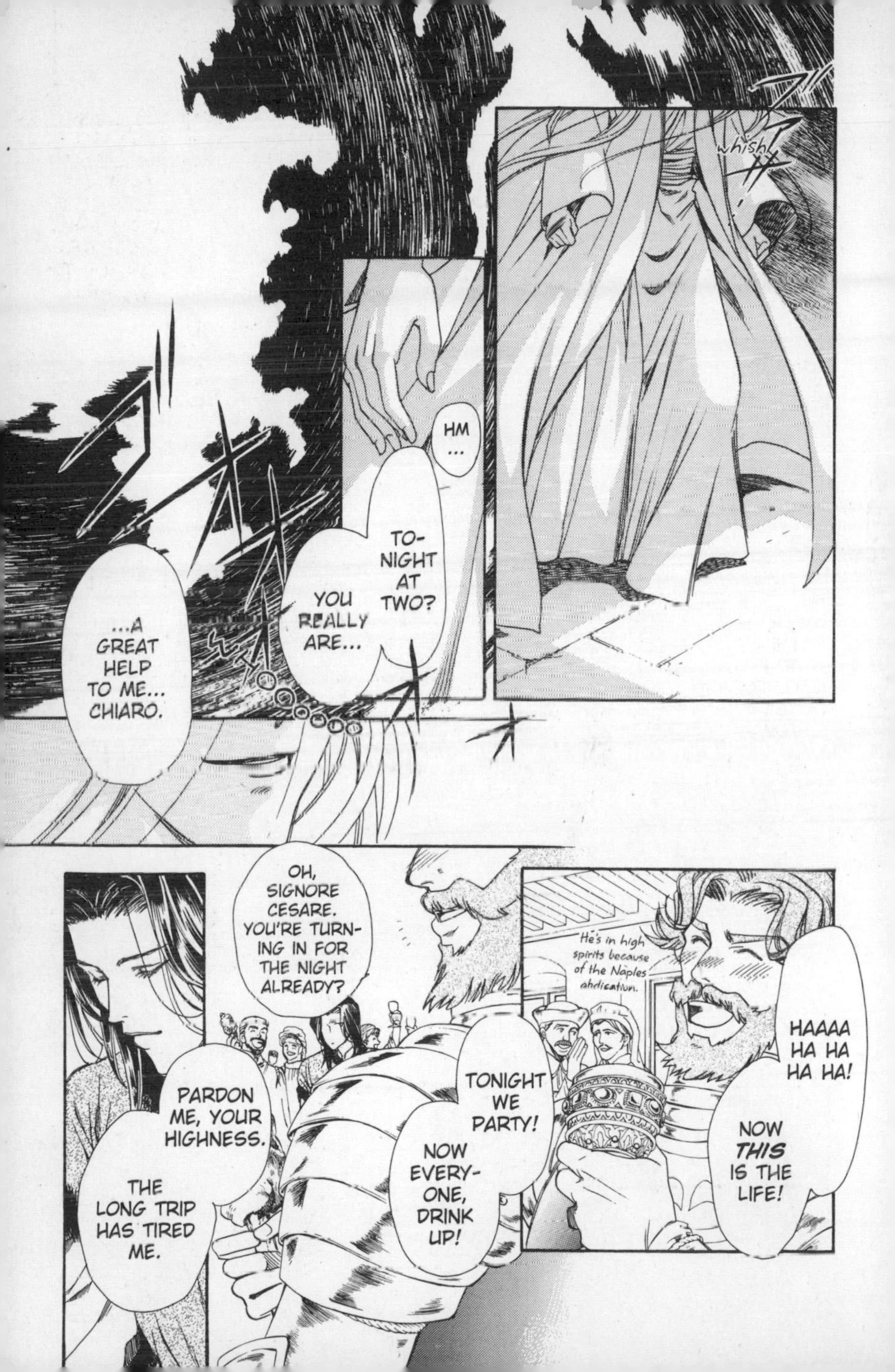
whish!
HM...
TO-NIGHT AT TWO?
YOU REALLY ARE...
...A GREAT HELP TO ME... CHIARO.
HAAAA HA HA HA HA!
NOW THIS IS THE LIFE!
He's in high spirits because of the Naples abdication.
TONIGHT WE PARTY!
NOW EVERY-ONE, DRINK UP!
OH, SIGNORE CESARE. YOU'RE TURNING-ING IN FOR THE NIGHT ALREADY?
PARDON ME, YOUR HIGHNESS.
THE LONG TRIP HAS TIRED ME.

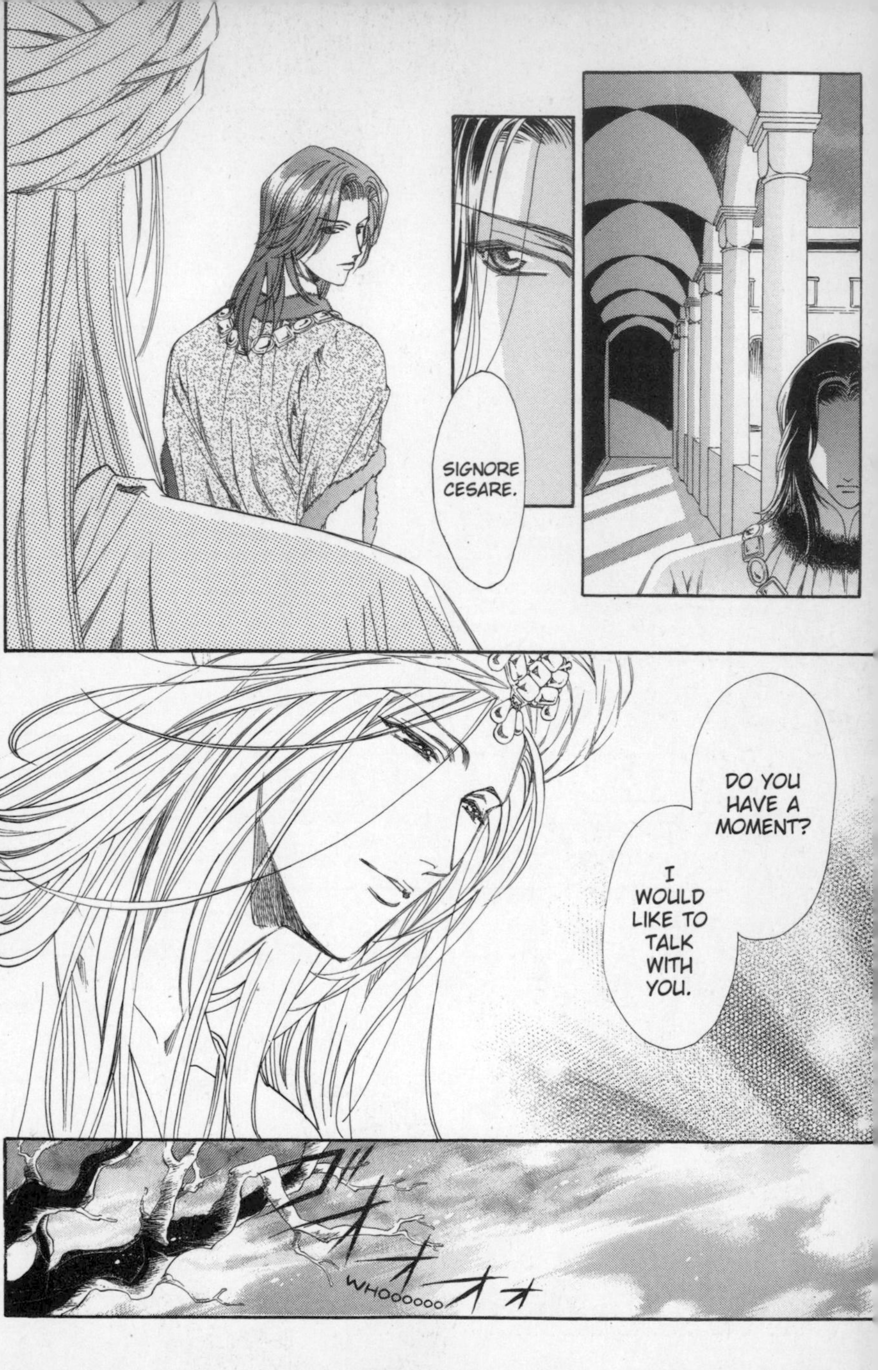
SIGNORE CESARE.
DO YOU HAVE A MOMENT?
I WOULD LIKE TO TALK WITH YOU.
WHOOOOOO

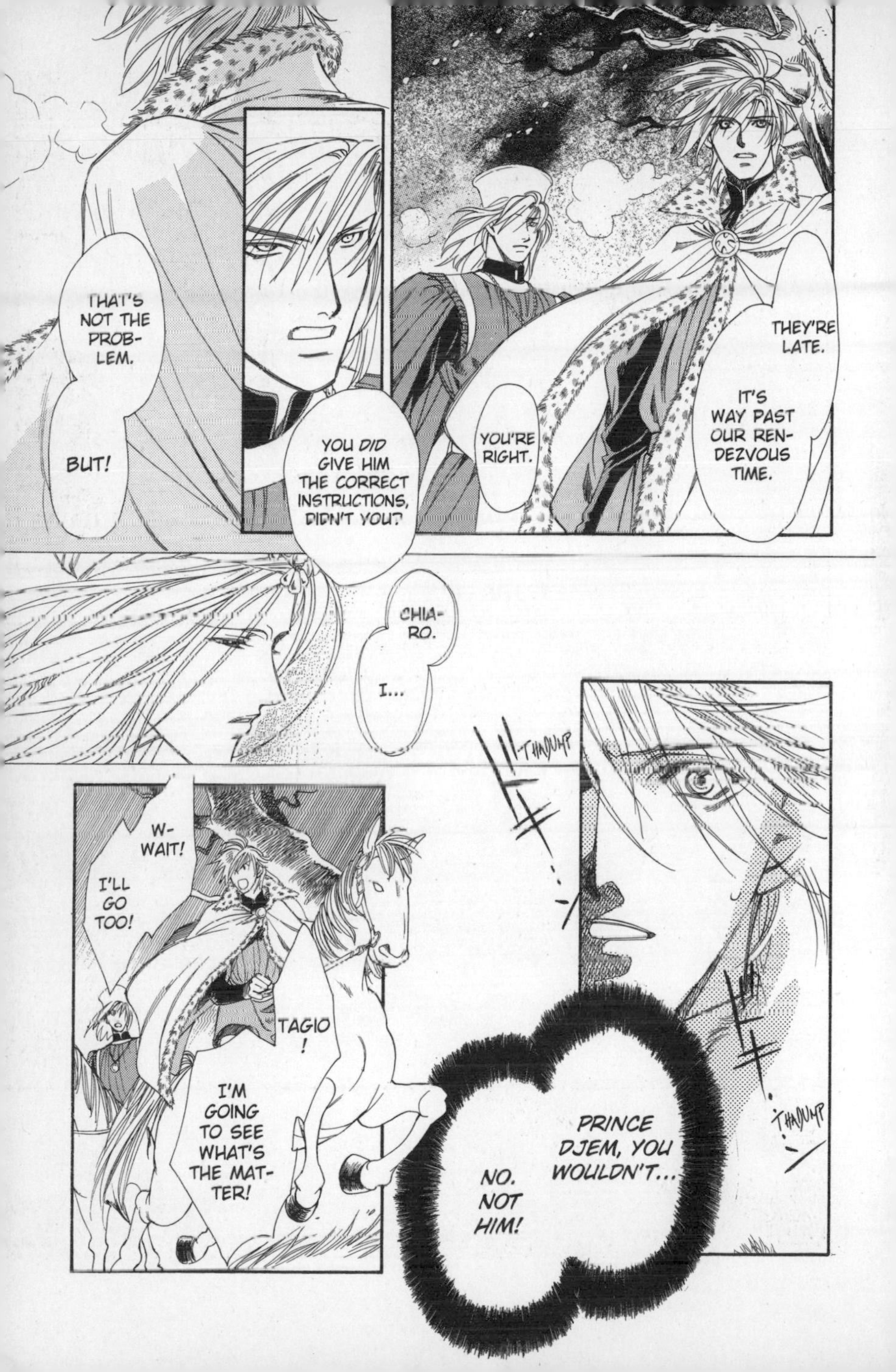
THEY'RE LATE.
IT'S WAY PAST OUR RENDEZVOUS TIME.
YOU'RE RIGHT.
YOU *DID* GIVE HIM THE CORRECT INSTRUCTIONS, DIDN'T YOU?
THAT'S NOT THE PROBLEM.
BUT!
CHIARO.
I...
THADUMP
THADUMP
PRINCE DJEM, YOU WOULDN'T...
NO. NOT HIM!
TAGIO!
I'M GOING TO SEE WHAT'S THE MATTER!
W-WAIT!
I'LL GO TOO!

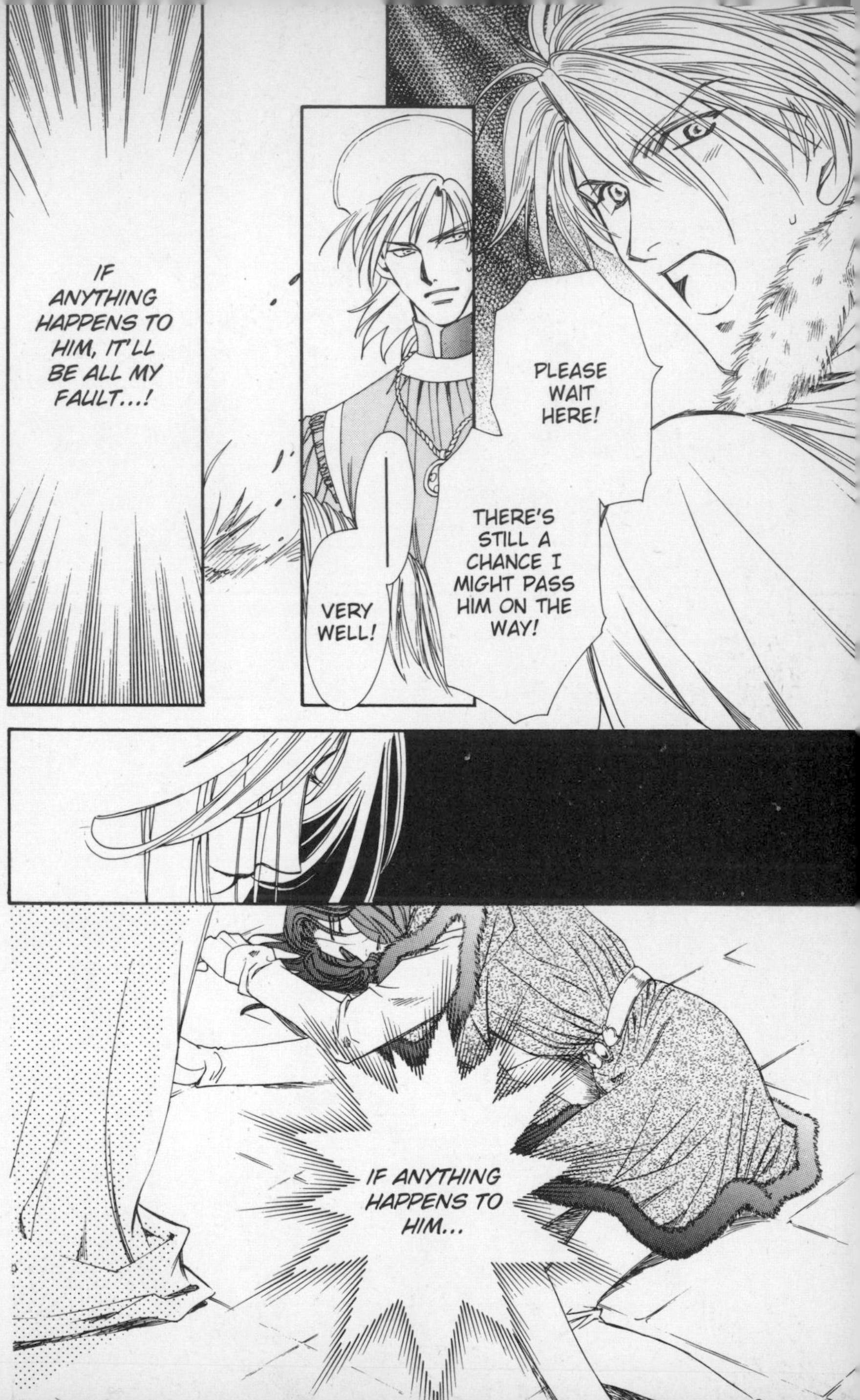
PLEASE WAIT HERE!
THERE'S STILL A CHANCE I MIGHT PASS HIM ON THE WAY!
VERY WELL!
IF ANYTHING HAPPENS TO HIM, IT'LL BE ALL MY FAULT...!
IF ANYTHING HAPPENS TO HIM...

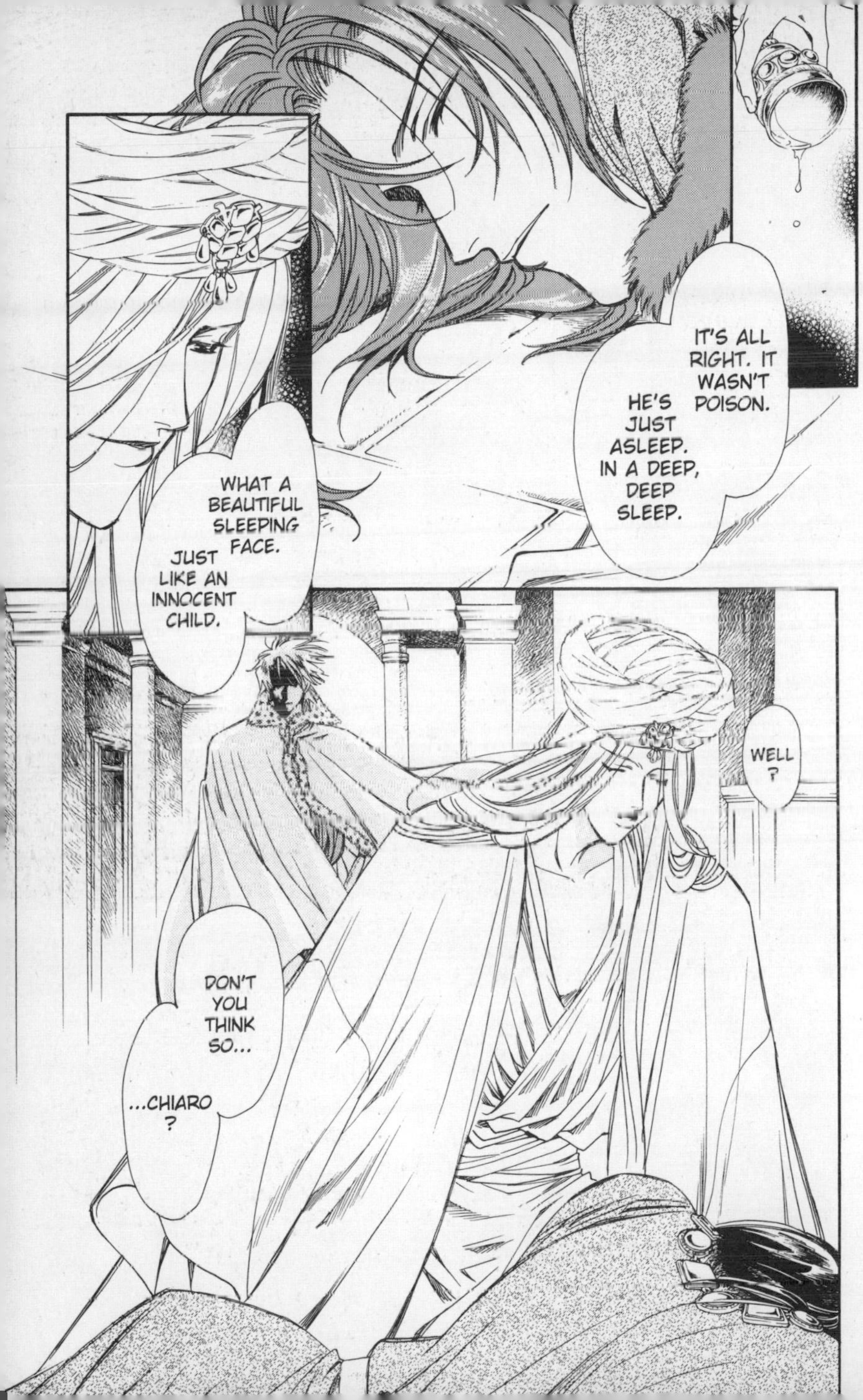
IT'S ALL RIGHT. IT WASN'T POISON.
HE'S JUST ASLEEP. IN A DEEP, DEEP SLEEP.
WHAT A BEAUTIFUL SLEEPING FACE.
JUST LIKE AN INNOCENT CHILD.
WELL?
DON'T YOU THINK SO...
...CHIARO?

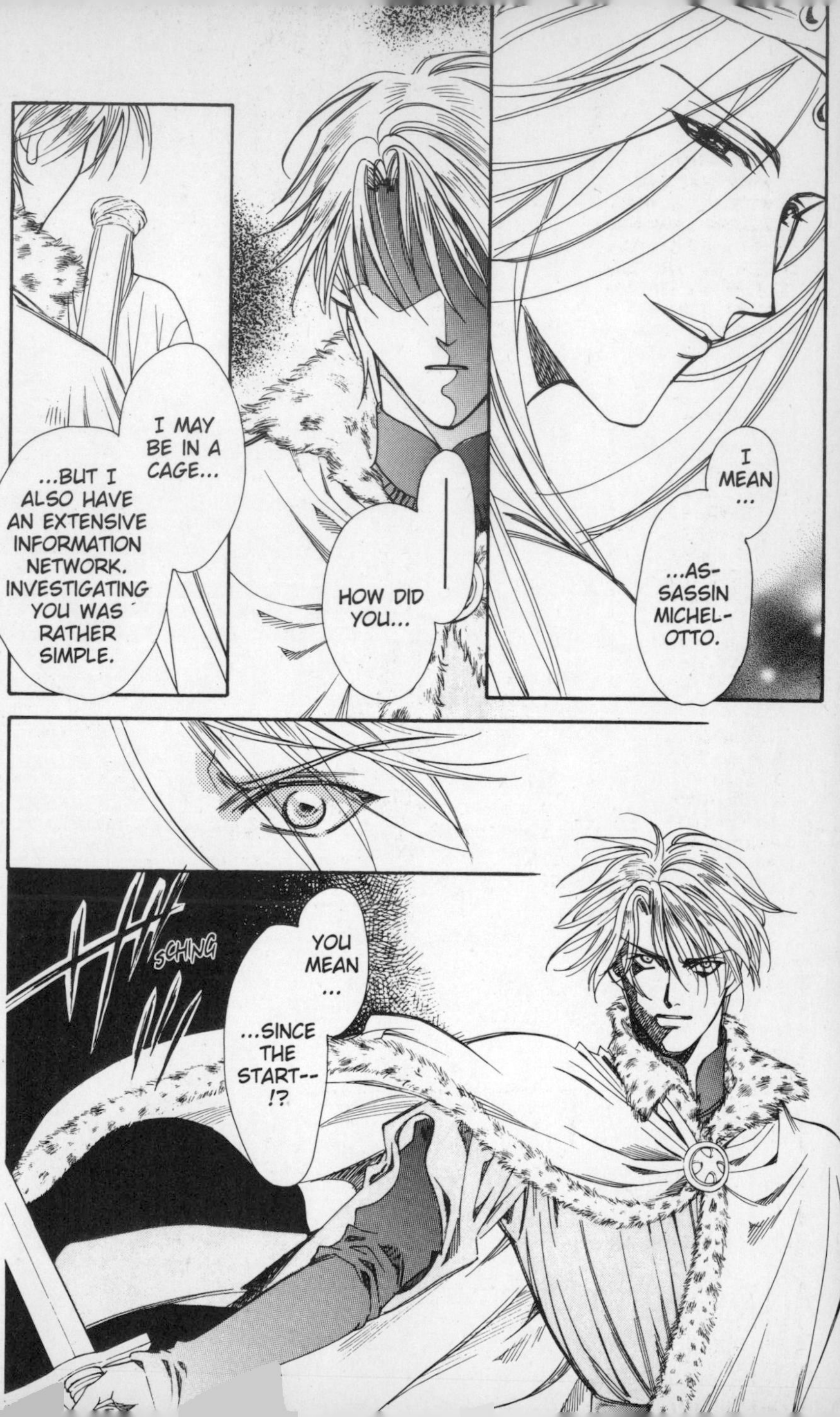
I MEAN ...
...AS-SASSIN MICHEL-OTTO.
HOW DID YOU...
I MAY BE IN A CAGE...
...BUT I ALSO HAVE AN EXTENSIVE INFORMATION NETWORK. INVESTIGATING YOU WAS RATHER SIMPLE.
YOU MEAN ...
...SINCE THE START--!?
SCHING

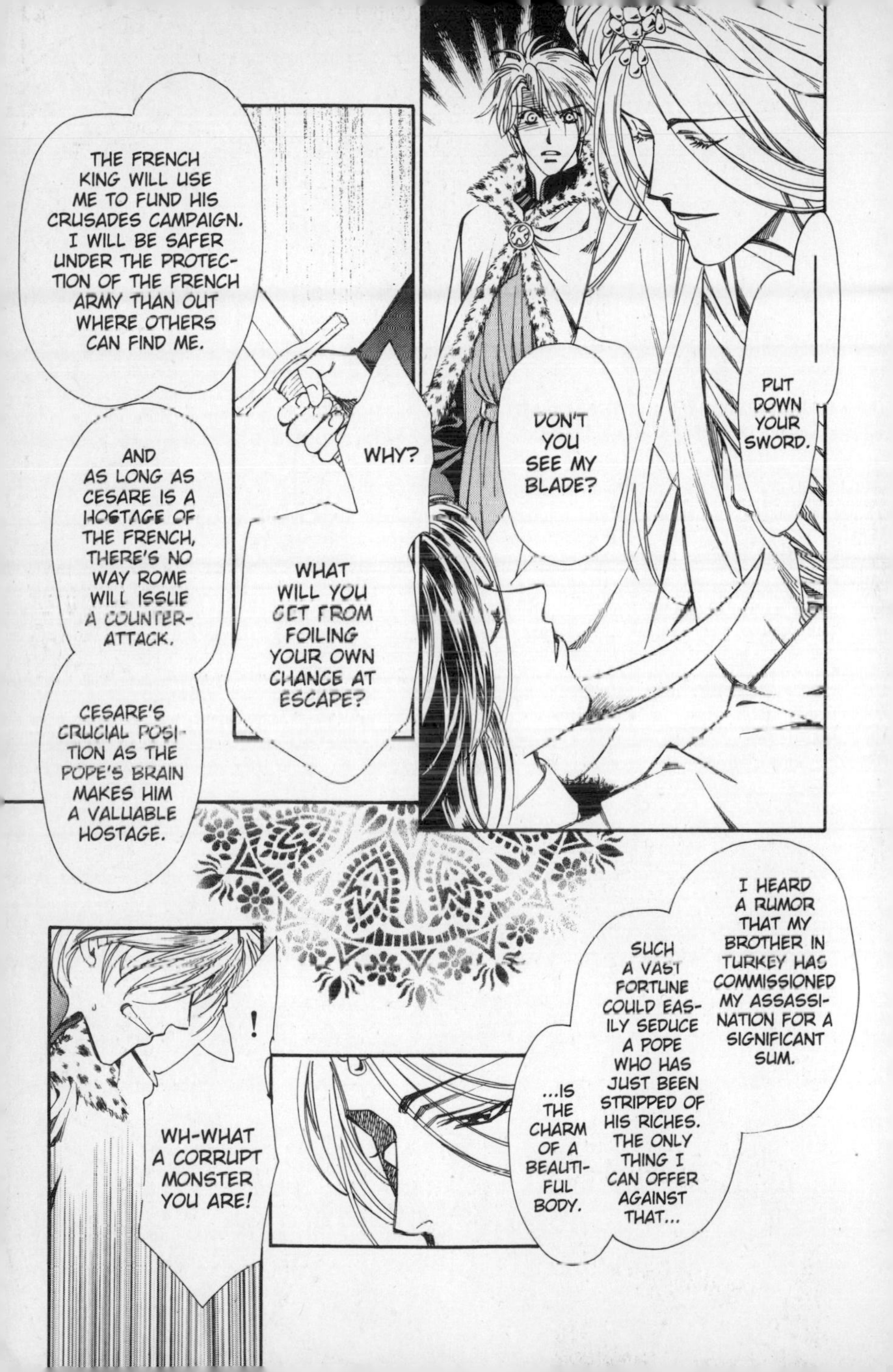
PUT DOWN YOUR SWORD.
DON'T YOU SEE MY BLADE?
WHY?
WHAT WILL YOU GET FROM FOILING YOUR OWN CHANCE AT ESCAPE?
THE FRENCH KING WILL USE ME TO FUND HIS CRUSADES CAMPAIGN. I WILL BE SAFER UNDER THE PROTECTION OF THE FRENCH ARMY THAN OUT WHERE OTHERS CAN FIND ME.
AND AS LONG AS CESARE IS A HOSTAGE OF THE FRENCH, THERE'S NO WAY ROME WILL ISSUE A COUNTER-ATTACK.
CESARE'S CRUCIAL POSITION AS THE POPE'S BRAIN MAKES HIM A VALUABLE HOSTAGE.
I HEARD A RUMOR THAT MY BROTHER IN TURKEY HAS COMMISSIONED MY ASSASSINATION FOR A SIGNIFICANT SUM.
SUCH A VAST FORTUNE COULD EASILY SEDUCE A POPE WHO HAS JUST BEEN STRIPPED OF HIS RICHES. THE ONLY THING I CAN OFFER AGAINST THAT...
...IS THE CHARM OF A BEAUTIFUL BODY.
!
WH-WHAT A CORRUPT MONSTER YOU ARE!

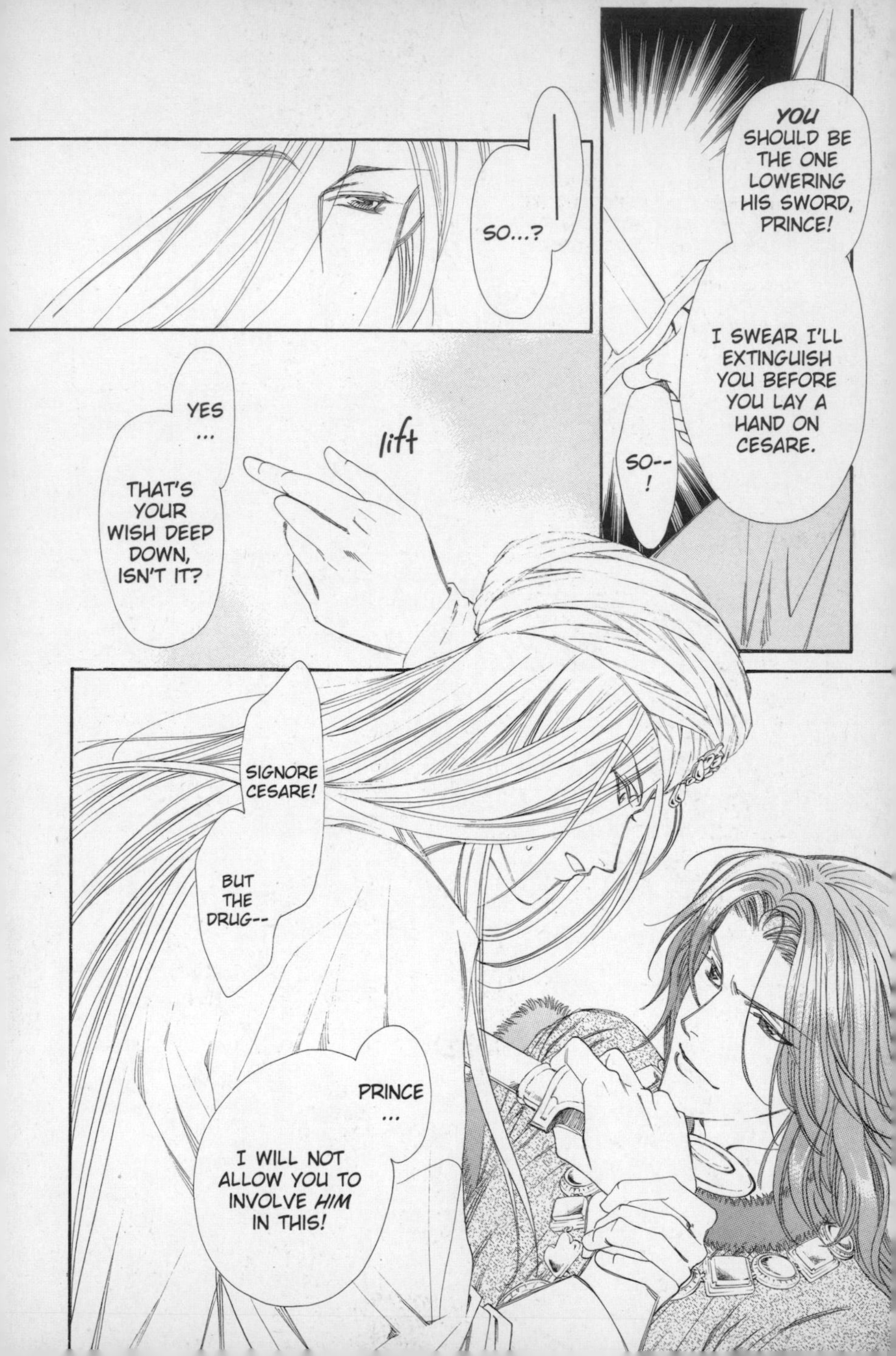
YOU SHOULD BE THE ONE LOWERING HIS SWORD, PRINCE!
I SWEAR I'LL EXTINGUISH YOU BEFORE YOU LAY A HAND ON CESARE.
SO--!
SO...?
lift
YES ... THAT'S YOUR WISH DEEP DOWN, ISN'T IT?
SIGNORE CESARE!
BUT THE DRUG--
PRINCE ...
I WILL NOT ALLOW YOU TO INVOLVE HIM IN THIS!

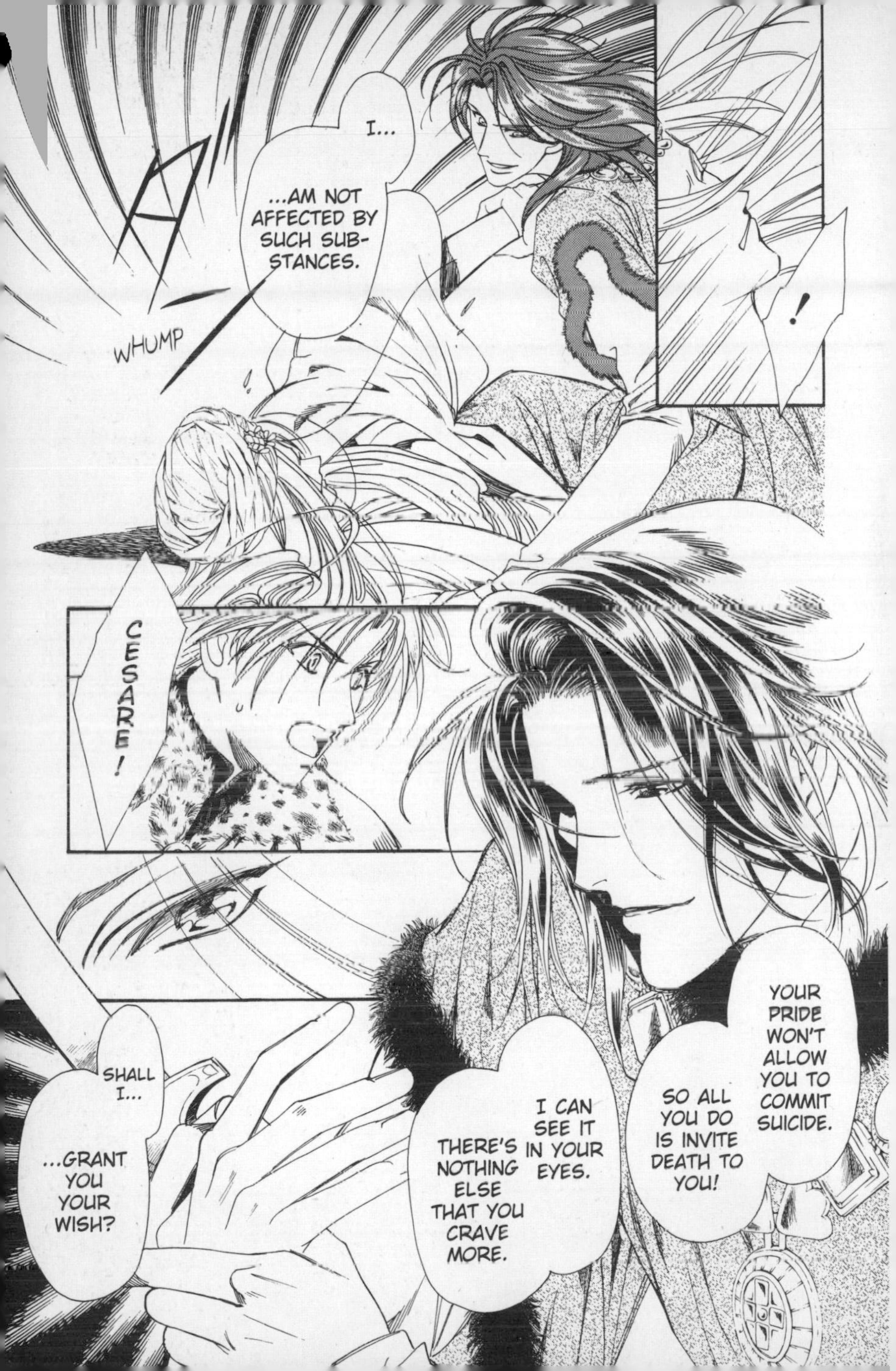
!
I...
...AM NOT AFFECTED BY SUCH SUB-STANCES.
WHUMP
CESARE!
YOUR PRIDE WON'T ALLOW YOU TO COMMIT SUICIDE.
SO ALL YOU DO IS INVITE DEATH TO YOU!
I CAN SEE IT IN YOUR EYES.
THERE'S NOTHING ELSE THAT YOU CRAVE MORE.
SHALL I...
...GRANT YOU YOUR WISH?

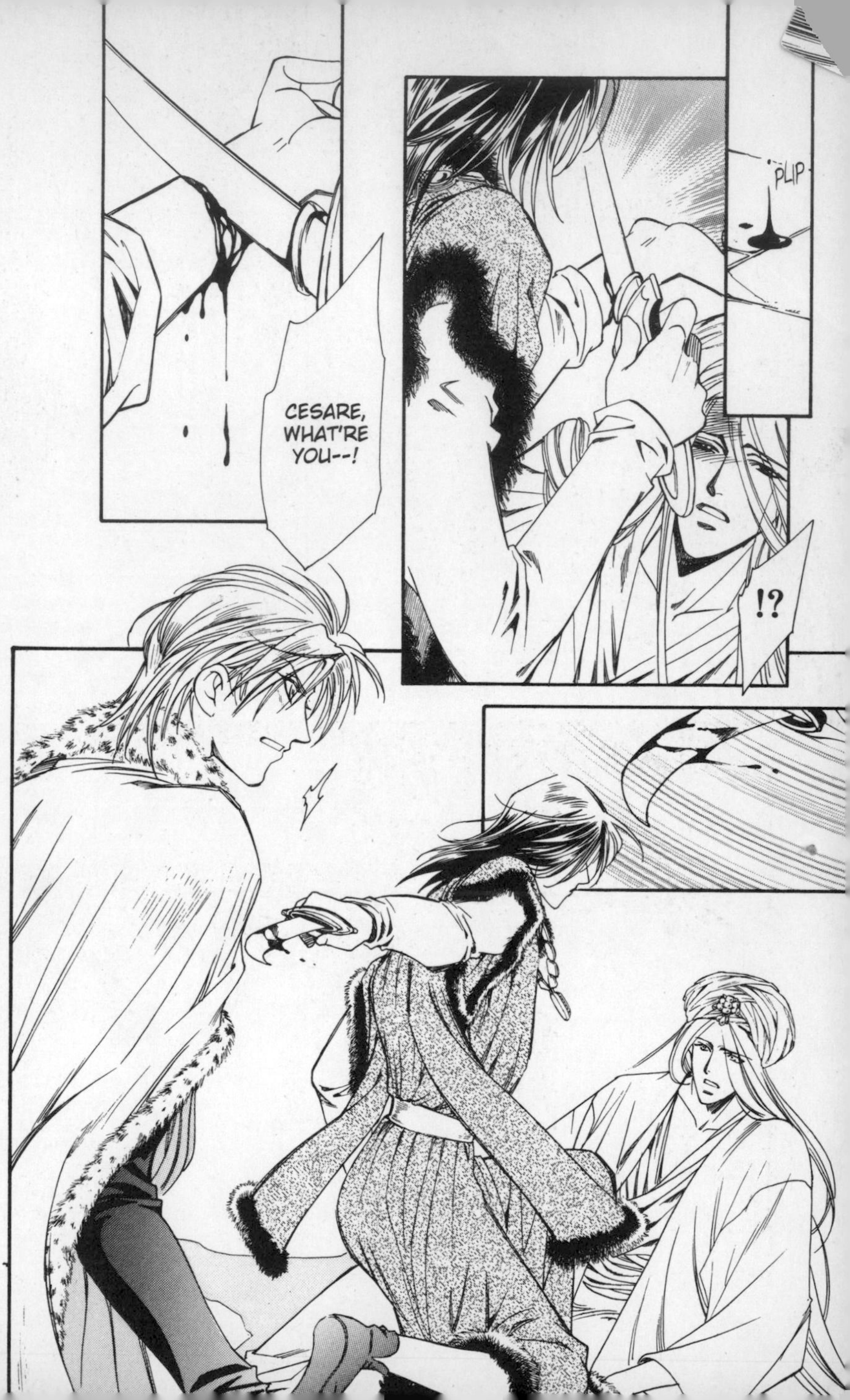
PLIP
!?
CESARE, WHAT'RE YOU--!

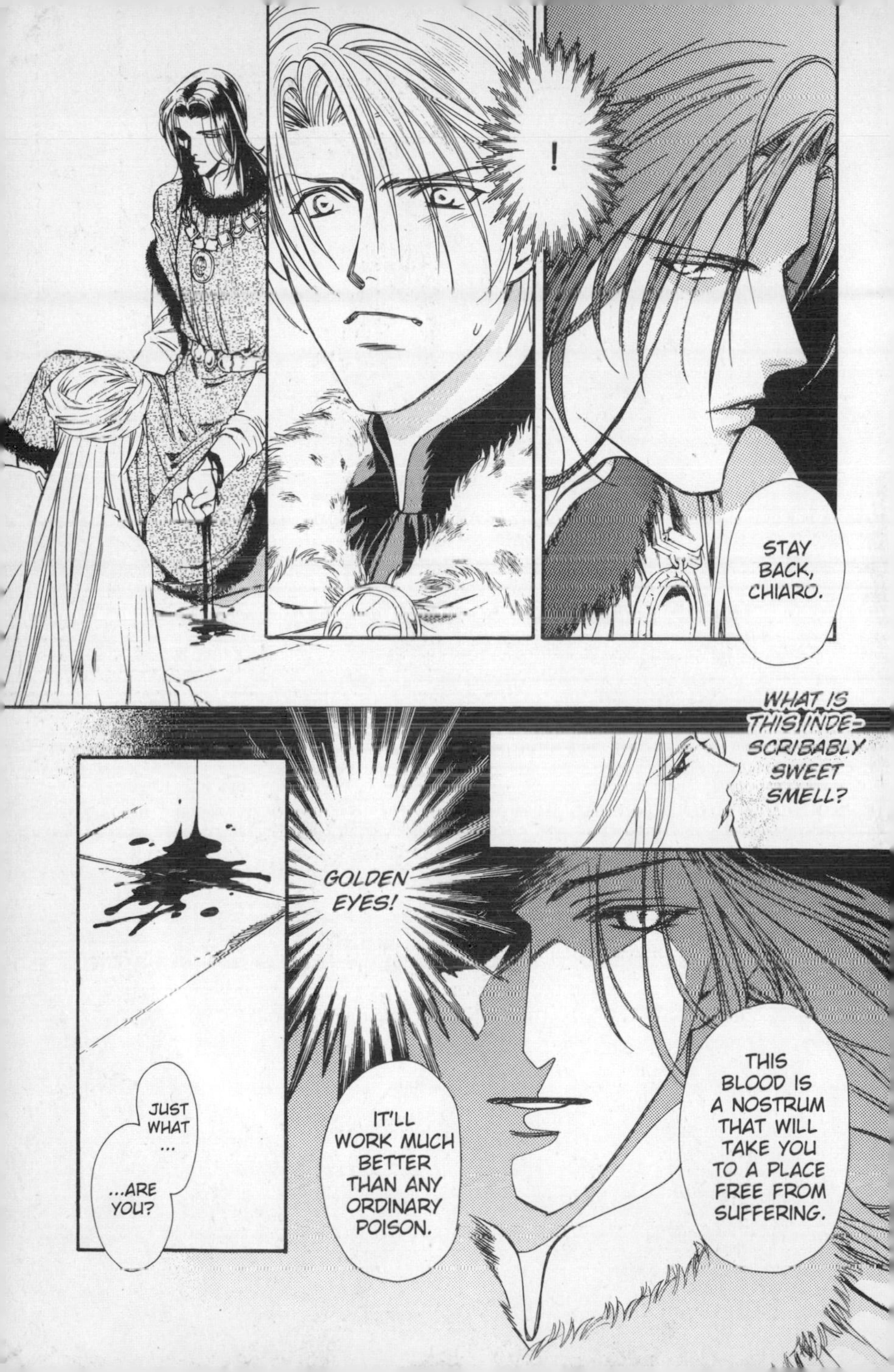
!
STAY BACK, CHIARO.
WHAT IS THIS INDE-SCRIBABLY SWEET SMELL?
GOLDEN EYES!
THIS BLOOD IS A NOSTRUM THAT WILL TAKE YOU TO A PLACE FREE FROM SUFFERING.
IT'LL WORK MUCH BETTER THAN ANY ORDINARY POISON.
JUST WHAT ...
...ARE YOU?

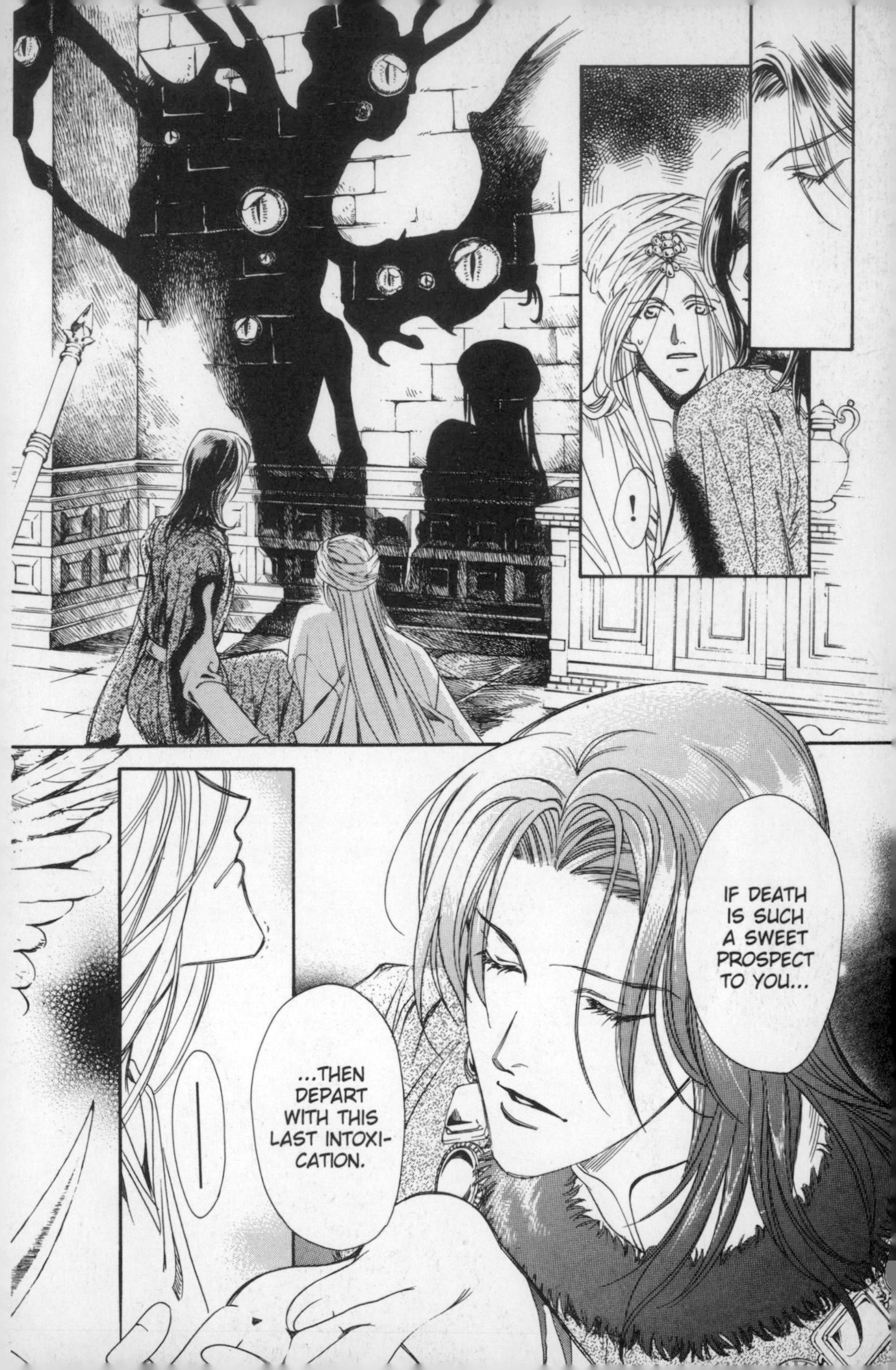
!
IF DEATH IS SUCH A SWEET PROSPECT TO YOU...
...THEN DEPART WITH THIS LAST INTOXI-CATION.

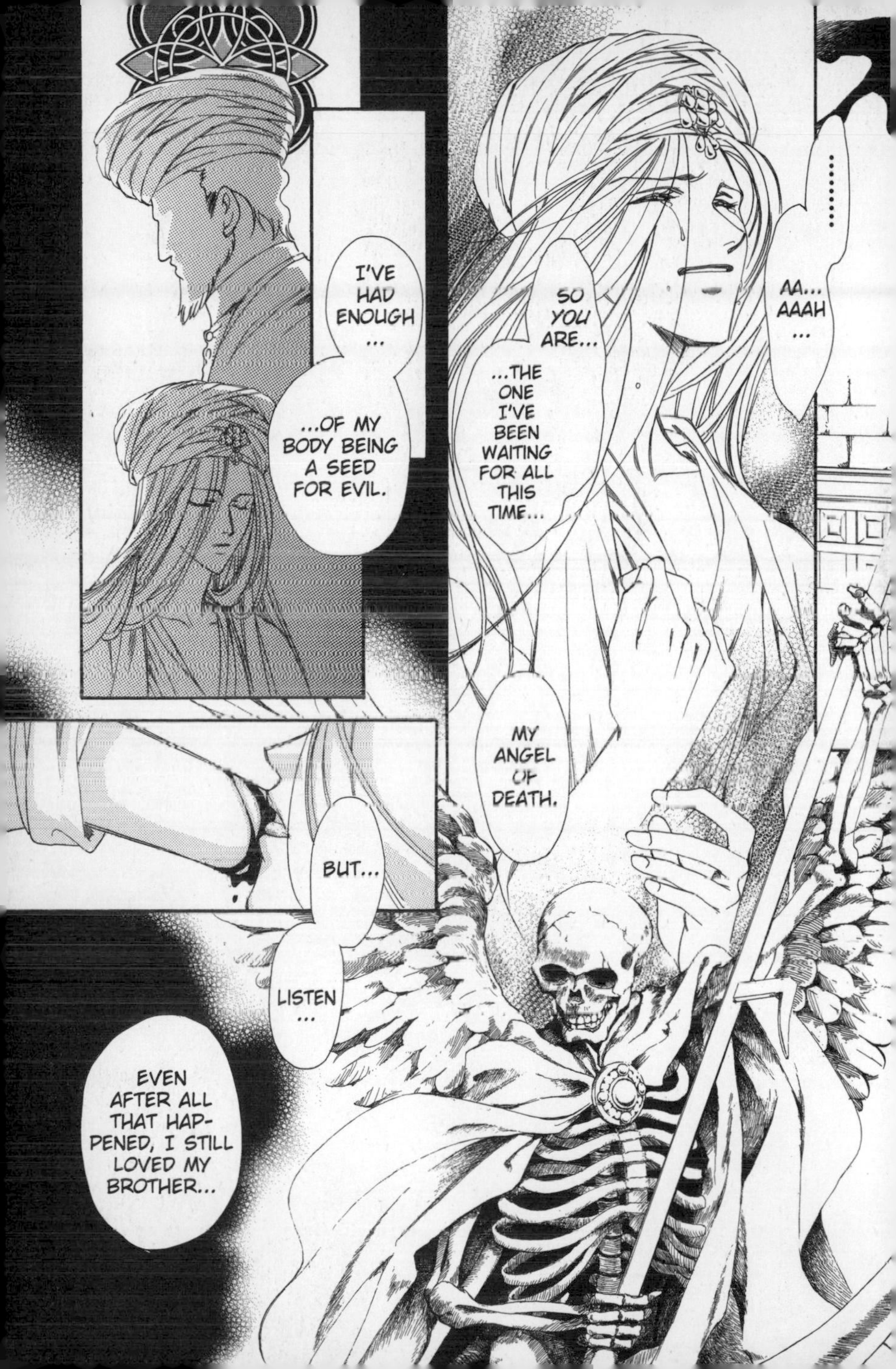
......
AA... AAAH...
SO YOU ARE...
...THE ONE I'VE BEEN WAITING FOR ALL THIS TIME...
MY ANGEL OF DEATH.
I'VE HAD ENOUGH...
...OF MY BODY BEING A SEED FOR EVIL.
BUT...
LISTEN...
EVEN AFTER ALL THAT HAP-PENED, I STILL LOVED MY BROTHER...

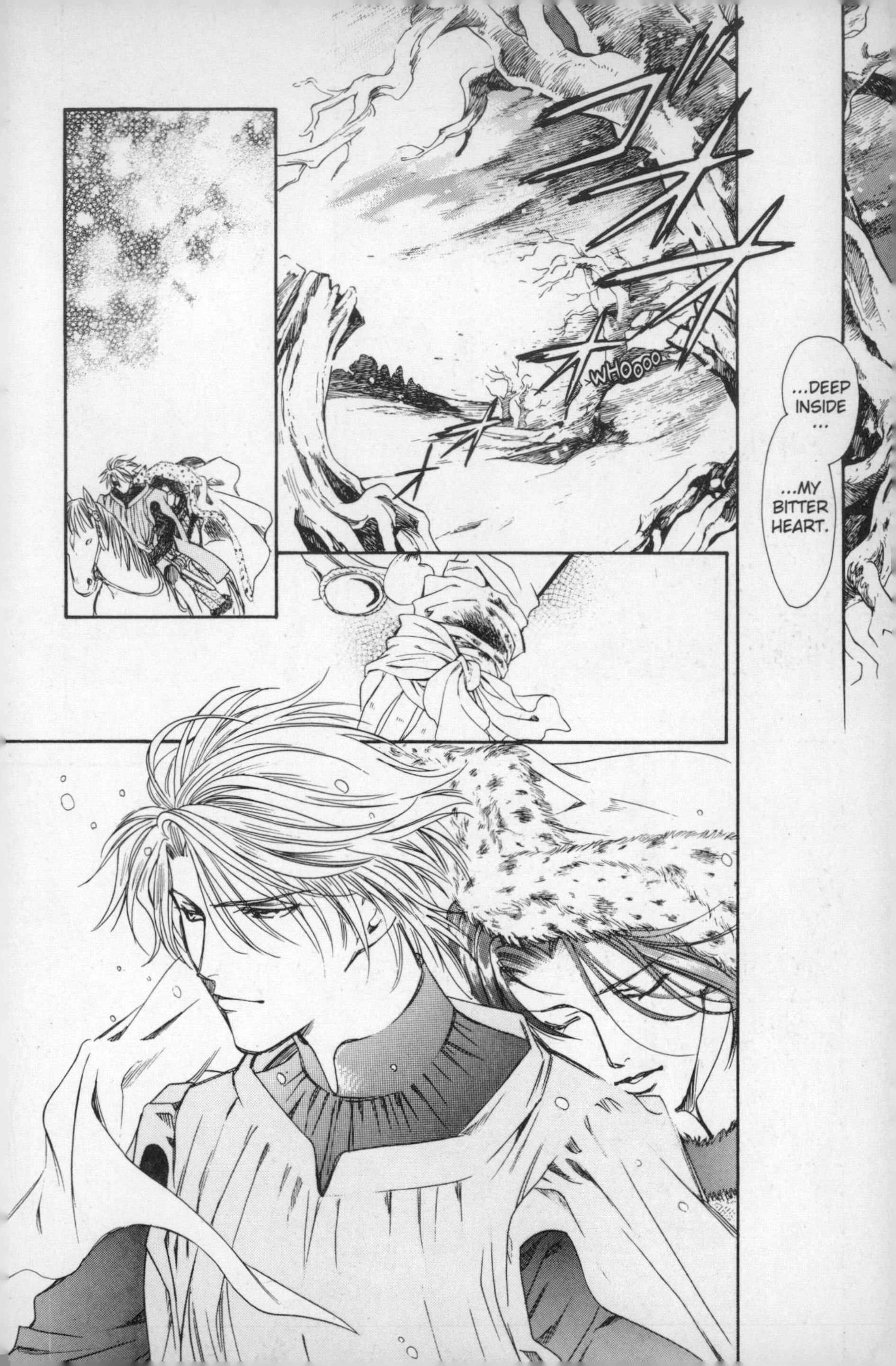
...DEEP INSIDE ...
...MY BITTER HEART.
WHOooo

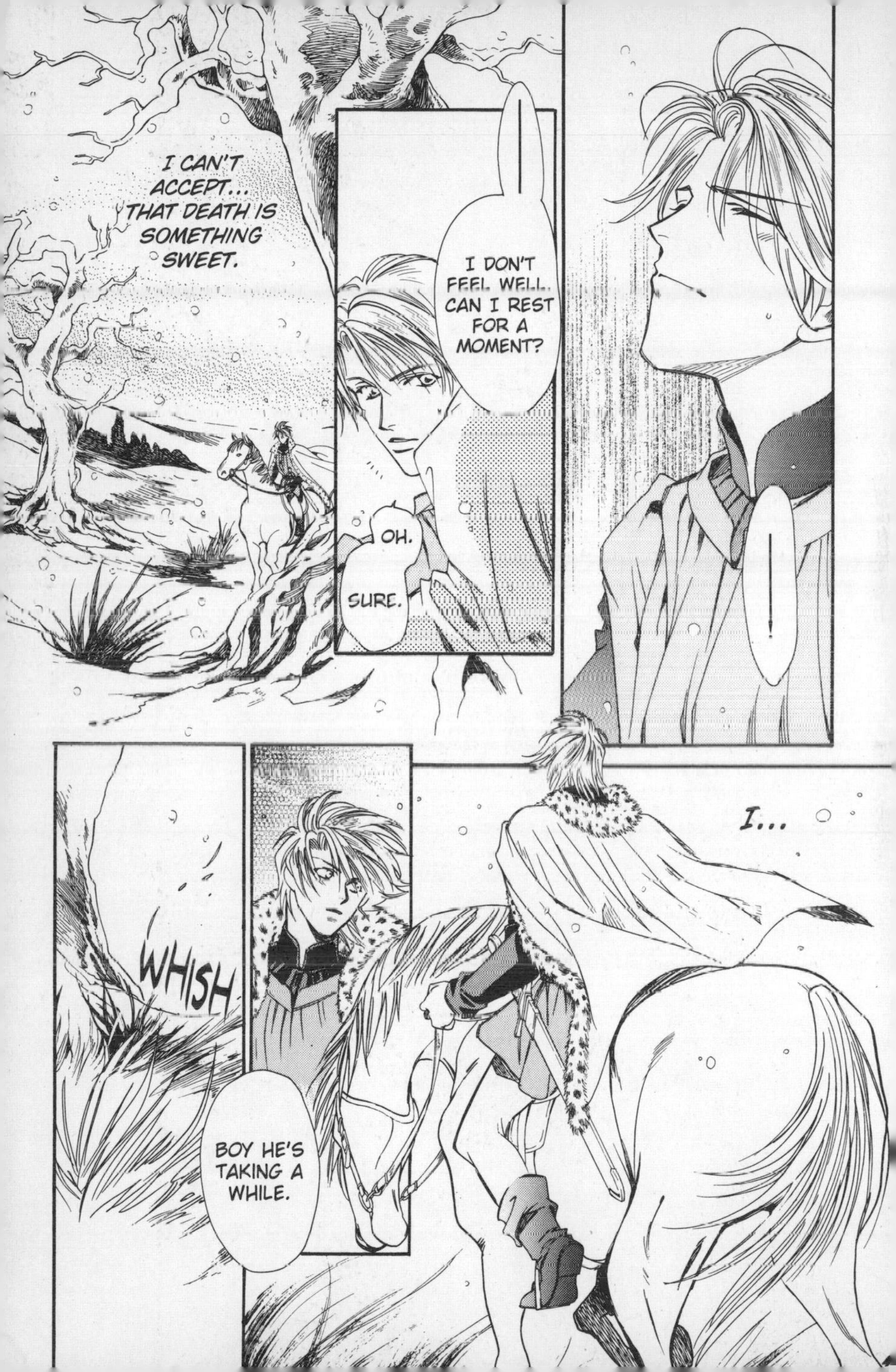
!
I DON'T FEEL WELL. CAN I REST FOR A MOMENT?
OH.
SURE.
I CAN'T ACCEPT... THAT DEATH IS SOMETHING SWEET.
I...
BOY HE'S TAKING A WHILE.
WHISH

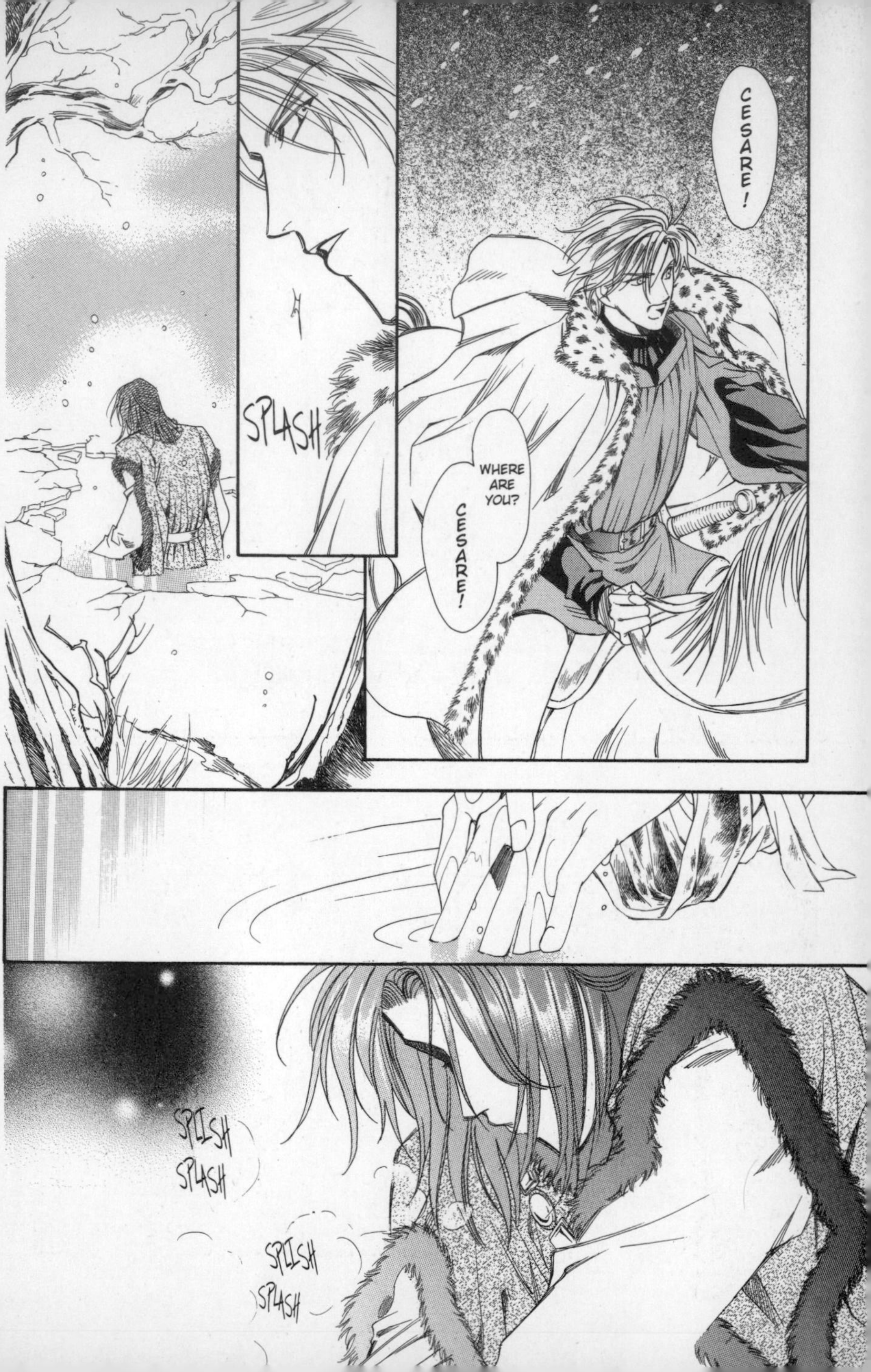

CESARE!
WHERE ARE YOU?
CESARE!
SPLASH
SPLISH
SPLASH
SPLISH
SPLASH

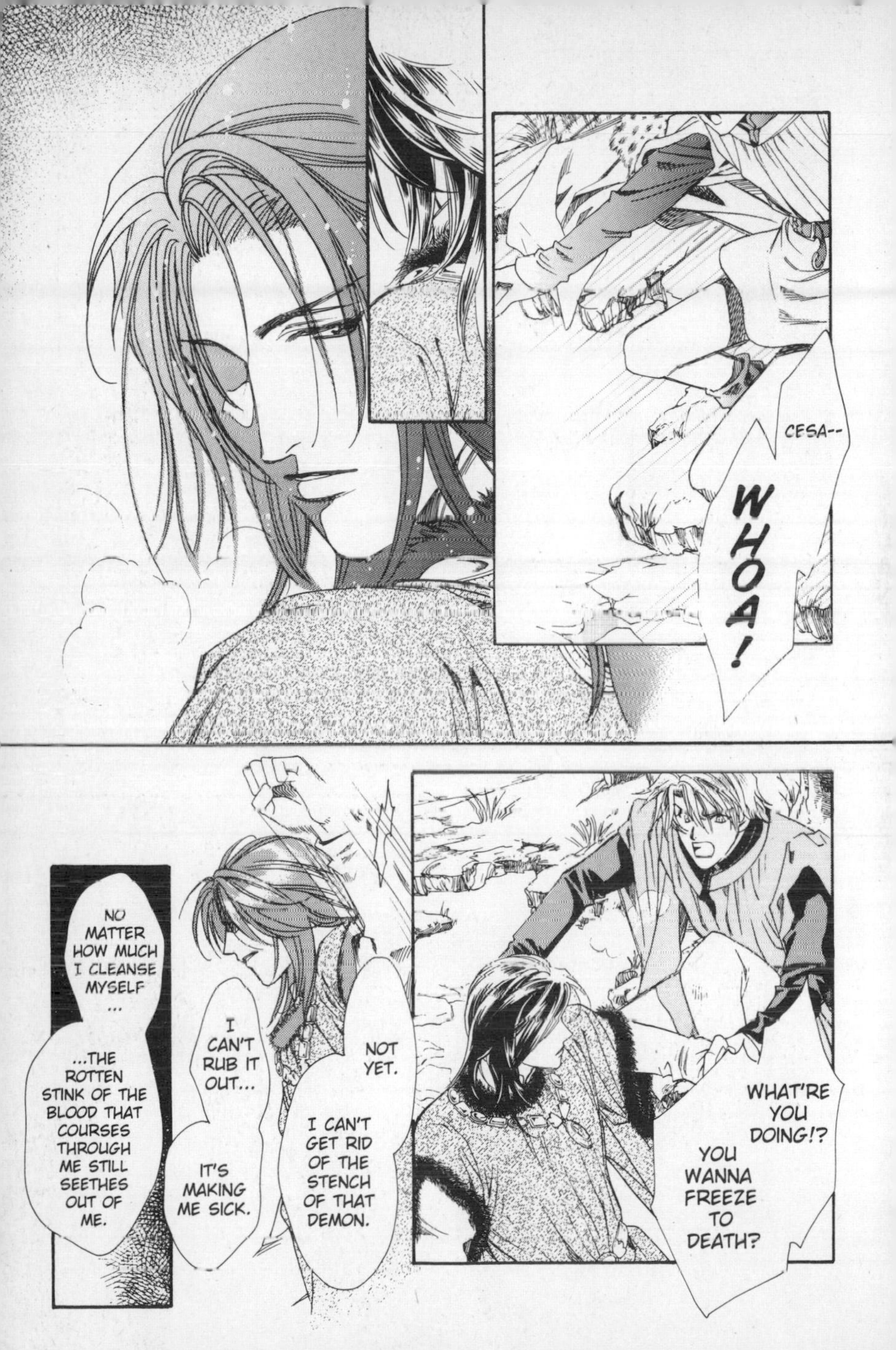
CESA--
WHOA!
WHAT'RE YOU DOING!?
YOU WANNA FREEZE TO DEATH?
NOT YET.
I CAN'T GET RID OF THE STENCH OF THAT DEMON.
I CAN'T RUB IT OUT...
IT'S MAKING ME SICK.
NO MATTER HOW MUCH I CLEANSE MYSELF...
...THE ROTTEN STINK OF THE BLOOD THAT COURSES THROUGH ME STILL SEETHES OUT OF ME.

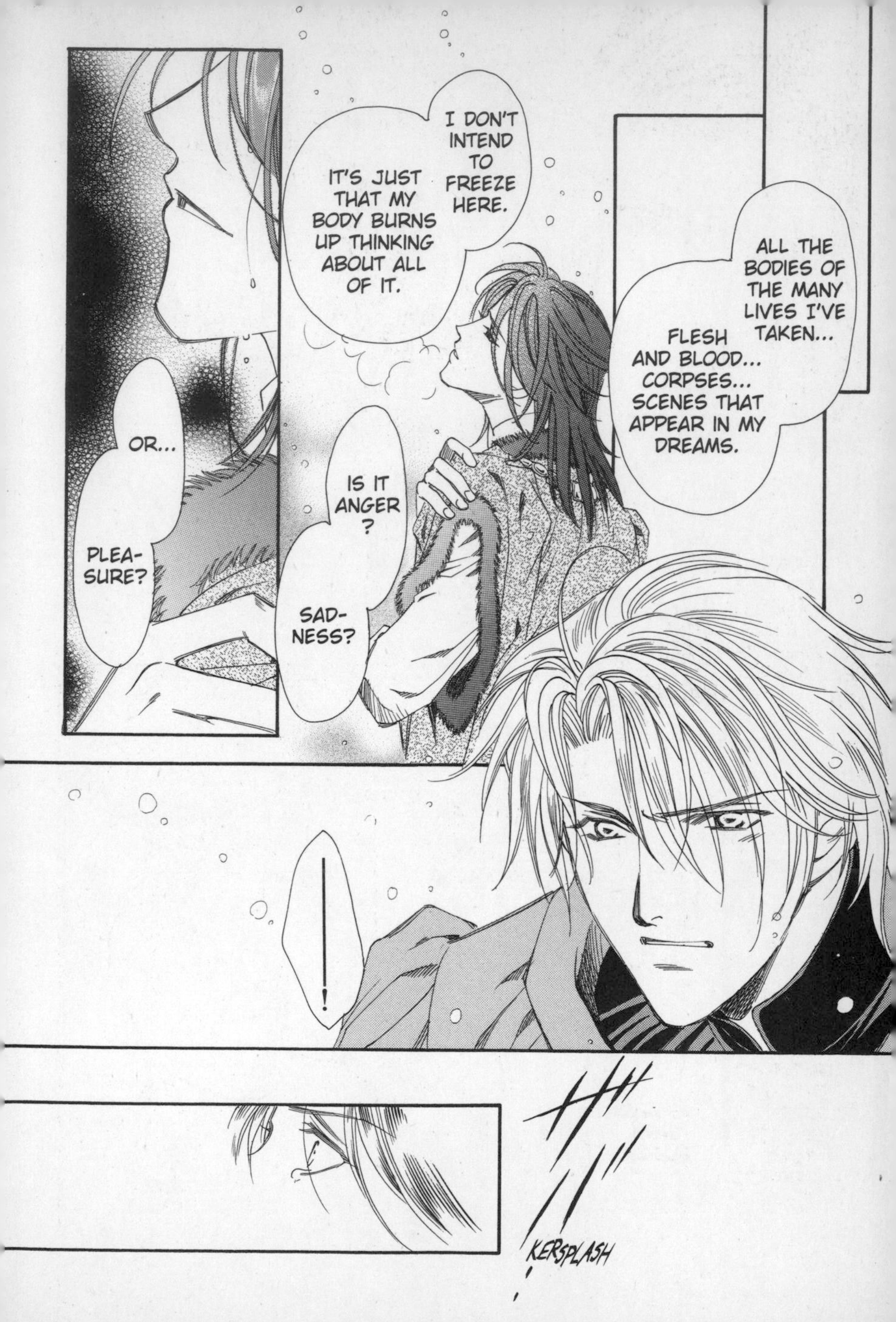
I DON'T INTEND TO FREEZE HERE.
IT'S JUST THAT MY BODY BURNS UP THINKING ABOUT ALL OF IT.
ALL THE BODIES OF THE MANY LIVES I'VE TAKEN...
FLESH AND BLOOD... CORPSES... SCENES THAT APPEAR IN MY DREAMS.
IS IT ANGER?
SADNESS?
OR...
PLEA-SURE?
!
KERSPLASH

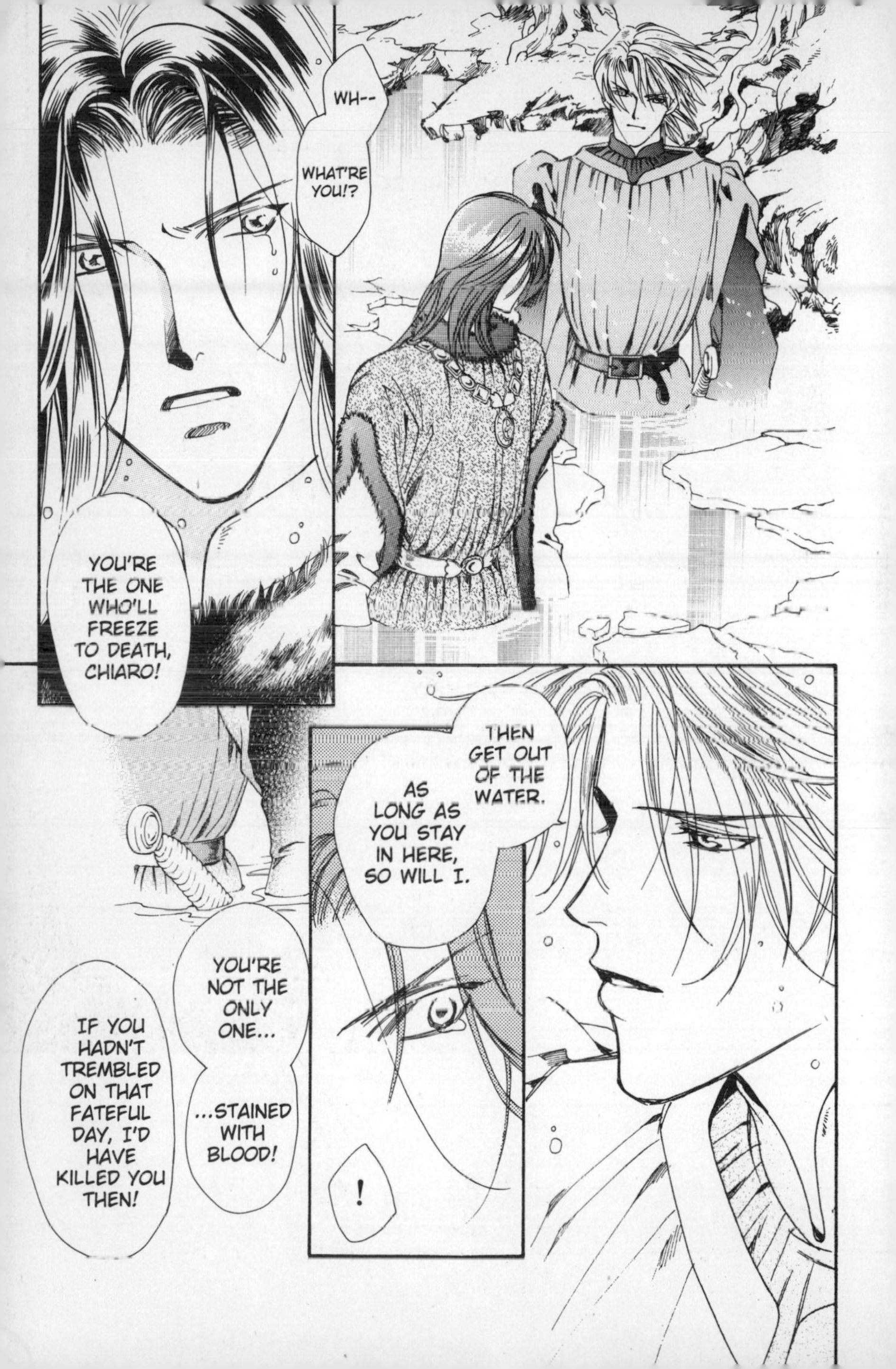
WH--
WHAT'RE YOU!?
YOU'RE THE ONE WHO'LL FREEZE TO DEATH, CHIARO!
THEN GET OUT OF THE WATER.
AS LONG AS YOU STAY IN HERE, SO WILL I.
!
YOU'RE NOT THE ONLY ONE...
...STAINED WITH BLOOD!
IF YOU HADN'T TREMBLED ON THAT FATEFUL DAY, I'D HAVE KILLED YOU THEN!

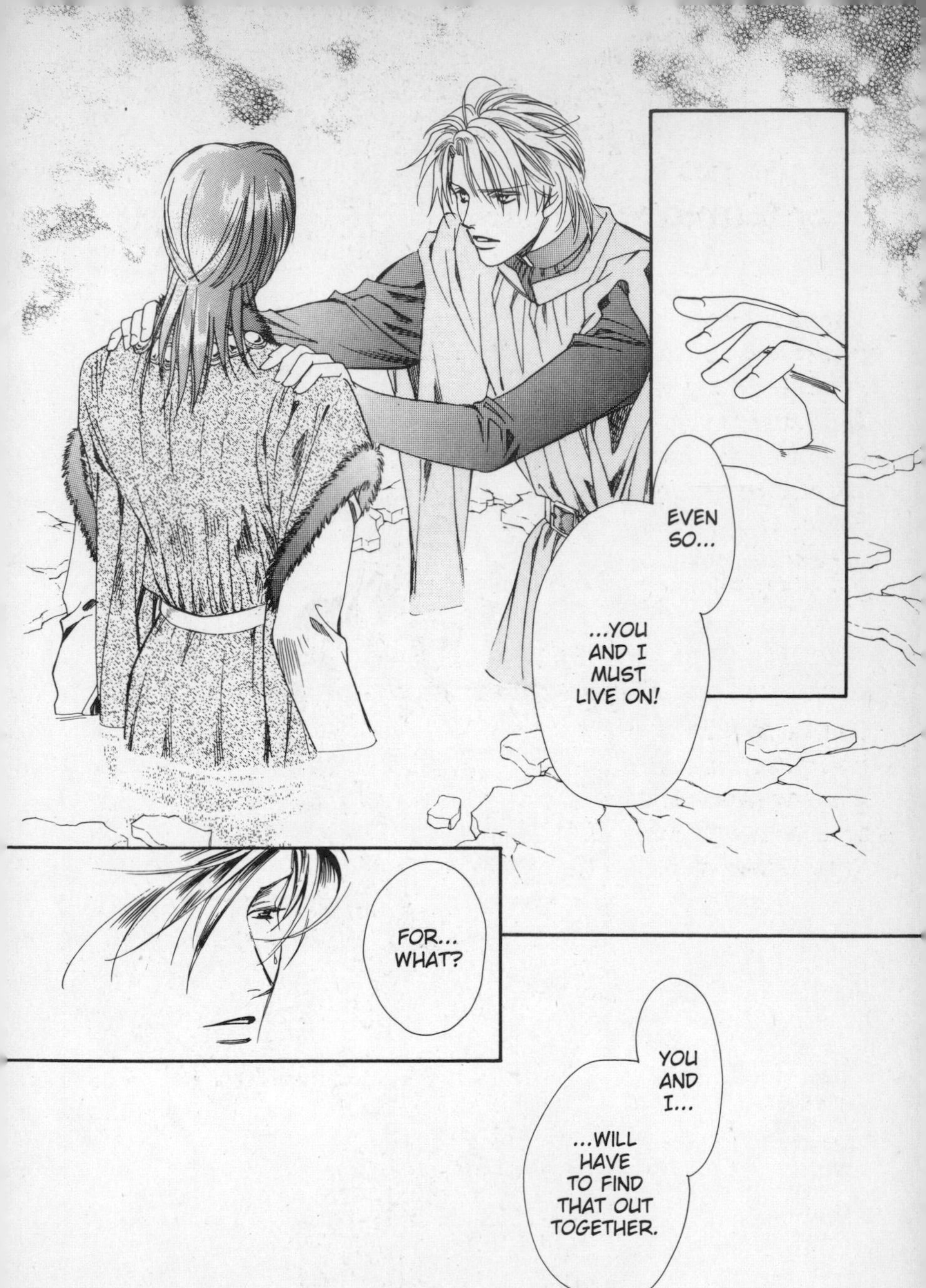
EVEN SO...
...YOU AND I MUST LIVE ON!
FOR... WHAT?
YOU AND I...
...WILL HAVE TO FIND THAT OUT TOGETHER.

To be continued in Cantarella vol. 4

In the next volume of Cantarella...

Tempted by the incestuous passion of his little sister... Tormented by forbidden feelings for his closest friend... Haunted by a deadly apparition come to devour his heart...

Cesare Borgia must face his greatest demons if he is to satisfy his terrible ambition...

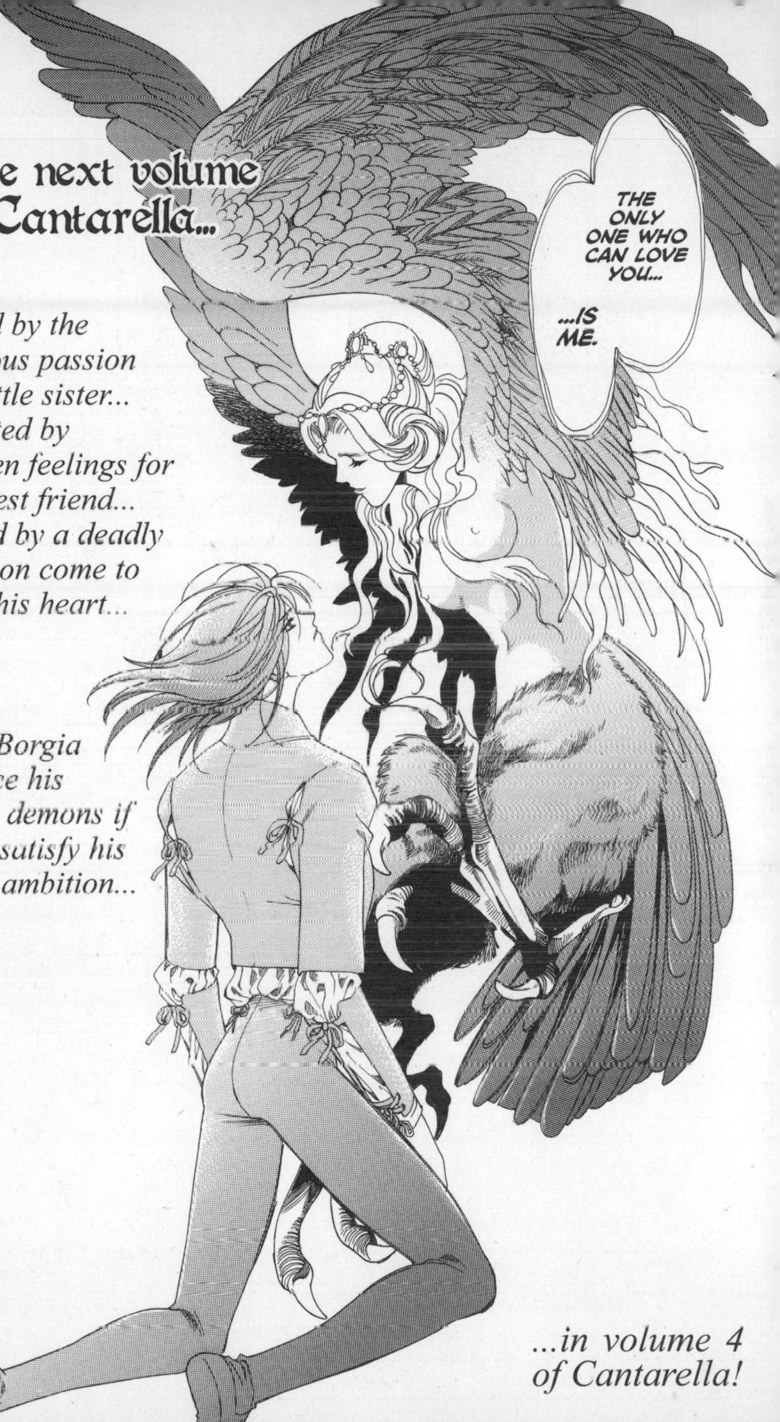
THE ONLY ONE WHO CAN LOVE YOU...
...IS ME.

...in volume 4 of Cantarella!

Post Script

I am fascinated by Italian history. No matter how much I research it, I just can't get enough. Especially when it comes to the chaos and confusion of the Renaissance period (an age fraught with civil war). During this period, each region bore forth its own geniuses, heroes, powerful families, and champions. A tumultuous time, indeed! As of yet, I have not been able to grasp how it all came to be this way.

I did my best to structure the story in a way that would make it comprehensible even to those readers who don't like history. I'm sure there are still some parts that are inevitably confusing. Doubtless there will be people who think, "Dang, this series is tiring!" I'm hoping they'll also think, "Hot damn, that Cesare's one helluva thinker!" I promise that amidst all the historical mayhem, I'll make sure the contorted love triangle between Michelotto, Lucrezia and Cesare continues to bend and twist for as long as I can possibly torture them with it.

Anyway, I'm running out of reference materials. I really need to fly to Italy and take some photos, but I just don't have the time! I've been so busy it's making my head spin so much I feel like I could faint. It's all stuff I love to do, but I'm beginning to feel like I'd like a life with at least a little bit of free time. I'm really in a spot. I'm nothing but trouble for my editors. Just thinking about this depresses me, so I'm going to make an effort to be more positive. I've begun to realize that the work one crafts as a writer can influence one's emotional state.

Before I knew what I was doing, I'd drawn my own emotions into Cesare -- and the sudden realization that I'd exposed myself like that turned me as blushing red as his robes. I'm afraid your Higuri tends to do that with her male characters. And then when I get to the female characters, it feels like I'm dragging my feet. I wonder why? I feel I have many flaws as a creator, but I hope you as my readers will continue to watch over me.

I was thinking that if I had time for it in my Afterword, I'd include some simplified explanation of the history of this period. It looks like I won't be able to do it this time around. Maybe I'll do it in the next volume. Do you think it needs one? A little history lesson, I mean. If you guys come up with any other good ideas, please send them to me! I'll be waiting!

I received a lot of help in the creation of this manga. Thank you Akari Izumi, Naoko Naktsuji, Makoto Hondo, Kaoru Matsuri, Wasao Miyakoshi, Mitsuru Fuyutsuki, Kenkichi Takanashi, Kinoko-san, Junko Fukashi, Mikiko Iwahashi, Kyoko Akimura, Yuki Mizutani, Kuro Takedamaru, Atsushi Umikyo, and Chief Assistant Ryoka Oda. From the bottom of my heart -- thank you.

I'm thinking about you, I-bashi-san and Y-yama-san... I'm going to be a good girl from now on, so please don't abandon me. (heart) hee hee (heart)

To the printing press and Akita Shoten too, and to all of you who purchased this book, my most sincere appreciation! The next volume will also be a tempest of a creation! To the best of us all in the future!!

February 2002
You Higuri

I'll be waiting for your letters:

YOU HIGURI
c/o Audry Taylor
Go! Media Entertainment, LLC
5737 Kanan Rd. #591
Agoura Hills CA 91301

Or visit her official website in English at:
http://www.youhiguri.com

The Life and Death of a Pope's Mistress

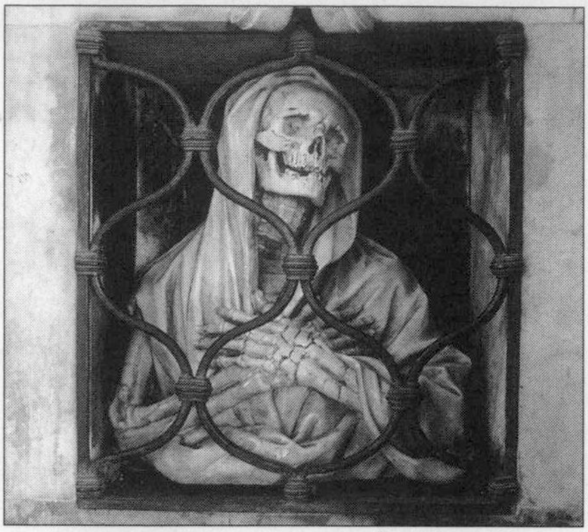

Photo: George Mastellone

A mysterious figure greets those who enter Santa Maria del Popolo, the original resting place of Vanozza dei Catanei's remains.

Vanozza dei Catanei -- one of the most tragic figures in *Cantarella.* (Speaking of which, if you haven't finished reading this volume, you might not want to read this extra feature yet!) But what of the real Vanozza, who loved and suffered five hundred years ago? Was her end as heart-rending as the one in You Higuri's gripping epic?

Born in 1442, Vanozza dei Catanei could hardly have anticipated that she would become the mother and mistress of several of the most infamous characters in Italian history. She was living in near-poverty with her first husband, a respectable lawyer named Domenico da Rignano, when she met the notorious womanizer Cardinal Rodrigo Borgia. They hit it off and a few months later when her husband died, Vanozza found herself moving to a respectable home at 58 Via Pellegrino, where she soon gave birth to Cesare Borgia.

Via del Pellegrino (which translates as Pilgrim Street) was a street from early medieval days that connected the Porticus of Octavia with the Ponte Sant'Angelo -- a very familiar name in the history of Borgia family. Still in existence today as an arts & books shopping district, the facades of several buildings on the street hark from the 16th century.

Vanozza's second husband, Giorgio della Croce, was as content as her first husband had been to share his wife (rather profitably) with

Cardinal Rodrigo, and by the time Lucrezia was born, della Croce and Vanozza had relocated to the grand Piazza Pizzo di Merlo. Perhaps the most important feature of this estate was its close proximity to the marvelous palace that the Cardinal used as his personal residence.

Foreseeing the inevitable fading of the Cardinal's romantic feelings for her, Vanozza secured her future by investing the money he gave her. When they split up around 1482, she became the wealthy owner of three hotels in the most fashionable sections of Rome -- including the famous Campo dei Fiori market, which still thrives to this day. If you walk down the market street called Vicolo del Gallo (on which Cesare and Lucrezia most likely rode when visiting their beloved mother), you will find a stone plaque above house number 13, which was placed there by Vanozza herself. This plaque is divided into 4 parts: the upper right section symbolizes the Catanei family; the upper left and the lower right sections bear the crests of the Borgia family; and the final section bears the crest of Vanozza's final husband, Carlo Canale.

The events that occur in this volume of Higuri-Sensei's *Cantarella* are mostly fictional -- but it is true that during the French invasion of Rome, Vanozza's house was utterly ransacked by enemy forces. She, however, lived to tell the tale at many a rousing party afterwards.

On 14 June, 1497, Vanozza held a *festa* for her beloved children, as she was still on good terms with her ex-lover Rodrigo, now Pope Alexander VI. Cesare and Juan were both in attendance, and left the party together at a rather late hour. To discuss what happened that black night in the alleyways of Rome would be to despoil future events in *Cantarella*. Let us just say that in both the factual version and the fantastical one the appalling horror must have been far greater than any mother could possibly bear.

As for the death of the real Vanozza...hers was a peaceful, quiet end at the age of 76. Vanozza's remains were entombed inside Santa Maria del Popolo, and gradually came to be surrounded by master artworks from later decades, including works by Raphael, Pinturicchio, and Gian Lorenzo Bernini. More than 150 years after her passing, the monks there were still saying masses for her soul.

The Borgia family bore bitter enemies through long centuries, and the plaque on Vanozza's tomb bearing a loving inscription of all the names of her children was eventually vandalized by one of these enemies. As a result, her tomb had to be relocated to the Church of San Marco, in the Palazzo Venezia in Rome. ❦

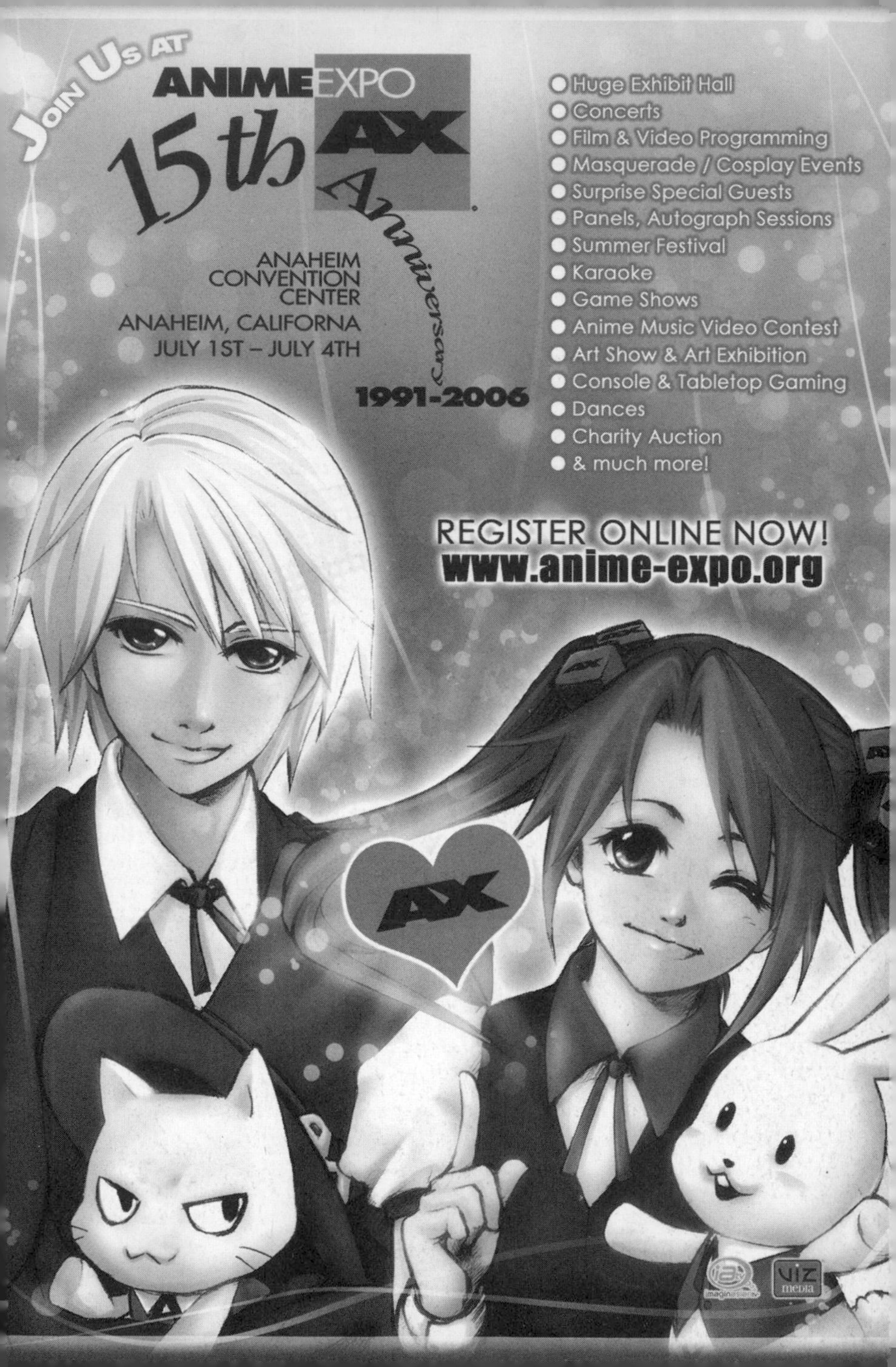

JOIN US AT
ANIME EXPO
15th
AX
Anniversary
ANAHEIM CONVENTION CENTER
ANAHEIM, CALIFORNA
JULY 1ST – JULY 4TH
1991-2006
Huge Exhibit Hall
Concerts
Film & Video Programming
Masquerade / Cosplay Events
Surprise Special Guests
Panels, Autograph Sessions
Summer Festival
Karaoke
Game Shows
Anime Music Video Contest
Art Show & Art Exhibition
Console & Tabletop Gaming
Dances
Charity Auction
& much more!
REGISTER ONLINE NOW!
www.anime-expo.org
AX
viz media

AUTHOR'S NOTE

The year 2001 was "The Year of Italy" in Japan and I was so happy because reference material flooded the television. Still, I'd rather go on a trip myself to gather materials!

Visit You Higuri online at
www.youhiguri.com